ASIAN POLITICAL, ECONOMIC AND SECURITY ISSUES SERIES

INDIA AND THE U.S: FUTURE RELATIONS, BUSINESS AND BACKGROUND

Asian Political, Economic and Security Issues Series

North Korea: Issues and U.S. Policy
Samuel P. Massingame (Editor)
2009. ISBN: 978-1-60692-845-5

North Korean Foreign Relations in the Post-Cold War World
Lyman R. Rechter (Editor)
2009. ISBN: 978-1-60692-806-6

The Land and Maritime Boundary Disputes of Asia
Rongxing Guo
2009. ISBN: 978-1-60741-629-6

United States and India Strategic Cooperation
Henry Sokolski (Editor)
2010. ISBN: 978-1-60692-385-6

India and the U.S: Future Relations, Business and Background
Tim S. Macleod (Editor)
2010. ISBN: 978-1-60741-197-0

ASIAN POLITICAL, ECONOMIC AND SECURITY ISSUES SERIES

INDIA AND THE U.S: FUTURE RELATIONS, BUSINESS AND BACKGROUND

TIM S. MACLEOD
EDITOR

Nova Science Publishers, Inc.
New York

For permission to use material from this book please contact us:
Telephone 631-231-7269; Fax 631-231-8175
Web Site: http://www.novapublishers.com

LIBRARY OF CONGRESS CATALOGING-IN-PUBLICATION DATA

India and the U.S. : future relations, business and background / editor, Tim S. Macleod.
p. cm.
Includes index.
ISBN 978-1-60741-197-0 (hardcover)
1. United States--Foreign relations--India. 2. India--Foreign relations--United States. 3. United States--Foreign economic relations--India. 4. India--Foreign economic relations--United States. 5. India--Economic conditions--21st century. I. Macleod, Tim S. II. Title: India and the US. III. Title: India and the United States.
JZ1480.A57I4 2009
327.73054--dc22

2009032063

Published by Nova Science Publishers, Inc. ✣ New York

CONTENTS

Preface **vii**

Chapter 1 The Environment for Agricultural and Agribusiness Investment in India **1**
Maurice Landes1

Chapter 2 The Role of Policy and Industry Structure in India's Oilseed Markets **43**
Suresh Persaud and Maurice R. Landes

Chapter 3 U.S. Nuclear Cooperation with India: Issues for Congress **101**
Paul K. Kerr

Chapter 4 India-U.S. Relations **145**
K. Alan Kronstadt

Chapter 5 Emerging Trends in the Security Architecture in Asia: Bilateral and Multilateral Ties Among the United States, Japan, Australia, and India **215**
Emma Chanlett-Avery and Bruce Vaughn

Chapter 6 More Than Just the 123 Agreement: The Future of U.S.-Indo Relations: Hearing Before the Subcommittee on the Middle East and South Asia of the Committee on Foreign Affairs House of Representatives **231**
United States Government Printing Office

Chapter Sources **279**

Index **281**

PREFACE

Long considered a "strategic backwater" from Washington's perspective, South Asia has emerged in the 21st century as increasingly vital to core U.S. foreign policy interests. India, the region's dominant actor with more than one billion citizens, is often characterized as a nascent major power and "natural partner" of the United States, one that many analysts view as a potential counterweight to China's growing clout. Washington and New Delhi have been pursuing a "strategic partnership" since 2004, based on shared values such as democracy, pluralism, and rule of law. This book describes the numerous economic, security, and global initiatives, including plans for "full civilian nuclear energy cooperation," which are underway. This book also explores the concerns of Congress with regards to the abuses of human rights, its tensions with Pakistan and religious freedoms in India.

Chapter 1 - Despite strong overall economic growth and strengthening food demand, investment in Indian agriculture and agribusiness has remained sluggish, and growth in farm output has slowed, since the early 1990s. An array of policies and regulations affecting agricultural production, marketing, and food processing—along with weak infrastructure and a lack of market services—have discouraged private investment by farmers and large, vertically integrated agribusinesses. The policy environment has grown more investor friendly since the late 1990s and private investment appears to be responding, but significant barriers remain and the pace of future reforms remains uncertain.

Chapter 2 - High tariff and nontariff protection of the Indian oilseed sector imposes costs on consumers, supports an inefficient processing industry, and has led to negligible gains in oilseed output. Model-based simulations indicate that higher levels of protection would increase the burden on consumers, but do little to meet key policy goals of supporting producers and reducing import dependence. A shift to direct support of oilseed producer prices would increase output, but may be complex to implement and subject to WTO discipline. Liberalization of oilseed imports, by permitting large gains in processing efficiency, could generate a stream of benefits that would allow producers, consumers, and processors to be better off, and also improve the trade balance.

Chapter 3 - On July 18, 2005, President Bush announced he would "work to achieve full civil nuclear energy cooperation with India" and would "also seek agreement from Congress to adjust U.S. laws and policies," in the context of a broader, global partnership with India.

India, which has not signed the Nuclear Nonproliferation Treaty (NPT) and does not have International Atomic Energy Agency safeguards on all nuclear material in peaceful nuclear activities, exploded a "peaceful" nuclear device in 1974, convincing the world of the need for greater restrictions on nuclear trade. The United States created the Nuclear Suppliers Group (NSG) as a direct response to India's test, halted nuclear exports to India a few years later, and worked to convince other states to do the same. India tested nuclear weapons again in 1998.

U.S. nuclear cooperation is governed by the Atomic Energy Act (AEA). P.L. 109-401, which President Bush signed bill into law on December 18, 2006, provides waivers of several provisions of the AEA (Sections 123 a. (2), 128, and 129). It requires that several steps occur before nuclear cooperation can proceed. On September 10, President Bush submitted to Congress a written determination that these requirements discussed above have been met. That same day, the President submitted the text of the proposed agreement, which has not yet been signed. The President also submitted a written determination (also required by the AEA) "that the performance of the proposed agreement will promote and will not constitute an unreasonable risk to, the common defense and security." In addition, President Bush submitted several documents, including classified and unclassified versions of a Nuclear Proliferation Assessment Statement, which is required by section 123 of the AEA. The Department of State has also submitted a report required by P.L. 109-401 on various aspects of the agreement.

On September 27, 2008, the House passed H.R. 7081, which approves the agreement. The Senate Committee on Foreign Relations approved identical legislation, S. 3548, September 23. The Senate passed H.R. 7081 October 1. President Bush signed P.L. 110-369 into law October 8. Secretary of State Condoleezza Rice and India's External Affairs Minister Shri Pranab Mukherjee signed the agreement October 10, but it has not yet entered into force.

Chapter 4 - Long considered a "strategic backwater" from Washington's perspective, South Asia has emerged in the 21st century as increasingly vital to core U.S. foreign policy interests. India, the region's dominant actor with more than one billion citizens, is often characterized as a nascent major power and "natural partner" of the United States, one that many analysts view as a potential counterweight to China's growing clout. Washington and New Delhi have since 2004 been pursuing a "strategic partnership" based on shared values such as democracy, pluralism, and rule of law. Numerous economic, security, and global initiatives, including plans for "full civilian nuclear energy cooperation," are underway. This latter initiative, launched by President Bush in July 2005 and provisionally endorsed by the 109th Congress in 2006 (P.L. 109-401, the "Hyde Act"), would reverse three decades of U.S. nonproliferation policy. It requires, among other steps, a Joint Resolution of Approval by Congress. Also in 2005, the United States and India signed a ten-year defense framework agreement that calls for expanding bilateral security cooperation. Since 2002, the two countries have engaged in numerous and unprecedented combined military exercises. Major U.S. arms sales to India are planned. The influence of a growing and relatively wealthy Indian-American community of more than two million is reflected in Congress's largest country-specific caucus.

Further U.S. interest in South Asia focuses on ongoing tensions between India and Pakistan rooted in unfinished business from the 1947 Partition, competing claims to the Kashmir region, and, in more recent years, "cross-border terrorism" in both Kashmir and major Indian cities. In the interests of regional stability, the United States strongly encourages an ongoing India-Pakistan peace initiative and remains concerned about the potential for conflict over Kashmiri sovereignty to cause open hostilities between these two nuclear-armed countries. The United States seeks to curtail the proliferation of nuclear weapons and ballistic missiles in South Asia. Both India and Pakistan have resisted external pressure to sign the major nonproliferation treaties. In 1998, the two countries conducted nuclear tests that evoked international condemnation. Proliferation-related restrictions on U.S. aid were triggered, then later lifted through congressional-executive cooperation from 1998 to 2000. Remaining sanctions on India (and Pakistan) were removed in late 2001.

India is in the midst of major and rapid economic expansion. Many U.S. business interests view India as a lucrative market and candidate for foreign investment. The United States supports India's efforts to transform its once quasi-socialist economy through fiscal reform and market opening. Since 1991, India has taken major steps in this direction and coalition governments have kept the country on a general path of reform, yet there is U.S. concern that such movement is slow and inconsistent. India is the world's fourth-largest emitter of greenhouse gases. Congress also continues to have concerns about abuses of human rights, including caste- and gender-based discrimination, and religious freedoms in India. Moreover, the spread of HIV/AIDS in India has been identified as a serious development.

Chapter 5 - Some analysts have questioned whether U.S. security interests in the Asia Pacific region are best served by its existing framework of bilateral alliances. The region is now facing an array of changes: deepening trade links, the formation of new regional institutions, and increased attention to the threat of Islamic terrorism. Against this backdrop, China's rise represents the key driver in the evolving security landscape in Asia. China is now attracting regional states with its economic power and is offering competing vision to the U.S.-centric "hub and spoke" system of alliances. In essence, China's increasing economic, diplomatic, and military strength is compelling countries to rethink existing security arrangements and take initial steps that may lead to the formation of regional groupings of nations with common interests and values. At the same time, the Bush Administration has pursued stronger defense relations with Australia, Japan, and India.

Bilateral defense ties have also developed between Canberra, Tokyo, and New Delhi, with varying degrees of engagement. Fledgling initiatives for trilateral efforts among the nations have emerged; some defense planners see these efforts as building on existing security cooperation to further U.S. goals in the region by combining forces among partners and allies. As trilateral initiatives have taken shape, some officials have begun promoting a quadrilateral grouping, which would tie together the United States, Japan, Australia, and India. Although no formal quadrilateral groupings exist, the *Malabar 07* military exercises among the four countries in September 2007 provided an opportunity to test naval cooperation. Some observers caution that moving forward too fast with such a grouping could trigger a negative response from China.

Pursuit of multilateral security arrangements holds a number of potential challenges and opportunities for the United States. Of the four leaders who championed the trilateral and quadrilateral groupings, two left office in 2007 and two face significant political challenges. Japan's constitutional restraints on military involvement may limit the scope of its cooperation, and both Australia and India have some degree of reluctance to fully engage in any forum that might alienate Beijing. Increasing capabilities among like-minded nations could enhance stability and provide a platform for responding to natural disasters and humanitarian emergencies in the region, or to potential aggression by other countries, but it also risks threatening China, potentially spurring dangerous countermeasures. Finally, there is the risk that other Asian allies, such as South Korea, Thailand, and the Philippines, could feel excluded from multilateral initiatives among the United States, Japan, Australia, and/or India.

Chapter 6 - The subcommittee met, pursuant to notice, at 2:33 p.m., in room 2172, Rayburn House Office Building, Hon. Gary L. Ackerman (chairman of the subcommittee) presiding.

Over the past year and a half, the subcommittee has examined a variety of issues and has, at least on their side, been very critical of the President, his administration and the state of affairs that the next President will inherit across the Middle East and South Asia as a result of the current President's policies. So today will be a change of pace, because, if there is one area in the subcommittee's jurisdiction where President Bush got the policy right, it is toward India.

In: India and the U.S: Future Relations…
Editor: Tim S. Macleod, pp.1-41

ISBN: 978-1-60741-197-0

Chapter 1

The Environment for Agricultural and Agribusiness Investment in India

Maurice Landes

Abstract

Despite strong overall economic growth and strengthening food demand, investment in Indian agriculture and agribusiness has remained sluggish, and growth in farm output has slowed, since the early 1990s. An array of policies and regulations affecting agricultural production, marketing, and food processing—along with weak infrastructure and a lack of market services—have discouraged private investment by farmers and large, vertically integrated agribusinesses. The policy environment has grown more investor friendly since the late 1990s and private investment appears to be responding, but significant barriers remain and the pace of future reforms remains uncertain.

Keywords: India, agriculture, agribusiness, investment, trade policy, domestic policy, infrastructure

Acknowledgments

Holly Higgins, P.K. Joshi, Ashok Gulati, Mary Anne Normile, and an anonymous reviewer made valuable comments on earlier drafts of this report. Indian Agribusiness Systems, Ltd of Okhla, Uttar Pradesh, India provided assistance in data collection. The report was edited by Dale Simms and the graphics were provided by Vic Phillips. Financial support for this study was provided by the USDA Emerging Markets Program.

Summary

Although rising incomes are contributing to expanding and diversifying food demand, investment in Indian agriculture has remained low relative to other sectors and grown slowly since the early 1990s. Lagging private investment in agriculture and agribusiness has corresponded with burdensome regulatory policies, poor infrastructure, and weak institutional support for agricultural markets. Even though India has one of the world's largest agricultural economies, Indian agribusiness is characterized by a multitude of small-scale, nonintegrated processing and marketing firms that use mostly outdated technology and are uncompetitive in global markets.

What Is the Issue?

India, with one of the world's fastest growing and most populous economies and one of its largest farm sectors, is emerging as a potentially large market for global agricultural trade and investment. Despite the rapid productivity gains occurring in India's service and manufacturing sectors, average crop yields remain below potential, agricultural markets are underdeveloped, and growth in farm output has slowed. Policymakers are increasingly focused on how to strengthen agricultural investment and growth, raise rural incomes, and help sustain rapid overall gains in income growth and poverty reduction.

What Are the Major Findings?

Both public and private investment in Indian agriculture and agribusiness have remained weak since the early 1990s, despite accelerating growth in the overall economy and a large domestic market for agricultural products. Growth in farm output has slowed since the early 1990s, and although a turnaround is seen as critical for sustained economic growth, consensus on agricultural reforms has proven difficult.

India's numerous domestic policy interventions—along with weak infrastructure and limited institutional support for agricultural markets—have been a deterrent to agricultural investment, particularly in large vertically integrated agribusinesses. Interventions have included restrictions on transporting, storing, and marketing of agricultural commodities, restrictions on the size of agribusiness firms, high taxes on processed products, high-cost credit, and complex food laws. The climate for private investment is also undermined by weak transport and power infrastructure and lack of key services such as market information, risk management tools, and grading/inspection systems.

For farmers, disincentives have included trade and price policies that maintained low domestic prices for many farm commodities, inefficient markets that dampen returns to growers, and few public and private marketing services. Onfarm investment may also be constrained by India's many small and marginal farmers, who account for nearly 40 percent of farmland, and often have limited access to input and output markets and more limited investment options.

Since 2000, the policy environment seems to be improving and investment in agriculture to be strengthening, as evidenced by higher market prices and input subsidies for farmers. Movement and storage restrictions on essential commodities, like wheat and rice, are becoming less common, restrictions on firm size have been largely removed, State marketing laws are evolving to accommodate private marketing channels, and taxes on agricultural products are being reduced and simplified. And although power, transport, and other infrastructure problems will likely be solved only in the longer term, there is evidence that private investment is now on the rise in those sectors. Food marketing ventures oriented toward development of supply chains and retail outlets represent a turnaround in investor confidence.

Recent investment in India's food marketing sector includes a number of ventures by U.S. and other foreign investors, mostly in collaboration with Indian firms. Since India does not permit foreign direct investment by multi-brand retailers, foreign investment has taken the form of wholesale (or "cash and carry") trading enterprises, or partnerships with Indian franchisees who own the retail outlets.

How Was the Study Conducted?

This study was based on analysis of literature and secondary data from published and online sources, together with interviews of representatives from Indian agribusinesses. Data collection and interviews in India were facilitated by Indian Agribusiness Systems, Ltd, of Okhla, Uttar Pradesh. Financial support for this study was provided by the USDA Emerging Markets Program.

INTRODUCTION

Economic growth in India has accelerated since the early 1990s, when a package of market-oriented reforms to domestic, trade, and exchange rate policies sparked investment and productivity gains in the industrial and services sectors. But agricultural investment has lagged investment in the rest of the economy since the 1980s. Output growth has slowed since the early 1990s (table 1), and agreement on reforms to strengthen agricultural performance has proven difficult.[1] With rising incomes, urbanization, and youthful demographics boosting demand for an increasingly diverse array of food and agricultural products, slowed growth in farm output is translating into rising real prices for some foods, as well as more agricultural imports. Although agricultural imports remain low compared with the size of the Indian economy, they have grown about 13 percent annually in real terms since the early 1990s, and India has emerged as a major global importer of edible oils, pulses, and, most recently, wheat.[2]

Despite the robust gains elsewhere in the economy, the poor performance of India's agricultural sector—including both production agriculture and marketing—has become a key concern of Indian policymakers. Agriculture accounts for about 21 percent of economic output (2003/04-2005/06 average; Reserve Bank of India, 2007) and is the primary source of employment and income for about 58 percent the population (Government of India, Ministry of Statistics and Program Implementation, 2005), including a large share of Indians living below the poverty line. Lagging performance in such a large segment of the economy jeopardizes the sustainability of the economy's strong overall growth. It has also prompted political resistance to extending market-oriented domestic and trade policy reforms into a farm sector comprised mostly of small farmers and agribusinesses that are seen as vulnerable and unready to compete in international markets.

Table 1. Growth of real gross domestic product (GDP) and gross fixed capital formation (GFCF) in India

Period	Gross domestic product Total	Gross domestic product In agriculture	Gross fixed capital formation Total	Gross fixed capital formation In agriculture
			Growth rates (percent per year)[1]	
1960s	3.7	2.2	5.9	5.9
1970s	3.2	1.6	4.6	5.1
1980s	5.3	3.4	6.0	0.6
1990-04	5.8	2.9	6.1	2.4
1997-04	5.8	1.8	11.3	3.9

[1]Growth rates between 3-year averages centered on years indicated.

Sources: Government of India, Ministry of Program Planning and Implementation, Central Statistical Organization; Government of India, Ministry of Finance, Economic Survey.

The lack of substantive yield growth and the inefficiency of markets in Indian agriculture are correlated with low levels of public and private investment in agriculture and agribusiness. In contrast to the dynamism evident in other sectors, investment in Indian agriculture and agribusiness—public and private, domestic and foreign—has been low and, until very recently, has shown little growth. Public investment has been partially constrained by the large and increasing costs of farm subsidies. Private onfarm investment has been hampered by policies that have historically taxed producers by maintaining relatively low domestic farm prices, inefficient markets that dampen market returns, and weak institutional support for growers, especially small and marginal farmers. Private agribusiness investors, in turn, have faced state and central regulatory policies—including marketing, interstate movement, storage, and taxation policies—that create disincentives for investment, particularly in larger, integrated agribusiness enterprises. Although foreign direct investment is permitted in most agribusiness—the key exception being retailing—the regulatory policies that impede domestic investors have also been a deterrent to foreign investment.

TRENDS IN AGRICULTURAL INVESTMENT

Output and investment in Indian agriculture have not been showing the same robust growth as in the overall economy. For the economy as a whole, real growth in gross domestic product (GDP) and in investment—as captured by gross fixed capital formation (GFCF)—have both been strengthening, particularly since the early 1990s (table 1). In agriculture, however, output growth has been slowing, and investment has continued to lag that in the overall economy. The annual share of GDP that is invested in GFCF averaged a robust 27 percent for the overall economy during 2005-07; by contrast, GFCF in agriculture was only about 7 percent of agricultural GDP during the same period. And while the rate of investment in the overall economy has continued to rise, the rate of investment in agriculture generally declined through 2000 before turning up slightly during 2000-07 (Figure. 1).

Although overall agricultural investment in India is low and growing slowly compared with investment in the rest of the economy, some categories of investment have shown signs of growth. Among these are investments in agriculture-related infrastructure and services, and in investment by the private as opposed to the public sector.

Investment "In" and "For" Agriculture

The data on capital formation in agriculture (shown in table 1) include primarily onfarm investment in construction, farm equipment, irrigation, and other land improvements. Omitted from these accounts are investments in off-farm agriculture-related infrastructure such as markets, storage facilities, rural roads, and rural electrification. Trends in these off-farm investments— **termed investments "for" agriculture**—are characterized in table 2 (Ministry of Agriculture, 2003). These data, which are available only through 2000, show that investment for agriculture has been growing much faster than investment in agriculture, though it too lags overall investment in the economy. And investments both in and for agriculture, combined, still represent a small share of agricultural GDP—about 15 percent during 1998-2000—compared with the 26-percent share of investment in the overall economy during that period.

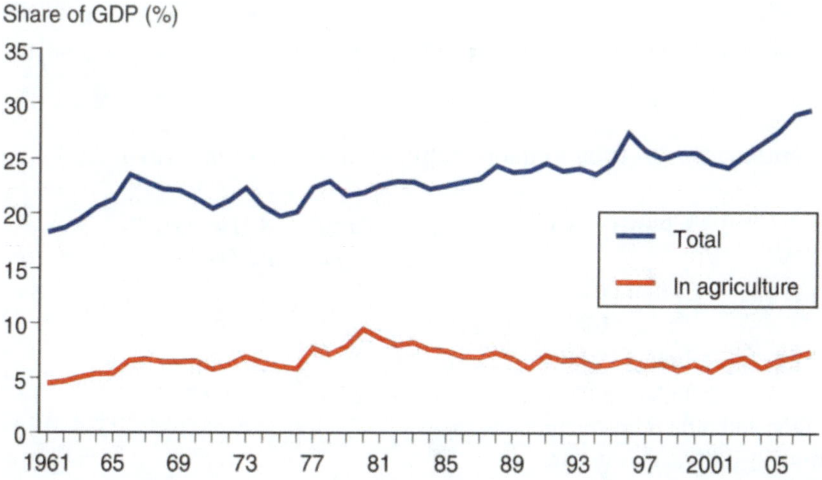

Figure 1. Gross fixed capital formation in India as share of Gross Domestic Product (GDP)
Source: Reserve Bank of India, Handbook of Statistics on Indian Economy.

Agricultural Investment in India Compared With Other Countries

Comparing agricultural investment across countries is complicated by limited availability of data and by differences in definitions and methods used to report data. Some data are available for China and Brazil which, like India, are large developing economies with large agricultural sectors. Both China (using a narrow definition of agricultural investment) and India (using either a narrow or broad definition) have substantially lower rates of investment in agriculture than in the overall economy (table 3). By contrast, in Brazil, where the data employ a broad definition of agricultural investment, the rate of agricultural investment is substantially higher than for the economy as a whole.

Table 2. Growth in public and private gross fixed capital formation in and for agriculture in India

Period	GFCF in Agriculture			GFCF for Agriculture			GFCF in/for Agriculture		
	Public	Private	Total	Public	Private	Total	Public	Private	Total
	Growth rate (percent per year)								
1982-92	-4.3	5.1	1.2	-1.3	5.1	2.0	-2.5	5.2	1.6
1992-99	-0.3	2.4	1.7	1.3	3.0	2.7	0.8	3.5	2.3
1992-97	1.3	2.4	2.0	1.7	3.4	3.2	1.5	4.2	2.8
1997-99	-4.0	2.6	0.7	0.4	2.2	1.3	-1.1	1.8	1.1
	Shares of agricultural GDP (percent)								
1981-83 avg.	4.3	4.0	8.3	6.0	4.7	10.7	10.3	8.6	19.0
1991-93 avg.	2.0	4.8	6.8	3.8	5.7	9.5	5.9	10.4	16.3
1996-98 avg.	1.8	4.5	6.4	3.5	5.9	9.4	5.4	10.4	15.8
1998-00 avg.	1.6	4.5	6.1	3.4	5.8	9.1	5.0	10.3	15.3

Source: Government of India, Ministry of Agriculture, Directorate of Economics and Statistics, 2003.

Table 3. Comparisons of total and agricultural investment in Brazil, China, and India

Country/year	Total	Agriculture
	Percent of GDP	
Brazil (2001-03 average)	16.2	48.4[1]
China (2003-05 average)	42.8	9.6[2]
India (1998-00 average)	25.7	15.3[1]
India (2003-05 average)	27.3	6.62

[1] Includes onfarm and rural infrastructure investment.

[2] Includes primarily onfarm investments.

Sources: Banco Central do Brasil; National Bureau of Statistics of China; Reserve Bank of India; Government of India, Ministry of Agriculture, Directorate of Economics and Statistics, 2003.

Agricultural investment averaged 9.6 percent of agricultural GDP in China during 2003-2005. The Chinese data are based on a definition of investment that compares most closely with investment "in" agriculture in India, which averaged 6.6 percent during the same period. Brazilian data, which include investment in rural infrastructure and agribusiness, show investment in agriculture averaging 48 percent of agricultural GDP during 2001-2003 (table 3). By comparison, Indian investment "in" and "for" agriculture, the broadest measure available for India, averaged 15.3 percent of agricultural GDP during 1998-2000, the most recent period for which data are available. While these comparisons suggest that agricultural investment in India is low compared with two other large, developing agricultural countries, definitional differences in the data make it difficult to draw firm conclusions.

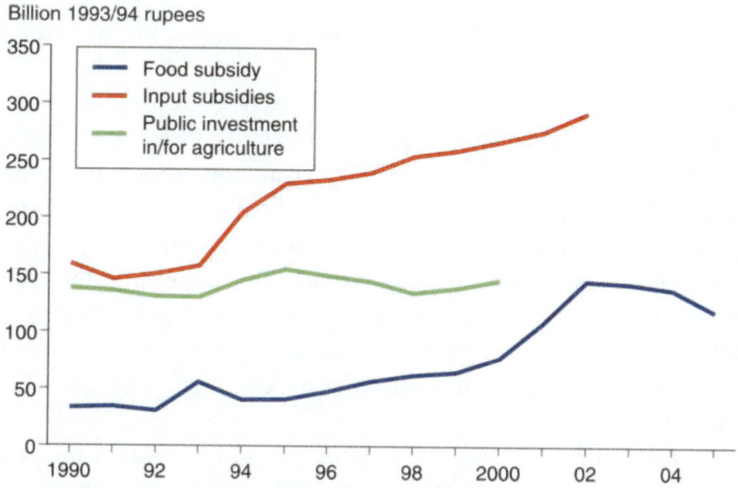

Figure 2. Public investment and subsidies in Indian agriculture

Source: Government of India, Ministry of Agriculture, Directorate of Economics and Statistics, 2003; Government of India, Ministry of Finance, Economic Survey; Mullen, Orden, and Gulatia, 2006.

Public and Private Investment

Public investment in and for agriculture has averaged roughly half the size of private investment, and grew much more slowly than private investment during both the 1980s and 1990s (table 2). Public investment in agriculture actually declined during the 1980s and showed little growth in the 1990s. Weak public investment in agriculture has corresponded with rapid expansion of public expenditures on price subsidies for the sector (Figure. 2), including price supports and subsidized storage and distribution for wheat and rice (the so-called "food grain subsidy"), as well as price subsidies for electricity, irrigation water, and fertilizer (Srinivasan et al., 2007; Landes and Gulati, 2004). No explicit link is apparent between the divergent trends in public outlays on investments versus subsidies in agriculture. However, public investment in irrigation—the major category of public investment in agriculture—has been declining since the mid-1990s. During the same period, political pressure has grown to compensate farmers for rising costs and price instability through input and output price subsidies (Landes and Gulati, 2004).

Studies of investment in Indian agriculture (Chand, 2000; Chand and Kumar, 2004) found that changes in private investment between the early 1980s and the mid-1990s could be explained by the availability of institutional credit for agriculture and improvements in the barter terms of trade—or the ratio of prices received to prices paid—for agriculture. While a significant complementary relationship between public and private investment was evident during the 1960s and 1970s, no such evidence exists since the early 1980s. Further, state-by-state analysis revealed a highly significant positive relationship between private investment and both agricultural output and productivity growth nationally and in most States. Overall, the evidence suggests that since the early 1980s, public investment in agriculture has been less important to overall investment in the sector—and to growth in output and productivity—

than has the environment for private investment, defined as profitability and credit availability compared to other sectors.

More recent data indicate that improving terms of trade for agriculture—as determined by the ratio of agricultural product prices to prices of manufactured and other nonagricultural goods—may have been an important factor in expanding private investment in and for agriculture through the end of the 1990s (Figure. 3). Improvements in the agricultural terms of trade during the 1990s were driven by two key factors (Landes and Gulati, 2004). First, liberalizing reforms to industrial and manufacturing sector policies in the early 1990s led to declining real prices for many nonagricultural goods. Second, agricultural commodity prices tended to strengthen during the late 1990s when the Government implemented large increases in support prices for wheat and rice—India's **major farm** products and food staples (Srinivasan et al., 2007).

Strengthening terms of trade for agriculture are also reflected in producer support estimates (PSEs) for Indian agriculture (Figure. 4). These estimates, which account for input subsidies and policy-induced differentials between domestic and international reference prices (termed market price support), indicate that India transitioned from taxing agriculture during the early and mid-1990s to supporting it during 1997-2002. This trend was driven by steadily increasing support of farmers through input subsidies and, particularly, by substantial increases in market price support in the late 1990s.

Increased producer support and strengthening terms of trade for agriculture suggest improved incentives for private investment by farmers and agribusinesses during the late 1990s and early 2000s. Although the most recent available data on the terms of trade for agriculture indicate some weakening during 2004-2005, more recent increases in world and domestic agricultural commodity prices have likely sustained price incentives for domestic producers.

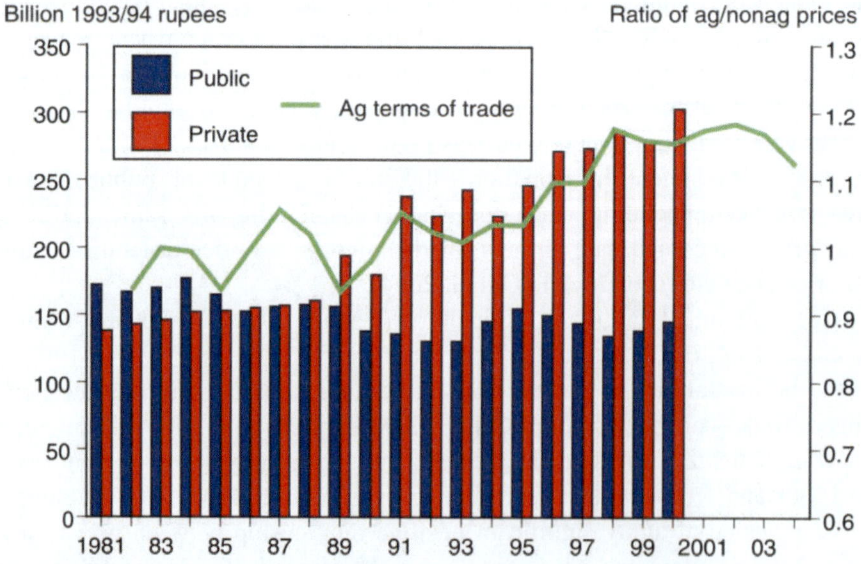

Figure 3. Public and private gross fixed capital formation in and for Indian agriculture

Source: Government of India, Ministry of Agriculture, Directorate of Economics and Statistics, 2003; Government of India, Ministry of Finance, Economic Survey.

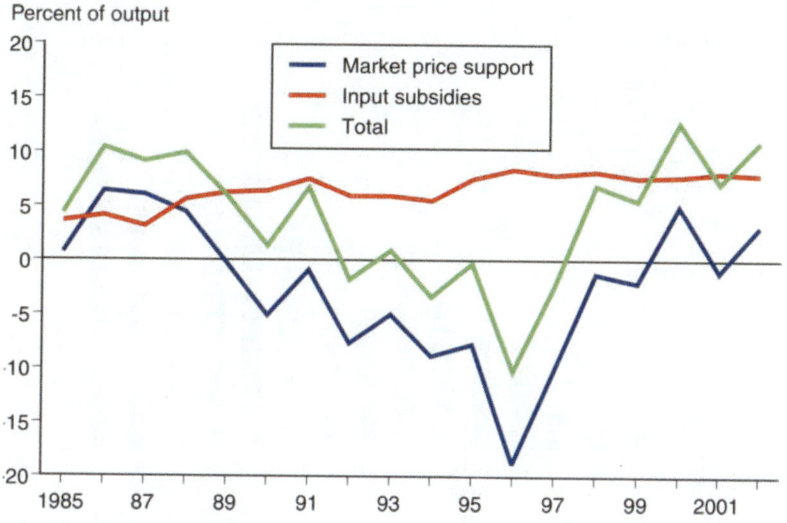

Figure 4. Producer support estimates for India

Source: Mullen, Orden, and Gulati, 2004.

Foreign Direct Investment

Prior to 1991, foreign direct investment (FDI) was negligible in the Indian economy because of highly restrictive policies regarding the permissible types of projects and foreign ownership shares, and the repatriation of earnings. In 1991, the Government began to liberalize FDI policies, initially giving automatic approval for up to 51 percent foreign ownership in 34 industries, including food processing, but with continued restrictions on imports and earnings repatriation.

FDI began to flow into India immediately following the 1991 reforms, growing about 36 percent annually in real terms between 1990-92 and 200305, but with only small amounts flowing into agriculture. Overall FDI growth has been aided by the implementation of additional reforms that have further eased the approval process, increased permissible sectors and foreign ownership shares, and loosened foreign exchange balancing restrictions. Still, FDI continues to make only a small contribution to annual fixed capital formation in India—now averaging about 4 percent (Figure. 5).

Although many agricultural sectors have been open to FDI since the early 1990s, FDI in Indian agriculture has not been significant. Leading sectors for FDI in India have been electrical equipment (17 percent of total FDI during 1991-2006), telecommunications (11 percent), transport (10 percent), services (9 percent), and power/petroleum refining (8 percent). Of the $38.9 billion in total FDI inflows during 1991-2006, about $1.7 billion—or 4 percent—has been in industries that can be identified as specific to agriculture. Food processing accounted for $1.2 billion of FDI, with agricultural machinery ($166 million), timber products ($107 million), and fertilizers ($78 million) accounting for most of the remainder. Some additional FDI that is classified in general activities, such as trading and services, might also be attributed to the agricultural sector.

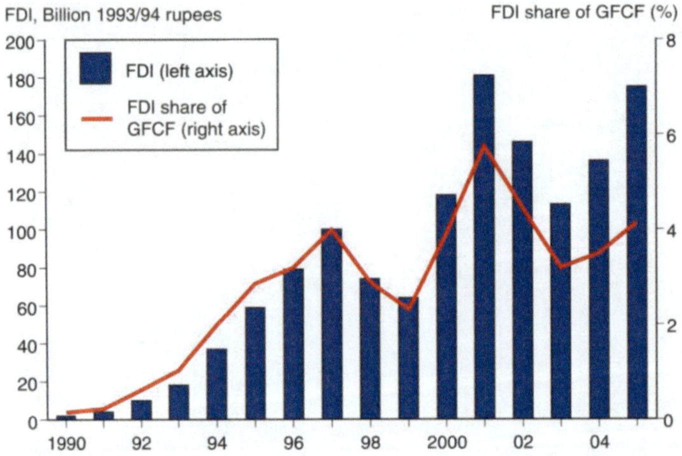

Figure 5. Foreign direct investment (FDI) in India and share of gross fixed capital formation (GFCF)

Source: Reserve Bank of India, Handbook of Statistics on Indian Economy.

Sources of Foreign Direct Investment

The United States has been the second largest single-country source of FDI in India, accounting for about 15 percent of Indian FDI during 1991-2006 (Figure. 6). The largest source of FDI to India, accounting for 37 percent of the total during 1991-2006, has been the island nation of Mauritius. A bilateral double taxation treaty affords favorable treatment to funds that move through Mauritius, a situation that likely disguises the true origin of much of the FDI flows to India. Other major sources are the European Union, collectively accounting for about 24 percent of FDI into India during 19912006, and the countries of East Asia (13 percent).

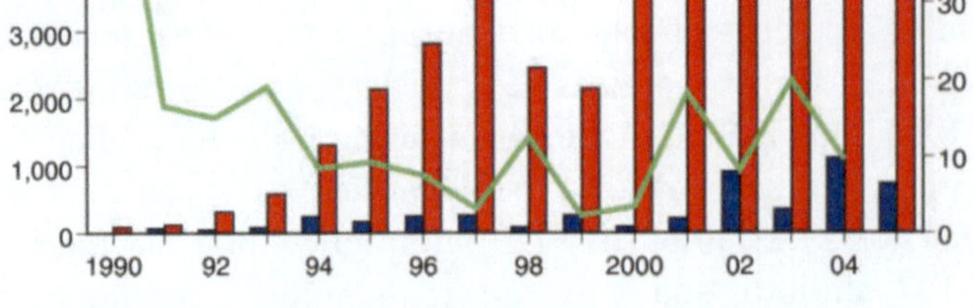

Figure 6. Total and U.S. foreign domestic investment (FDI) in India

Source: Reserve Bank of India, Handbook of Statistics on Indian Economy; U.S. Department of Commerce, Bureau of Economic Analysis.

Indian data on inward FDI by industry and country of origin are not available, but U.S. sources suggest that U.S. FDI in food-related industries there has been minor—about $18 million over 1990-2005. However, data for several years are not reported in order to protect the confidentiality of the small number of firms investing.

THE PRIVATE INVESTMENT CLIMATE

Prospects for agricultural investment hinge largely on the environment for private investment by farmers and agribusinesses. Private investment accounts for the bulk of total investment in agriculture, while fiscal constraints—including growing subsidy outlays—may continue to restrict public investment. Key factors likely to shape the climate for private investment by farmers and agribusinesses include (1) the extent to which domestic demand for agricultural products makes investment potentially profitable; (2) a range of government regulatory, credit, tax, and other policies that affect incentives for domestic and foreign investment in Indian agriculture; and (3) infrastructure constraints.

Consumer Demand

Consumer demand for food products in India has registered significant growth and diversification since the early 1990s, when a package of reforms to industrial, trade, and exchange rate policies launched India on a path of relatively strong income growth. India's youthful demographics and rapid urbanization also bode well for further growth and diversification of food demand (Joshi et al., 2007; Pingali and Khwaja, 2004).

Income growth in India, as measured by growth in real gross domestic product (GDP), has averaged more than 6 percent annually since the early 1990s, and more than 8 percent since 2003, establishing India as one of the fastest growing economies in the world. Rising incomes have contributed to a steady decline in the share of the population living in poverty, with poverty defined as the level of per capita income needed to purchase a nutritionally adequate diet (Figure. 7). Although growth has been strong, India's per capita income remains at a level—about $588 annually in 2006—where most households continue to spend a large share of new income on food, both to increase caloric intake and to diversify and upgrade diets (World Bank, 2007).

India's youthful demographics—about 34 percent of the population was age 14 or under in 2001 compared with 25 percent in China—is also a driver of food demand (Figure. 8). Not only can average levels of daily food intake be expected to rise as more children grow to adulthood, but young adults are often more likely to try new foods and diversify their diets beyond traditional foods. Urbanization is another force that typically contributes to dietary change, through more intense exposure to foods from other cultures and increased demand for convenience foods to accommodate the schedules of two-earner households. The urban share of India's population was 27.8 percent (285 million) in 2001 and is rising steadily. In 2001, India had 35 cities with a population of 1 million or more, with these larger urban areas accounting for more than 10 percent of India's total population of more than 1 billion.

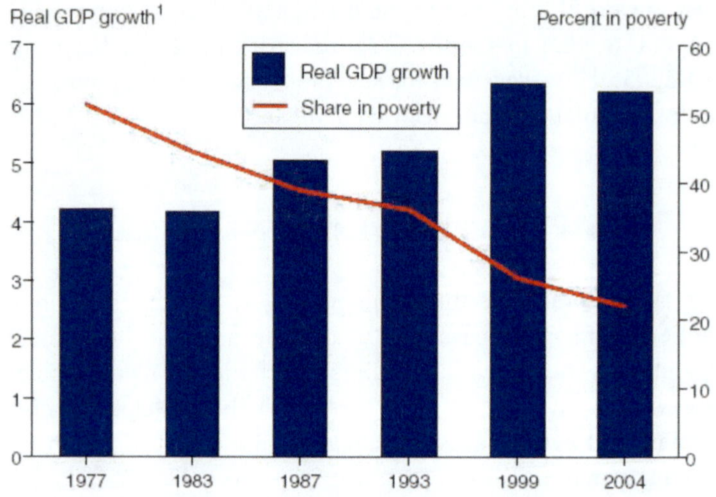

Figure 7. Income growth and poverty reduction in India

[1]Real GDP growth for 5 years preceding year indicated.
Source: Government of India, Ministry of Finance, Economic Survey.

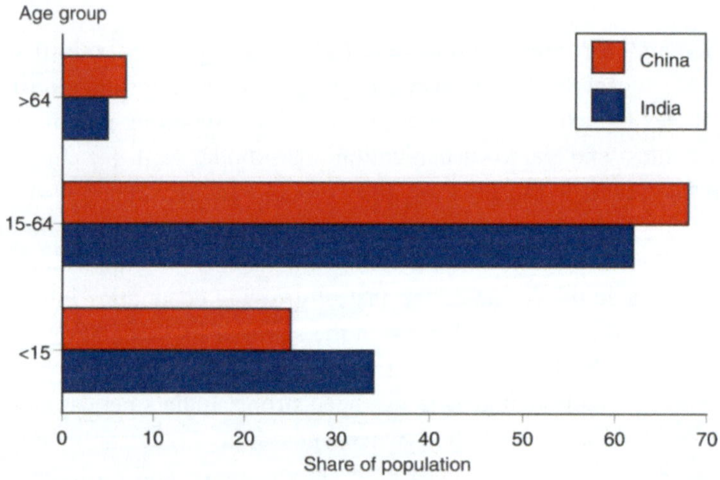

Figure 8. Age composition of India's **and China's populations**

Source: Census of India, 2001.

Data on food consumption by major food groups demonstrate the impact of rising incomes, demographics, and urbanization on the growth and diversification of food demand since the early 1990s (Figure 9). While consumption of traditional items such as cereals and pulses continues to expand, other food categories—including vegetable oils, eggs, fruit, vegetables, milk, and meats—have been exhibiting substantially more rapid growth in demand.[3] These patterns are also evident from Indian consumer surveys that provide expenditure data by food group and expenditure class. Expenditures on cereals—the traditional food staples that still account for the bulk of average consumer food expenditure—tend to decline among higher income consumers (Figure. 10). For higher valued foods groups, however, consumer expenditure tends to accelerate as incomes rise. Foods in greater demand as incomes rise include not only fruit, vegetables, and edible oils, but also animal-based products such as milk, eggs, and meat (Figures 11-13).

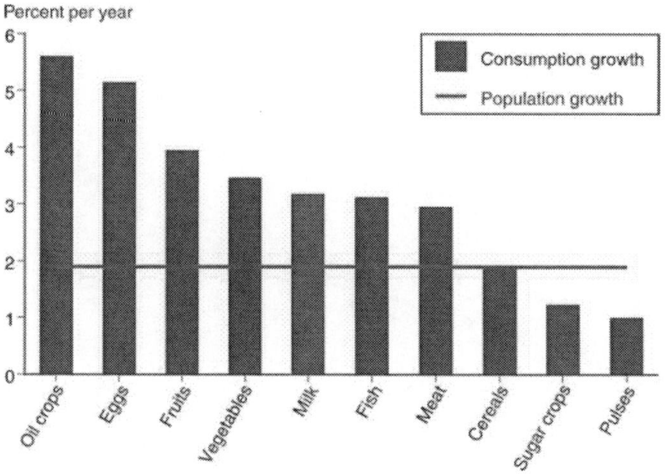

Figure 9. Consumption growth by food group in India, 1991-2004[1]

[1] Endpoints based on 3-year year averages centered on middle year; 1991 = 1990-92 average.
Source: Food and Agriculture Organization, FAOSTAT database.

Overall, the robust prospects for growth and diversification of food demand in India contrast sharply with sluggish agricultural investment. Constraining new investment in and for agriculture are policies that diminish incentives for both domestic and foreign investors, as well as infrastructure constraints that increase costs.

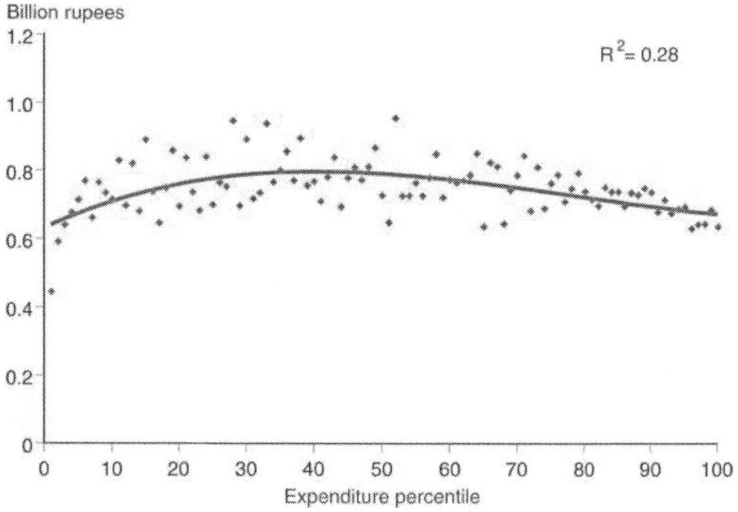

Figure 10. Consumer expenditures on cereals by expenditure percentile in India

Source: National Samply Survey, 1999/2000.

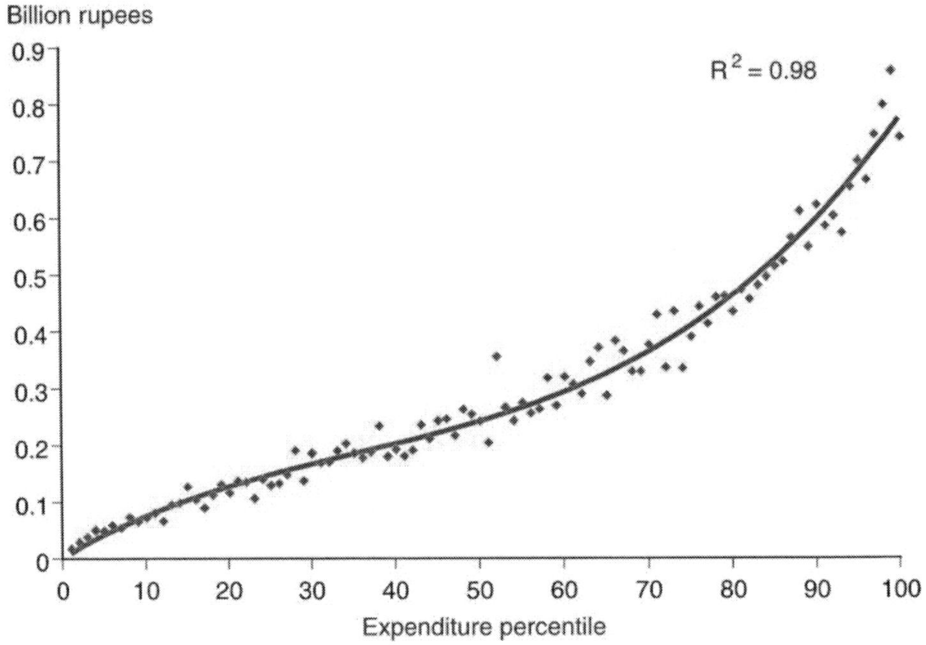

Figure 11. Consumer expenditures on milk products by expenditure percentile in India

Source: National Samply Survey, 1999/2000.

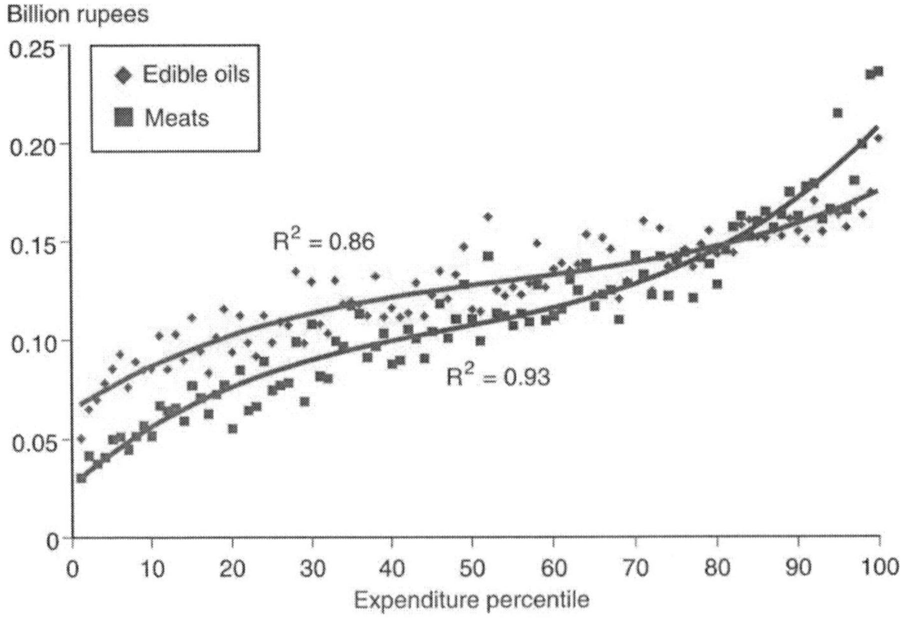

Figure 12. Consumer expenditures on edible oils and meats by expenditure percentile in India

Source: National Samply Survey, 1999/2000.

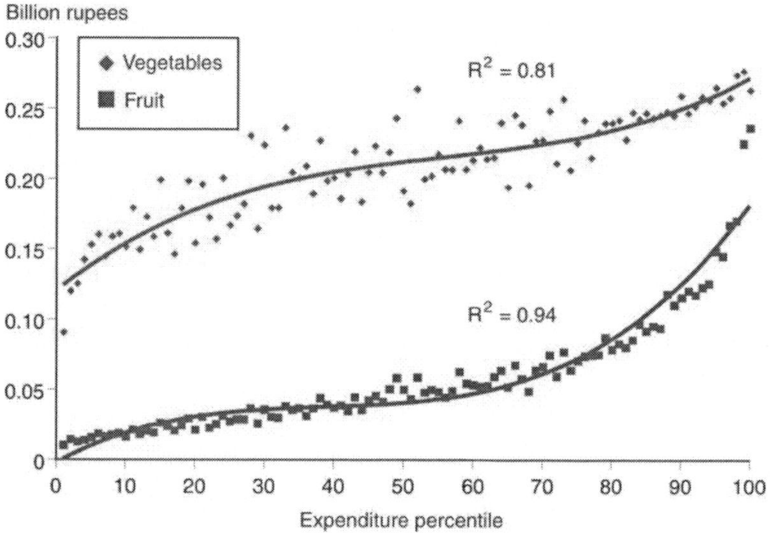

Figure 13. Consumer expenditures on fruit and vegetables by expenditure percentile in India

Source: National Samply Survey, 1999/2000.

Policy Factors Affecting Investment

India's agricultural sector—including most aspects of agricultural production, marketing, processing, and trade—has traditionally been heavily regulated. Although an earlier study (Chand and Kumar, 2004) identified the importance of credit availability in driving private investment, a broader range of Indian policies and regulatory interventions is at play in shaping the environment for private investment by farmers and agribusiness. To the extent that regulatory and institutional disincentives for investment have resulted in inefficient markets, they can also limit the potential for farmers—including India's many small farmers—to benefit from and respond to signals from India's expanding and diversifying consumer markets.

The primary goals of regulation have been to enhance food security by ensuring adequate supplies of food staples at affordable prices and to support employment growth through labor-intensive import substitution. Historically, regulation of agriculture has included strict controls on foreign trade, domestic marketing and interstate movement of agricultural produce, the scale of agricultural processing firms, and land ownership (in addition to the taxation, labor, and investment measures that applied to all areas of the economy). While regulation has eased since the early 1990s, there has been less reform in agriculture than in the manufacturing or service sectors of the Indian economy.

India's Constitution vests the governments of India's 35 States and Union Territories with most of the authority to make and implement regulations and policies affecting the agricultural sector. Central government influence over the regulations and policies promulgated by the States stems largely from the extent to which States are dependent on the central government for funds. Many States tend to have unique regulations and policies, which complicates the regulatory climate facing agribusinesses when operating across State lines. The necessity for obtaining State-by-State legislation and implementation can also slow the process of reform.

India has made progress in reforming market interventions and improving the climate for private investment by farmers and agribusiness since the late 1990s. Plant-scale restrictions have been eliminated for most agribusinesses. Regulation of private movement and storage of farm produce is now less restrictive in many States, and restrictions on the private marketing of farm produce are undergoing reform in most States. Farmers and agribusiness face an improved credit environment. Business taxes are being reduced, food laws are being simplified, and tariff barriers, though high, are declining for some commodities. However, most reforms are being implemented gradually and the lack of a clear political consensus on reducing government intervention in agriculture is likely to continue to slow progress and create risk for investors. In addition, political sensitivity has prevented real progress in several key areas of concern to domestic and foreign investors, including easing restrictive labor laws and developing legal systems to support equitable and efficient rental and sale markets for agricultural land.

Overall, the analysis of individual factors below indicates that the regulatory and policy climate is becoming more supportive of new investment by farmers and agribusiness, but it is not clear if the completed reforms will be adequate to stimulate rapid growth in investment, or if the process of implementing reforms will be sustained.

The Essential Commodities Act

The Essential Commodities Regulation & Enforcement Act of 1955 (or ECA) authorizes the Central and State Governments to make broad ranging interventions in the markets for essential food products to ensure their availability and to protect consumers from possible exploitation by commercial traders (Government of India, Ministry of Consumer Affairs, Food, and Public Distribution, 2007). Under the ECA, Ministries and Departments of the Central Government may issue rules for regulating production, distribution, quality standards, movement, and pricing of essential commodities, including cereals, pulses, edible oils, and sugar. Regulations are implemented through "control orders" issued by State Governments, with monitoring and oversight by the Central Government.

The ECA gives authority to the Central and State Governments to intervene at any level of the supply chain, including:

Regulating production or manufacture of essential commodities;
Controlling the price at which essential commodities are bought or sold ;
Prohibiting the withholding from sale of any essential commodity ordinarily kept for sale (stock holding limits);
Restricting or preventing private movement of essential commodities across district or State borders.

Control orders under the ECA can be issued by State authorities at any time without Central or State legislative action. State governments may, for example, issue control orders when local prices of essential commodities rise sharply, or if there is suspicion of "hoarding" or black market activities by traders.

Although there is evidence that the imposition of ECA-related restrictions has been declining over time—perhaps because of improved local supplies of cereals and other foods—all States continue to have ECA laws and many have some operative controls over commodity storage and movement (World Bank, 1999). Examples include ongoing controls on the storage, sale, and movement of rice in the State of Tamil Nadu, and recent restrictions on wheat and pulse storage in the State of Maharashtra (Government of Tamil Nadu, 2007; Government of Maharashtra, 2007). Even with declining use, the continued existence of the legal authority to restrict commercial trading and movement of commodities is a source of risk for private investors.

Small-Scale Industry Reservations

The small-scale industry (SSI) sector is a major component of the Indian economy, with about 3.6 million firms accounting for about 39 percent of total industrial value added, 20 million jobs, and 45 percent of total exports. From shortly after independence in 1947 until the late 1990s, most of the food processing sector was, by law, reserved for small-scale firms with a prescribed maximum investment. According to the Industries (Development and Regulation) Act of 1951, this policy was intended to promote the small-scale sector with two objectives: (1) ensuring increased production of consumer goods in the small-scale sector, and (2) expanding employment opportunities through small-scale industries (Government of India, Ministry of Micro, Small, and Medium Enterprises, 2007).

The limit for fixed capital assets for small-scale industries (SSIs) has been increased over time and is currently set at Rs 10 million (about $247,000). These limits effectively prevented the establishment of large-scale or vertically integrated food processing firms in the past, and continue to do so in the sectors that remain reserved for SSIs. Additionally, the manufacture of most agricultural machinery and many types of food processing machinery was reserved for SSIs before being "dereserved" during 1997-2007. These constraints limited the availability of modern farm equipment and food processing technology. Although some firms received waivers of SSI restrictions to operate larger enterprises, these special licenses have mostly been made available to firms exporting at least 50 percent of their output (Government of India, Ministry of Micro, Small, and Medium Enterprises, 2007).

Since 1997, when rice and wheat milling were removed from the SSI list, food processing industries reserved for the small-scale sector have grown fewer. At present, just six food processing industries remain on the reserved list (Government of India, Ministry of Micro, Small, and Medium Enterprises, 2007):

Pickles and chutneys
Bread
Pastry
Hard-boiled sugar candy
Rapeseed, mustard, sesame, and groundnut oil (except solvent extracted)
Ground and processed spices (other than spice oil and oleoresin spices).

Perhaps as important as SSI policies to the structure of Indian food processing and marketing are the very small-scale, "unorganized sector" firms. These small enterprises operate outside the legal, tax, and regulatory systems that are pervasive in agricultural processing and marketing, and account for about 75 percent of food processing industry output (Government of India, Ministry of Food Processing, 2007). The unorganized sector firms—which the State, local, and Central governments generally choose not to try to control—benefit from avoidance of taxes and regulations and are often competitive with both SSIs and larger firms in supplying small volumes of relatively low-quality goods.

Although only a few food processing industries continue to be reserved for the small-scale sector, the legacy of the SSI policy is an agricultural processing and marketing industry characterized by small, nonintegrated firms and a generally low level of technology. While this structure is beginning to change—with some former SSIs either supplying larger firms, expanding themselves, or closing—agribusiness investors currently face a general lack of competitive suppliers of intermediate goods and services, which may also discourage new investment.

State Agricultural Produce Marketing Committee Acts

Under the authority of India's Agricultural Produce Marketing Act of 1972 (and its amendments), most Indian States have similar acts (Agricultural Produce Marketing Committee, or APMC, Acts) that regulate the establishment of markets and the marketing of agricultural produce. These acts are intended to ensure that all (or most) trade between farmers and initial buyers occurs through a regulated market, primarily to protect farmers from unfair or exploitative trading practices. But the requirement to market all produce through the regulated markets also facilitates the collection of marketing taxes and fees for State and local governments.

The APMC policies have led to the establishment of more than 7,500 regulated markets in India, each operated by a local marketing committee and supported by the marketing fees collected on each transaction. Marketing fees typically range from 1 to 2 percent, on top of which a market levy is often imposed to support State or local investments in market infrastructure. In general, the quality of marketing infrastructure and services—including roads, marketing floor, weighing, storage, grading, and market information— is poor (Patnaik, 2006). Studies have also found that transactions in regulated markets, where licensed traders can have significant market power, often lack transparency and lead to exploitation of farmers (World Bank, 2006)

The Indian Government has acknowledged that policies established under the APMC Acts have hampered the development of India's agricultural markets and is now promoting reforms by the State governments (Government of India, Ministry of Agriculture, 2000). In addition to the cost, quality, and performance issues already noted, the policies have prevented private investment in agricultural markets and infrastructure, and have largely prevented development of coordinated or integrated market structures, such as contracting, that more directly connect farmers and buyers. Although some States have permitted contracts between growers and buyers for specific products, the APMC requirement to trade in regulated markets tended to prevent the emergence of contract farming. Although views differ, some analysts and policymakers have noted the potential advantages of contract farming in India, both in helping growers manage risk and in engaging the private sector in the delivery of inputs and technology (Birthal, 2007; Singh, 2007).

Table 4. Status of State Agricultural Produce Marketing Act reforms (as of January 2007)

Stage of reform	Number	States and Union Territories
Reforms completed as suggested by the model act.	12	Andhra Pradesh, Arunachal Pradesh, Chandigarh, Chatti-sgarh, Himachal Pradesh, Madhya Pradesh, Maharashtra, Nagaland, Orissa, Punjab, Rajasthan, Sikkim
Reforms suggested by the model act partially completed.	5	Delhi, Gujarat, Haryana, Karnataka, Uttar Pradesh
Existing act already provides for reforms suggested by the model act.	1	Tamil Nadu
No existing act; no reforms required.	7	Andaman & Nicobar Islands, Bihar, Dadra & Nagar Haveli, Daman & Diu, Kerala, Lakshadweep, Manipur
Reforms suggested by the model act initiated but not completed.	10	Assam, Goa, Jammu & Kashmir, Jharkhand, Meghalaya, Mizoram, Pondicherry, Tripura, Uttaranchal, West Bengal

Source: Ministry of Agriculture, Government of India, 2007.

The Ministry of Agriculture is currently promoting the reform of State APMC regulations, including those impeding contract farming and private investment in primary markets, by urging States to conform to a new "model" agricultural marketing act (Government of India, Ministry of Agriculture, Department of Agriculture and Cooperation. 2007). Significant progress has been made in implementing the suggested policy changes, with 25 of India's 35 States and Union Territories having completed or partially completed the suggested reforms as of January 2007 (table 4). With these reforms and past waivers granted by States to specific enterprises, contract farming activities, particularly for horticultural crops and poultry, are becoming increasingly common. In addition, the recent initiatives by central and State governments to build new terminal markets in Punjab, Haryana, Chandigarh, and Madhya Pradesh, and by the National Dairy Development Board to build the new Safal fruit and vegetable market in Bangalore—all with majority private-sector ownership—indicate an improved climate for private investment (Sharma, 2007; Patnaik, 2006).

Land Tenure Policies

Operational holdings of agricultural land in India are small and fragmented, reflecting the pressure of a large rural population on available cultivable land, as well as laws that set landownership ceilings and weak legal frameworks to support the sale and rental markets for farmland. About 63 percent of India's land is farmed in operational holdings of less than 4 hectares, and holdings are becoming more fragmented as farms are divided through inheritance (table 5). India's average operational holding of just 1.3 hectares is larger than in China and some other developing countries, but small relative to holdings in other major agricultural regions such as the United States, the EU, Brazil, Argentina, Canada, and Australia.

Such small operational holdings discourage agribusiness investment by complicating vertical coordination or integration by traders and processors because of the need to assemble produce from so many farmers. Throughout India, national and State laws prevent private companies, as opposed to individuals, from owning agricultural land except for specific approved purposes, such as producing seed or conducting scientific research. It is unclear whether Indian marketing firms and processors will be able to work successfully with large numbers of small farmers. If unsuccessful, this factor could limit the economic viability or scale of vertically integrated food marketing and processing enterprises.

Table 5. Distribution of operational agricultural landholdings in India

Size	1995/96		2000/01	
	Share of holdings	Share of area	Share of holdings	Share of area
		Percent		
Marginal (< 1 hectare)	61.6	17.2	63.0	18.8
Small (1-2 hectares)	18.7	18.8	18.9	20.2
Semi-medium (2-4 hectares)	12.3	23.8	11.7	24.0
Medium (4-10 hectares)	6.1	25.3	5.4	23.8
Large (>10 hectares)	1.2	14.8	1.0	13.2

Source: Ministry of Agriculture, Directorate of Economics and Statistics, *Agricultural Statistics at a Glance 2006.*

With laws typically capping landholdings at 15-20 hectares, far above the current average holding size, progress in improving land rental markets may be an important step in allowing operational holdings to grow to more efficient scales. Land rental and tenancy laws vary by State, with relative freedom of land rental in some States (Assam, Punjab and Haryana), and a total ban on rentals in others (Bihar, Gujarat, Karnataka, Kerala, Manipur, Orissa, Rajasthan, Jammu & Kashmir and Uttar Pradesh). Lack of clear landownership records is often a key impediment to reform, although a number of States have made progress in land registration and computerization of land records. Also, legal frameworks often place landowners at risk by giving tenants ownership rights after land is rented and operated for several years. This precedent reportedly discourages the rental of farmland and results in near-term rentals that discourage investment in land improvement.

Some States, including West Bengal, have achieved success in improving tenant registration and strengthening land rental and sales markets. Recent policy statements—including the National Agricultural Policy, 2002, and 10th Five-Year Plan document—urge the reformulation of tenancy laws to encourage advanced commercialization of agriculture.

Credit Policies

India's agricultural credit system—an extensive network of cooperative, public sector, and commercial banks—has significantly improved both the availability and terms of credit for agriculture and allied activities since the late 1990s. Following sluggish growth in availability during most of the 1990s, institutional agricultural credit has expanded about 19 percent annually in real terms since 2000, with private commercial banks accounting for most of the expansion (Figure 14). The surge in credit availability has been particularly strong since the announcement of a "Farm Credit Package" in 2004 that aimed at doubling farm credit within 3 years, but has exceeded its annual targets with increases of 37 percent and 40 percent in the first 2 years of implementation.

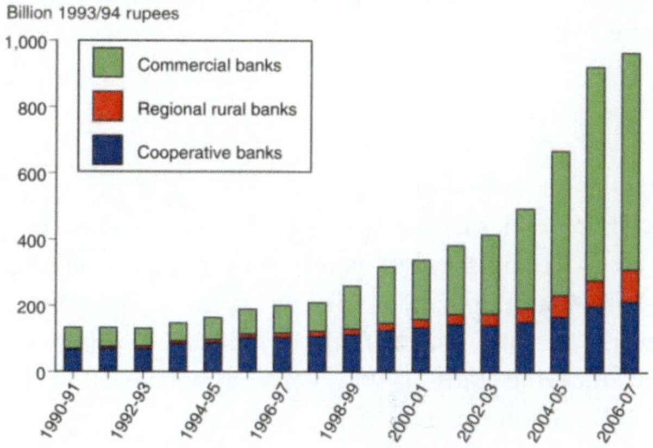

Figure 14. Direct institutional credit for agriculture and allied activities in India

Source: Reserve Bank of India; Government of India, Ministry of Agriculture, Statistics at a Glance, 2006.

An important mechanism for expanding the availability and use of credit by producers has been "Kisan (Farmer) Credit Cards." The cards were introduced in 1998 and, by 2006, were available to about 64.5 million farmers (Government of India, Ministry of Finance, Economic Survey, 2008). Despite the improved availability of institutional credit, about 41 percent of Indian farmers, often those with smaller landholdings, remain dependent on traditional moneylenders at other noninstitutional sources of credit (Government of India, Ministry of Statistics and Program Implementation, 2005).

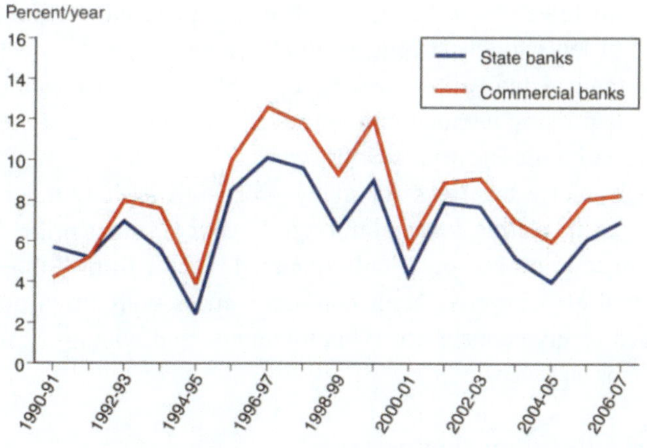

Figure 15. Prime real lending rates in India

Source: Reserve Bank of India; Government of India, Ministry of Agriculture, Statistics at a Glance, 2006.

Credit availability has also improved—and interest rates have generally declined—for business investors. Ensuring a supportive monetary and interest rate environment for investment has been a top policy priority of the Indian Government. Despite rapid economic growth, inflation has averaged about 5 percent and interest rates have generally declined since the late 1990s. Overall, business investors have enjoyed relatively low and stable real interest rates since 2000 (Figure 15).

Tax Policies

Indirect taxes, including tariffs on imported goods and excise taxes on domestically manufactured products, are a major source of government revenue in India, accounting for about 52 percent of the tax receipts and 41 percent of the total revenue receipts of the central government. Agricultural marketing and retail sales taxes are also important sources of State revenue. Declining excise tax rates and tariffs have reduced the share of indirect taxes in total government revenues since the early 1990s, while direct taxes on personal and business income have accounted for an increasing share of revenues.

In 2005, the Central and State governments began implementing a central value-added tax (VAT) system that will eventually unify the central excise and State sales tax systems across all States. The VAT system imposes taxes only on the value added at each step of the supply chain through a system of firm credits for taxes paid on purchased intermediate inputs, thus preventing the cascading of taxes on final products. Introduction of the VAT, together with simplification and reduction of State sales and marketing taxes and indirect taxes, will lower business costs, particularly for larger and integrated firms operating across multiple States.

Excise taxes

India's traditionally high excise taxes have been reduced significantly since economywide reform began in the early 1990s (fig. 16). The excise tax system has been steadily simplified with fewer basic rates, and peak tax rates have been reduced from 110 percent (ad valorem) in 1991 to 24 percent by 2004. However, despite declining rates, excise tax revenues have remained buoyant—growing more than 9 percent annually in real terms since 1999/2000—due to rising demand and improved tax compliance (Government of India, Ministry of Finance, Economic Survey, various issues).

Traditionally high excise tax rates for many processed agricultural products have also been reduced (table 6), stimulating demand through lower consumer prices and improving the investment climate for food processors. For "organized" sector firms—those that pay taxes—lower excise taxes will also improve their competitiveness with firms qualifying as small-scale industries, which receive concessional tax treatment, and with unorganized sector firms, which often pay little or no taxes.

State sales and agricultural marketing taxes

State taxes on retail sales and transactions in regulated agricultural markets are typically major sources of State revenue. Tax rates vary by State as well as by product. In 2005, prior to introduction of the value added tax (VAT) system, sales tax rates for processed agricultural products ranged from 8 to 23 percent, with most of the largest States imposing taxes of 12-16 percent. With the VAT, these rates will likely decline and converge across States, although it is not clear how quickly this will happen (World Bank, 2005).

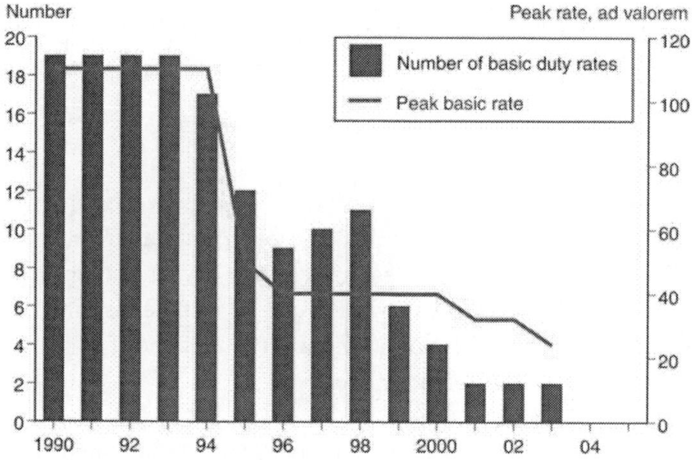

Figure 16. Trend in central excise taxation in India

Source: Government of India, Ministry of Finance, Economic Survey various issues.

Table 6. Changes in India's excise taxation of food products since 2001

Year and product	From	To
2001/02:		
Fruit & vegetable preps	16%	0
2002/03:		
Tea	2 rupees/kg	1 rupee/kg
2003/04:		
Branded, packed refined edible oils	0	8%
2004/05:		
Processed meat, fish, and poultry prod.	16%	8%
Cakes and pastries	8%	16%
2005/06:		
Surcharge on refined edible oils	1 rupee/kg	0
2006/07:		
Condensed milk	16%	0
Ice cream	16%	0
Processed meat, fish, and poultry prod.	8%	0
Pasta	16%	0
Ready-to-eat processed foods	16%	8%
2007/08		
Packed biscuits	16%	0

Source: Government of India, Ministry of Finance, Economic Survey, various issues.

Agricultural marketing taxes imposed on all agricultural produce at the first point of sale also vary significantly by State. These taxes typically include marketing fees of 1-2 percent and development or infrastructure "cesses" (fees) as high as 5 percent, on top of mandatory commissions and fees for cleaning, weighing, bagging, and other services paid to private agents in the market (World Bank, 2005). The reform of State Agricultural Produce Marketing Committee laws—already underway—may create more competition with private markets and eventually reduce these fees.

Direct taxes

India has also taken steps to extend direct tax incentives to the food processing industry. In 2004/05, the Government announced a package of incentives for new firms that process, preserve, and package fruits and vegetables, including a 5-year waiver of direct taxes plus a 25percent reduction in taxes for the next 5 years. In 2005, India also increased tax incentives for the development of Special Economic Zones (SEZs) and for firms, including agro-processing firms, operating in SEZs, among them:

Duty-free import of goods for development, operation, and maintenance of SEZ units;
100-percent income tax exemption on exports from SEZ units for the first 5 years, 50-percent exemption for years 6-10, and a 50-percent exemption of reinvested export profits for years 11-15;
External commercial borrowing by SEZ units up to $500 million/year, without restriction, through recognized banking channels;
Exemption from central Government sales and service taxes;
Exemption from State sales taxes and other State levies.

As of April 2008, six new food and agri-processing SEZs have been approved. How quickly the SEZ policy will improve investment in these sectors is uncertain due to ongoing disputes over the acquisition of land— particularly agricultural land—to accommodate the SEZs.

Tariff Policy

Import tariffs have also been simplified and reduced since the early 1990s (Figure 17). Peak tariffs—the rates charged for the most highly protected products—for nonagricultural goods dropped from 300 percent in 1991 to 12.5 percent by 2006. In agriculture, import access has improved due to the removal of quantitative restrictions in 2001 and some reductions in applied tariffs, but bound agricultural tariffs remain high relative to other sectors of the Indian economy, and relative to most other countries. Although the Government has been reluctant to reduce agricultural tariffs that protect India's many small farmers and small-scale agribusinesses, many agricultural tariffs are now set well below World Trade Organization bound rates (table 7). There has been a tendency in recent years to reduce tariffs when domestic shortages lead to significantly higher consumer prices for essential food commodities. Setting applied tariffs well below bound rates has led to India's emergence as a major importer of pulses and vegetable oils since the 1990s. More recently, India has reduced its applied tariffs for wheat and corn to zero and sharply lowered its tariffs on palm oil products to help augment domestic supplies and stabilize prices.

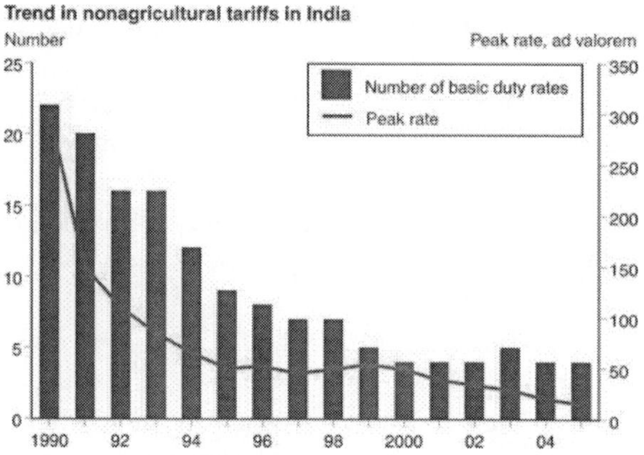

Figure 17. Trend in nonagricultural tariffs in India

Source: Government of India, Ministry of Finance, Economic Survey various issues.

Table 7. India's bound and applied tariffs for selected agricultural products

	Bound rate	Applied rate[1]
	Percent	
Grain and oilseeds		
Pulses	100	0
Wheat	100	0
Rice	70	70
Corn	70	0
Oilseeds	100	30
Horticulture		
Apples	50	50
Oranges, lemons, grapes	100	30
Potato	100	30
Onions	100	5
Meats		
Poultry, whole	100	30
Chicken, leg	150	100
Processed products		
Wheat flour	150	0
Milk powder	60	60
Cheese	40	30
Sugar	150	60
Frozen vegetables	150	30
Oilcake	100	15
Crude soybean oil	45	40
Crude palm oil	300	45
Refined soybean oil	45	45
RBD palm olein	300	52.5

[1] As of January 2008.

Source: Ministry of Agriculture, Directorate of Economics and Statistics, *Statistics at a Glance, 2007*.

Reduced tariff protection presents both challenges and opportunities for investors in agriculture and agribusiness. On the challenge side, lower tariffs imply more competitive pressure to reduce costs and improve quality through increased scale, improved technology, and vertical integration. Reduced agricultural tariffs may tend to discourage some new investment aimed at serving rising domestic demand. However, competitive pressure could foster gains in efficiency and quality that allow agriculture and agribusinesses to expand in both domestic and global markets. Some agribusinesses may benefit from freer trade in raw materials and intermediate products. For example, greater access to imported oilseeds could benefit producers and consumers by allowing greater oilseed processing efficiency (Persaud and Landes, 2006). And, access to competitively priced feed can be critical to contain production costs and maintain growth in consumption and production of poultry meat and eggs (Landes et al., 2004).

Labor Policies

Under the Indian constitution, labor law is on the "concurrent list," giving both the Central and State governments the authority to enact legislation on most labor matters. India's comprehensive labor laws—aimed primarily at protecting the rights of employees—are often seen as a disincentive to new investments by larger, organized sector firms. For example, firms with more than 100 employees are required to obtain government permission before laying off workers and can remain obligated to pay workers even after a unit has gone out of business. There are approximately 45 central government laws addressing labor practices and roughly four times that number of additional laws enacted by States (Basu, 2006). Some of the major central government laws are:

Workmen's Compensation Act, 1923: Specifies compensation to be paid in case of injury or death of a worker.

Payment of Wages Act, 1936: Specifies when and how wages must be paid and what deductions are permitted.

Industrial Employment (Standing orders) Act, 1946: Requires employers to clearly define the conditions of employment in conformance with model "standing orders" dealing with worker classification, holidays, shifts, payment of wages, leaves, termination etc.

Industrial Disputes Act, 1947: Provides for investigation and settlement of disputes; sets conditions for laying off workers.

Minimum Wages Act, 1948: Sets minimum wages for all employees.

Employees Provident Fund and Miscellaneous Provisions Act, 1952: Requires minimum employee and employer contributions to "Provident Fund" or retirement accounts.

Maternity Benefit Act, 1961: Requires payment of maternity benefits and/or medical bonus and maternity leave for women employees.

Payment of Bonus Act, 1965: Requires payment of specified bonuses to employees of firms with 20 or more employees.

Payment of Gratuity Act, 1972: Requires payment of specified gratuity, or separation allowance, to employees of firms with 10 or more employees, (Embassy of India, 2007).

Significant reform to India's labor laws to give employers more flexibility in hiring and laying off workers has proven difficult at the central government level, but several States have made changes to support growth in the information technology industry or to attract foreign investment. To avoid falling under the purview of these laws, many larger firms prefer hiring contract labor or organizing into a number of units small enough to avoid the regulations. Locating within an SEZ, where labor laws are sometimes less restrictive, may also be increasingly attractive to new investors.

Food Laws

Until the new Food Safety and Standards Bill was passed in August 2006, India's food processing industry was subject to regulation by eight government ministries administering more than a dozen legislative acts dating as far back as 1954. The complex, overlapping, and sometimes contradictory regulatory environment was seen as a deterrent to investment and innovation in food processing.

The 2006 bill, which awaits implementation, consolidates the laws relating to food and establishes a Food Safety and Standards Authority of India to set science-based food standards and regulate the manufacture, import, processing, distribution, and sale of food. The "Food Authority" is to be established in the Ministry of Health and supported by scientific committees and panels in setting standards. According to the legislation, the goal is to have an effective and transparent regulatory framework that will allow the food industry to work efficiently and attract investment. The new legislation is to be enforced by State Governments, State Commissioners for Food Safety, and local government bodies.

Foreign Direct Investment Policy

Indian investment rules currently permit FDI up to 100 percent ownership in most sectors, and in most cases with automatic approval. This includes investment in India's Export Oriented Units and, more recently, in India's planned Special Economic Zones. Key agricultural areas where FDI is currently not permitted (Government of India, Ministry of Finance, Union Budget, various issues) are:

Retail trading, except for wholesale trading and single-brand retailing.

Agricultural production, except for floriculture, horticulture, development of seeds, animal husbandry, fisheries, cultivation of vegetables under controlled conditions, tea plantations, and services related to agriculture and allied sectors.

Housing and real estate.

Foreign investors and firms can enter India as either incorporated or unincorporated entities. Incorporated firms can be established through joint ventures with existing firms, or as wholly owned subsidiaries of foreign companies. Unincorporated entities can take the form of liaison, project, or branch offices of foreign firms. All profits, dividends, and foreign investment may be freely repatriated, except for special cases where nonresident Indians invest in specific schemes that do not permit repatriation (Government of India, Ministry of Commerce and Industry).

Restrictions on agricultural production and, particularly, multi-brand retailing likely deter some foreign firms from investing in Indian agribusiness. In the absence of a competitive and efficient domestic food retailing industry, the inability to integrate forward into retailing likely reduces the potential profitability of investments in food supply chains by multinational retailers. However, it is likely that foreign investors are as discouraged— and perhaps even more so—by the same regulatory and policy disincentives faced by domestic firms investing in agribusiness.

Infrastructure Factors Affecting Investment

The climate for agribusiness investment in India is also shaped by the availability, quality, and costs of various infrastructural services required by agricultural producers, traders, and processors. In general, India's transport, power and water infrastructure, while often available at low cost, is of poor quality. Similarly, the institutions that provide important agricultural services, such as market information and grading/inspection services, are generally considered to be weak, while the agricultural research and extension system is criticized for being unresponsive to emerging needs of the farm sector. These infrastructural and institutional deficiencies impose additional costs and risks for new investors.

Power

India's economy labors under a chronic shortage of electrical power. During 2003-2005, the average energy deficit was more than 7 percent and the average peak shortage was about 11 percent, gaps that have not been closed significantly in the last decade. About 64 percent of India's power is generated by thermal plants, 25 percent from hydroelectric facilities, 8 percent from wind and other renewable sources, and 3 percent from nuclear plants (Ministry of Power, 2008). Plans to reduce the energy deficit by expanding public and private investment in power generation and transmission are ambitious, but have generally fallen below target.

Table 8. Estimated average power tariffs and costs in Indian States, 2001-02

Category	India average	Andhra Pradesh	Uttar Pradesh	Rajasthan	Tamil Nadu	Haryana
			Rupees per kilowatt-hour			
Agriculture	0.42	0.14	1.19	0.46	0.01	0.48
Domestic	1.95	1.74	1.81	1.90	1.81	2.80
Industry	3.79	4.41	4.82	3.95	3.95	4.51
Overall	2.40	2.22	2.59	2.21	2.37	2.25
Cost of supply	3.50	3.61	3.83	3.68	3.09	4.12

Source: Planning Commission, May 2002.

Low cost recovery is a fundamental problem of the power sector, leading to underinvestment in new generation and transmission capacity, as well as poor maintenance of existing capacity. Large subsidies on household and agricultural power use, together with significant theft, are key sources of low cost recovery. Power rates for agricultural uses are heavily subsidized throughout India, while industrial users are charged high power rates that cross-subsidize agricultural and household users. Overall, however, the average power tariff accounts for only about 70 percent of the costs of generation and transmission (table 8).

Power costs for both agricultural and household (domestic) uses in India are low by international standards (Figure 18). This cost advantage for farmers and farm households is at least partially offset by power rationing, frequent power interruptions, and voltage fluctuations that damage pumps and make water supplies unreliable. In addition, India's power subsidies are hastening the depletion of groundwater resources due to the low cost of operating electric irrigation pumps (Gulati and Narayanan, 2003).

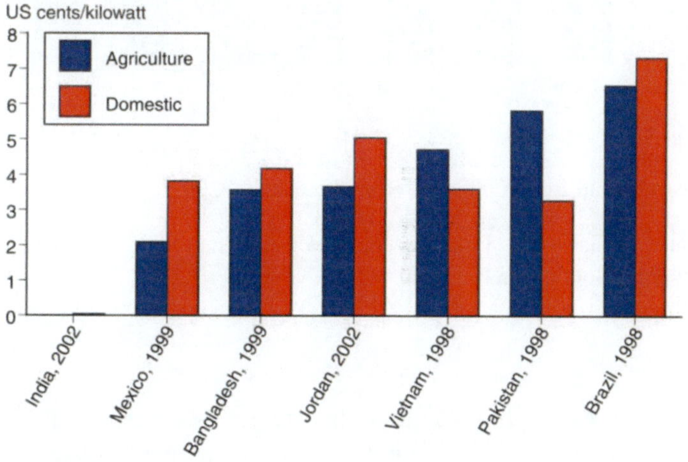

Figure 18. Agricultural and domestic (household) power tariffs, selected countries

Source: Kapoor and Barnes, 2003.

The industrial and commercial sectors account for about 36 percent of India's power use, compared with 29 percent by agriculture, 21 percent by households, and 14 percent by other users. However, because of problems with power availability and quality and the high cost of power to industrial users, a growing number of firms (and households) are investing in their own "captive" power generation facilities to supplement supplies from the power grid. Captive power capacity is estimated to be about 20,000MW, or 16 percent of the total capacity operated by public utilities (Hindu Business Line, 2005; Government of India, Ministry of Power, 2008).

In June 2003, the Government of India enacted the Electricity Act, which provides a framework for comprehensive power sector reforms. The act authorizes the Central Government to harmonize central and State laws, enforce national policies, and establish a competitive environment for the power sector. Power generation no longer requires a license, and new rules are established to strengthen transmission and support private investment in power generation and distribution. The act progressively reduces cross-subsidies and moves tariffs toward the actual cost of supply. Progress on power reform has been mixed. Additions to generating capacity are expected to meet only 57 percent of the current 5-year planning target, while the weighted-average power tariff increased 13.4 percent between 2003 and 2007, led by large hikes in agricultural tariffs (Government of India, Ministry of Finance, Economic Survey, 2006/07).

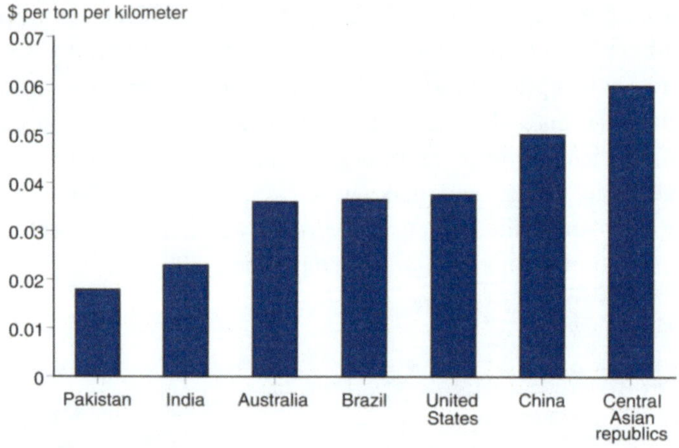

Figure 19. Average truckload freight rates in selected countries, 2002

Source: World Bank, India Road Transport Service Efficiency Study, Energy and Infrastructure Operations Division, South Asia Regional Office, November 1, 2005.

Transportation

More than two-thirds of India's **domestic freight** is transported by road, with the remainder shipped primarily by rail. Although India has an extensive rail transport system, the use of road transport grew from 51 percent of all freight in 1991 to 67 percent by 1998. Users have grown to regard road transport as more readily available, reliable, and cost-effective than rail transport (Cook et al., 1999; World Bank, 2005a).

India's **road freight** transport sector, while competitive and low-cost compared with other countries (fig. 19), tends to be slow and unreliable. For example, average transit time for the 1,408-kilometer (875 mile) trip between Delhi and Mumbai is 3 days, and for the 2,019-kilometer (1,255 mile) trip from Delhi to Bangalore it is 4-5 days, both about twice the time that would be expected in the United States. Slow and unreliable transit times stem from low speeds associated with poor roads and mixed traffic, lack of urban bypasses, and delays for inspection and fee collection at internal border checkpoints. Checkpoint delays alone typically account for 15-25 percent of the transit time (World Bank, 2005a).

Both road and rail transport systems have very limited capacity for bulk handling and transport of agricultural commodities. With a few exceptions, cereals, oilseeds, and other basic agricultural commodities in India are handled and transported in gunny sacks via standard, multi-purpose trucks or railway wagons. Refrigerated rail or road transport of perishable agricultural products is also limited. However, private investment in refrigerated road transport is growing, with subsidized financing available through government programs.

Water

Growth in irrigated area has boosted Indian farm output through both higher yields and increased cropping intensity. About 54 million hectares—or 30 percent of all agricultural land—is now irrigated, making India second only to China in irrigated area (fig. 20). The largest share of and most of the growth in irrigated area is associated with private investment in wells and diesel/electric pumps for groundwater irrigation. Power subsidies have prompted the expansion of groundwater irrigation. Surface-water irrigation—which is dependent on public investment in dams, reservoirs, and canals—accounts for about a third of irrigated area, a share that has been declining. Rising public investment costs for new surface-water projects, together with the cost of subsidies for canal water, are contributing to the slowed growth of surface irrigation. In some areas, particularly in north India where intensively irrigated wheat and rice have become common, agriculture is increasingly threatened by water logging and salinity problems associated with high rates of canal irrigation and extraction of groundwater (Gulati and Narayanan, 2003; Gulati et al., 2005).

With the expansion of irrigation, agriculture now accounts for 84 percent of total water use in India (Government of India, Planning Commission, 2002). Many regions face a growing challenge as agricultural, industrial, and household uses compete for water resources. Industrial uses now account for 3-5 percent of water use, about half from surface-water and half from groundwater sources. While most States promise adequate water supplies as part of their industrial policies, highly water-dependent industries tend to locate facilities only in water-surplus areas. Water demand by domestic and industrial users is projected to grow 27 percent and 14 percent, respectively, between 2010 and 2025 (Rosegrant et al., 2002), necessitating more government emphasis on water use regulation, pricing of water, and water resource development.

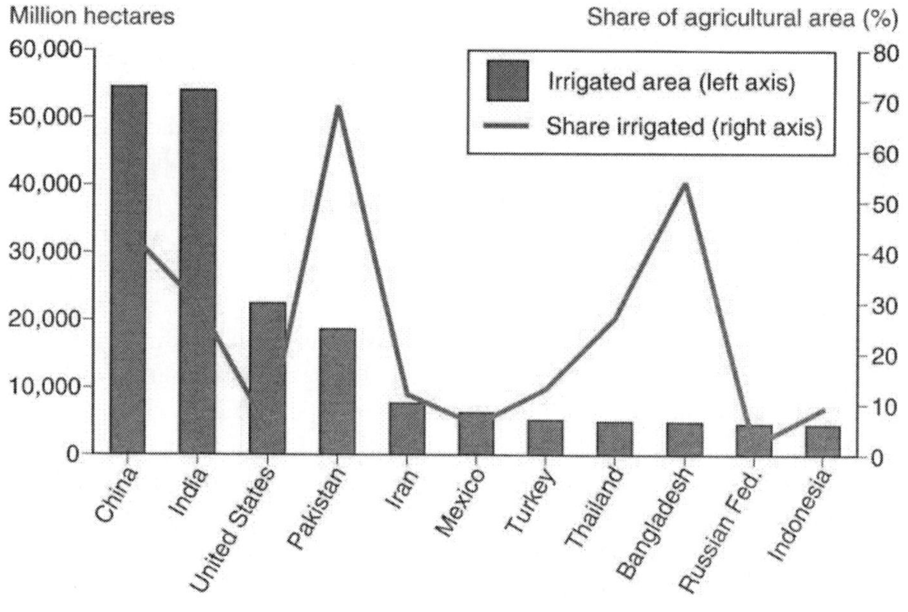

Figure 20. Countries with the largest irrigated area

Source: Food and Agriculture Organization, FAOSTAT database.

Agricultural Research and Extension

India has one of the largest public sector agricultural research and extension systems in the world, as well as a growing private sector research and extension industry. Both public and private research and extension have been important factors in agricultural productivity growth in India, with public research accounting for about 30 percent of total factor productivity growth between 1956 and 1987 and private sector research accounting for about 11 percent (Evenson et al., 1999).

The public agricultural research system—governed by the Indian Council for Agricultural Research (ICAR)—includes 47 central research institutes, 32 national research centers, and 37 State agricultural universities with more than 30,000 research staff (Government of India, Ministry of Agriculture, Indian Council of Agricultural Research, 2007). ICAR and the public research system have been criticized for failing to adapt research priorities to the changing economic and scientific environment for agriculture (Government of India, Planning Commission, 2005; World Bank, 2004). Key issues include making research more demand based to meet the needs of an increasingly diverse agricultural consumption basket, adapting research and extension to new agricultural technologies, and developing more effective public-private research partnerships. A new multi-year National Agricultural Innovation Project funded by the World Bank seeks to address these issues through research capacity building and the formation of public-private consortia focusing on research questions across agricultural supply chains.

Private sector participation in agricultural research is increasing. Government efforts to promote biotechnology research and recent steps to strengthen and clarify intellectual property protections—including passage of the Plant Variety Protection and Farmers' Rights Act (2002) and formulation of the National Seed Policy (2002) and the National Seed Act (in draft)—provide an impetus for private sector involvement in research. At present, private sector research tends to focus on higher value crops (Bt cotton, Bt eggplant, etc.) and on plant types (hybrid seeds) with high expected returns to private investment.

Historically, public investment in agricultural research in India has been low relative to many other countries (Figure 21), but investment has increased since the late 1990s (Figure 22). During 2000-2007, available data indicate that public investment grew about 6 percent annually in real terms, implying a continued increase in investment as a share of agricultural output.

Public agricultural extension is primarily the responsibility of State governments, and has been much criticized for lack of effectiveness (Government of India, Ministry of Agriculture, Department of Agriculture and Cooperation, 2002; Planning Commission, 2005). Key problems include understaffing, lack of coordination, and difficulty in shifting from the historical focus on food grain production to a more diverse set of crop and marketing issues. The Government's New Policy Framework for Agricultural Extension (2002) seeks to instill a new approach that concentrates on increasing farm household income through agricultural diversification. The goal is to make the extension system more market-oriented and farmers more competitive in domestic and international markets.

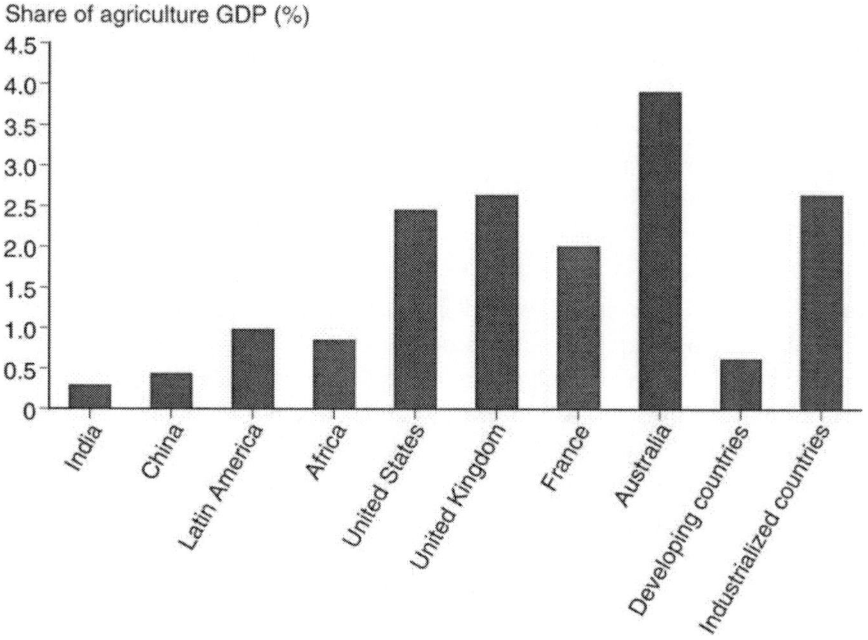

Figure 21. Public agricultural research expenditures in selected countries and regions[1]

[1] 1995 data for all countries except the United States (1993) and Australia (1994).
Source: Pal and Byerlee, 2003.

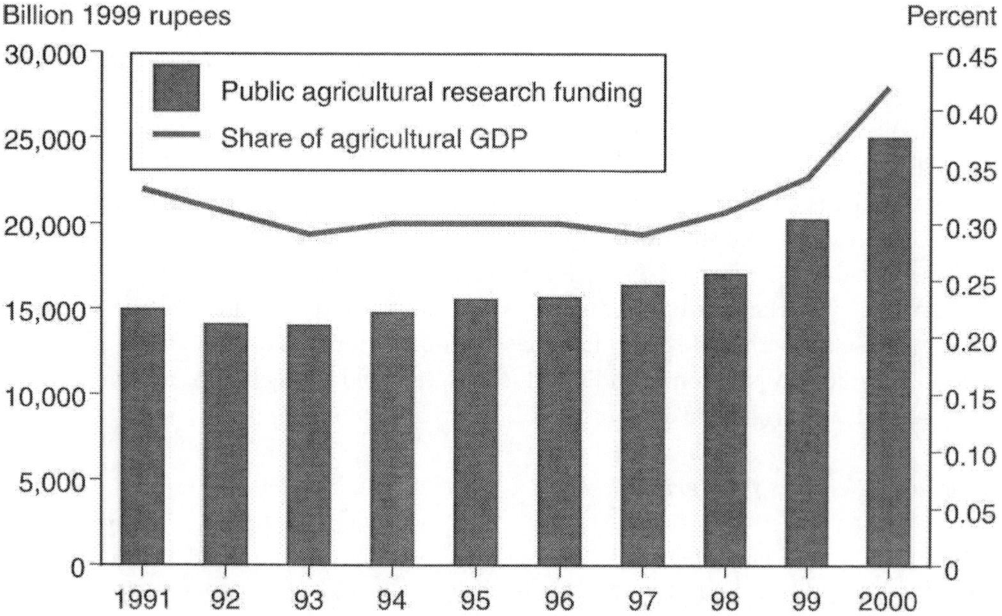

Figure 22. Public agricultural research funding in India

Source: Pay and Byerlee, 2003.

Along with the government effort to strengthen and improve funding for public extension services, private companies and nongovernmental organizations (NGOs) are becoming more active in providing extension services. Models employed by private firms and NGOs include fee-for-service extension, extension linked to input supply or marketing services, and extension linked to contract farming or vertical coordination (World Bank, 2004).

Cold Chain Capacity

Although cold chain capacity is expanding due to public and private investments, India's capacity for cold storage and refrigerated transport of perishable food products is limited. Cold storage capacity in 2006 was 21.7 million tons, reflecting growth of about 11 percent since 2004 (Government of India, Ministry of Food Processing, 2007). As of 2003, approximately 90 percent of total cold storage capacity was used to store potatoes, with other fruit and vegetable products accounting for about 7 percent and dairy products about 1 percent.

Only a few integrated cold chains are established in India, including two serving the dairy industry (Gujarat Cooperative Milk Marketing Federation, and Mother Dairy Foods Processing Ltd), one serving the franchises of McDonald's India, and Snowman Frozen Foods Ltd, which operates the only countrywide cold storage and refrigerated transport network. Most cold storage and refrigerated transport capacity is operated by small, nonintegrated firms that do not make use of state-of the-art technology or management practices (U.S. Trade and Development Agency, 2006).

A number of programs now aim at expanding investment in cold chain capacity:

A capital investment subsidy scheme for construction, expansion, and modernization of cold storage for produce is being implemented by the National Horticulture Board of the Ministry of Agriculture. Between 2001 and 2004, this scheme facilitated private investment in about 4.7 million tons of new cold storage capacity (Government of India, Ministry of Agriculture, Department of Agriculture and Cooperation, 2005).

The Central Warehousing Corporation (CWC), the largest owner of warehouse capacity in India, is developing a large cold storage facility near Delhi, with plans to develop other modern cold storage facilities throughout the country.

The Agricultural Processed Food Products Export Development Authority (APEDA), part of the Ministry of Commerce and Industry, is promoting the development of world-class perishable cargo facilities at air cargo terminals.

The Container Corporation of India Ltd is building cold storage units across the country, as well as refrigerated containers, to support agricultural exports.

Institutional Services for Agriculture

Many of the institutional services needed to support agricultural markets are in the early stages of development in India. In some cases—such as grades/standards and market information—the services have been the responsibility of government agencies that have not adapted to provide the services needed by expanding and diversifying markets. In other cases— such as futures trading—government policies that have regulated markets to protect consumers or farmers have prevented or slowed the evolution of market services.

Grades and standards

The Agricultural Produce (Grading and Marketing) Act of 1937 empowers the Government to fix quality grades, authorize commodity grading, specify labeling and packaging requirements, and confiscate substandard produce. In practice, government decisions on grades and standards issues are seldom rendered in cooperation with the private sector. Although government agencies establish and revise grades and standards for many commodities, there are generally no inspection services in Indian markets and commodities are seldom bought and sold based on these grades and standards. Most Indian grain, for example, is traded based on the broad standard of "fair-to-average quality (FAQ)" with no formal grading, although some private buyers and sellers trade grains at premiums or discounts to the FAQ price based on their independent quality assessments.

Market information

There is a critical shortage of objective, reliable, and timely public information on most major Indian commodity markets, including traded volumes and prices, production, consumption, and stock levels. Although public market reporting by the Ministry of Agriculture and State governments is improving, current reporting includes a limited range of variables—mostly wholesale prices and production estimates—of uncertain quality. The lack of adequate public market information tends to raise the transaction costs and price risk faced by market participants, creates the potential for information asymmetry between large and small players in the market, likely reduces marketing efficiency, and limits information available to support policy formulation. Several private sector firms now sell market information based on their proprietary data collection, and others provide marketing data through their village-level agricultural service centers.

Futures trading

The Government removed its longstanding prohibition on futures trading in most agricultural commodities in 2003/04, leading to the immediate formation of several exchanges to trade futures contracts in major farm commodities (Government of India, Ministry of Finance, Union Budget, 2004/05). However, except for a few commodities that have had a longer history of futures trading—most importantly soybean oil, which has been traded since 2000—traded volumes remain small compared with overall market size and contracts often lack liquidity, thus limiting the utility of the markets for hedging risk.

While the availability of futures contracts and traded volumes have tended to increase, there continues to be concern over the impact of speculators and unscrupulous traders on the stability of consumer prices for essential commodities. In 2006/07, a government panel determined that futures market activity was contributing to a runup in consumer wheat and rice prices, leading the Government to announce a cessation of wheat and rice trading in February 2007, which remains in effect (U.S. Department of Agriculture, Foreign Agricultural Service, 2007). As a result of limited contract liquidity and uncertain government policy, prospective investors in agricultural production, marketing, and processing enterprises continue to face limited and uncertain access to risk management tools.

Prospects for Agricultural Investment

Continued sluggish private investment in Indian agriculture and agribusiness since the early 1990s, despite sustained high growth in consumer incomes and food demand, suggests that policy and infrastructure factors have been a deterrent to new investment. Historically, extensive policy intervention in markets and industries has created disincentives and risks for investments in agriculture, including farmers and agribusinesses, and particularly large-scale vertically integrated agribusinesses.

During much of the 1990s, agricultural trade and price policies resulted in taxation of agricultural production despite substantial and rising farm subsidies. At the same time, movement, storage, and private marketing restrictions for agricultural commodities, scale restrictions on agribusinesses, high taxes on processed products, the high cost of credit, and complex food laws were among the disincentives and risk factors facing investors. This uncertainty was compounded by weak transport and power infrastructure and lack of key market services such as market information, risk management tools, and grading/inspection systems. Through the late 1990s, public investment in agriculture remained sluggish despite rising food demand, while more public funds went to meet the rising cost of subsidies on food grains and farm inputs.

Since 2000, however, there is evidence that the policy environment is improving and that investment in agriculture and agribusiness is beginning to strengthen. Movement and storage restrictions on essential commodities are less common, plant scale limitations have been largely removed, State marketing laws are beginning to permit development of private marketing channels, and taxes on agricultural products are being reduced and simplified. And, although power, transport, and other infrastructure problems will likely be solved only in the longer term, private investment is seemingly on the rise. Private investment in food marketing ventures has increased noticeably in the last several years (table 9). These new ventures collectively amount to \$10-\$20 billion over the next 5-7 years to develop supply chains and "front-end" retail outlets. This activity represents a turnaround in investor confidence.

Recent investment in India's food marketing sector includes a number of ventures by foreign investors, including a Wal-Mart collaboration with the Indian conglomerate Bharti. Since India does not permit foreign direct investment (FDI) by multi-brand retailers, foreign investment has taken the form of wholesale (or "cash and carry") trading enterprises, or partnerships with Indian "franchisees" who own the retail outlets. Other than multi-brand retailing, all other areas of agricultural processing and marketing are open to FDI. While the FDI restrictions on retailing may be deterring some foreign investment in agricultural marketing, the increased activity in chain food retailing by many of India's largest domestic companies indicates their confidence in a supportive policy environment.

While there is evidence that the investment climate is improving for agriculture and agribusiness and that private investment is beginning to respond, it is unclear how quickly or how much agricultural productivity and marketing efficiency will respond. If rapid income growth is sustained, the growth and diversification of food demand will likely continue to outpace production for the next several years, leading to continued pressure on domestic food prices and demand for imports. However, given India's extensive land and water resources and low current farm yields, there is scope to expand output of many farm products and become more globally competitive in the longer term.

Table 10. Growth of India's chain food retailing industry, 2007

Retailer	Year entered	Ownership	Formats	Outlets/ plans	Locations
Nilgiri's	1971	Local (Part own-ership by Actis, UK)	Supermarkets, convenience stores	40; plans for 500 sto-res by 2010	Major cities in south India
Trinethra & Fabmill	1986	Local (Aditya Birla Group)	Supermarkets, convenience stores	170	Major cities in Andhra Pradesh, Tamil Nadu, Karnataka, and Kerala
Margin Free	1994	Local Coopera-tive (Consumer Protection and Guidance society)	Discount stores, supermarkets	350	Major cities in Kerala, Tamil Nadu and Karnataka
Spencers	1996	Local (RPG Group)	Hypermarkets, supermarkets, convenience stores	97; plans to add 50 hyp-ermarkets by 2008	Major cities in South India
Subhiksha	1997	Local (Subik-sha Trading Services Pvt. Ltd.)	Discount stores	520; plans for 1,200 stores all over the country by 2007/08	Major cities in Tamil Nadu, Andhra Pradesh, and Pond-icherry, and Delhi region
Foodworld	1999	Local (Subsi-diary of Dairy Farm Interna-tional)	Supermarkets	55; plans to expand in south India	Bangalore, Hyderabad
Trumart	2001	Local (Pyramid Retail)	Supermarkets, convenience stores	29; plans for 90 sto-res by end of 2007	Maharashtra and Gujarat; Bang-alore, Chennai, Hyderabad, and Kolkata
Food Bazaar	2002	Local (Future Group)	Hypermarkets, supermarkets	90; Plans for 250 stores by 2010	National (major metros and large cities)
Metro Cash & Carry*	2003	Foreign (Metro AG, Germany)	Wholesale "cash & carry"	3; plans to add 1518 new outlets by 2009	Bangalore, Hyderabad, Mumbai, Kolkata, Chennai
My Dollar Store	2004	Local (Franch-isee of My Dollar Store of the U.S.)	Convenience stores	50; plans for 400 sto-res by 2010	Nationwide
Shoprite	2004	Local (Subsidiary of Shoprite (PTY) Ltd., South Africa)	Hypermarket	1; plans to add 2-3 new outle-ts by 2007	Mumbai
Star India Bazaar	2004	Local (Trent; division of Tata Group)	Hypermarket	3; plans to add 23	Nationwide

Table 10. (Continued)

Retailer	Year entered	Ownership	Formats	Outlets/ plans	Locations
Reliance Retail	2006	Local (Relia-nce Industries Ltd.)	Hypermarkets, supermarkets, Convenience stores	230; plans for 3,000 stores, 2,500 super-markets and 500 hy-permarkets by 2010	Nationwide
Spinch	2006	Local (Wadhawan Retail)	Supermarkets	89; plans to add 1,500 stores in 90 cities by 2010	Nationwide
Max Hyper-markets	2007	Local-foreign joint venture (SparInter-national, Neth.)	Hypermarkets	Plans to develop 7 stores by 2009	Nationwide
Bharti[1]	2007	Local (Bharti Enterprises)	Hypermarkets, supermarkets	Plans to invest $2.5 billion by 2014	Nationwide
Bharti Walmart	2007	Local-foreign joint venture (Wal-Mart USA)	Wholesale "cash & carry"	Plans for 15 stores by 2014	Nationwide

[1]Retail partner of Walmart.

Source: U.S. Department of Agriculture. Foreign Agricultural Service. 2006; updated from various press reports.

REFERENCES

Banco Central do Brasil: Anuário Estatístico do Crédito Rural, (2007). http://www.agricultura.gov.br/images/MAPA/estatisticas/06.19.xls

Basu, K. (2006). "*Why India's Labour Laws Are a Problem*," BBC News, 18 May. http://news.bbc.co.uk/2/hi/south_asia/4984256.stm

Birthal, Pratap. (2007). "*Conditions for Success of Contract Farming*," NCAP-USDA-IFPRI Workshop on Contract Farming: Methods and Experiences, New Delhi, May 5-6.

Chand, R. & Kumar, P. (2004). "Determinants of Capital Formation and Agriculture Growth: Some New Explorations," *Economic and Political Weekly, V.39 (52)*: 5611-5616.

Chand, R. (2000). "*Emerging Trends and Regional Variations in Agricultural Investments and Their Implications for Growth and Equity*," NCAP Policy Paper No. 11, New Delhi.

Cook, P. D., Das, S., Aeppli, A. & Martland, C. (1999). "Key Factors in Road-Rail Mode Choice in India: Applying the Logistics Cost Approach," *in Proceedings of the 31st Winter Simulation Conference, Vol. 2*, ACM Press (NY), pp. 1280-1286.

Evenson, R. E., Pray, C. & Rosegrant, M. W. (1999). *Agricultural Research and Productivity Growth in India*. Research Report 109. International Food Policy Research Institute, Washington, DC.

Government of India. Embassy of India (Washington, DC). (2007). Labour Laws. http://www.indianembassy.org/newsite//Doing_business_In_India/ Labor_Laws.asp

Government of India, Ministry of Agriculture. (2007). "Status of Market Reforms in Agriculture (APMC Act amendments) as of 31st January, 2007." http://agricoop.nic.in/PolicyIncentives/progress.pdf

Government of India, Ministry of Agriculture, Department of Agriculture and Cooperation, (2005). http://agricoop.nic.in/ncpm.htm

Government of India. Ministry of Agriculture. Directorate of Economics and Statistics. (2003). *Report of the Committee on Capital Formation in Agriculture, March.* http://agricoop.nic.in/Capital%20Formation/FinalReport.doc

Government of India, Ministry of Agriculture. (2003). *Report of the High-Level Expert Committee on Cold Storage and Storage*, Nov.

Government of India, Ministry of Agriculture, (2002). *Report of Inter-Ministerial Task Force on Agricultural Marketing Reforms.* May 27. http://agmarknet. nic.in/taskrep.htm

Government of India, Ministry of Agriculture, (2000). *National Agricultural Policy.* http://agricoop.nic.in/agpolicy02.htm

Government of India, Ministry of Agriculture, Department of Agricultural Research and Education, Indian Council of Agricultural Research. (2004). *Annual Report, 2003/04.*

Government of India, Ministry of Agriculture, Department of Agriculture and Cooperation. (2007). *Model Rules*, http://agricoop.nic.in/ FINAL%20Model%20Rule%20as%20corrected%20on%2007%2011%20 07.pdf

Government of India, Ministry of Agriculture, Department of Agriculture and Cooperation, Extension Division. (2002). *Policy Framework for Agricultural Extension.*

Government of India, Ministry of Commerce and Industry. Department of Industrial Policy and Promotion. (2003). *Foreign Direct Investment in India—Policy and Procedures*, New Delhi, May. http://dipp.nic.in/manual/manual_0403.pdf

Government of India, Ministry of Finance. *Economic Survey*, various issues.

Government of India, Ministry of Finance. *Union Budget*, various issues.

Government of India, Ministry of Consumer Affairs, Food, and Public Distribution, Department of Consumer Affairs. (2007). *Essential Commodities Act, 1955*, http://fcamin.nic.in/Events/EventDetails.asp?EventId=600&Section=Acts%20 and%20Rules &ParentID=0&Parent=1&c heck=0#

Government of India, Ministry of Food Processing. (2007). Answer to parliamentary question, August 21.

Government of India, Ministry of Micro, Small, and Medium Enterprises. (2007). http://www.laghu-udyog.com/ssiindia/statistics/economic.htm

Government of India, Ministry of Power. (2006). *Annual Report 2005/06.*

Government of India, Ministry of Statistics and Program Implementation, (2005). *National Sample Survey, 59th Round; 2005, Situation Assessment Survey of Farmers: Indebtedness of Farmer Households*, May. http://mospi.nic.in/rept%20_%20pubn/ ftest.asp?rept_id=498&type=NSSO

Government of India, Ministry of Statistics and Program Implementation, (2005). *National Sample Survey, 61st Round; 2004-2005.* http://mospi.gov.in/mospi_nsso_rept_pubn.htm

Government of India, Planning Commission. *Annual Reports*, various issues.

Government of India, Planning Commission, Agriculture Division. (2005). *Report of the Task Group on Revamping and Refocusing of National Agricultural Research*, Jan.

Government of India, Planning Commission, Power and Energy Division. (2002). *Annual Report (2001-02)*, May.

Government of Maharashtra; Food, Civil Supplies and Consumer Protection Department. (2007). Mantralaya, Mumbai, India, March 7. http://fcs.maharashtra.gov.in/data/gr/marathi/2007/03/07/20070309103540001.pdf

Government of Tamil Nadu. (2007).http://www.tn.gov.in/rti/proactive/cfcp/control_orders_manual3/TN _essential_trade_articles_regulation.pdf

Gulati, A., Meinzen-Dick, R. & Raju, K. V. (2005). *Institutional Reforms in Indian Irrigation*. International Food Policy Research Institute, Sage Publications, New Delhi.

Gulati, A., & Narayanan, S. (2003). *The Subsidy Syndrome in Indian Agriculture*. Oxford University Press, New Delhi, 297 pages.

Hindu Business Line. (2005). "Govt to Tap India Inc's Captive Power Capacity," May 16.http://www.thehindubusinessline.com/2005/05/16/sto ries/2005051601950300.htm

Joshi, P. K., Gulati, A. & Birthal, P. S. (2007). "Agricultural Diversification in India: Status, Nature and Pattern," in *Agricultural Diversification and Smallholders in South Asia*, P.K. Joshi, A. Gulati, and R. Cummings Jr (eds.), Academic Foundation, New Delhi, pp. 219-242.

Kapoor, S. & Barnes, D. (2003). "*Agricultural Pricing and Rural Electrification in India: Some International Comparisons*." Draft Paper, World Bank, Washington, DC.

Landes, M. R. (2004). "The Elephant Is Jogging: New Pressures for Agricultural Reform in India," *Amber Waves* 2(1):28-35, Feb., U.S. Department of Agriculture, Economic Research Service, http://www.ers.usda.gov/AmberWaves/February04/pdf/features_ elephant.pdf

Landes, R. & Gulati, A. (2004). "Farm Sector Performance and Reform Agenda," *Economic and Political Weekly* (Mumbai), Aug. 7-13, pp. 36113619.

Landes, M., Persaud, S. & Dyck, J. (2004). *India's Poultry Sector: Development and Prospects*, Agriculture and Trade Report No. WRS0403, U.S. Department of Agriculture, Economic Research Service, Feb. http://ers.usda.gov/ publications/WRS0403/

Mullen, K., Orden, D. & Gulati, A. (2005). "Agricultural Policies in India: Producer Support Estimates, 1985-2002." MTID Discussion Paper No. 82, International Food Policy Research Institute, Feb.

National Bureau of Statistics of China. (2006). China Statistical Yearbook, http://www.stats.gov.cn/tjsj/ndsj/2006/indexeh.htm

Pal, S. & Byerlee, D. (2003). "*The Funding and Organization of Agricultural Research in India: Evolution and Emerging Policy Issues*," Policy Paper 16, National Centre for Agricultural Economics and Policy Research (ICAR), New Delhi, India, February.

Patnaik, G. (2006). "*State Level Marketing Reforms: A Status Report, Federation of Indian Chambers of Commerce and Industry*," Oct. www.ficci.com/media-room/speeches-presentations/2006/oct/ agri/SessionI/GokulPatnaik.pdf

Persaud, S. & Landes, M. (2006). *The Role of Policy and Industry Structure in India's Oilseed Markets*, Economic Research Report No. 17, U.S. Department of Agriculture, Economic Research Service, April. http://ers.usda.gov/ publications/err17/

Pingali, P. & Khwaja, Y. (2004). "*Globalization of Indian Diets and the Transformation of Food Supply Systems*," Keynote Address, 17th Annual Conference, Indian Society of Agricultural Marketing, Hyderabad, Feb. 5-7.

Reserve Bank of India. (2007). *Handbook of Statistics on Indian Economy*, Sept.

Sharma, Ashok B. (2007). "Punjab, Haryana, Madhya Pradesh Likely to Have Modern Terminal Markets," *Financial Express* (India), Aug. 26. http://www.financial express.com/news/Punjab-Haryana-Madhya-Pradeshlikely-to-have-modern-terminal-mkts/212766/).

Singh, Sukpal. (2007). "*Understanding Contract Farming in India: Models and Learnings*," NCAP-USDA-IFPRI Workshop on Contract Farming: Methods and Experiences, New Delhi, May 5-6.

Srinivasan, P. V., Jha, S. & Landes, M. (2007). Indian Wheat and Rice Sector Policies and the Implications of Reform, ERR-41, Economic Research Service, U.S. Department of Agriculture, May.

U.S. Department of Agriculture, Foreign Agricultural Service. (2007). *India: Agricultural Situation, Weekly Highlights and Hot Bites*, #9 Gain Report IN7018, March 2. http://www.fas.usda.gov/gainfiles/200703/146280326.pdf

U.S. Department of Agriculture. Foreign Agricultural Service. (2006). *India Report: Retail Food Sector*, Gain Report IN- 6111, Dec. 12, http://www.fas.usda.gov/gainfiles/200612/146269832.pdf

U.S. Trade and Development Agency. (2006). *India Cold Chain Improvement Program: Definitional Mission Report*, USTDA-06-Q-21-143, Arlington, VA.

World Bank. (2007). World Development Indicators Database.

World Bank. (2005a). *India Road Transport Service Efficiency Study*. Energy and Infrastructure Operations Division, South Asia Regional Office, Nov.

World Bank, (2005b), *Review of India Agricultural Marketing*. WB0262, Programme of Advisory Support Services for Rural Livelihoods, Department for International Development, Final Technical Output, Nov. http://www.passlivelihoods.org.uk/default.asp?project_id=254

World Bank. (2004). *Re-energizing the Agricultural Sector to Sustain Growth and Reduce Poverty*. Report No. 27889-IN, Rural Development Unit, South Asia Region, Washington, DC, July 30.

World Bank. (1999). *India Foodgrain Marketing Policies: Reforming to Meet Food Security Needs, Vols I & II.* Rural Development Sector Unit, South Asia Region, Washington, DC, Aug. 17.

World Bank. (1998). *India: Water Resources Management Sector Review; Groundwater Regulation and Management Report*. Washington, DC.

END NOTES

[1]Calculation of representative growth rates in Indian agriculture is complicated by weather-induced fluctuations in annual performance. To minimize the influence of these fluctuations, growth rates are calculated between endpoints based on 3-year average levels of agricultural GDP (see table 1).

[2]Agricultural exports grew just 8 percent annually during the same period, but agricultural exports continue to average about double the size of agricultural imports.

[3] The same pattern of growth across food groups is reflected in consumer survey data collected for selected years by India's National Sample Survey Organization (Government of India, Ministry of Statistics and Program Implementation). The FAO data used here provide broader commodity coverage within food groups and allow use of more stable 3-year average endpoints when computing annual growth rates.

In: India and the U.S: Future Relations…
Editor: Tim S. Macleod, pp.43-99

ISBN: 978-1-60741-197-0

Chapter 2

THE ROLE OF POLICY AND INDUSTRY STRUCTURE IN INDIA'S OILSEED MARKETS

Suresh Persaud and Maurice R. Landes
Electronic Report from the Economic Research Service

ABSTRACT

High tariff and nontariff protection of the Indian oilseed sector imposes costs on consumers, supports an inefficient processing industry, and has led to negligible gains in oilseed output. Model-based simulations indicate that higher levels of protection would increase the burden on consumers, but do little to meet key policy goals of supporting producers and reducing import dependence. A shift to direct support of oilseed producer prices would increase output, but may be complex to implement and subject to WTO discipline. Liberalization of oilseed imports, by permitting large gains in processing efficiency, could generate a stream of benefits that would allow producers, consumers, and processors to be better off, and also improve the trade balance.

Keywords: India, oilseeds, soybeans, vegetable oil, meal, processing industry, industry structure, policy, trade liberalization.

ACKNOWLEDGMENTS

The authors thank Praveen Dixit, John Dunmore, Barry Krissoff, Erik Dohlman, James Hansen, Thomas St. Clair, V. Shunmugam, and Samarendu Mohanty for their reviews. Dale Simms, editor, and Anne Pearl, designer, provided excellent publication support. Financial support for this project was provided by the Emerging Markets Program of USDA's Foreign Agricultural Service.

SUMMARY

Oilseeds and oilseed products emerged during the 1990s as one of the fastest-growing components of global and U.S. agricultural trade, with developing countries accounting for most of the growth in both supply and demand. India is the world's second most populous country, the third largest economy in Asia, and one of the world's fastest growing developing economies. India is also a major producer and consumer of oilseeds and their products, emerging in the late 1990s as one of the world's largest importers of vegetable oils. Higher incomes, low productivity in domestic oilseed production, and more liberal policies for edible oil imports are all expanding trade.

What is the Issue?

Stronger income growth in India is likely to be sustained, leading to continued strong demand for oils and oil meals, as well as other foods. Without significant improvement in yields, India is likely to have a growing deficit in vegetable oils to be met by imports of either oils or oilseeds for processing. And, without improved oilseed productivity, particularly for soybeans, rapid growth in meal demand is likely to continue to reduce India's oil meal surplus, eventually creating a deficit in feed protein.

Current policies, which aim to support oilseed producers by imposing high tariffs on oil and prohibitive restrictions on oilseed imports, have not led to significant gains in oilseed area or yields. In addition to imposing substantial costs on all consumers of oil, oil and oilseed import barriers have propped up a processing sector that is technically inefficient and heavily underutilized. As a result, policy change is likely to determine the future growth and composition of India's oilseed and product trade. This report reviews recent developments in India's oilseed sector and, with a model- based evaluation of alternate scenarios, assesses the implications of current and potential policies for oilseed producers, processors, Indian consumers, and international trade.

What Did the Project Find?

India's current policy of high tariffs on oilseeds and oil affords little benefit to oilseed producers, while supporting processors and imposing high costs on consumers. Direct support of domestic oilseed prices would help growers more, and at lower cost to consumers, but could be costly and difficult to implement so as to ensure processor incentives.

Liberalization of tariff and nontariff barriers to oilseed imports, with high oil tariffs continuing, would lead to large-scale imports of oilseeds, primarily soybeans, as imports of the raw material substitute for imports of the processed commodity. Improved access to oilseeds would allow processors in India to boost capacity utilization, resulting in lower processing costs, and increased net revenues and employment. The windfall gains in processing efficiency and processor returns could be reallocated to producers and consumers through adjustments in oilseed and oil tariffs, with the potential for growers, consumers, and processors to all be better off than under existing policies.

The ongoing process of consolidation of ownership in India's oilseed processing sector is likely to generate benefits for Indian producers and consumers, as larger, consolidated processors compete more effectively for scarce raw materials and pass on economies associated with increased scale, process integration, and capacity utilization. In this context, liberalization of oilseed imports that boosts raw material supplies may allow smaller-scale processors to remain competitive.

The United States is a minor player in India's edible oil market because Latin American soybean oil and Asian palm oil are less costly than U S soybean oil. However, the United States is a competitive supplier of soybeans, and U.S. producers stand to gain if India follows some other developing countries—most notably China—by reducing barriers to oilseed imports. Although U.S. soybeans and products would still face considerable competition from Latin American suppliers, trade liberalization that results in India's substituting imports of soybeans for imports of oil is likely to improve U.S. trade prospects.

How Was the Project Conducted?

The ERS India Oilseed Sector Model illustrates the impacts of alternative oilseed policies on India's supply, demand, and trade of oilseeds and their products, including implications for producers, consumers, and processors. The model incorporates supply, demand, and trade relationships for each of India's major oilseeds (soybean, peanut, rapeseed, and sunflower) and their products, as well as demand relationships for palm oil. The model first generates a 10-year projection (2001-11), or reference scenario, for India's oilseed sector. The reference scenario is based on existing policies and assumed changes in key exogenous variables, including income growth, exchange rates, and world prices. Policy scenarios analyzed are (1) increased oil tariffs, (2) increased oilseed price supports, (3) oilseed import liberalization, (4) increased ownership consolidation in the oilseed processing industry, and (5) composite scenarios involving changes in both oilseed and oil tariffs. Data were collected from secondary sources and through ERS interviews with oilseed traders, processors, and industry representatives in India. Support for this study was provided by the ERS-India Emerging Markets Project.

INTRODUCTION

Oilseeds and oilseed products emerged during the 1990s as one of the fastest growing components of global and U.S. agricultural trade, with developing countries accounting for most of the growth in both supply and demand. Many developing countries—including the rapidly expanding economies of China and India—have become the principal source of growth in demand for feed proteins and edible oils. And following a period of rapid production growth, soybean products from Latin America and palm oil from Southeast Asia now meet most of the growth in oilseed product demand.

U.S. exports of oilseeds and oilseed products—mostly soybeans and products—now account for declining shares of global trade in these products. This stems largely from the comparative advantage of Latin American soybean and Southeast Asian palm oil producers

(Schnepf et al., 2001). Policies that affect production, trade, and processing in importing and exporting countries have also affected trade growth and the mix of raw materials and processed products that is traded. For example, government land, credit, and export tax policies support the expansion of production and processing infrastructure for soybeans in Latin America and palm oil in Southeast Asia. In China, rising incomes and trade policy reforms have fueled rapid growth in demand for vegetable oil and feed protein, as well as its shift from an importer of oilseed products to an importer of raw materials.

India is the world's second most populous country, the third largest economy in Asia, and one of the world's fastest growing developing economies since 1990. India is also a major producer and consumer of oilseeds and their products, emerging in the late 1990s as one of the world's largest importers of vegetable oils. Higher incomes, low productivity in domestic oilseed production, and more liberal policies for edible oil imports have driven expanding trade. Despite more open oil import policies, extensive policy intervention continues to affect oilseed production, trade, and processing in India, and policy change is likely to play a major role in the future growth and composition of India's oilseed and product trade.

India's Oilseed Sector

India, the world's seventh largest producer of oil crops (2001-03 average), is a major producer of soybeans, rapeseed, peanuts, cottonseed, and sunflowerseed and their derived products. India is traditionally an importer of vegetable oils and an exporter of protein meals, but a negligible trader in oilseeds. Oil imports have been on the rise as a result of strengthening consumer demand and import liberalization measures implemented in 1994. During 2001-03, India was the second largest edible oil importer in the world, behind the European Union (EU-25) and ahead of China. India is also the world's fifth largest exporter of oil meals, although exports of soybean and other meals have slowed due to rapid growth in domestic feed demand. And, despite substantial excess capacity in the domestic oilseed processing industry, imports of oilseeds remain restricted by tariff and non- tariff policies (Dohiman et al., 2003).

Oilseed Product Demand

India has been among the fastest growing developing economies since the late 1980s, with real growth in gross domestic product (GDP) averaging more than 6 percent annually. Rising incomes and steady growth in urbanization are stimulating demand for a more diverse array of foods, including fruit, vegetables, edible oils, milk, eggs, and poultry meat. Demand for these products is now outpacing demand for traditional food staples.

India's improved growth has been accompanied by a dramatic improvement in its balance of payments—once a chronic source of weakness. Although a large current account deficit persists, increased export competitiveness associated with more liberal trade and domestic policies has improved India's capacity to import and to borrow foreign capital. The improved payments position provides more flexibility for additional import liberalization.

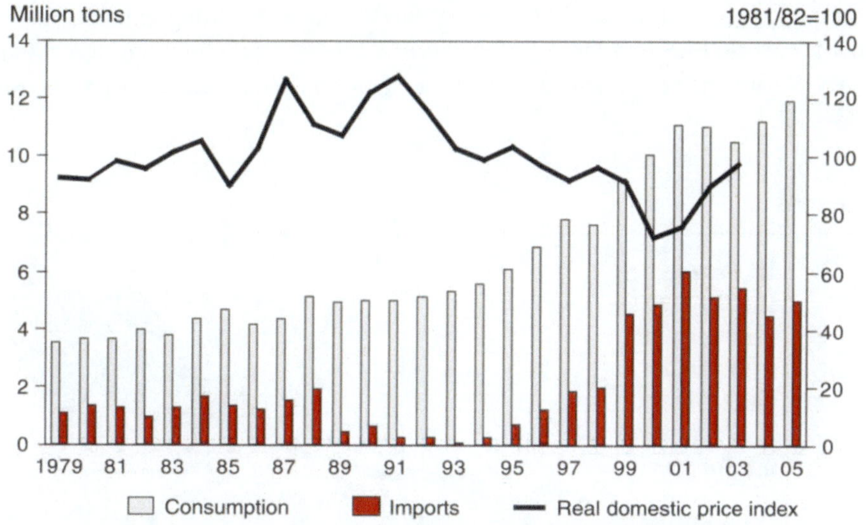

Figure 1. Edible oil consumption, imports, and prices, India

Source. USDA Production, Supply, and Distribution database; Economic Survey, Government of India.

Oil demand

Indian edible oil consumption is now growing at more than 6 percent annually, but per capita consumption (9.6 kg) remains below the world average of 11.1 kg. Most oil is used in food preparation, mostly in the home, but also in food shops, restaurants and, to a lesser extent, food processing firms. Driving consumption growth has been rising incomes and a more open trade regime, which has led to increased edible oil supplies and lower domestic prices (Figure 1). In 1994, India shifted from a restrictive state trading regime for oil to unrestricted imports (subject to tariffs) by private traders. Although tariffs remain high, imported oils—mostly palm and soybean oils—have accounted for most of the growth in consumption. Together, these nontraditional imported oils now account for about half of the oil consumed in India, replacing the higher priced, domestically produced oils such as peanut and rapeseed oil.

Indian consumers spend a large share of their income on food—about 55 percent compared with just 10 percent in the United States (USDA, 2005a)—and are generally highly responsive to prices. Middle- and lower income consumers, in particular, substitute items in and out of the diet based on relative prices. Despite high tariffs, prices for edible oils—led by imported palm and soybean oils—have tended to decline compared with other foods since the early 1990s, stimulating increased per capita oil consumption (Figure 2).

Meal demand

Faster income growth is also strengthening demand for animal products and the derived demand for coarse grain and oil meal for feeding. India has a large animal product sector, and both supply and demand have responded to stronger income growth. Since the early 1990s, the dairy, poultry, egg, and aquaculture sectors have registered strong expansion. The dairy sector—now the world's second largest after the EU-25—is expanding at 4 percent annually, eggs at nearly 5 percent, poultry meat at 12.5 percent, and freshwater fish production at 6.1 percent.

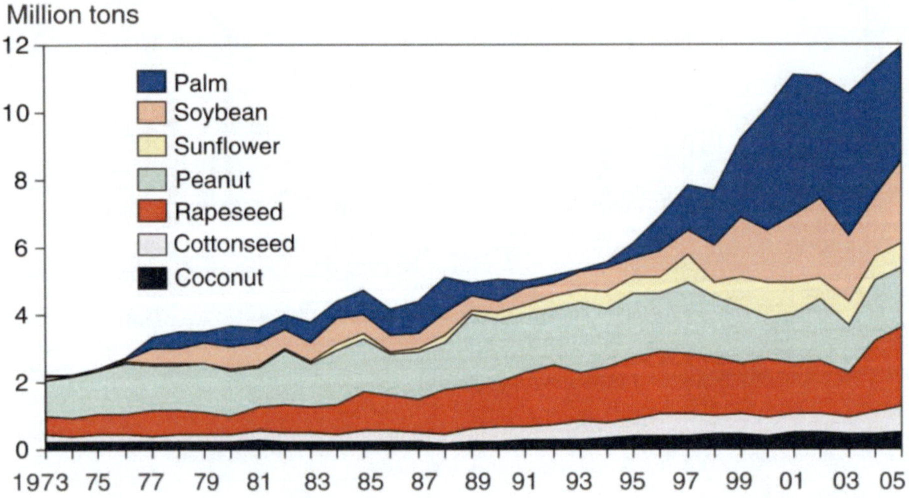

Figure 2. Oil consumption in India by major type

Source: USDA Production, Supply, and Distribution database.

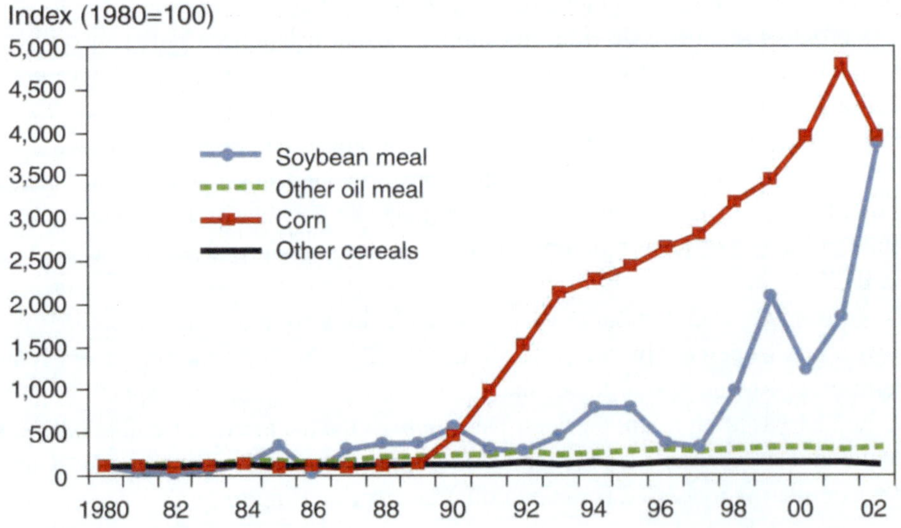

Figure 3. Growth in Indian feed demand

Source: FAOSTAT, May 2005.

The surge in animal product production has been accompanied by accelerated growth in feed use (Figure 3). The poultry and egg sectors—which rely heavily on rations of corn and soybean meal—have been the main drivers of commercial feed demand. During 1990-2001, feed demand for corn and soybean meal grew at annual rates of 21 percent and 17 percent.

The consumer-driven emergence of India's animal products sector, and accompanying growth in demand for commercial feeds, is significant for the future development of India's oilseed and products industry. Historically, returns to oilseed processors and producers have been undermined by weak domestic demand for oilseed meals for feed purposes. Since meals account for the largest physical fraction of most oilseeds, poor market returns from meal have tended to reduce the profitability of processing and returns to growers. Meal exports have buoyed demand and prices for soybeans and soybean meal, but most other meals face weak domestic and export demand and are of poor quality, with significant shares traditionally disposed of as fertilizer.[1] The expanding domestic feed market may reduce India's exportable surpluses of meal, but also strengthen the returns to domestic oilseed production and processing and improve the quality of the meal produced.

Oilseed and Product Trade

The role of trade in India's oilseed economy is determined primarily by trade policy (see box). India's recent large imports of edible oil have been the result of reduced border protection beginning in 1994. Oilseed imports, though no longer restricted by quantitative measures, are prevented by prohibitive tariffs and sanitary regulations. Exports of oil meals have been aided both by traditionally weak domestic feed demand and by the implicit support that the protected oil market affords to domestic oilseed processors.

Edible Oil Trade Policy

From the 1970s until 1994, most edible oil imports were conducted by the Government's State Trading Corporation, with annual import quantities determined by an interministerial committee based on domestic supply, demand, and balance-of-payment conditions. Imports were particularly restricted during 1989-94, a period corresponding with the Technology Mission on Oilseeds, a government initiative to boost self-sufficiency in edible oils. Since 1994, when India began conforming to WTO rules and replacing quantitative trade restrictions with tariffs, oil imports have been placed under Open General License (OGL), allowing unlimited imports by private traders subject to applied tariffs (Table 1).

INDIA'S OILSEED AND PRODUCT TARIFFS

India's applied tariffs for soybeans and products—as well as other oilseeds and products—are high by global standards. For soybeans, for example, India's seed, meal, and oil tariffs are all sharply higher than for any of the world's major producing and consuming countries. The principal reason for India's high tariffs is to protect the welfare of oilseed producers, most of whom are small-scale, limited resource farmers operating under conditions of erratic rainfall.

Although India's soybean and product tariffs are higher than for other major countries, it is common for soybean producing countries, including the United States, to provide tariff protection for their soybean and product sectors. For nearly all major producers, the common pattern of protection is to place higher tariffs on products than on raw materials, thus supporting higher margins for processors than without protection. As a result, tariff policies play a role not only in where soybeans are produced, but also where they are processed.

Applied soybean oil tariffs for major importers

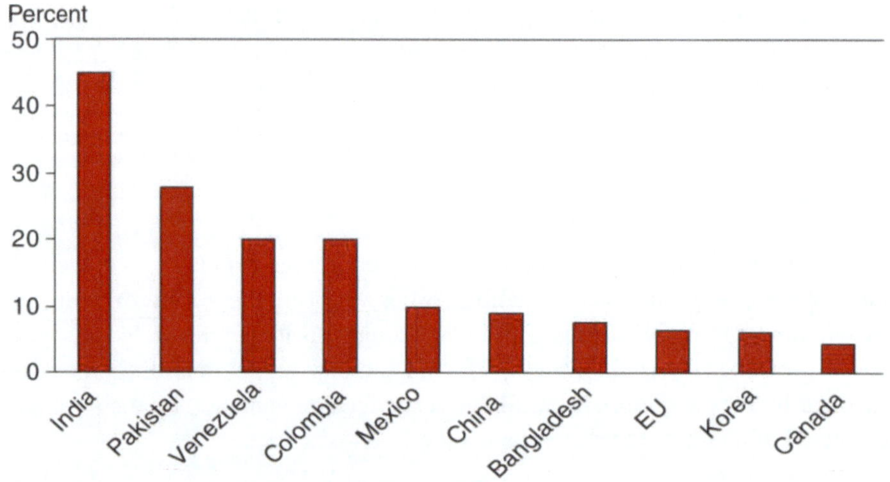

Source: Agricultural Market Access Database (AMAD).

Applied soybean and product tariffs for major producers and consumers (ranked by 2002-04 average production)

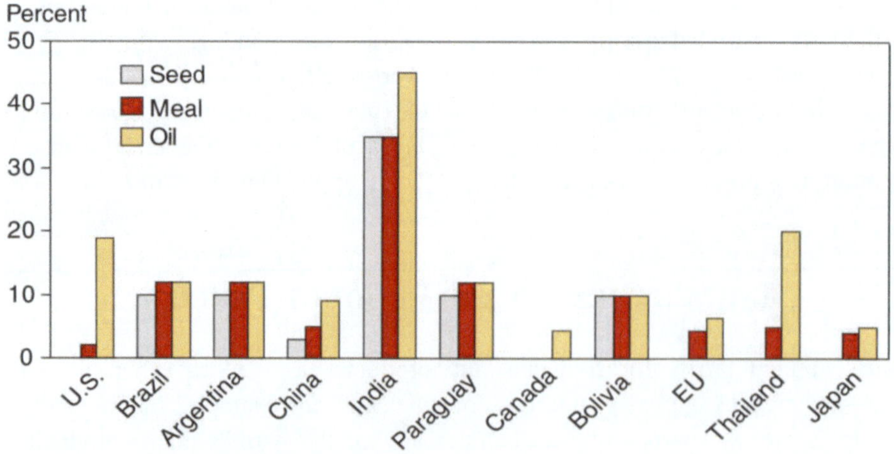

Source: Agricultural Market Access Database (AMAD).

Table 1. Bound and Applied Tariffs in India's Oilseed Sector

Commodity	Bound rate	Applied rate[1]
	Percent, ad valorem	
Oilseeds	30	30
Oils		
Crude		
Soybean	45	45
Palm oil	300	80
Peanut	300	75
Sunflower[2]	300	50/75
Rapeseed	75	75
Refined		
Soybean	45	45
Palm oil	300	90
Peanut	300	85
Sunflower	300	85
Rapeseed[3]	75	45/85
Oilmeals	100	30

[1] Applied sales as of March 2006.
[2] Applied rate of 50 percent within 150,000-ton quota; 85 percent above quota.
[3] Applied rate of 45 percent within 150,000-ton quota; 75 percent above quota.
Source: Ministry of Commerce and Industry, Government of India; USDA/Foreign Agricultural Service attache reports.

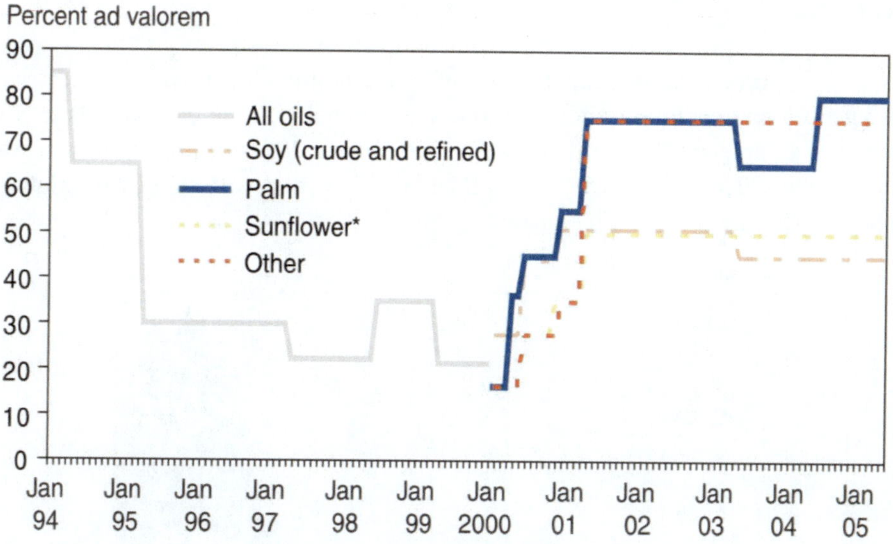

Figure 4. Applied crude vegetable oil tariffs in India

*Tariffs for imports within tariff-rate quota.
Source: Ministry of Commerce and Industry, Government of India; USDA/Foreign Agricultural Service attache reports.

Since the introduction of a tariff-based import regime in 1994, applied tariffs have evolved from initially high rates (65-85 percent) during 1994-1995 to lower (20-30 percent) tariffs during 1996-2000. They escalated again during 2001-04 (Figure 4). High WTO bound rates of 300 percent for most oils have afforded India the flexibility to adjust tariffs upward. The major exceptions are crude and refined soybean oils, which are bound at 45 percent. Crude sunflowerseed oil (50 percent) and refined rapeseed oil (45 percent) also have relatively low bound tariffs within 150,000-ton tariff-rate quotas, but only small amounts of these higher priced oils are imported.

The comparatively low 45-percent bound tariff on soybean oil has tended to limit the scope for upward adjustment of applied tariffs on other oils. This has been controversial among Indian policymakers who would like to increase protection for domestic oil and oilseed producers. Large differentials between soybean and palm oil tariffs, such as the current 35 percentage points, create a market advantage for soybean oil that forces palm oil suppliers to cut prices. The scope for reducing oil imports by raising palm oil tariffs has been limited because palm oil exporters reduce prices to remain competitive with soybean oil, and because importers substitute soybean oil for palm oil.

In addition to adjusting tariffs, the Government influences the cost of imported oils through a system of "tariff rate values," or administered import prices used to calculate the tariff revenue due to the Government for each ton of imported oil. These were introduced in 2000 to prevent under-invoicing of prices by importers. The tariff values are adjusted periodically based on world prices. On occasion, however, tariff-rate values for soybean oil have been above actual market prices, resulting in an effective tariff above the 45-percent bound rate (Dohlman et al., 2003).

Edible Oil Trade

India's oil imports expanded rapidly following the removal of quantitative restrictions in 1994, rising from an average of about 200,000 tons annually in the early 1990s to 5 million tons, or about 44 percent of domestic consumption, during 2003-05 Import growth was most rapid during 1996-2000, when tariffs were relatively low, and was slowed by higher tariffs during 2001-05 (Figure 5).

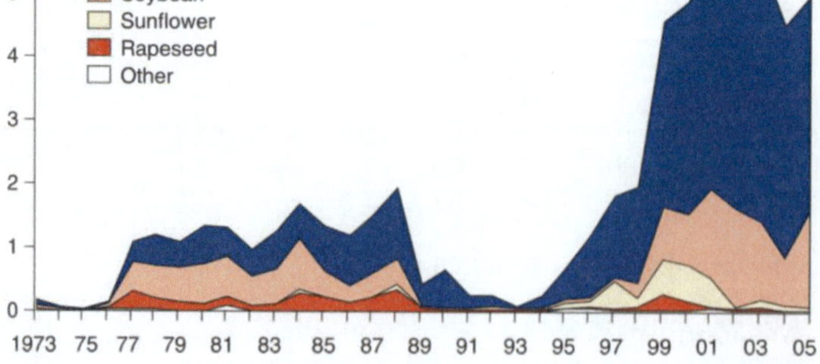

Figure 5. Edible oil imports by type, India.

Source: USDA, Production, Supply, and Distribution database.

Mindful of the price sensitivity of Indian consumers, India's oil importers have been highly price sensitive in determining the composition of oils imported. Palm oil, generally the lowest priced oil, has dominated Indian imports since the mid-1990s, accounting for about 75 percent of oil imports during 2003-05. Soybean oil, generally the second cheapest oil in the market, accounted for about 23 percent of imports during 2003-05. Higher priced oils—including sunflower oil and oils traditional to the Indian diet, such as peanut and rapeseed oil—were imported in only small amounts.

Price is also a key determinant of the origin of oils purchased by Indian importers. The U.S. share of the Indian soybean oil market declined sharply when U.S. exports shifted from concessional shipments to commercial sales after the mid-1990s. The Indian soybean oil market is dominated by Argentina and Brazil, who offer consistently lower prices than U S suppliers (Dohlman et al., 2003; Schnepf et al., 2001).

Meal Trade

India is the fifth largest exporter of both soybean meal and total oil meals, although its exports trail those of the major global suppliers—Argentina, Brazil, and the United States—by a wide margin. Indian soybean meal is more competitive in world markets in terms of both quality and price than other domestically produced meals (fig. 6). Because soybeans (and sunflowerseed) have been cultivated in India only since the 1970s, they are processed in relatively modern, small- and medium-scale solvent extraction facilities Indian soybean meal is competitive in small, regional markets that favor India's bagged, as opposed to bulk, product.

The once strong growth in India's exports of soybean meal has slowed due to expanding domestic feed use and slower growth in soybean production. Rapid growth in demand from domestic poultry meat and egg producers has increased domestic soybean meal prices relative to world prices, reducing their competitiveness in world markets and their appeal to exporters.

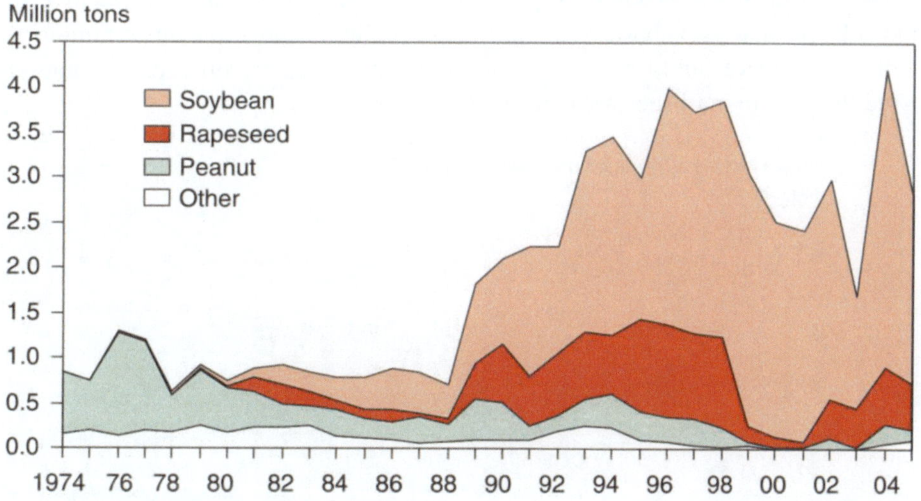

Figure 6. Oilmeal exports by major type, India

Source: USDA, Production, Supply, and Distribution database.

Oilseed Trade

India is not a significant trader in oilseeds for processing. Oilseed imports are restricted by both a 30-percent tariff and by nontariff barriers. Imports of genetically modified oilseeds are not permitted unless approved by the Government's Genetic Engineering Approvals Committee (GEAC). The GEAC currently has no policy that would permit such approvals. In addition, a 2002 Plant Quarantine Order requires that shipments be certified free of certain pests or that seeds be "devitalized." At present, the only permissible means of "devitalization" is to mechanically split the seed, a process that adds considerable cost and, if done at the point of origin, would lead to unacceptable deterioration in quality during transit.

Oilseed Production

India produces a broad range of oilseeds, ranking among the world's largest producers of peanut, rapeseed, soybean, cottonseed, and a number of minor oilseeds. Oilseed yields, however, remain well below world averages, with limited success in sustaining productivity growth. Government policy gives priority to protecting oilseed producers by placing quantitative restrictions or high tariffs on imports of oilseeds and products.

Trends in Oilseed Area and Yields

Area planted to oilseeds has generally responded to changes in domestic prices associated with changes in trade policy, and in price policy for competing crops. Growth in oilseed area accelerated—and grew faster than the world average—during the 1980s, when stricter controls on imports of oilseeds and products strengthened oilseed prices relative to competing crops (table 2, Figure 7). However, during 1990-2002—a period that includes the liberalization of oil imports—domestic prices of oilseeds and oils declined relative to other crops and oilseed area growth slowed significantly. Higher Government minimum support prices (MSPs) for wheat and rice, important competing crops for oilseeds in some regions, also slowed the growth in oilseed area during the late 1990s.

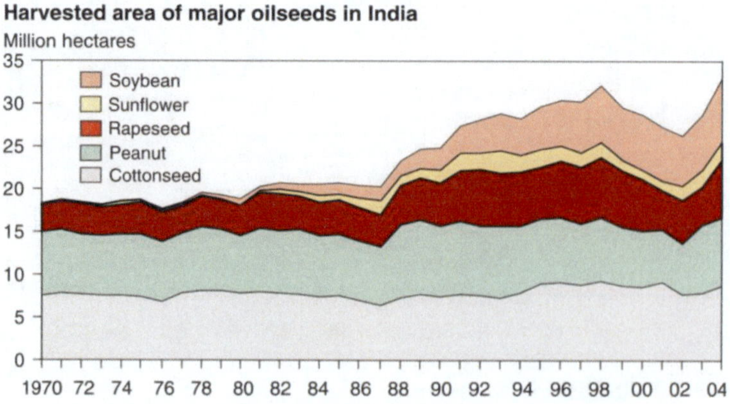

Figure 7. Harvested area of major oilseeds in India
Source: FAOSTAT, May 2005.

Table 2. Growth Rates of Oilseed Area, Yield, and Production, India and World Average

Oilseed	Area			Yield			Production		
	1970-80	1980-90	1990-02	1970-80	1980-90	1990-02	1970-80	1980-90	1990-02
	Percent change								
India									
Cottonseed	0.4	-0.5	0.5	1.6	3.4	0.8	1.9	2.9	1.3
Peanuts	-0.3	1.8	-1.2	0.6	0.5	-0.1	0.3	2.4	-1.1
Rapeseed	1.7	3.4	0.3	-0.4	5.8	0.7	1.4	9.4	1.1
Soybeans	32.3	17.6	7.2	4.5	2.5	0.5	38.3	20.4	7.8
Sunflowerseed	7.1	26.7	1.1	-1.7	-0.1	0.3	5.4	26.5	1.4
Five oilseeds	0.7	2.8	1.0	0.6	2.5	0.5	1.3	5.3	1.6
World									
Cottonseed	0.0	-0.3	-0.2	1.9	2.8	0.7	1.9	2.5	0.5
Peanuts	-0.4	0.8	1.7	0.8	1.6	1.3	0.4	2.4	3.1
Rapeseed	3.7	4.6	2.1	1.8	3.5	1.2	5.4	8.3	3.3
Soybeans	5.6	1.2	3.1	1.4	0.9	1.5	7.0	2.1	4.7
Sunflowerseed	3.7	2.9	2.1	0.0	1.5	-0.8	3.7	4.5	1.2
Five oilseeds	2.5	1.3	2.0	1.8	1.6	1.2	4.3	3.0	3.2

Source: Computed from FAOSTAT data.

India's average yields for major oilseeds are 40-60 percent below world averages and, with the exception of the 1980s, have been growing at a substantially lower rate (Figure 8). Most oilseeds are grown by small-scale, limited-resource farmers in areas that are dependent on erratic monsoon rainfall, with only about 24 percent of oilseed area irrigated. Faced with considerable weather-related risk, oilseed producers invest little in improved seeds, fertilizer, and pesticides. Oilseed farmers also face considerable price risk because the minimum support prices set for oilseeds are typically either too low to influence market prices or are not adequately defended by Government purchases. Government initiatives to extend credit and technology to oilseed producers, including the 1988-94 Technology Mission on Oilseeds, have had very fleeting impact.

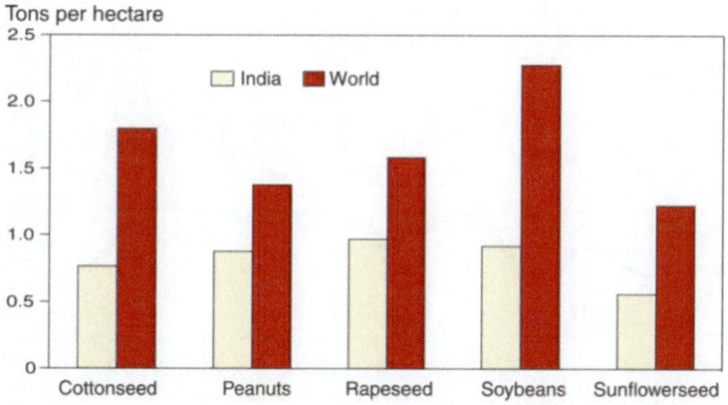

Figure 8. Oilseed yields, Indian and world average, 2002-04 Tons per hectare

Source: FAOSTAT, May 2005.

Soybeans and rapeseed are the two oilseeds that may have the most potential for improvements in area, yield, and production. Soybean area continues to expand outside the traditional area of Madhya Pradesh into the neighboring areas of Rajasthan and Maharashtra, where it competes for land with other dryland crops, including sorghum, millet, and pulses. Returns to soybean cultivation are helped by strong demand for soybean meal and by excess capacity in solvent extraction, which creates some competition for supplies of raw material.

Rapeseed, grown in the winter often in competition with wheat, is the most heavily irrigated of all the oilseeds, with about 63 percent of area irrigated. Rapeseed area and yield increased during the 1980s and early 1990s when high prices boosted plantings on irrigated land. Rapeseed production was slowed by large hikes in wheat MSPs during the late 1990s, but higher oil tariffs and lower relative wheat prices could now stimulate another expansion of output.

Producer Price Policy

The MSP system has had little impact on oilseed prices, which are formed primarily by trade policy and domestic and world market prices for oilseeds and products. With India's large-scale imports, domestic prices for edible oils are linked closely to tariff-adjusted world prices, although domestic supplies affect prices during the harvest period. Similarly, domestic prices of traded oil meals are linked to world prices and domestic seasonal factors, although some meals are often priced below world levels. With oilseed imports restricted by tariff and nontariff barriers, domestic oilseed prices are shaped largely by the prices of their derivative products, their respective oil and meal extraction rates, and processing costs.

Historical trends in prices for oilseeds reflect the impact of trade policy (Figure 9). Oilseed prices tended to rise relative to other crops through the early 1990s when vegetable oil imports were restricted, then decline following the liberalization of oil imports. Oilseed prices have turned up in the early 2000s, reflecting oil tariff hikes during 2000-2002 and, possibly, the impact of higher oilseed MSPs.

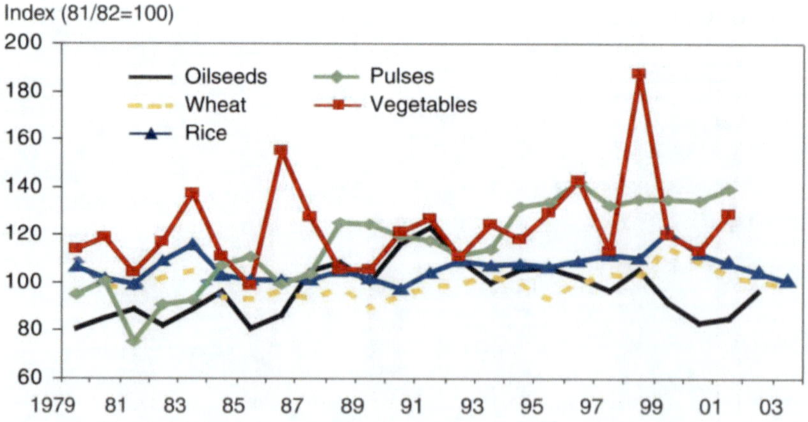

Figure 9. Trends in real wholesale prices for selected crops, India

Source: Government of India, Ministry of Finance.

Although oil and oilseed tariffs emerged as primary policy instruments during the 1990s, it is unclear how effectively-and how efficiently-higher tariffs can achieve the avowed policy objectives of supporting small oilseed producers and reducing dependency on oil imports. Because oil accounts for the smallest physical fraction of the oilseed—ranging from 18 percent for soybeans to 40 percent for sunflower—the impact of oil tariffs on the oilseed price is also proportionally small. Benefits to producers are further reduced if processors and traders fail to transmit the full impact of the oil tariff into the oilseed price. Another constraint is that high oil tariffs place most of the proportionally large cost burden of supporting oilseed producers on India's mostly low-income consumers.

Oilseed Processing

The Indian oilseed processing sector is characterized by a large number of relatively small-scale, low-technology plants and substantial excess capacity. The structure of the industry has been heavily influenced by Government policies that have: regulated plant scale, capital intensity, and oilseed/product marketing; provided incentives for building new capacity; and prevented imports of oilseeds for processing. Also shaping the industry has been a domestic demand preference for crude traditional oils, weak effective demand for quality feed protein, and diverse and erratic supplies of domestic oilseeds for processing.

Processing Sector Structure, Capacity and Costs

The Indian oilseed processing industry includes three major processing technologies: (1) traditional mechanical crushing, or expelling, used for oilseeds with relatively high oil content; (2) solvent extraction for processing oilseeds and expeller cake 3). The traditional mechanical crushing industry has two segments: the very small-scale "ghanis" and the small-scale expellers. The processing industry also includes an oil refining sector, which primarily refines domestic solvent-extracted oils and imported crude and solvent-extracted oils, and a "vanaspati" (hydrogenated oil) sector that refines and hydrogenates domestic and imported oils.

Table 3. India: Structure of the Oilseed Processing Sector

Process	Units		Capacity[1]	
		Total	Average	Use rate
	Number	*Million tons*	*Tons/day*	*Percent*
Mechanical crushing:				
"Ghanis"	130,000	2.0	0.05	10
Expellers	20,000	40.5	7	30-40
Solvent extraction[2]	766	36.0	157	30-40
Vanaspati	241	4.8	66	35
Oil refining	800	4.7	20	35

[1] Capacity and use based on raw material; 300 days/year, 24 hours/day basis.
[2] Includes expander units.
Source: Solvent Extractors' Association of India.

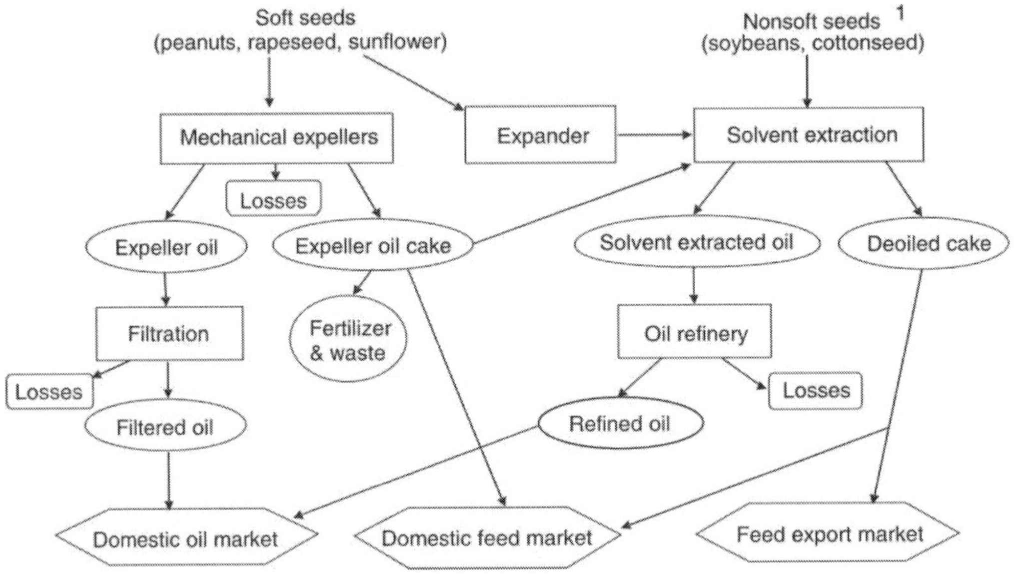

Figure 10. India's oilseed processing sector

[1] Solvent extraction is used for raw materials, such as soybeans,cottonseed, and expeller oilcake with less than 20 percent oil content.

Each segment of India's oilseed processing industry has small capacities and low technical efficiency compared with other major processing countries. On average, India's solvent extraction plants are about one-sixth the size of those in the United States and the EU and use significantly more power, steam, and hexane solvent per unit of oilseeds processed. Even India's largest integrated expeller-solvent extraction plants are small and high-cost by international standards.

Indian processing units also have more excess capacity than units in other major processing countries. On average, Indian expeller and solvent extraction plants operate only around the domestic raw material harvest, or at tion plants operate only around the domestic raw material harvest, or at about 30-40 percent of capacity. This contrasts with capacity utilization rates of 92-96 percent for U.S. plants (Reca, 2003). Low rates of capacity use compound relatively poor technical efficiency and further increase the average and marginal costs of processing raw materials, because fixed costs must be recouped over fewer units of output (Figure 11).

Additional inefficiency arises because some processes are not well integrated. While it is common to see an oil refinery and/or vanaspati unit combined with a solvent extraction plant, expeller units are often not integrated with solvent extraction units. As a result, oil and meal production is lost because significant amounts of expeller cake are not solvent-extracted. In addition, the costs of solvent-extracting the expeller cake rise, and processing delays reduce the quality of the oil and de-oiled cake.

India's oilseed processors are able to operate profitably despite their high costs largely because of the high border protection afforded to vegetable oils. In addition, because the price of oilseeds is determined by the cost of processing—together with the market value of the derived oil and meal—high processing costs dampen oilseed prices, partially offsetting benefits to producers from India's tariffs on oilseeds and oils.

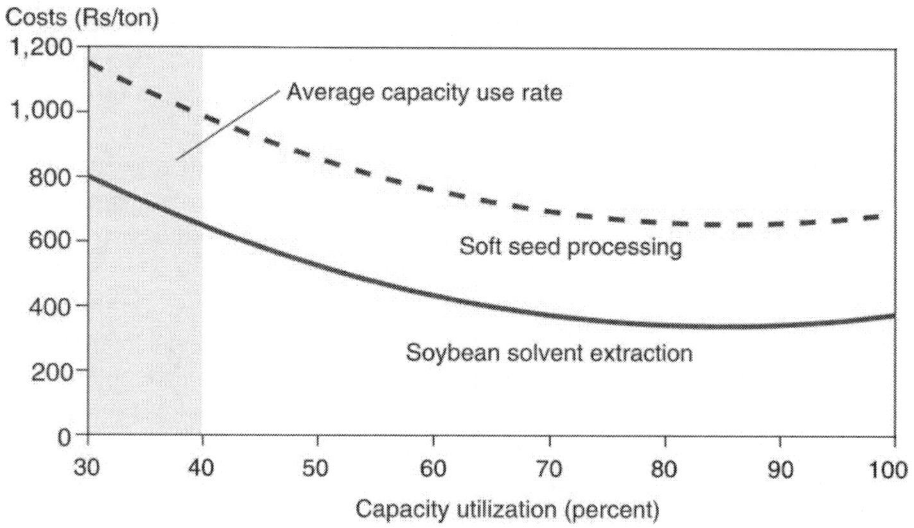

Figure 11. Average cost curves for oilseed processing in India

Source: ERS estimates.

In the short run—with existing processing capacity and low capacity use—India's processors operate their plants at a level where average costs are high. They can reduce unit processing costs by increasing capacity use. In the long run, costs can drop further if larger, more technically efficient plants are built and can operate at high levels of capacity use. Lower processing costs would create a stream of benefits to processors that could be shared with producers (in the form of higher oilseed prices) and consumers (in the form of lower oil prices).

Processing Sector Policies

The fragmentation, low technical efficiency, and excess capacity of India's oilseed processing industry are largely the result of government regulatory and trade policies:

Plant scale restrictions. Under the Small Scale Industry (SSI) reservation policy, expelling of peanut, rapeseed, sesame, and safflower oils is restricted to units with investment of Rs 0.5-7 5 million ($10,000$170,000), effectively restricting capacities to units small by international standards. In addition, firms that manufacture oilseed crushing equipment are subject to the same scale limits, restricting use of more modem technology. These restrictions do not apply to the processing of soybeans or sunflowerseed, or to the manufacture of solvent extraction equipment, so these commodities are processed in relatively large units.

Movement and storage restrictions. The central and state Governments have the authority, through the Essential Commodities Act (ECA) and an array of control orders, to regulate and restrict movement and storage of farm commodities, including oilseeds and products. These regulations are now seldom enforced, but remain a source of risk that reduces incentives to invest in larger or vertically integrated units.

Selective credit controls. Oilseed processors face restrictions on the availability and cost of credit from commercial banks for storage of oilseeds and oils. The regulations raise the cost of credit and further limit the size and capacity use of processing firms.

Restrictions on oilseed imports. Tariff and nontariff barriers to oilseed imports limit average capacity use in the processing industry to what can be achieved from low and variable domestic production. This raises average processing costs.

Taxes and tax incentives. Oilseeds and products are subject to taxes at the point of sale and—if transported across state borders—to turnover, entry, and central sales taxes. These taxes raise the cost of operating larger enterprises that assemble raw materials or transport products across state borders. Central, state, and local governments also provide tax exemptions and other tax incentives to promote construction of new processing plants, particularly in backward areas. This contributes to excess processing capacity and to the location of plants where they are not economically viable or sustainable (World Bank, 1997).

Futures trading restrictions. From the 1960s until very recently, futures trading in nearly all oilseeds and products was illegal and oilseed processors were unable to legally use futures contracts to manage price risk. The recent legalization of futures trading may eventually provide an effective risk management tool but, at present, traded volumes remain small.

Industry Consolidation

The last several years have witnessed a trend toward consolidation of ownership of oilseed processing units by larger domestic and multinational companies. The trend appears to be driven partly by short-term factors, particularly financial distress in the industry following several poor harvests. But these larger players are also responding to the potential for cutting costs and increasing profitability, as well as the appeal of participating in a large and expanding market.

Key to larger players' efficiency advantage is the cost of investment and operating capital. Multinational and large domestic firms typically have access to capital near the London Inter-Bank Offer Rate (LIBOR), which has averaged between 1 and 4 percent over the last 3 years. In contrast, domestic firms must borrow commercially at rates ranging from 14-16 percent for smaller firms to 8-10 percent for larger ones. As a result, the consolidating companies will be better able to acquire and store raw material and boost capacity use rates. Consolidating firms are also likely to achieve cost savings by establishing backward (to primary markets or farmers) and forward (to wholesaling and retailing) links They may also have the advantage of investing in larger, more efficient solvent extraction plants.

Consolidating firms face risks from enforcement of movement or storage restrictions under the ECA, as well as higher costs from taxes on interstate movements So far, these factors have not been significant deterrents to consolidation. It is not yet clear how significant the consolidation trend will become, but it could lead to closure of some surplus capacity as smaller firms with high operating costs and low capacity use find it difficult to compete.

IMPLICATIONS OF POLICY AND STRUCTURAL CHANGE

Future trends in India's production, consumption, and trade in oilseeds and oilseed products are likely to be shaped by changes in domestic and border policies. Current policies appear not to be achieving stated policy goals of benefiting small farmers and reducing import dependence. They are, however, imposing large costs on consumers and creating an inefficient processing sector. Eventually, pressures to improve the performance of the sector, combined with rising demand for animal products and feed protein, are likely to lead to policy reform in the oilseed sector.

Potential changes in domestic and border policies would have differing effects on India's supply, demand, and trade of major oilseeds and products. To help assess how Indian policymakers might view the alternative policy options, we use an economic model of India's oilseed sector that incorporates supply, demand, trade, and processing behavior for major Indian oilseeds and products (see appendix 1 for details). We first generate a 10- year projection, or reference scenario, for India's oilseeds sector beginning in 2001 and ending in 2011. The reference scenario is based on existing policies and assumed changes in key exogenous variables, including income growth, exchange rates, and world prices. Alternative scenarios are then evaluated relative to the reference scenario.

We examine five alternative scenarios:

Changes in oil tariffs.
Changes in oilseed price supports.
Oilseed import liberalization.
Consolidation in oilseed processing.
Two composite scenarios, favoring producers and consumers alternately.

Reference Scenario

The reference scenario provides projections for India's oilseeds sector through 2011 based on data available and policies in place as of June 2005. Assumptions for all other variables exogenous to the model (Table 4) are consistent with the most recent USDA baseline projections (USDA, 2005c).[2]

In the reference scenario, supply, demand, and price variables track actual historical developments through 2004, and are determined by model assumptions and results for 2005 through 2011. Real world prices of oilseeds and meals rise during 2001-04, decline during 2005-06, and remain roughly constant thereafter (Figure 12). World oil prices follow a slightly different path, peaking in 2003 and declining during 2004-06 before leveling off. Domestic prices of oils and meals follow world prices, adjusted for tariffs and estimated transport and marketing costs. Although Indian oilseeds are not traded, domestic oilseed prices track world prices because they are determined primarily by the prices of their derived products—oil and meal—which are traded. The exception is the peanut market. Since Indian peanuts and peanut oil are usually not traded in significant volumes, their prices are determined by domestic supply and demand conditions rather than world prices.

Table 4. Summary of Reference Scenario Assumptions

Variable	Assumption		
	1991-2001	2001-05	2005-11
	Annual percent change		
Income/capita, real	4.0	5.8	4.6
Exchange rate, real[1]	2.5	0.4	1.5
Yield trends:[2]			
Soybeans	0.5	1.2	1.2
Peanuts	-1.3	1.0	1.0
Rapeseed	-0.5	1.0	1.0
Sunflower	0.6	1.5	1.5
World prices, real:			
Soybeans	-3.7	14.5	-8.0
Soybean meal	-3.1	-2.3	0.1
Soybean oil	-3.8	7.0	-3.4
Tariffs:			
Oilseeds	NA	30	30
Oil meals	NA	30	30
Oils, crude:			
Soybean	NA	45	45
Palm	NA	80	80
Rapeseed	NA	75	75
Sunflower	NA	50	50

NA = Not available.

[1] Positive numbers indicate real depreciation against the U.S. dollar.

[2] Assumptions are for technical yield trends. Model yields also respond to oilseed prices.

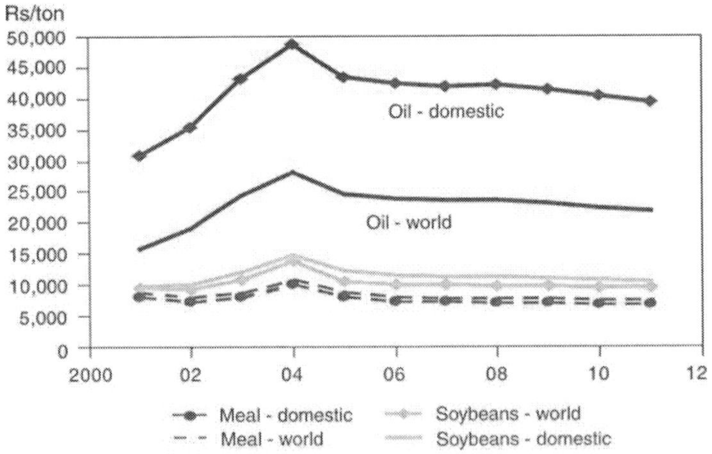

Figure 12. Reference scenario price trends for soybeans and products, India
Source: ERS, India oilseed sector model.

Supply and demand projections in the reference scenario broadly reflect underlying price movements (table 5). Higher world prices, coupled with higher Indian oil tariffs, boost domestic oilseed prices and output during 2001-05, before leveling off during 2006-11. Consistent with the recent pattern, soybean and rapeseed continue to show the strongest production growth, while peanuts grow the slowest.

Table 5. Summary of Reference Scenario Results

Variable	1990-92 average	2001 base	2011	Growth rates 1991-01	Growth rates 2001-11
	Million tons			*Percent*	
Oilseeds:					
Area (Mil. ha)	19.7	21.9	24.6	1.0	1.2
Soybean	3.1	6.0	6.5	6.7	0.8
Yield (Kgs/ha.)	0.86	0.9	1.0	0.2	1.4
Soybean	0.88	0.9	1.1	0.2	2.3
Production	17.0	19.0	24.4	1.1	2.6
Soybean	2.7	5.4	7.4	7.0	3.2
Crush	14.6	15.7	20.3	0.7	2.6
Soybean	2.5	4.6	6.2	6.5	3.0
Imports	0	0.0	0.0		
Soybean	0	0.0	0.0	--	--
Domestic price (Rs/ton)	NA	12,239	15,569	NA	2.4
Soybean	NA	9,545	10,266	NA	0.7
Oils:					
Production	4.2	4.8	6.2	1.4	2.6
Soybean	0.4	0.9	1.1	6.8	3.0
Consumption	4.4	9.8	13.3	8.3	3.0
Soybean	0.5	2.4	2.9	17.6	1.7
Imports	.20	5.0	7.0	38.3	3.5
Soybean	0.0	1.5	1.7	43.3	1.0
Domestic price (Rs/ton)	NA	32,453	41,671	NA	2.5
Soybean	NA	30,818	39,450	NA	2.5
Meals:					
Production	8.3	8.9	11.6	0.7	2.7
Soybean	2.0	3.7	5.0	6.5	3.0
Consumption	5.7	6.0	8.6	0.5	3.6
Soybean	0.4	1.3	2.8	11.0	8.3
Exports	2.6	2.9	3.0	1.1	0.3
Soybean	1.5	2.4	2.2	4.8	-1.1
Domestic price (Rs/ton)	NA	7,136	5,997	NA	-1.7
Soybean	NA	8,118	6,856	NA	-1.7
Processing:					
Capacity (Mil. tons)	NA	52.3	52.3	NA	0.0
Capacity use (percent)	NA	30.0	39.1	NA	2.7
Soybean	NA	30.0	40.3	NA	3.0
Avg. cost (Rs/ton)	NA	1,017	887	NA	-1.4
Soybean	NA	800	665	NA	-1.8
Quasi-profit (Rs/ton)	NA	1,466	1,571	NA	7.2
Soybean	NA	1,457	1,457	NA	0.0
Quasi-profit (Rs mil.)	NA	22,994	31,840	NA	3.3
Soybean	NA	6,744	9,067	NA	3.0
Net imports (Rs bil.)	NA	-53.6	-119.1	NA	8.3
NA = Not available.					

-- = Cannot be calculated.

Source: ERS-India oilseed sector model.

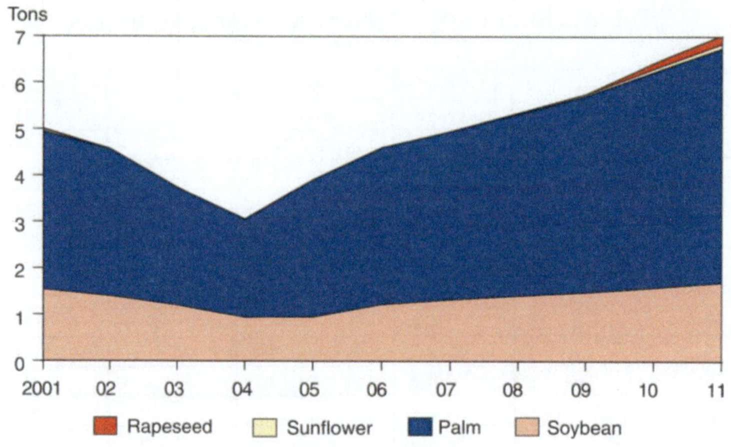

Figure 13. Reference scenario trends in vegetable oil imports, India

Source: ERS, India oilseed sector model.

Both imports and consumption of total oils initially decline in the reference scenario, reflecting the drought-induced decline in domestic supplies in 2002/03, as well as higher world prices and oil tariffs (Figure 13). Oil consumption and imports resume growth after 2003, the result of steady growth in domestic supplies, lower world and domestic prices, and the assumption of constant oil tariffs. As has been the case since the early 1990s, palm and soybean oils account for most of the projected growth in oil imports and consumption. Rapeseed and sunflower oil consumption also exhibit stronger growth, reflecting gains in domestic supplies and—given projected world prices—rising imports. Peanut oil, which again is not imported based on projected world prices, continues to show the highest domestic price and slowest consumption growth of the major oils.

In the reference scenario, demand for oil meal continues to be led by growth in soybean meal for feed, which expands about 8 percent annually, consistent with recent trends. Other meals grow more slowly, reflecting the weaker preference for these meals by the poultry and egg industries. Growth in soybean meal demand continues to outstrip production, leading to a steady decline in exports of soybean meal and total meal.

The reference scenario assumes that processing capacity remains fixed at current levels, and that real prices for processing inputs, other than raw material, remain constant.[3] With these assumptions, rising oilseed production leads to modest gains in capacity use in the processing industry, but rates remain low and unit processing costs high by world standards. Increased capacity use generates modest declines in unit processing costs, but processor "quasi-profits"[4] per unit of production remain constant in real terms because the benefits of cost reductions are passed on to oilseed producers in the form of higher oilseed prices.[5] Domestic oilseed producer prices, which are linked to changes in world oil and meal prices, tariffs, and processing costs, are thus able to grow somewhat faster than world prices. Although processors do not realize higher quasi-profits per unit, they benefit from higher total profits because of increased volumes processed and marketed. Total processor profits expand more than 3 percent annually.

Impacts of Changes in Oil Tariffs

To evaluate the impacts of oil tariffs, we analyze the impacts of increasing them by 10 percentage points. Because India's current soybean oil tariff (45 percent) and in-quota tariffs on crude sunflower oil (50 percent) and refined rapeseed oil (45 percent) are already set at their bound maximums, actual increases in these tariffs would be violations of WTO disciplines. Increases in these tariffs are analyzed only to demonstrate the impacts relative to other policies. Actual hikes in these bound rates would entail negotiated compensation to trading partners involving costs not accounted for in this analysis. All other assumptions remain as they are in the reference scenario.[6]

The increase of 10 percentage points in oil tariffs leads to smaller percentage increases in average domestic wholesale prices of oil (4.5 percent) and farm prices of oilseeds (2.9 percent) (table 6). World and domestic meal prices are unchanged. Oilseed production and crush increase, but the gains are small—averaging about 2.0 percent—relative to the increase in oil tariffs. Higher prices reduce oil consumption. Oil imports fall due to larger domestic supplies and reduced consumption, while larger supplies allow meal exports to rise. Impacts for peanuts are small compared with other oilseeds because of weak price response among peanut producers, and because prices for peanut oil are linked to domestic supply and demand rather than world prices. Even with the benefit of lower unit processing costs (resulting from higher capacity use) passed on to oilseed producers, the quasi-profits of oilseed processors increase relative to the reference scenario, mostly because larger quantities are processed and marketed.

The impacts of a 10-percent decrease in oil tariffs would be symmetrical with the tariff increase scenario (see appendix 4 for complete results). With lower oil tariffs, lower domestic oil and oilseed prices would result in much smaller percentage declines in oilseed production and crush, and in lower meal exports. Processor quasi-profits would shrink due to higher unit costs associated with lower capacity use, as well as smaller quantities processed and marketed, but would remain substantially positive. Consumers, by contrast, would receive significant benefits as the average domestic price of oil would fall 4.5 percent, consumption would rise 2.5 percent, and imports would rise 6.7 percent over the reference scenario.

The analysis of tariff impacts highlights several important issues. First, as expected, the impacts on oilseed producers and processors are opposite the impacts on consumers. The size of the producer and consumer impacts are determined by several factors:

- Oil accounts for a small physical fraction of the oilseed, so changes in oil prices tend to yield proportionally small changes in oilseed prices.
- Based on the elasticities of oilseed supply and oil demand used in the model, consumers are more responsive to changes in oil prices than are farmers to changes in oilseed prices.
- Changes in processing costs associated with different levels of capacity use can affect oilseed prices and oilseed production.

Second, oilseed processors are clear gainers from higher oil tariffs but, even with lower tariffs, would continue to earn significant unit profits. With higher oil tariffs, processors gain from higher returns to oil, as well as increased quantities processed when domestic raw material supplies respond to higher oil prices.

Table 6. Scenario Results: 10-Percentage-Point Increase in Oil Tariffs

Variable	2011 result	Scenario/reference
	Million tons	*Percent change*
Oilseeds:		
Production	24.9	2.0
Soybean	7.6	2.8
Crush	20.7	2.2
Soybean	6.4	3.0
Imports	0.0	1
Soybean	0.0	1
Domestic price (Rs/ton)	16,022	2.9
Soybean	10,682	4.1
Oils:		
Production	6.4	2.2
Soybean	1.2	3.0
Consumption	12.9	-2.5
Soybean	2.8	-2.1
Imports	6.6	-6.7
Soybean	1.6	-5.6
Domestic price (Rs/ton)	43,556	4.5
Soybean	41,626	5.5
Meals:		
Production	11.9	2.6
Soybean	5.1	3.0
Consumption	8.6	0.0
Soybean	2.8	0.0
Exports	3.3	10.2
Soybean	2.3	6.7
Domestic price (Rs/ton)	5,993	-0.1
Soybean	6,856	0.0
Processing:		
Capacity (Mil. tons)	52.3	0.0
Capacity use (%)	40.0	2.4
Soybean	41.5	3.0
Avg. cost (Rs/ton)	874	-1.5
Soybean	651	-2.1
Quasi-profit (Rs/ton)	1,584	0.8
Soybean	1,457	0.0
Quasi-profit (Rs mil.)	32,820	3.1
Soybean	9,337	3.0
Net imports (Rs bil.)	107.0	-10.2

[1] Imports are zero in the reference scenario.
Source: ERS-India oilseed sector model.

Third, higher oil tariffs tend to reduce foreign exchange costs (the cost of oil imports less earnings from meal exports), while lower oil tariffs would tend to raise foreign exchange costs. However, the net foreign exchange impacts of the scenarios analyzed are small in the context of India's overall balance of payments.

Impacts of Oilseed Price Supports

A major justification for maintaining high oil tariffs is to provide support to oilseed producers. However, oil tariffs may be a relatively inefficient means of supporting farmers. Another approach would be to make the existing system of minimum support prices (MSPs) more effective in supporting oilseed prices. This would provide direct support to oilseed producers and help diversify production away from food grains and toward crops in short supply (such as oilseeds), another stated policy goal.

The scope for using the MSP program to provide direct support to oilseed producers may, however, be restricted by multilateral commitments and budgetary costs. Oilseed MSPs set above import parity (the international reference price for the commodity plus transport and handling costs) would constitute "domestic support" under current World Trade Organization rules. To the extent that support exceeded WTO permitted levels, an oilseed MSP program could be subject to WTO discipline. Such a program would also imply some government budgetary costs for procurement, handling, and storage of oilseeds purchased to defend the MSP. These costs must be weighed against any estimated benefits of such a policy.

Two scenarios analyze the potential impacts of supporting oilseed prices with the MSP program. Both scenarios raise producer prices for each oilseed by an amount equal to the impact of a 10-percent increase in oil tariffs. This permits comparison of the impacts of providing the same amount of producer support via the MSP (directly) versus the oil tariff (indirectly). The difference between the two MSP scenarios is in the mechanism for supporting higher oilseed prices. In the first scenario, the Government pays the difference between the market price and the MSP, while processors continue to operate based on market prices of raw materials and products. In the second scenario, processors pay for the program by paying the MSP for oilseeds and absorbing the costs by reducing their margins.

These two mechanisms essentially bracket the available options for operating an oilseed MSP. When the Government pays the full cost of supporting oilseed prices above market prices, processor returns are not directly affected. Government costs would include the difference between the MSP and the market price for all of the oilseeds procured in price support operations, as well as any storage and handling costs. Storage periods and costs may be small for oilseeds because of excess demand in the form of idle processing capacity. At the other extreme, when processors are required to pay the new MSP for raw materials, government costs are limited to handling and (likely short-term) storage for oilseeds procured in price support operations. But, with this option, processors will likely cease operations if the oilseed MSP becomes too high relative to market prices of oil and meal and processing margins become negative. Intermediate scenarios would involve some sharing of program costs, with the Government selling procured oilseeds to processors at a price between the market price and the MSP.

With a government-financed MSP, oilseed producer prices rise an average of 2.9 percent (table 7). Prices for traded oils and meals—which remain linked to world prices—are mostly unchanged from the reference scenario. In contrast to the higher oil tariff scenario—which afforded little benefit to peanut producers—peanut prices and production rise, leading to lower prices for peanut oil and higher consumption. Overall, gains in oilseed production and crush, as well as oil and meal production, average about 2 percent, the same as when oil tariffs were increased 10 percent. However, with oil prices mostly unchanged, oil consumption is also unchanged and oil imports fall. Meal exports rise due to higher production and unchanged consumption.

Table 7. Scenario Results: Raising Oilseed Minimum Support Prices (MSPs)

Variable	2011 result		Scenario/reference	
	Government pays	Processor pays	Government pays	Processor pays
	Million tons		*Percent change*	
Oilseeds:				
Production	24.9	24.9	2.0	2.1
Soybean	7.6	7.6	2.9	2.9
Crush	20.7	20.7	2.3	2.3
Soybean	6.4	6.4	3.1	3.1
Imports	0.0	0.0	1	1
Soybean	0.0	0.0	1	11
Domestic price (Rs/ton)	16,025	16,024	2.9	2.9
Soybean	10,697	10,697	4.2	4.2
Oils:				
Production	6.4	6.4	2.3	2.3
Soybean	1.2	1.2	3.1	3.1
Consumption	13.3	13.3	0.0	0.0
Soybean	2.9	2.9	0.0	0.0
Imports	6.9	6.9	-2.0	-2.0
Soybean	1.7	1.7	-2.1	-2.1
Domestic price (Rs/ton)	41,663	41,663	0.0	0.0
Soybean	39,450	39,450	0.0	0.0
Meals:				
Production	11.9	11.9	2.7	2.7
Soybean	5.1	5.1	3.1	3.1
Consumption	8.6	8.6	0.0	0.0
Soybean	2.8	2.8	0.0	0.0
Exports	3.3	3.3	10.4	10.5
Soybean	2.4	2.3	7.0	7.0
Domestic price (Rs/ton)	5,993	5,993	-0.1	-0.1
Soybean	6,856	6,856	0.0	0.0
Processing:				
Capacity (Mil. tons)	52.3	52.3	0.0	0.0
Capacity use (percent)	40.0	40.0	2.4	2.4
Soybean	41.6	41.6	3.1	3.1
Avg. cost (Rs/ton)	873	873	-1.5	-1.5
Soybean	650	650	-2.2	-2.2
Quasi-profit (Rs/ton)	1,584	1,076	0.8	-31.5
Soybean	1,457	1,040	0.0	-28.6
Quasi-profit (Rs mil.)	32,831	22,310	3.1	-29.9
Soybean	9,347	6,673	3.1	-26.4
Net imports (Rs bil.)	113.7	113.7	-4.5	-4.6'

[1] Imports are zero in the reference scenario.

Source: ERS-India oilseed sector model.

Although the benefits of lower unit processing costs accrue to producers, the quasi-profits of oilseed processors rise because of increased capacity use and sales. Budgetary costs associated with the government-financed MSP are difficult to estimate. Assuming that just 220,000-290,000 tons of oilseeds would have to be removed from the market for an average of 3 months to support a 2.9-percent average price increase, the cost would be about Rs123-164 million ($2.7-$3.6 million).[7] These costs are balanced by producer and processor gains from higher prices and output.

When processors pay the new higher MSP, impacts on production, consumption, and trade are identical to the "government pays" scenario. But processor quasi-profits, while remaining positive, fall about 30 percent compared with the reference scenario. Average returns to processors of peanuts turned negative for some years, meaning that at least some processors would cease operations rather than incur losses.

The MSP scenarios indicate that, by supporting oilseed prices directly rather than indirectly through the oil tariff, producer support is achieved with less adverse impact on oil consumers and with a net savings of foreign exchange. The MSP approach, unlike oil tariffs, also supports peanut producers. But such a policy would entail costs to the Government and/or processors, and may also be subject to WTO disciplines regarding domestic support. A "processor pays" approach is likely to reduce government costs, but may result in private fmancial losses and supply disruptions. Intermediate solutions that share costs between the government and processors may mitigate private losses, but would add regulatory complexity and, possibly, create processor dependence on government outlays.

Impacts of Oilseed Import Liberalization

Liberalization of oilseed imports, which are now effectively prohibited by tariff and sanitary/phytosanitary (SPS) restrictions, is an additional policy option open to the Indian Government. The oilseed tariffs are intended to protect oilseed producers but, in fact, domestic oilseed prices are determined more by the economics of processing, including oil and meal prices, oil and meal extraction rates, and unit processing costs. Generally, domestic oilseed prices are not afforded protection equivalent to the 30-percent import tariff. Domestic oilseed prices-except in the case of rapeseed-are typically below import parity prices (world reference prices adjusted for transport and handling costs to the farm gate), and well below import parity prices plus the tariff (table 8).

The oilseed import liberalization scenario assumes reduced oilseed tariffs and the removal of-or zero-cost solutions to-existing SPS barriers.[8] All other assumptions on exogenous variables, including oil tariffs and the fixed availability of processing capacity, remain the same as in the reference scenario. To implement this scenario, three important changes are introduced into the analytical framework:

The scenario is conducted in a way that prevents oilseed imports from leading to losses for oilseed producers. Producer prices are not allowed to fall below reference scenario prices. This is a realistic approach because of the priority that policymakers place on producer welfare. When necessary, producer prices are maintained at the reference scenario level by allowing non-zero tariffs sufficient to maintain reference scenario producer prices. Based on market price conditions during the period analyzed, non-zero tariffs are required for rapeseed only.

With import liberalization, domestic oilseed prices become linked directly to world oilseed prices rather than domestic oil and meal prices. The only remaining protection of domestic oilseeds and products arises from oil tariffs, plus the "natural" protection afforded by international and domestic transport and handling costs. A key implication of oilseed import liberalization is that India's high oil tariffs would have little or no impact on the oilseed prices received by Indian producers or paid by processors. Processors would, however, continue to benefit from high domestic oil prices and crush margins resulting from oil tariffs. Oilseed producers may also receive less price benefit than they would in a protected market, as increased use of processing capacity reduces processing costs. Any portion of this benefit that would raise oilseed producer prices above import parity would be retained by processors, unless redirected by other policies.

Table 8. Domestic and Import Parity Prices for Major Oilseeds, India

Oilseed	Unit	2000	2001	2002	2003
Soybeans:					
World price	$/ton	208	200	203	240
Freight/ins.	$/ton	30	25	36	61
Border price	$/ton	238	225	239	301
Border price	Rs/ton	10,738	10,605	11,336	14,016
Domestic trans.	Rs/ton	783	800	821	849
Import parity price	Rs/ton	11,521	11,405	12,157	14,866
Domestic price[1]	Rs/ton	9,497	10,318	12,268	14,040
Rapeseed:					
World price	$/ton	190	202	220	284
Freight/ins.	$/ton	30	25	36	61
Border price	$/ton	220	227	256	345
Border price	Rs/ton	9,926	10,683	12,142	16,064
Domestic trans.	Rs/ton	783	800	821	849
Import parity price	Rs/ton	10,709	11,483	12,963	16,913
Domestic price[2]	Rs/ton	12,134	13,046	15,265	18,121
Sunflower:					
World price	$/ton	214	219	287	289
Freight/ins.	$/ton	30	25	36	61
Border price	$/ton	244	244	323	350
Border price	Rs/ton	11,008	11,483	15,320	16,297
Domestic trans.	Rs/ton	783	800	821	849
Import parity price	Rs/ton	11,791	12,283	16,141	17,146
Domestic price[3]	Rs/ton	10,225	12,622	14,508	15,573

[1] Soybean: Indore; Source: Solvent Extractors' Association of India.
[2] Rapeseed: Jaipur; Source: Solvent Extractors' Association of India.
[3] Sunflowerseed: Average of Khamgaon (Maharashtra), Jalna (Maharashtra), and Gulbargo Karnataka); Source Government of India, Ministry of Agricuture.

Table 9. Scenario Results: Liberalizing Oilseed Imports[1]

Variable	2011	Scenario/reference
	Million tons	*Percent change*
Oilseeds:		
Production	24.8	1.4
Soybean	7.7	4.1
Crush	29.3	44.5
Soybean	14.5	133.1
Imports	8.7	2
Soybean	8.0	2
Domestic price (Rs/ton)	15,816	1.6
Soybean	11,039	7.5
Oils:		
Production	8.1	29.2
Soybean	2.7	133.1
Consumption	13.3	0.0
Soybean	2.9	0.0
Imports	5.2	-25.9
Soybean	0.2	-89.7
Domestic price (Rs/ton)	41,673	0.0
Soybean	39,450	0.0
Meals:		
Production	18.6	60.6
Soybean	11.6	133.1
Consumption	8.6	0.0
Soybean	2.8	0.0
Exports	10.0	237.5
Soybean	8.8	301.4
Domestic price (Rs/ton)	6,273	4.6
Soybean	6,856	0.0
Processing:		
Capacity (Mil. tons)	52.3	0.0
Capacity use (percent)	67.6	72.9
Soybean	94.0	133.1
Avg. cost (Rs/ton)	637	-28.2
Soybean	367	-44.9
Quasi-profit (Rs/ton)	1,320	-16.0
Soybean	982	-32.6
Quasi-profit (Rs mil.)	38,679	21.5
Soybean	14,250	57.2
Net imports (Rs bil.)	118.2	-1.0

[1] The removal of SPS barriers on all oilseeds with zero tariffs on soybeans, rapeseed, sunflowerseed, and peanuts. Rapeseed tariff is maintained to prevent a decline in domestic prices.

[2] Imports are zero in the reference scenario.

Source: ERS-India oilseed sector model.

With no prohibitive restrictions on imports of raw material, processors would likely behave as profit maximizers, importing and processing raw material until marginal revenue equals marginal cost. Additional cost factors include the costs of transporting imported oilseeds to processing plants and, as long as India has a meal surplus, transporting surplus meal back to ports for export.

This scenario includes assumptions on transportation and handling costs for imported oilseeds and exported meal. These costs vary by unit according to distance from ports, access to rail transport, the quality of roads, and other factors. Some processing units may be too remote and inaccessible for imports to be feasible. Based on available information on transport and handling costs and the location of processing capacity, it is assumed that about 76 percent of India's processing capacity could process imported oilseeds, with an average transport and handling cost of Rs800 ($17.78) per ton.[9]

With liberalization of oilseed imports, producer prices rise an average of 1.6 percent (table 9). Soybean and sunflowerseed prices rise 7.5 percent and 6.4 percent because import parity prices are above initial domestic prices. Despite the higher price of imported raw materials, lower average processing costs and increased volumes make soybean and sunflowerseed imports profitable for processors. However, a 34-percent tariff is needed to maintain rapeseed prices at reference scenario levels, and peanuts continue to be untraded with no change in price relative to the reference scenario.[10] Domestic prices of oils and meals remain linked to world prices and are unchanged from the reference scenario.

Soybean and sunflowerseed production increase 4.1 percent and 1.3 percent, while oilseed crush and production of meal and oil rise sharply due to imports of about 8.7 million tons of oilseeds. Soybeans (8 0 million tons in 2011) are the major oilseed imported, followed by rapeseed (0.5 million) and sunflowerseed (0.2 million). Domestic oil and meal consumption are mostly unchanged so, with the large gains in oil and meal production, oil imports fall 26 percent and meal exports more than triple relative to the reference scenario. Soybean processors reap windfall gains in quasi-profits, with smaller gains for processors of other oilseeds. Although the cost of soybeans and sunflowerseed rises, processors benefit from high oil tariffs, the retained benefits of lower unit processing costs, and large increases in volumes processed and marketed.

Under oilseed import liberalization, soybeans, rather than sunflowerseed and rapeseed, account for the bulk of imports. This occurs despite the fact that both rapeseed and sunflowerseed contain a larger oil fraction and are currently protected by higher oil tariffs than soybeans. The reason for this outcome is that India imports only small amounts of rapeseed and sunflower oils. With oilseed import liberalization, these oilseeds are imported only until the derived oil output replaces imports of the oils; larger imports of the oilseeds would drive down domestic prices of the oils and reduce processor profits.

The oilseed import liberalization scenario demonstrates the potential for efficiency gains from using idle processing capacity. Oilseed producers gain on average, consumers are largely unaffected and, with high oil tariffs in place, processors reap large windfall gains. This result may not be optimal for the economy as a whole but, as later scenarios indicate, there is scope to reallocate processor gains so that consumers and/or producers receive more of the benefits.

While gains for processors are large, producer and processor impacts would likely vary by plant and region, and over time. Larger plants with greater scale economies are likely to have an advantage over smaller units. As a result, peanut and rapeseed processors, who are restricted to small-scale units, may receive smaller gains than sunflower and soybean processors. Processors located near ports would have cost advantages over inland units for imports of raw material and exports of meal. While the scenario assumes that processing capacity remains fixed at the 2001 level, larger and more technically efficient units may eventually be built near ports and have a competitive advantage over most existing units. In this event, the least competitive existing units would likely close, and the remaining inland units would tend to process domestic raw materials, selling both oil and meal in the domestic market.

Table 10. Scenario results: Consolidation of oilseed processing[1]

Variable	2011	Scenario/reference
	Million tons	*Percent change*
Oilseeds:		
Production	24.7	1.1
Soybean	7.5	1.9
Crush	20.5	1.2
Soybean	6.3	2.0
Imports	0.0	2
Soybean	0.0	2
Domestic price (Rs/ton)	15,860	1.9
Soybean	10,564	2.9
Oils:		
Production	6.3	1.1
Soybean	1.2	2.0
Consumption	13.3	0.0
Soybean	2.9	0.0
Imports	7.0	-0.9
Soybean	1.7	-1.4
Domestic price (Rs/ton)	41,647	-0.1
Soybean	39,450	0.0
Meals:		
Production	11.8	1.4
Soybean	5.1	2.0
Consumption	8.6	0.0
Soybean	2.8	0.0
Exports	3.1	5.7
Soybean	2.3	4.5
Domestic price (Rs/ton)	5,999	0.0
Soybean	6,856	0.0
Processing:		
Capacity (Mil. tons)	21.8	-58.2
Capacity use (percent)	93.9	140.3
Soybean	94.0	133.1
Avg. cost (Rs/ton)	549	-38.1
Soybean	367	-44.9
Quasi-profit (Rs/ton)	1,573	0.2
Soybean	1,457	0.0
Quasi-profit (Rs mil.)	32,281	1.4
Soybean	9,248	2.0
Net imports (Rs bil.)	116.5	-2.3

[1] Linear reduction of processing capacity so that processing capacity utilization rate is 94 percent by 2011.

[2] Imports are zero in the reference scenario.

Source: ERS-India oilseed sector model.

Impacts of Consolidation in Oilseed Processing

The recent trend in oilseed processing toward consolidation of ownership by larger domestic and multinational firms, though not driven by policy change, is a potentially significant development. With the formation of larger consolidated firms, smaller, less efficient firms are likely to be pressured to exit the industry. As firms exit, average capacity use will rise and average costs of processing will fall. While there would be local employment losses associated with firm exits, benefits would accrue to producers and consumers due to lower average processing costs. Economywide employment effects may be minimal if the overall volume processed by the industry does not change.

Some of the impacts of industry consolidation are analyzed with a scenario that reduces processing capacity at a constant rate during the projection period. By 2011, capacity is reduced to the point where overall capacity use reaches about 94 percent, roughly the rate maintained in other major oilseed processing countries such as the United States, Argentina, and Brazil.[11] All other assumptions remain the same as the reference scenario.

With this consolidation scenario, oilseed producer prices rise modestly when-as in the reference, tariff change, and MSP scenarios-the benefits of higher capacity use and lower processing costs are passed to producers, but domestic oil and meal prices are unchanged (table 10). Increased oilseed production and crush raise oil and meal output, but oil and meal consumption are unchanged. As a result, oil imports drop slightly and meal exports rise. Processor quasi-profits rise as the gains associated with increased volumes more than offset the modest increase in raw material prices.

Under this scenario, even with plants moving out of production, both the processing industry and oilseed producers benefit. Although there would be local employment losses associated with plant closures—and smaller, more labor-intensive firms may exit first—the increase in volume processed makes the change in total employment uncertain.

The recent consolidation trend, because of excess capacity and limited raw material supplies, threatens the least efficient oilseed processors under existing domestic and trade policies. Increased Government support, perhaps through higher oil tariffs, may continue to protect less efficient processors, but would result in additional costs to consumers and, in the case of soybean oil, require renegotiation of the WTO bound tariff. Liberalizing oilseed imports would, however, provide an opportunity for more processors to stay in business if they are sufficiently competitive with other firms.

Composite Scenarios: Distributing Benefits to Producers and Consumers

The analysis so far has shown that each of the policy options available to the Government—adjusting oil tariffs, providing price supports to oilseed producers, and liberalizing oilseed imports—has differing implications for producers, consumers, processors, government outlays and, in some cases, WTO disciplines. The results for individual policy changes suggest that some composite scenarios—scenarios that combine changes in multiple policies—may meet the goals of supporting oilseed producers and processors at a smaller cost to consumers.

Two such scenarios involve tapping the large potential for efficiency gains in processing associated with liberalizing oilseed imports, but then reallocating the gains to producers or consumers. The first scenario includes the same liberalization of oilseed imports analyzed previously (see table 9), but investigates whether it is possible to transfer the gains in processor quasi-profits to consumers by reducing oil tariffs. The second scenario also includes oilseed import liberalization, but investigates whether it is possible to transfer gains in processor quasi-profits to oilseed producers using oilseed tariffs.

Oilseed Imports with Benefits Shifted to Consumers

In this scenario, the bulk of any gains in processor quasi-profits (between the reference scenario and the oilseed import liberalization scenario) are shifted to consumers by reducing oil tariffs. This type of transfer appears possible for the soybean sector and, to a lesser extent, for rapeseed, but not for the sunflower or peanut sectors (table 11). The overall decline in domestic oil prices is relatively small—about 1 percent—as the significant consumer gains are confined to soybean oil.

In this scenario, impacts on producers are the same as in the oilseed import liberalization scenario; soybean and sunflower prices and production rise, while peanut and rapeseed production and prices are almost unchanged.

Consumer prices fall for soybean and rapeseed oils, and consumption rises, as processor gains from oilseed imports are transferred to consumers by reducing oil tariffs. Tariffs on soybean oil are reduced from 45 percent to 37 percent, and for rapeseed oil from 75 percent to 74 percent, leading to declines in consumer prices for soybean and rapeseed oils of about 4 percent and 1 percent, respectively. (The relatively small tariff reduction for rapeseed oil is linked to the relatively small impacts on rapeseed imports and processing costs in the oilseed import liberalization scenario.) Soybean oil tariffs and prices fall the most because soybean processors benefit the most from oilseed import liberalization, thus generating more efficiency gains to transfer to consumers.

It was not possible to lower the sunflower oil tariff because any downward adjustment would reduce processor quasi-profits below the reference scenario. However, sunflower processors, on average, appear to earn significantly higher unit surpluses than other processors, both in the base period and the reference scenario. As a result, there may be more scope for transferring sunflower processor quasi-profits to oil consumers than accounted for in this analysis. Transferring benefits to peanut oil consumers by this approach is not possible because these products continue to be untraded under oilseed import liberalization.

Oilseed Imports with Benefits Shifted to Farmers

In this scenario, the bulk of any gains in processor quasi-profits are shifted to producers by upward adjustments to oilseed tariffs. This policy approach is feasible for all oilseeds except peanuts.

With processor quasi-profits transferred to producers, oilseed producer prices and oilseed production rise relative to both the reference scenario and the oilseed import liberalization scenario (table 11). Oilseed producer prices rise an average of 2.4 percent. The largest price and output gains are for soybeans, again because soybean processors experience the largest efficiency gains from liberalization of oilseed imports. The soybean tariff rises from zero to 4 percent and the rapeseed tariff rises from 34 percent to 37 percent. Producer prices rise 10.9 percent for soybeans and 1.5 percent for rapeseed.

Table 11. Scenario Results: Composite Scenarios

Variable	2011 result		Scenario/reference	
	Oilseed import liberalization with benefits to:			
	Consumers	Producers	Consumers	Producers
	Million tons		*Percent change*	
Oilseeds:				
Production	24.8	25.0	1.4	2.5
Soybean	7.7	7.9	4.1	7.2
Crush	29.3	29.3	44.6	44.5
Soybean	14.5	14.5	133.1	133.1
Imports	8.7	8.5	1	1
Soybean	8.0	7.8	1	1
Dom. price (Rs/ton)	15,845	15,945	1.8	2.4
Soybean	11,039	11,388	7.5	10.9
Oils:				
Production	8.1	8.1	29.3	29.2
Soybean	2.7	2.7	133.1	133.1
Consumption	13.3	13.3	0.4	0.0
Soybean	2.9	2.9	2.1	0.0
Imports	5.3	5.2	-25.1	-25.9
Soybean	0.2	0.2	-86.2	-89.7
Dom. price (Rs/ton)	41,228	41,674	-1.1	0.0
Soybean	37,709	39,450	-4.4	0.0
Meals:				
Production	18.6	18.6	60.7	60.6
Soybean	11.6	11.6	133.1	133.1
Consumption	8.6	8.6	0.0	0.0
Soybean	2.8	2.8	0.0	0.0
Exports	10.0	10.0	237.7	237.5
Soybean	8.8	8.8	301.4	301.4
Dom. price (Rs/ton)	6,273	6,273	4.6	4.6
Soybean	6,856	6,856	0.0	0.0
Processing:				
Capacity (Mil. tons)	52.3	52.3	0.0	0.0
Capacity use (percent)	67.6	67.6	72.9	72.9
Soybean	94.0	94.0	133.1	133.1
Avg. cost (Rs/ton)	637	637	-28.2	-28.2
Soybean	367	367	-44.9	-44.9
Quasi-profit (Rs/ton)	1,111	1,099	-29.3	-30.0
Soybean	661	633	-54.6	-56.6
Quasi-profit (Rs mil.)	32,564	32,197	2.3	1.1
Soybean	9,586	9,182	5.7	1.3
Net imports (Rs bil.)	119.4	115.5	0.2	-3.1

[1] Imports are zero in the reference scenario.
Source: ERS-India oilseed sector model.

Sunflowerseed prices, while higher than in the reference scenario, are consistent with the oilseed import liberalization scenario because higher farm prices would reduce processor quasi-profits below the reference scenario. However, the high level of quasi-profits (per unit) apparently earned from sunflowerseed processing may suggest more scope to transfer gains to producers than shown in this analysis. Since peanuts used for processing are not traded, there is no scope to raise producer prices by this mechanism.

Impacts on oil consumers are unchanged from the reference scenario and the oilseed import liberalization scenario. Oilseed processor quasi-profits match those of the reference scenario. Oil and meal trade implications remain the same as under the oilseed import liberalization scenario, but increased oilseed production leads to smaller oilseed imports.

This analysis demonstrates how oilseed import liberalization—with oilseed tariffs set in a way that enables higher processing efficiency while protecting producers—could benefit most oilseed producers with no loss to consumers or processors. In the longer term, if processors respond to oilseed import liberalization by building larger, more efficient plants, even larger efficiency gains may be shared among producers, consumers, and processors than estimated in this analysis. These larger efficiency gains could be channeled to consumers (through reductions in oil tariffs) or to producers (through WTO-legal adjustments in oilseed tariffs) without making other players worse off.

CONCLUSIONS

Stronger income growth in India is likely to be sustained, leading to continued strong demand for oils and oil meals, as well as other foods. Without significant improvement in yields, India is likely to have a growing deficit in vegetable oils to be met by imports of either oils or oilseeds for processing. And, without improved oilseed productivity, particularly for soybeans, rapid growth in meal demand is likely to continue to reduce India's oil meal surplus, eventually creating a deficit in feed protein.

Current policies, which aim to support oilseed producers by imposing high tariffs on oil and prohibitive restrictions on oilseed imports, have not led to significant gains in oilseed area or yields. In addition to imposing substantial costs on all consumers of oil, oil and oilseed import barriers have propped up a processing sector that is technically inefficient and heavily underutilized. The analysis also suggests that future trade or domestic policy changes aimed at improving the performance of the sector could have trade implications of potential significance for world and U.S. trade.

Our analysis indicates that further hikes in oil tariffs are likely to generate limited producer gains and add to already high consumer costs, while providing further support to an inefficient processing sector. By contrast, lower oil tariffs provide significant benefits (reduced costs) for consumers, with only minor adverse impacts on processors and producers.

More effective implementation of the minimum support price (MSP) system to boost oilseed prices would provide direct benefits to producers and processors with negligible consumer impacts, and may be consistent with current priorities for diversifying agricultural production. Such a policy would likely entail budgetary costs and be complex to implement in a way that ensures processor incentives, and may also conflict with WTO domestic support disciplines.

Because of India's large surplus of processing capacity, liberalization of oilseed imports with current oil tariffs in place would lead to windfall gains for processors. Most oilseed producers would benefit from somewhat higher prices, although rapeseed producers would require continued tariff protection to avoid losses. Impacts on consumers, who would continue to pay tariff adjusted world prices for oil, would be negligible. Analysis suggests that when processor gains from oilseed import liberalization are reallocated to consumers (through lower oil tariffs) or to producers (through a small oilseed tariff), producers, consumers, and processors may all be better off than under existing policies. This assessment, however, assumes that an acceptable, low-cost solution can be found to nontariff barriers that currently restrict oilseed imports.

The ongoing consolidation of India's oilseed processing capacity by larger domestic and multinational which have relatively low costs of investment and operating capital and may achieve further economies in vertical integration and marketing—threatens the viability of inefficient processors even under existing policies. Over time, larger consolidated units will likely put less efficient smaller units out of business. However, the resulting gains in processing efficiency indicate potential benefits for producers and consumers, and for the processing sector as a whole.

It is unclear which policy approach India will adopt to meet growing demand for oilseeds and products, while addressing policy goals concerning producers, consumers, and processors. Most major producing countries, while affording some tariff protection for producers and/or processors, provide much lower levels of protection than India. This translates into lower oil prices and more efficient processing, as well as higher average oilseed yields, than in India. China is a recent example of a developing country that lowered protection in its oilseed and products sector to serve dynamic growth in edible oil and feed demand (Tuan et al., 2004).

In the Indian case, the analysis suggests that a large surplus of processing capacity creates the potential to liberalize trade in a way that provides benefits to producers, consumers, and processors. In the long run, if domestic processors invest in larger, more efficient plants that vertically integrate more processing and marketing enterprises, the potential gains to be shared by producers and consumers would be even larger than indicated in this study. Access to imported raw materials would help transform oilseed processing from an inefficient and underutilized industry dependent on high oil tariffs to a more efficient and dynamic sector that better serves producers and consumers.

Finally, if India were to allow oilseed imports, the United States, which tends to be more competitive at exporting soybeans than soy oil, may benefit. Although the United States would still face considerable competition from Brazilian soybeans, oilseed trade liberalization would improve the U.S. competitive position as Indian imports of South American soybean oil are replaced by imports of soybeans.

REFERENCES

Agricultural Market Access Database. www.amad.org.

Chandvaria, Munendra Singh (1991). *Acreage Response of Oilseeds in India,* Radha Publications, New Delhi.

Chaudhary, Sudhir (1997). "Government Intervention and Trends in the Indian Oilseeds Sector: An Analysis of Alternative Policy Scenarios," Working Paper 97-WP 179, Ames: Center for Agricultural and Rural Development, Iowa State University, June.

Dey, A. K. & B. N. Banerjee. (1991). *Production and Marketing of Pulses and Oilseeds,* Mittal Publications, New Delhi, 1991.

Dohlman, E., Persaud, S. C. & Landes, M. R. (2003). "India's Edible Oil Sector: Imports Fill Rising Demand," OCS090301, U.S. Dept. Agr., Econ. Res. Serv., Nov.

Government of India, Ministry of Agriculture, Directorate of Economics and Statistics (2004). *Statistics at a Glance.*

Government of India, Ministry of Finance (2005). *Economic Survey, 2004/05.*

Gulati, Ashok, Sharma, A. & Kohli, D. (1996). "Self-Sufficiency and Allocative Efficiency: Case of Edible Oils," *Economic and Political Weekly,* March 30.

Gulati, V. P. & Phansalkar, S. J. (1994). *Oilseeds and Edible Oil Economy of India,* Vikas Publishing House Pvt. Ltd., New Delhi.

Kumar, P. (1998). *Food Demand and Supply Projections for India,* Agricultural Economics Policy Paper 98-01, Indian Agricultural Research Institute: New Delhi, India.

Landes, M. R., S. C. Persaud & Dyck, J. (2004). *India's Poultry Sector: Development and Prospects,* WRS-04-03, U.S. Dept. Agr., Econ. Res. Serv., Jan.

Mahendra, Dev, Ravi, C. Viswanathan, Brinda, Gulati, Ashok & Ramachander Sangamitra. (2004). *Economic Liberalisation, Targeted Programmes and Household Food Security: A Case Study of India.*

MTID Discussion Paper No. 68, International Food Policy Research Institute, Washington, DC.

Narappanavar, S. R. (1989). *The Oils and Oilseeds Economy of India: An Econometric Analysis,* Himalaya Pub. House, Bombay.

Reca, Alejandro (2001). "Oilseed Crushing in Argentina: Increasing Supplies, Better Margins and Further Restructuring," *Industry Note, Food & Agribusiness Research,* Rabobank International, Issue 028-2001, Sept.

Reca, Alejandro (2003). "Competition, Economies of Scale and Product Differentiation," *2003 U.S. Food and Agribusiness Outlook,* Rabobank International and Sparks Companies Inc.

Schnepf, R. D., Dohlman, E. & Bolling, C. (2001). *Agriculture in Brazil and Argentina: Developments and Prospects for Major Field Crops.* WRS013, U.S. Dept. Agr., Econ. Res. Serv., Dec.

Solvent Extractors' Association of India (2003). *32nd Annual Report, 200203,* Mumbai, India.

Srinivasan, P. V. (2004). *Managing Price Volatility in an Open Economy Environment: The Case of Edible Oils and Oilseed in India.* MTID Discussion Paper No. 69, International Food Policy Research Institute, Washington, DC, May.

Tuan, Francis C., Cheng Fang & Zhi Cao (2004). "*China's Soybean Imports Expected To Grow Despite Short-Term Disruptions.*" OCSO4J01, U.S. Dept. Agr., Econ. Res. Serv., Oct.

U.S. Department of Agriculture, Foreign Agricultural Service (2005b). USDA PS&D database.

U.S. Department of Agriculture, Office of the Chief Economist (2005c). *USDA Agricultural Baseline Projections to 2014.* OCE-2005-1, Feb.

U.S. Department of Agriculure, Economic Research Service (2005a). Food, CPI, & Expenditures Briefmg Room. www.ers.usda.gov/Briefing/CPIFoodAndExpenditures/threetypesoffoodexpendituresseries.htm

World Bank (1997). *The Indian Oilseed Complex: Capturing Market Opportunities,* Report No. 15677-IN, Rural Development Sector Unit, South Asia Region, Washington, DC.

APPENDIX 1: INDIA OILSEED MODEL CHARACTERISTICS

The ERS India Oilseed Sector Model was developed specifically to analyze the impacts of alternative oilseed sector policies on India's supply, demand, and trade of oilseeds and products, as well as implications for producers, consumers, and processors. The commodity coverage for this report includes soybeans, rapeseed, groundnut, sunflower, and palm oil. The behavioral equations include India's domestic use of the derivative oils and meals, as well as the area and yield of the oilseeds, excluding palm oil.

India's demands for the various oils and meals are linear functions of income, own-price, and substitutes. Farm production of the oilseeds is an identity, computed as the product of area and yield. Crop areas are specified as functions of lagged own-price and competing crop prices. For soybeans and rapeseed, 1-year lags of price variables provided the best results, while distributed lag structures worked best for peanuts and sunflowers. Yield is a function of a lagged own-price and a trend variable representing technological improvements. India's palm oil production is negligible, and hence the quantity consumed is made equal to imports. Imports for the other oils and exports of the meals are treated as residuals. Groundnut oil is an exception, in that imports are consistently zero, implying that the domestic price is that which clears India's supply and demand, i.e., an endogenously formed autarchy price. The model incorporates domestic use of oilseeds for seed, feed, and waste as a fixed percentage of domestic production. Food use of oilseeds grows at a trend rate throughout the projection period, apart from sunflower seed where USDA data do not report food consumption.

The analytical framework for this study illustrates possible impacts on farmers, processors, and consumers of permitting imports of the raw material, taking into account that processors currently operate on the high average cost (downward sloping) part of their cost curves due to low capacity utilization. If imports of the raw material are permitted and processors continue to pay the same input prices, processors find it profitable to increase capacity use and move down their cost curves. Thus, processors gain in two key ways: their unit costs fall and their sales volumes increase. Moreover, liberalizing imports of raw materials may be supportive of lower output prices charged to consumers.

Reference (disequilibrium). The impacts of allowing imports of raw material are illustrated in appendix Figure 1.1. The quantity shown on the X-axis is defined as the amount of raw material provided by farmers to produce output purchased by consumers. That is, the output is placed on a farm product equivalent basis. The Y-axis, which is in monetary terms, represents prices and costs. Average processing costs (AC) include labor, electricity, steam, interest, other costs, and most importantly, the price of raw material. In general form, average costs are written as:

AC = AC(Labor, Electricity, Steam, Interest, Other Costs, Oilseed).

The reference scenario assumes fixed processing capacity, implying that an increase in quantity leads to higher capacity utilization, resulting in an initial decline in unit costs. As quantity continues to expand, unit costs attain a minimum and subsequently begin to rise.

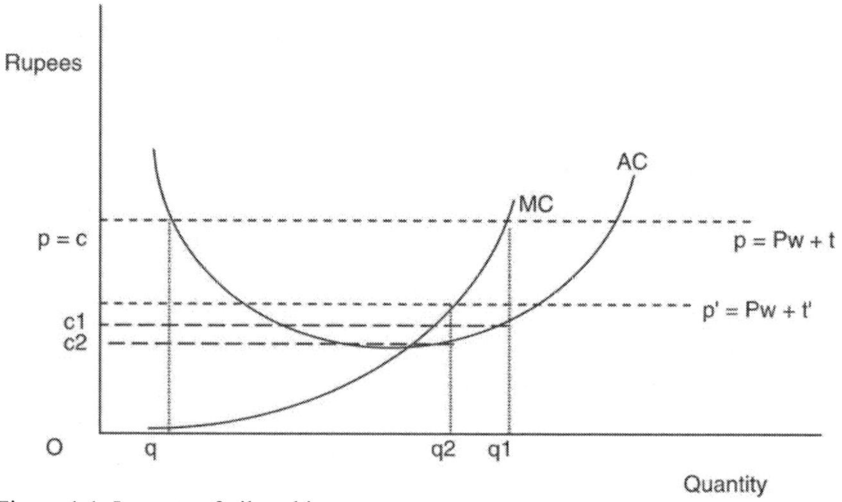

Appendix Figure 1.1. Impacts of oilseed imports

In the disequilibrium case, which serves as the reference scenario, the quantity of the raw material processed is identical to the pre-determined level of domestic farm production, denoted as q in appendix Figure 1.1. The fixed quantity, q, in turn determines the cost of crush, c, on the downward sloping part of the cost curve. The processor would prefer not to operate on the downward sloping part of the cost curve because doing so implies foregone profits. However, over-investment in processing plants and policies preventing raw material imports lead to an artificially depressed rate of capacity use and a relatively high cost, as reflected in the figure. The output price, p, is exogenously determined from a world price (Pw) and a tariff (t), i.e.,

$$p = Pw + t.$$

For simplicity, it is assumed that p is identical to the unit cost, c. The cost of producing at q is given by the rectangle with width Oq and length Oc, i.e., (Oq)(Oc). The revenues obtained from producing q are given by the rectangle with width Oq and length Op, i.e., (Oq)(Op). But since p = c, profits, computed as

((Oq)(Op) - (Oq)(Oc), are zero.

Farmers' revenues are computed as the product of the raw material (Oilseed) price and the quantity produced (Oq),

(Oq)(Oilseed).

Oilseed imports. In this scenario, nontariff barriers on imports of raw material are removed and tariffs reduced. Nonzero tariffs are used to prevent imports of a raw material from depressing domestic prices below the reference scenario. Since the cost of raw material, as well as all other inputs, does not change, the cost curves do not shift. In other words, the tariff is set to eliminate the price advantage of imported raw materials, thereby controlling for shifts in the cost curves. However, processors operate at a different point (ql), where p intersects marginal cost (MC). That is, processors fmd it profitable to increase the quantity produced using imported raw materials, where the quantity of imports is given by the difference, ql-q. Consequently, capacity utilization rises and unit costs fall to c1. The total cost of processing ql is the rectangle (0q1)(0c1). If the world price of the output and its tariff remain constant, the output price remains at p, leading to revenues of (0q1)(0p). Profits, which are now positive, exceed those in the reference (disequilibrium) case, implying that processors benefit:

$$((0q1)(0p) - (0q1)(0c\ 1) > (Oq)(Op) - (Oq)(Oc)$$

This result is noteworthy since it is based on an assumed tariff on raw material imports that protects farmer welfare. Farmer revenues, which are the same as in the reference case, are once again computed as the product of the raw material price (Oilseed) and the quantity produced (q),

$$(Oq)(Oilseed).$$

Finally, consumers neither gain nor lose because the price of the output has not changed.

The analysis is taken a step further to determine if lower trade barriers on imports of the raw material can be used to compensate processors for reduced duties on imports of the output. The price of the output is reduced to p' from p due to a reduction in the tariff to t' from t. Imports of raw material are curtailed, leading to a decrease in the quantity processed to q2 from ql. With unit costs at c2 and the output price at p', profits are now (Op')(0q2) - (0c2)(0q2), which still exceeds zero, the level of profits in the reference scenario. In other words, processors are still better off even with reduced output tariffs, since the benefits of improved access to raw materials more than offset the impacts of lower output prices. The tariff on raw material imports maintains farm revenues at (Oq)(Oilseed), implying that farmers are indifferent to the policy package. Consumers benefit from the reduction in the output price to p' from p. Thus, reductions in the output tariffs transfer rents from processors to consumers.

Although it is not shown in appendix Figure 1.1, there could also be scope for transferring processor rents to farmers by imposing a higher tariff on oilseeds, such that the import price exceeds the autarchy level. This would have the effect of shifting the cost curves upward due to higher raw material costs. Processors would then have to weigh the benefits of moving down a higher cost curve via oilseed imports, against operating at the autarchy crush level on the original cost curve.

This model illustrates the key role of the shape of the cost curve in determining the optimal quantity of oilseed crush, the likely gains to processors under various oilseed import scenarios, and the scope for transferring rents to consumers and/or farmers. The following sections demonstrate the key role of the cost schedule in the quantitative assessment of oilseed trade liberalization, using soybeans as an example.

Cost schedule. Operating costs in India reportedly fall by roughly half to 375 rupees per ton (appendix table 1.1), when moving from 30-percent utilization to full capacity, although, as shown in Figure 11, costs attain a minimum between 85- and 90-percent utilization. The quadratic equation that fits the processing cost data for oilseed i is given by:

$$CRcost_i = CR^1_i*CapUtil_i**2 + CR^2_i*CapUtil_i + CR^0_i$$
$$= 0.1176*CapUtil_i**2 - 21.356*CapUtil_i + 1334.9, \quad (1)$$

where CRcosti is the average variable cost of crush, CapUtili is capacity utilization, the operator is for multiplication, and `**2' indicates squared. Total crush costs ($TCRcost_i$) are,

$$TCRcost_i = SCrush_i*(0.1176*(SCrush_i/Cap_i)**2 - 1.356*(SCrush_i/Cap_i) + 1334.9) + FC_i, \quad (2)$$

where $SCrush_i$ is the quantity of soybean crush, FC_i is the fixed cost, and Cap_i is the soybean crush capacity, such that capacity utilization ($CapUtil_i$) is given by $SCrush/Cap_i$ in (2).

Optimal crush quantity. In the reference scenario, India's trade policies are such that no imports of oilseeds occur. Thus, oilseed crush is simply a residual: the predetermined level of domestic oilseed production less the exogenous quantities of seed, feed, waste, and food uses (see Appendix 2, equation A.7, autarchy case). The stock of crush capacity remains constant throughout the projection period, implying that once the quantity of crush is known, capacity utilization can be computed from equation A.6 (Appendix 2). We assume that costs of crushing, such as labor, hexane, energy expenses, etc., are constant in real terms, so capacity utilization is the only variable that causes the real cost of crushing to vary throughout the projection period. Given a level of capacity utilization, the model computes the cost of crush. The autarchy wholesale price of oilseeds is formed by subtracting the cost of crushing from a weighted-sum of the oil and meal prices, where the weights are the oil and meal extraction rates (equation (A.19), autarchy case). The farm price of the oilseed is then computed by subtracting a margin from the autarchy wholesale price of the oilseed. The farm price determines the production of oilseeds in the subsequent period.

Appendix Table 1.1. Estimated Cost of Indian Oilseed Processing at 30-Percent and 50-Percent Capacity Use

	Rapeseed		Groundnut		Soybeans		Sunflower	
	(30)	(50)	(30)	(50)	(30)	(50)	(30)	(50)
	Rupees							
Power	325	215	333	275	210	150	210	150
Steam	155	65	175	100	150	90	150	90
Hexane	125	70	108	55	134	100	134	100
Labor	255	195	210	140	128	100	128	100
Interest	156	156	157	157	120	96	120	96
Other	170	170	130	130	58	25	108	75
Total	1,186	871	1,112	857	800	561	850	611

Note: At full utilization, the costs for rapeseed, groundnut, soybean, and sunflower are Rs680, Rs696, Rs375, and Rs425, respectively. A breakout of individual cost items is not available.
Source: World Bank (1997), ERS estimates.

In the scenarios where oilseed imports are permitted, crush quantities cannot be computed as a residual because optimal oilseed crush may exceed domestic production. The optimizing framework computes the level of oilseed crush to maximize processor surplus, subject to the cost equation and given the output and input prices.

$$\underset{SCrush_i}{\text{MAXIMIZE}} \{OEXT_i*OPriceW_i + MEXT_i*MPriceW_i - TCRcost_i - SPriceW_i\}, \tag{3}$$

where $OEXT_i$ is the soybean oil extraction rate, $OPriceW_i$ is the domestic price of soy oil, $MEXT_i$ is the soybean meal extraction rate, $MPriceW_i$ is the domestic price of soy meal, and $SPriceW_i$ is the domestic price of the raw material (soybeans). Substituting (2) into (3) for the crush cost yields,

$$\underset{SCrush_i}{\text{MAXIMIZE}} [OEXT_i*OPriceW_i + MEXT_i*MPriceW_i - SPriceW_i - \{SCrush_i*(0.1176*(SCrush_i/Cap_i)**2 - 21.356*(SCrush_i/Cap_i) + 1334.9) + FC_i\}]. \tag{4}$$

Rather than solving explicitly for the crush demand, the optimization framework iterates to compute the profit maximizing quantity of oilseed crush. A non-deterministic approach is preferable, since the cost curves are nonlinear and it is difficult to obtain closed form solutions. Crush levels that exceed domestic production give rise to oilseed imports. Domestic oil, meal, and oilseed prices, which are influenced by world prices, transport costs, and tariffs (in the case of oils and oilseeds) affect the profit maximizing level of crush. Additionally, the ratio of the tariffs on oils to oilseeds affect the crush and oilseed import decision. All other things equal, an increase in the oil tariff relative to the oilseed tariff favors oilseed imports. Similarly, the ratio of world prices of the outputs (oil and meal) to world oilseed prices, coupled with the ratio of the transport costs of oils to oilseeds, will influence the oilseed import decision. This information is summarized in the crush margins that prevail in the domestic market.

It is important to note that, in the scenarios where oilseed imports are permitted, the wholesale price of oilseeds is *not* simply the lesser of the autarchy and import prices. Oilseed imports may be feasible at import prices that exceed the autarchy prices for two reasons: (1) unit crush costs will fall below the autarchy level because imports allow greater capacity use, (2) total processor profits rise above the autarchy level because oilseed imports allow substantially greater volumes of sales. If oilseed imports are feasible, i.e., profit enhancing even with raw material costs that are somewhat higher, then the domestic wholesale price of oilseeds equals the import price, even if it exceeds the autarchy price due to a tariff wedge and/or transport costs. Clearly, if the import price of oilseeds is too far above the autarchy level, then the benefits of importing oilseeds do not justify the costs and, in this case, the domestic wholesale price is the autarchy price.

APPENDIX 2 : INDIA OILSEED MODEL: EQUATIONS AND VARIABLE LIST

Oilseed Block

(A.1) Oilseed Area $\quad SArea_i = SA^1_i * lag(SArea_i) + SA^2_i * lag(SPriceF_i) + SA^0_i$

(A.2) Oilseed Yield $\quad SYield_i = SY^1_i * lag(SYield_i) + SY^2_i * lag(SPriceF_i) + SY^0_i$

(A.3) Oilseed Production $\quad SProd_i = SArea_i * SYield_i$

(A.4) Non-crush demand $\quad SNonCrushi = NC_i * SProd_i$

(A.5) Total Crush Cost $\quad TCRcosti = [CR^1_i * CapUtil_i ** 2 + CR^2_i * CapUtil_i + CR^0_i] * SCrush_i + FC_i$

(A.6) Capacity utilization $\quad CapUtili = SCrush_i / Cap_i$

(A.7) Oilseed crush $\quad SCrushi =$

$$\left\{ \begin{array}{l} \textbf{Autarchy:} \\ SProd_i - SNonCrush_i \\ \\ \textbf{Oilseed Trade:} \\ \underset{SCrush_i}{MAX} \left\{ \begin{array}{l} OEXT_i * OPriceW_i + MEXT_i * MPriceW_i \\ - TCRcost_i - SPriceW_i \end{array} \right\} \end{array} \right\}$$

(A.8) Oilseed imports $\quad IMSi = SCrush_i + SNonCrush_i - SProd_i$

Oil Block

(A.9) Oil Production $\quad OProdi = OEXT_i * SCrush_i$

(A.10) Oil Demand $\quad ODemandi = OD^1_i * OPriceW_i + OD^2_i * GDP + OD^3_i * OOPriceW_i + OD^0_i$

(A.11) Oil imports (identity) $\quad IMOili = ODemand_i - OProd_i$

Meal Block

(A.12) Meal Production $\quad MProdi = MEXT_i * SCrush_i$

(A.13) Meal Demand $\quad MDemandi = MD^1_i * MPriceW_i + MD^2_i * GDP + MD^3_i * MMPriceW_i + MD^0_i$

(A.14) Meal exports (identity) $\quad EXMeali = MProd_i - MDemand_i$

Oil, Meal, and Seed Price Block

(A.15) Wholesale price of oil $\quad OPriceWi = (1 + t_{Oi}) * OPriceREF_i + Margin_{Oi}$

(A.16) Oil margin MarginOi $= OCEAN_{Oi} + Inland_{Oi}$

(A.17) Wholesale price of meal MPriceWi $= MPriceREF_i - Margin_{Mi}$

(A.18) Farm price of seed SPriceFi $= SPriceW_i - SHandle_i$

(A.19) Wholesale price of seed SPriceWi $=$

$$\left\{ \begin{array}{l} \textbf{Autarchy}: \\ OEXT_i * OPriceW_i + MEXT_i * MPriceW_i - TCRcost_i \\ \\ \textbf{Oilseed Trade}: \\ SPriceREF_i * (1 + t_{si}) + STRAN_i \} \end{array} \right\}$$

Variable List

$SArea_i$	Oilseed area
$SYield_i$	Oilseed yield
$SProd_i$	Oilseed production
$SNonCrush_i$	Non-crush demand
IMS_i	Oilseed imports
$SCrush_i$	Oilseed crush
$TCRcost_i$	Total crush cost
$CapUtil_i$	Capacity utilization
Cap_i	Oilseed processing capacity
FC_i	Fixed cost
$OProd_i$	Oil production
$OEXT_i$	Oil extraction rate
$ODemand_i$	Oil demand
$OPriceW_i$	Wholesale price of oil (own-price)
$00PriceW_i$	Wholesale prices of competing oils
GDP	Gross domestic product per capita
$IMOil_i$	Oil imports
$MProd_i$	Meal production
$MEXT_i$	Meal extraction rate
$MDemand_i$	Meal demand
$MPriceW_i$	Wholesale price of meal
$MMPriceW_i$	Wholesale prices of competing meals and complements
$EXMeal_i$	Meal exports
t_{oi}	Oil tariff
t_{si}	Oilseed tariff
$OPriceREF_i$	Reference price of oil
$Margin_{oi}$	Wholesale-reference price margin for oil (oil margin)
$OCEAN_{oi}$	Ocean freight & insurance for oil imports
$Inland_{oi}$	Inland transportation and marketing costs for oil

$MPriceW_i$	Wholesale price of meal
$MPriceREF_i$	Reference (border) price of meal
$Margin_{mi}$	Reference-wholesale price margin for meal (meal margin)
$SPriceF_i$	Farm price of oilseed
$SPriceW_i$	Wholesale price of seed
$SHandle_i$	Wholesale-farm price spread for oilseed
$SPriceREF_i$	Reference (border) price of seed
$STRAN_i$	Ocean freight plus inland transportation and handling cost for oilseed

APPENDIX 3 : INDIA OILSEED MODEL: ELASTICITIES AND BASE DATA

Demand and Supply Elasticities

Elasticities used in the model are given in appendix tables 3.1, 3.2, and 3.3, and are based on both ERS estimates and the literature. Existing literature does not provide formal estimates of demand elasticities for soybean, sunflower, and palm oils, which are relatively new in the Indian market, and time series price data provide relatively few observations for econometric estimation. Previous studies using household data provide elasticity estimates only for "edible oil" as an aggregate commodity group (Kumar, 1998; Dev et al. 2004). Narappanavar (1989) used time series data to estimate demand elasticities for traditional oils (rapeseed and peanut) and also provides a catalogue of estimates from previous studies. However, these studies are based on older time periods and do not capture substitution relationships between the traditional oils and new oils. The demand elasticities for this study are derived from a synthetic approach that generates a set of elasticities that are both theoretically consistent, and generate projections that roughly in line with recent historical data for 2001-05.

Existing literature does not provide elasticity estimates for India's domestic use of oilseed meals. For meals, initial estimates of domestic use were obtained using Ordinary Least Squares (OLS) and annual time-series data, with Gross Domestic Product (GDP) used as the shift variable and corn prices to represent the energy complement. Meal prices were export unit values, which are closely linked to domestic prices. The single-equation approach is less than ideal, but development of a more complete econometric system was judged too costly. Initial OLS estimates were then calibrated in accordance with the base year data and theoretical conditions.

In the context of poor data for generating reliable econometric estimates of the supply and demand elasticities needed for the analysis, the approach used—starting with available estimates, imposing theoretical consistency, and then calibrating the elasticities to replicate historical data—increases confidence in the model results. In calibrating the model, multiple combinations elasticities were experimented with and generated the same basic analytical outcomes.

BASE-YEAR PRICES AND QUANTITIES

Base year prices and quantities used in the model are given in appendix table 3.4. Due to sharp weather-induced swings in production and market conditions in 2002 and 2003, as well as data limitations, 2001 was used as the base year because it is the most recent normal crop year for which data are available. Policy changes in the alternate scenarios are enacted in 2005 and maintained through the terminal year of the annual simulation (2011).

Model parameters replicate India's domestic prices and quantities in the 2001 base year. India's oil and meal extraction rates and domestic supply and use of oilseeds, meals, and oils are from the USDA PS&D Database. Domestic wholesale prices of the oilseeds and oils are published by the Government of India, and domestic meal prices are from the Solvent Extractors' Association of India.

Through the projection period, India's real domestic wholesale prices of soybean oil are obtained from the vector of real world prices generated by the USDA Baseline (U.S. Dept. Agr., 2005c), adjusted by the tariff and the same margin that was used to replicate the base period. India's domestic soy meal prices are determined by adjusting the real world prices from the USDA Baseline by the same margin that was computed to replicate the base period. World prices for the oilseeds, the exchange rate for the rupee, and the GDP deflators through 2011 are from USDA baseline projections.

Appendix Table 3.1. Oil Demand Elasticities for India Oilseed Model

Commodity	Soy oil	Rape oil	Peanut oil	Sun oil	Palm oil	Income
Soy oil	**-0.44**	0.03	0.01	0.04	0.02	0.50
Rape oil	0.04	**-0.70**	0.15	0.02	0.15	0.90
Peanut oil	0.00	0.09	**-0.80**	0.02	0.02	0.90
Sun oil	0.12	0.04	0.07	**-0.30**	0.01	1.00
Palm oil	0.00	0.08	0.01	0.00	**-1.05**	1.20

Appendix Table 3.2. Meal Demand Elasticities for India Oilseed Model

Commodity	Soy meal	Rape meal	Peanut meal	Sun meal	Total protein
Soy meal	**-1.60**	0.04	0.00	0.01	1.70
Rape meal	0.12	**-0.20**	0.07	0.02	0.40
Peanut meal	0.10	0.10	**-0.25**	0.02	0.35
Sun meal	0.12	0.08	0.05	**-0.30**	0.43

Appendix Table 3.3. Farm Supply Elasticities for India Oilseed Model

	Soybeans	Rapeseed	Peanut	Sunflower	Tech chg.
Soybean area	**0.630**	0	-0.005	0	--
Yield	0.003	--	--	--	0.020
Rapeseed area	0	**0.640**	-0.002	0	--
Yield	--	0.003	--	--	0.013
Peanut area	-0.003	-0.002	**0.110**	-0.001	--
Yield	--	--	0.00001	--	0.004
Sunflowerseed	-0.001	-0.0008	-0.050	**0.500***	--
Yield	--	--	--	0.0004	0.022

* Longrun elasticity; shortrun is 0.1.

Appendix Table 3.4. Base Values for India Oilseed Model

Variable (Definition)	Unit	Soybeans	Rapeseed	Peanut	Sunflower	Palm oil
SArea (Oilseed area)	ha	6,000,000	5,250,000	8,200,000	2,400,000	—
SYield (Oilseed yield)	kgs/ha	0.9	0.9	0.9	0.6	—
SProd (Oilseed production)	mt	5,400,000	4,500,000	7,600,000	1,450,000	—
SCrush (Oilseed crush)	mt	4,629,000	3,985,000	5,750,000	1,325,000	—
SNonCrush (Noncrush demand)	mt	202,000	310,000	560,622	**0**	—
IMS (Oilseed imports)	mt	**0**	**0**	**0**	**0**	—
MProd (Meal production)	mt	3,700,000	2,431,150	2,243,000	530,000	—
OProd (Oil production)	mt	855,000	1,554,000	1,894,000	534,000	—
GDP (Per capita)	rs	21,649	21,649	21,649	21,649	21,649
ODemand (Oil demand)	mt	2,405,000	1,559,000	1,894,000	584,000	3,400,000
IMOil (Oil imports)	mt	1,550,000	5,000	**0**	50,000	3,400,000
MDemand (Meal demand)	mt	1,250,000	2,121,000	2,143,000	518,000	—
EXMeal (Meal exports)	mt	2,450,000	310,150	100,000	12,000	
SPriceW (Wholesale price seed)	rs/mt	9,924	13,139	15,668	12,622	--
OPriceW (Wholesale price oil)	rs/mt	30,818	33,078	42,908	40,250	26,160
MPriceW (Wholesale price meal)	rs/mt	8,118	6,097	7,119	5,117	--
t_o (Oil tariff)	%	0.45	0.75	0.75	0.75	0.65
OPriceREF (Reference price oil)	rs/mt	15,809	17,515	32,222	20,131	13,481
SPriceF (Farm price oilseed)	rs/mt	9,545	12,760	13,844	12,243	—
t_s (Oilseed tariff)	%	0.30	0.30	0.30	0.30	—
SPriceREF (Reference price seed)	rs/mt	9,428	9,507	29,254	10,318	—
TCRcost (Total crush cost)	rs/mt	800	1,186	1,112	850	—
Cap (Crush capacity)	mt	15,430,000	13,283,333	19,166,666	4,416,667	—
CapUtil (Capacity utilization)	%	30	30	30	30	—
FC (Fixed cost)	rs/mt	225	200	200	225	—
OEXT (Oil extraction rate)	%	18	39	33	40	—

Appendix Table 3.4. (Continued)

Variable (Definition)	Unit	Soybeans	Rapeseed	Peanut	Sunflower	Palm oil
MEXT (Meal extraction rate)	%	80	61	39	40	
$Margin_O$ (Wholesale-reference price margin for oil)	rs/mt	7,895	2,426		3,916	5,021
$OCEAN_O$ (Ocean freight & insurance for oil imports)	rs/mt	1,457	1,457		1,457	1,222
$Inland_O$ (Inland transport & marketing costs for oil)	rs/mt	6,438	969		2,459	3,799
MPriceREF (Reference (border) price of meal)	rs/mt	8,844	6,612	5,450	5,549	—
$Margin_M$ (Reference-wholesale price margin for meal)	rs/mt	726	515	-1,669	432	—
STRAN (Ocean freight, inland transport & handling cost for seeds)	rs/mt	1,974	1,974		1,974	—

— = Not required.

Appendix Table 4.1. Detailed Results for the Soybean Sector

Change over reference in 2011 (Percent)										
			Change oil tariffs		Oilseed price support				Composite scenario	
Variable (Unit)	**Base year 2001**	**Reference scenario 2011**	**Increase 10 percent**	**Decrease 10 percent**	**Processor pays**	**Government pays**	**Oilseed import liberalization**	**Processor consolidation**	**Government benefits**	**Producer benefits**
Soybeans:										
Area (1,000 ha)	6,000	6,529	2.7	-2.7	2.8	2.8	4.1	1.8	4.1	7.1
Yield (Tons/ha)	0.9	1.13	0.1	-0.1	0.1	0.1	0.1	0.0	0.1	0.2
Production (1,000 tons)	5,400	7,400	2.8	-2.8	2.9	2.9	4.1	1.9	4.1	7.2
Imports (1,000 tons)	0	0	[1]	[1]	[1]	[1]	[2]	[1]	[2]	[3]
Crush (1,000 tons)	4,629	6,223	3.0	-3.0	3.1	3.1	133.1	2.0	133.1	133.1
Farm price (Rs/ton)	9,545	10,266	4.1	-4.1	4.2	4.2	7.5	2.9	7.5	10.9
Processing sector:										
Utilization (Percent)	30	40	3.0	-3.0	3.1	3.1	133.1	133.1	133.1	133.1
Crush margin (Rs/ton)	2,257	2,122	-0.7	0.7	-20.3	-0.7	-36.4	-14.1	-51.6	-52.9
Processing cost:										
Seed cost (Rs/ton)	9,924	10,645	3.9	-3.9	4.1	0.1	7.3	2.8	7.3	10.5
Avg. cost (Rs/ton)	800	665	-2.1	2.2	-2.2	-2.2	-44.9	-44.9	-44.9	-44.9
Unit surplus (Rs/ton)	1,457	1,457	0.0	0.0	-28.6	0.0	-32.6	0.0	-54.6	-56.6

Appendix Table 4.1. (Continued)

Change over reference in 2011 (Percent)										
			Change oil tariffs		Oilseed price support				Composite scenario	
Variable (Unit)	Base year 2001	Reference scenario 2011	Increase 10 percent	Decrease 10 percent	Processor pays	Government pays	Oilseed import liberalization	Processor consolidation	Government benefits	Producer benefits
Quasi-profit (Rs mil.)	6,744	9,067	3.0	-3.0	-26.4	3.1	57.2	2.0	5.7	1.3
Soy oil sector:										
Consumption (1,000 tons)	2,405	2,854	-2.1	2.1	0.0	0.0	0.0	0.0	2.1	0.0
Production (1,000 tons)	855	1,149	3.0	-3.0	3.1	3.1	133.1	2.0	133.1	133.1
Imports (1,000 tons)	1,550	1,705	-5.6	5.6	-2.1	-2.1	-89.7	-1.4	-86.2	-89.7
Wholesale price (Rs/ton)	30,818	39,450	5.5	-5.5	0.0	0.0	0.0	0.0	-4.4	0.0
Soy meal sector:										
Consumption (1,000 tons)	1,250	2,778	0.0	0.0	0.0	0.0	0.0	0.0	0.0	0.0
Production (1,000 tons)	3,700	4,974	3.0	-3.0	3.1	3.1	133.1	2.0	133.1	133.1
Exports (1,000 tons)	2,450	2,196	6.7	-6.7	7.0	7.0	301.4	4.5	301.4	301.4
Wholesale price (Rs/ton)	8,118	6,856	0.0	0.0	0.0	0.0	0.0	0.0	0.0	0.0

[1] No change from reference scenario.
[2] Imports increase to 8.01 million tons.
[3] Imports increrase to 7.80 million tons.
Source: ERS-India oilseed sector model.

Appendix Table 4.2. Detailed Results for the Rapeseed Sector

Change over reference in 2011 (Percent)										
			Change oil tariffs		Oilseed price support				Composite scenario	
Variable (Unit)	Base year 2001	Reference scenario 2011	Increase 10 percent	Decrease 10 percent	Processor pays	Government pays	Oilseed import liberalization	Processor consolidation	Government benefits	Producer benefits
Rapeseed:										
Area (1,000ha)	5,250	5,785	3.8	-3.8	3.9	3.9	0.0	1.6	0.3	0.7
Yield (Tons/ha)	0.9	1.0	0.0	0.0	0.0	0.0	0.0	0.0	0.0	0.0
Production (1,000 tons)	4,500	5,812	3.9	-3.8	3.9	3.9	0.0	1.6	0.3	0.7
Imports (1,000 tons)	0	0	1	1	1	1	2	1	3	4
Crush (1,000 tons)	3,985	5,042	4.2	-4.2	4.3	4.3	10.0	1.8	10.3	10.0
Farm price (Rs/ton)	12,760	16,787	5.8	-5.8	5.9	5.9	0.0	2.3	0.8	1.5
Processing sector:										
Utilization (Percent)	30	38	4.2	-4.2	4.3	4.3	14.6	147.5	14.9	14.6
Crush margin (Rs/ton)	3,480	3,338	-0.8	0.8	-29.9	-0.8	0.0	-11.6	-7.9	-7.6
Processing cost:										
Seed cost (Rs/ton)	13,139	17,166	5.7	-5.7	5.8	0.2	0.0	2.3	0.8	1.5
Avg. cost (Rs/ton)	1,186	1,044	-2.5	2.6	-2.5	-2.6	-8.2	-37.0	-8.4	-8.2
Unit surplus (Rs/ton)	2,294	2,294	0.0	0.0	-42.3	0.0	3.7	0.0	-7.6	-7.4
Quasi-profit (Rs mil.)	9,142	11,566	4.2	-4.2	-39.8	4.3	14.1	1.8	1.9	1.9
Rapeseed oil:										
Consumption(1,000 tons)	1,559	2,162	-2.6	2.7	0.0	0.0	0.0	-0.1	0.3	0.0

Appendix Table 4.2. (Continued)

Change over reference in 2011 (Percent)										
			Change oil tariffs		Oilseed price support				Composite scenario	
Variable (Unit)	Base year 2001	Reference scenario 2011	Increase 10 percent	Decrease 10 percent	Processor pays	Government pays	Oilseed import liberalization	Processor consolidation	Government benefits	Producer benefits
Production (1,000 tons)	1,554	1,966	4.2	-4.2	4.3	4.3	10.0	1.8	10.3	10.0
Imports (1,000 tons)		5 196	-71.8	71.4	-43.7	-43.7	-100.0	-18.5	-100.0	-100.0
Wholesale price (Rs/ton)	33,078	44,781	5.4	-5.4	0.0	0.0	0.0	0.0	-0.7	0.0
Rapeseed meal:										
Consumption (1,000 tons)	2,121	2,621	0.0	0.0	0.0	0.0	0.0	0.0	0.0	0.0
Production (1,000 tons)	2,431	3,076	4.2	-4.2	4.3	4.3	10.0	1.8	10.3	10.0
Exports (1,000 tons)	310	455	28.7	-28.4	29.3	29.3	67.4	12.1	69.9	67.4
Wholesale price (Rs/ton)	6,097	4,985	0.0	0.0	0.0	0.0	0.0	0.0	0.0	0.0

[1] No change from reference scenario.
[2] Imports rise to 0.50 million tons.
[3] Imports rise to 0.51 million tons.
[4] Imports rise to 0.46 million tons.
Source: ERS-India oilseed sector model.

Appendix Table 4.3. Detailed Results for the Peanut Sector

Change over reference in 2011 (Percent)										
			Change oil tariffs		Oilseed price support				Composite scenario	
Variable (Unit)	**Base year 2001**	**Reference scenario 2011**	**Increase 10 percent**	**Decrease 10 percent**	**Processor pays**	**Government pays**	**Oilseed import liberalization**	**Processor consolidation**	**Government benefits**	**Producer benefits**
Peanuts:										
Area (1,000 ha)	8,200	9,183	0.1	-0.2	0.1	0.1	0.0	0.3	0.0	0.0
Yield (Tons/ha)	0.9	1.0	0.0	0.0	0.0	0.0	0.0	0.0	0.0	0.0
Production (1,000 tons)	7,600	8,859	0.1	-0.2	0.1	0.1	0.0	0.3	0.0	0.0
Imports (1,000 tons)	0	0	1	1	1	1	1	1	1	1
Crush (1,000 tons)	5,750	6,855	0.1	-0.2	0.1	0.1	0.0	0.3	0.0	0.0
Farm price (Rs/ton)	13,844	20,113	0.7	-0.6	0.5	0.5	0.0	1.4	0.0	0.0
Processing sector:										
Utilization (Percent)	30	36	0.1	-0.2	0.1	0.1	0.0	162.8	0.0	0.0
Crush margin (Rs/ton)	1,243	1,158	-0.1	0.1	-11.4	0.0	0.0	-30.1	0.0	0.0
Processing cost:										
Seed cost (Rs/ton)	15,668	21,937	0.6	-0.6	0.5	-0.1	0.0	1.3	0.0	0.0
Avg. cost (Rs/ton)	1,112	1,027	-0.1	0.1	-0.1	-0.1	0.0	-33.9	0.0	0.0
Unit surplus (Rs/ton)	131	131	0.0	0.0	-100.4	0.0	0.0	0.0	0.0	0.0
Quasi-profit (Rs mil.)	753	898	0.1	-0.2	-100.4	0.1	0.0	0.3	0.0	0.0
Peanut oil:										
Consumption (1,000 tons)	1,894	,258	0.1	-0.2	0.1	0.1	0.0	0.3	0.0	0.0
Production (1,000 tons)	1,894	2,258	0.1	-0.2	0.1	0.1	0.0	0.3	0.0	0.0
Imports (1,000 tons)	0	0	1	1	1	1	1	1	1	1
Wholesale price (Rs/ton)	42,908	62,604	0.6	-0.6	-0.1	-0.1	0.0	-0.3	0.0	0.0
Peanut meal:										
Consumption (1,000 tons)	2,143	2,554	0.0	0.0	0.0	0.0	0.0	0.0	0.0	0.0

Appendix Table 4.3. (Continued)

Change over reference in 2011 (Percent)											
			Change oil tariffs		Oilseed price support				Composite scenario	
Variable (Unit)	Base year 2001	Reference scenario 2011	Increase 10 percent	Decrease 10 percent	Processor pays	Government pays	Oilseed import liberalization	Processor consolidation	Government benefits	Producer benefits
Production (1,000 tons)	2,243	2,674	0.1	-0.2	0.1	0.1	0.0	0.3	0.0	0.0
Exports (1,000 tons)	100	120	3.2	-3.7	2.5	2.5	-0.5	7.3	-0.9	-0.8
Wholesale price (Rs/ton)	7,119	6,342	0.0	0.0	0.0	0.0	0.0	0.0	0.0	0.0

[1] No change from reference scenario.

Source: ERS-India oilseed sector model.

Appendix Table 4.4. Detailed Results For The Sunflower Sector

Change over reference in 2011 (Percent)										
		Change oil tariffs			Oilseed price support				Composite scenario	
Variable (Unit)	Base year 2001	Reference scenario 2011	Increase 10 percent	Decrease 10 percent	Processor pays	Government pays	Oilseed import liberalization	Processor consolidation	Government benefits	Producer benefits
Sunflower seed:										
Area (1,000ha)	2,400	3,116	2.1	-2.3	2.3	2.0	1.3	0.5	1.1	1.3
Yield (Tons/ha)	0.6	0.8	0.0	0.0	0.0	0.0	0.0	0.0	0.0	0.0
Production (1,000 tons)	1,450	2,352	2.1	-2.3	2.3	2.0	1.3	0.5	1.1	1.3
Imports (1,000 tons)	0	0	[1]	[1]	[1]	[1]	[2]	[1]	[3]	[1]
Crush (1,000 tons)	1,325	2,149	2.1	-2.3	2.3	2.0	11.4	0.5	10.9	11.4
Farm price (Rs/ton)	12,243	12,131	7.0	-7.0	7.1	7.1	6.4	2.5	6.4	6.4
Processing sector:										
Utilization (Percent)	30	49	2.1	-2.3	2.3	2.0	11.4	91.8	10.9	11.4
Crush margin (Rs/ton)	5,646	5,511	-0.3	0.3	-15.6	-0.3	-14.1	-5.4	-14.1	-14.1
Processing cost:										

Appendix Table 4.4. (Continued)

Change over reference in 2011 (Percent)										
			Change oil tariffs		Oilseed price support				Composite scenario	
Variable (Unit)	Base year 2001	Reference scenario 2011	Increase 10 percent	Decrease 10 percent	Processor pays	Government pays	Oilseed import liberalization	Processor consolidation	Government benefits	Producer benefits
Seed cost (Rs/ton)	12,622	12,510	6.8	-6.8	6.9	0.1	6.2	2.4	6.2	6.2
Avg. cost (Rs/ton)	850	715	-2.0	2.0	-2.0	-2.0	-41.7	-41.7	-41.7	-41.7
Unit surplus (Rs/ton)	4,796	4,796	0.0	0.0	-17.7	0.0	-10.0	0.0	-10.0	-10.0
Quasi-profit (Rs mil.)	6,355	10,309	2.1	-2.3	-15.8	2.0	0.3	0.5	-0.2	0.3
Sunflower oil:										
Consumption (1,000 tons)	584	965	-0.2	0.2	0.0	0.0	0.0	0.0	-0.4	0.0
Production (1,000 tons)	534	866	2.1	-2.3	2.3	2.0	11.4	0.5	10.9	11.4
Imports (1,000 tons)	50	98	-20.4	22.4	-20.5	-17.9	-100.0	-4.4	-100.0	-100.0
Wholesale price (Rs/ton)	40,250	41,166	5.0	-5.0	0.0	0.0	0.0	0.0	0.0	0.0
Sunflower meal:										
Consumption (1,000 tons)	518	673	0.0	0.0	0.0	0.0	0.0	0.0	0.0	0.0
Production (1,000 tons)	530	860	2.1	-2.3	2.3	2.0	11.4	0.5	10.9	11.4
Exports (1,000 tons)	12	186	9.7	-10.8	10.7	9.3	52.4	2.2	50.2	52.4
Wholesale price (Rs/ton)	5,117	3,575	0.0	0.0	0.0	0.0	0.0	0.0	0.0	0.0

[1] No change from reference scenario.
[2] Imports rise to 0.22 million tons.
[3] Imports rise to 0.21 million tons.
Source: ERS-India oilseed sector model.

Appendix Table 4.5. Detailed Results For Palm Oil

Change over reference in 2011 (Percent)											
			Change oil tariffs			Oilseed price support				Composite scenario	
Variable (Unit)	Base year 2001	Reference scenario 2011	Increase 10 percent	Decrease 10 percent	Processor pays	Government pays	Oilseed import liberalization	Processor consolidation	Government benefits	Producer benefits
Palm oil:											
Consumption (1,000 tons)	3,400	5,036	-4.2	4.2	0.0	0.0	0.0	0.0	-0.1	0.0
Production (1,000 tons)	0	0	1	1	1	1	1	1	1	1
Imports (1,000 tons)	3,400	5,036	-4.2	4.2	0.0	0.0	0.0	0.0	-0.1	0.0
Wholesale price (Rs/ton)	26,160	32,307	5.3	-5.3	0.0	0.0	0.0	0.0	0.0	0.0

[1] No change from reference scenario.

Source: ERS-India oilseed sector model.

END NOTES

[1] Indian rapeseed varieties are high in glucosinolates (a growth inhibitor in livestock) and indigestible fiber, and low in metabolizable energy and key amino acids. They also contain erucic acid, which causes liver necrosis and thyroid enlargement. Indian peanut meal is low in quality due to aflatoxin, which results from poor postharvest handling.

[2] Although reference scenario assumptions are consistent with current USDA baseline projections, the reference scenario projections differ in some respects from the USDA baseline because of the availability of more recent data and differences in model base periods, specifications, and elasticities.

[3] Recent data suggest that solvent extraction capacity may be declining, in part because recent poor harvests led to closure of some units. Constant crush capacity is assumed in the reference scenario, with the effects of reduced processing capacity analyzed in the consolidation scenario.

[4] Quasi-profits, as used here, account for the major costs and revenues associated with processing, including the cost of raw materials, labor, interest, power, steam, and hexane, and revenues from sale of oil and meal. Excluded items include such costs as bags and brokerage for de-oiled cake, local and central taxes, and revenues from the sale of processing wastes such as sunflowerseed hulls and peanut pods.

[5] The extent to which changes in crush costs are transmitted to producer prices of oilseeds and consumer prices of products is determined in the model by (1) the price responsiveness of oilseed supply (own- and cross-price elasticities) and (2) the oilseed trade regime in the scenario being analyzed. When oilseeds cannot be imported, the impact of gains in processing efficiency tends to be bid into the price of oilseeds, which are in relatively fixed (inelastic) supply. When oilseeds can be imported, domestic oilseed prices are determined primarily by world market prices, and domestic crush costs have little bearing on domestic prices.

[6] World reference prices for oilseeds and products are maintained at reference scenario levels (consistent with 2005 USDA baseline projections) in all scenarios analyzed. Although India is a large trader in global oil and meal markets, the changes in trade in the scenarios analyzed are small compared with the volume of global trade and unlikely to have significant long-term impacts on world prices. The oilseed import liberalization scenario alters the composition of India's oilseed.

[7] The calculation assumes an average oilseed price elasticity of demand in the range of -0.30 to -0.40, implying that 0.87-1.16 percent of total supplies (220,000-290,000 tons) would have to be removed from the market to raise the average reference scenario price by 2.9 percent (Rs456/ton), yielding a cost of Rs99.0-132 million. Adding handling and administrative costs of Rs100/ton and storage costs, computed assuming 10-percent interest for an average storage period of 3 months, results in a budgetary cost estimate of Rs123-164 million ($2.7-3.6 million).

[8] Assessing the feasibility of removing existing SPS barriers to oilseed imports is beyond the scope of this study. For this analysis, it is assumed that the barriers can be reduced or complied with without creating unacceptable pest or disease risks, or unacceptable costs to oilseed processors.

[9] Oilseed transport and handling costs are accounted for in a way that avoids the detail of plant- or region-specific transport and handling cost data. It is assumed that all processing capacity within about 800 km of major ports could process imported oilseeds. This is reasonable because soybean processors in Madhya Pradesh-roughly 800 km from major ports-now pay the transport costs and earn profits from meal exports. Based on state data, about 76 percent of existing processing capacity meets this criterion (Solvent Extractors' Association of India, 2003). Processors farther from the port are assumed to rely on domestically produced oilseeds. The average costs of transporting oilseeds and meals from and to ports are based on data provided by processors in Madhya Pradesh (Rs850/ton by road, Rs750/ton by rail, Rs800/ton average). Oilseed imports might, in the short run, bid up the transport costs. But since many plants are located closer to ports than 800 km and large-scale imports could lead to investment in more efficient transport, current costs may also overestimate longrun costs.

[10] The 34-percent average tariff needed to maintain rapeseed producer prices is above the current 30-percent tariff, implying that the current tariff would not prevent rapeseed imports in the absence of nontariff barriers.

[11] In oilseed processing, the convention is to measure capacity based on 24-hour days and 300 days of operation, which builds in 65 days of closure for holidays and plant maintenance.

In: India and the U.S: Future Relations…
Editor: Tim S. Macleod, pp.101-145

ISBN: 978-1-60741-197-0

Chapter 3

U.S. NUCLEAR COOPERATION WITH INDIA: ISSUES FOR CONGRESS

Paul K. Kerr
Analyst in Nonproliferation Foreign Affairs,
Defense, and Trade Division

SUMMARY

On July 18, 2005, President Bush announced he would "work to achieve full civil nuclear energy cooperation with India" and would "also seek agreement from Congress to adjust U.S. laws and policies," in the context of a broader, global partnership with India.

India, which has not signed the Nuclear Nonproliferation Treaty (NPT) and does not have International Atomic Energy Agency safeguards on all nuclear material in peaceful nuclear activities, exploded a "peaceful" nuclear device in 1974, convincing the world of the need for greater restrictions on nuclear trade. The United States created the Nuclear Suppliers Group (NSG) as a direct response to India's test, halted nuclear exports to India a few years later, and worked to convince other states to do the same. India tested nuclear weapons again in 1998.

U.S. nuclear cooperation is governed by the Atomic Energy Act (AEA). P.L. 109-401, which President Bush signed bill into law on December 18, 2006, provides waivers of several provisions of the AEA (Sections 123 a. (2), 128, and 129). It requires that several steps occur before nuclear cooperation can proceed. On September 10, President Bush submitted to Congress a written determination that these requirements discussed above have been met. That same day, the President submitted the text of the proposed agreement, which has not yet been signed. The President also submitted a written determination (also required by the AEA) "that the performance of the proposed agreement will promote and will not constitute an unreasonable risk to, the common defense and security." In addition, President Bush submitted several documents, including classified and unclassified versions of a Nuclear Proliferation Assessment Statement, which is required by section 123 of the AEA. The Department of State has also submitted a report required by P.L. 109-401 on various aspects of the agreement.

On September 27, 2008, the House passed H.R. 7081, which approves the agreement. The Senate Committee on Foreign Relations approved identical legislation, S. 3548, September 23. The Senate passed H.R. 7081 October 1. President Bush signed P.L. 110-369 into law October 8. Secretary of State Condoleezza Rice and India's External Affairs Minister Shri Pranab Mukherjee signed the agreement October 10, but it has not yet entered into force. This report will be updated as necessary.

RECENT DEVELOPMENTS

India and the United States announced July 27, 2007, that they had reached agreement on the text of a nuclear cooperation agreement.[1] P.L. 109-401, the Henry J. Hyde United States-India Peaceful Atomic Energy Cooperation Act of 2006, which President Bush signed into law December 18, 2006, allows the President to waive such an agreement with India from several requirements of the Atomic Energy Act (AEA) of 1954, as amended.

President Bush submitted the text of the proposed agreement, which has not yet been signed, to Congress September 10. The President also submitted a written determination (also required by the AEA) "that the performance of the proposed agreement will promote and will not constitute an unreasonable risk to, the common defense and security." In addition, President Bush submitted several documents, including classified and unclassified versions of a Nuclear Proliferation Assessment Statement (NPAS), which is required by section 123 of the AEA. The Department of State has also submitted a report, which is required by section 104 of P.L. 109401, on various aspects of the agreement.[2]

President Bush also determined that P.L. 109-401's requirements for the President to exercise his waiver authority have been met. These requirements are (1) provision of a credible separation plan for India's nuclear facilities; (2) approval by the IAEA Board of Governors of India's new nuclear safeguards agreement; (3) substantial progress toward concluding an Additional Protocol; (4) India's active support for the conclusion of a treaty to ban fissile material production for nuclear weapons; (5) India's support for U.S. and international efforts to halt the spread of sensitive nuclear fuel cycle technologies (enrichment and reprocessing); (6) India taking necessary steps to secure nuclear and other sensitive materials and technologies through adherence to multilateral control regimes (like the NSG and the Missile Technology Control Regime [MTCR]); and (7) a consensus decision by the NSG to make an exception for India.

President Bush submitted the agreement after the IAEA Board of Governors approved India's safeguards agreement August 1. The NSG decided at the end of a September 4-6 Extraordinary Plenary meeting to exempt India from the Group's export guidelines.

Procedures for congressional approval of the nuclear cooperation agreement are described in both P.L. 109-401 and the AEA. According to P.L. 109-401, the agreement cannot enter into force without a joint resolution of approval from Congress. According to Section 123 b. of the AEA, the President is to submit the text of the agreement to the Senate Foreign Relations Committee and the House Committee on Foreign Affairs. The President is then to consult with the committees "for a period of not less than thirty days of continuous session." According to Section 123 d., the two committees shall, after that time, "each hold hearings on the proposed agreement for cooperation and submit a report to their respective bodies recommending whether it should be approved or disapproved." Therefore, the minimum amount of time that must elapse before Congress can vote on a joint resolution of approval is 30 days of continuous session, in addition to the amount of time Congress would take to hold hearings.

On September 27, however, by a vote of 298 - 117 (1 Present), the House passed H.R. 7081, which approved the agreement and waived "the provisions for congressional consideration and approval of a proposed agreement" contained in Sections 123 b. and 123 d. of the AEA. The Senate Foreign Relations Committee approved identical legislation, S. 3548, September 23. The Senate passed H.R. 7081 by a vote of 86-13 October 1. The Senate passed H.R. 7081 October 1. On October 8, President Bush signed P.L. 110-369, the United States-India Nuclear Cooperation Approval and Nonproliferation Enhancement Act, into law. The President's signing statement did not indicate any differences with the legislation.

According to its text, the July 2007 agreement "shall enter into force on the date on which the Parties exchange diplomatic notes informing each other that they have completed all applicable requirements for its entry into force." Secretary of State Condoleezza Rice and India's External Affairs Minister Shri Pranab Mukherjee signed the agreement October 10. P.L. 110-369 requires the President to sign and transmit to Congress two certifications in order for the two governments to exchange diplomatic notes (see below). Washington and New Delhi have not yet done so, although President Bush transmitted the certifications October 20.

BACKGROUND

The United States actively promoted nuclear energy cooperation with India from the mid-1950s, building nuclear power reactors (Tarapur), providing heavy water for the CIRUS research reactor, and allowing Indian scientists to study at U.S. nuclear laboratories. Although India was active in negotiations of the 1968 Nuclear Nonproliferation Treaty (NPT), India refused to join the treaty, arguing that it was discriminatory. India conducted a "peaceful" nuclear test in 1974, which reinforced the notion that nuclear technology transferred for peaceful purposes could be used to produce nuclear weapons.[3] Congress responded to that test by passing the Nuclear Non-Proliferation Act of 1978 (NNPA, P.L. 95-242), which imposed tough new requirements for U.S. nuclear exports to non-nuclear-weapon states — full-scope safeguards and termination of exports if such a state detonates a nuclear explosive device or engages in activities related to acquiring or manufacturing nuclear weapons, among other things.[4] The United States created the NSG, a voluntary nuclear export regime, in 1975. The NSG published guidelines in 1978 "to apply to nuclear transfers for peaceful purposes to help ensure that such transfers would not be diverted to unsafeguarded nuclear fuel cycle or nuclear explosive activities."[5]

The condition that non-nuclear-weapon states wishing to obtain U.S. nuclear exports must have full-scope safeguards created a problem for U.S. fuel supplies to India's reactors at Tarapur, which were built by U.S. firms and fueled by U.S. low-enriched uranium, pursuant to a 1963 nuclear cooperation agreement. After passage of the NNPA, the Carter Administration exported two more uranium shipments under executive order after the Nuclear Regulatory Commission (NRC) refused to approve an export license on nonproliferation conditions. Although the House voted to disapprove the President's determination, the Senate voted 46 to 48 on a resolution of disapproval. After 1980, all nuclear exports from the United States to India were cut off under the terms of the NNPA. France supplied fuel under the terms of the U.S. agreement with India until France also adopted a full-scope safeguards requirement in 1995. After the NSG adopted the full-scope safeguards condition in 1992, China supplied the reactor. Russia supplied fuel from 2001 to 2004.[6]

Although the NPT requires safeguards on items going to non-nuclear weapon states, it does not explicitly prohibit nuclear commerce with states outside the NPT. In 1995, at the NPT Extension Conference, states supported the principle that non-NPT parties should not be eligible for the same kinds of assistance as NPT parties in good standing. India tested several nuclear weapons in 1998.

GLOBAL PARTNERSHIP[7]

The Bush Administration had been considering a strategic partnership with India as early as 2001. Indian officials identified their growing energy needs as an area for cooperation, particularly in nuclear energy. The U.S.-India 2004 Next Steps in Strategic Partnership (NSSP) initiative included expanded cooperation in civil nuclear technology as one of three goals. Phase I of the NSSP, completed in September 2004, required addressing proliferation concerns and ensuring compliance with U.S. export controls.[8]

On July 18, 2005, President Bush announced the creation of a global partnership with India in a joint statement with Prime Minister Manmohan Singh.[9] Noting the "significance of civilian nuclear energy for meeting growing global energy demands in a cleaner and more efficient manner," President Bush said he would "work to achieve full civil nuclear energy cooperation with India" and would "also seek agreement from Congress to adjust U.S. laws and policies."

The Joint Statement noted that the United States "will work with friends and allies to adjust international regimes to enable full civil nuclear energy cooperation and trade with India, including but not limited to expeditious consideration of fuel supplies for safeguarded nuclear reactors at Tarapur." The United States committed to encouraging its partners to consider this request — a reversal in the U.S. position, which has been to ban fuel to Tarapur — and to consulting with its partners on Indian participation in ITER (collaboration on fusion research) and in the Generation IV International Forum for future reactor design.

Prime Minister Singh conveyed that India "would take on the same responsibilities and practices and acquire the same benefits and advantages as other leading countries with advanced nuclear technology, such as the United States."[10] India agreed to:

identify and separate its civilian and military nuclear facilities and programs;
declare its civilian facilities to the IAEA;
voluntarily place civilian facilities under IAEA safeguards;
sign an Additional Protocol for civilian facilities;
continue its unilateral nuclear test moratorium;
work with the United States to conclude a Fissile Material Cut Off Treaty (FMCT);[11]

refrain from transferring enrichment and reprocessing technologies to states that do not have them, as well as support international efforts to limit their spread;
secure its nuclear materials and technology through comprehensive export control legislation and through harmonization and adherence to MTCR and NSG guidelines.

ISSUES FOR CONSIDERATION

The AEA requires Congressional approval and oversight of peaceful nuclear cooperation agreements (details described below). As Senator Lugar has noted, "Ultimately the entire Congress ... must determine what effect the Joint Statement will have on U.S. efforts to halt the proliferation of weapons of mass destruction."[12] Congress held eight hearings in 2005 and 2006 on the global partnership and has consulted with the Administration on various aspects of the U.S.-India nuclear agreement.[13] The discussion of potential issues for consideration is drawn in part from the hearings and from the emerging debate.

Strategy vs. Tactics

The Bush Administration has described its "desire to transform relations with India" as "founded upon a strategic vision that transcends even today's most pressing security concerns."[14] There is clearly broad support for cultivating a close relationship with India, yet some members of Congress have suggested that civil nuclear cooperation may not be the most appropriate vehicle for advancing our relationship. In a House International Relations Committee hearing on September 8, 2005, Congressman Jim Leach stated,

> I don't know any member of Congress that doesn't want to have a warming of relations with the government of India.... I also don't know many members of Congress who are pushing for the precise commitment that the administration has made.[15]

Congressman Leach suggested instead that U.S. support for a permanent seat for India on the United Nations Security Council might have been a more appropriate gesture.

Other observers outside of Congress have questioned whether U.S. energy assistance should focus on expanding nuclear power, in contrast to other energy alternatives. Henry Sokolski of the Nonproliferation Policy Education Center has argued that Indian energy needs might be better met through free market allocation, including improved efficiency. He asserts that nuclear power is the least leveraged of India's options to meet India's energy needs, given that it currently provides only 2.7% of installed electrical capacity.[16] India's projections of its nuclear energy needs are predicated on an estimated annual growth rate of 8%, which some observers believe may be unrealistic.[17] One well-known Indian commentator, Brahma Chellaney, argued in the *International Herald Tribune* that the premise that India should meet its rapidly expanding energy needs through importing nuclear power reactors was flawed. Chellaney argued that a better approach for India would be to secure clean-coal and renewable energy technologies.[18]

The Senate Foreign Relations Committee's November 2, 2005 hearing sought, among other things, to answer the question of why civil nuclear cooperation was so important to the U.S.-Indian strategic relationship. Under Secretary of State Nicholas Burns told Committee members that "India had made this the central issue in the new partnership developing between our countries."[19]

Impact on U.S. Nonproliferation Policies

The Administration has characterized civil nuclear cooperation with India as a "win" for nonproliferation because it would bring India into the "nonproliferation mainstream." In short, the Administration is proposing that India should be courted as an *ally* in U.S. nonproliferation policy, rather than continue as a *target* of U.S. nonproliferation policy. According to this reasoning, India should become an allyfor three reasons: past policies have not worked; India has a relatively good nonproliferation record anyway, and India could be a useful ally in the nonproliferation regime.

Some observers, however, are concerned that India may not support U.S. nonproliferation policies sufficiently to warrant nuclear cooperation, particularly where the United States faces its greatest nuclear proliferation threat: Iran. For example, at the September 8 House International Relations Committee hearing, several members of Congress questioned whether the United States had obtained assurances from India of its support on Iran before it issued the July 18 joint statement.

Iran

Two factors may present challenges to Indian support for U.S. policies toward Iran. First, India has a growing strategic relationship with Iran, not limited to its interest in a proposed $7.4 billion, 2800-km-long gas pipeline between Iran, Pakistan, and India. Second, India has a strong tradition of foreign policy independence, as a long-time leader of the Non-Aligned Movement (NAM) states and as a vigorous opponent of the discriminatory nature of the Nuclear Nonproliferation Treaty.[20] One witness before the House International Relations Committee hearing on November 16, 2005, suggested that opposition from the United States on the gas pipeline project is considered to be "interference with India's autonomy in foreign relations, as well as disregard for its security and energy needs."[21]

On Iran's nuclear program, Indian officials have stated they do not support a nuclear weapons option for Tehran. However, they did not agree with the United States on the urgency of reporting Iran's nuclear program to the U.N. Security Council, which the United States has proposed since 2003, nor on the need to limit Iran's nuclear fuel cycle development. When the IAEA Board of Governors passed a resolution (GOV/2005/77) on September 24, 2005, finding Iran in noncompliance with its safeguards agreement, India voted with the United States, provoking significant domestic dissent. According to Indian Foreign Secretary Shyam Saran, India voted for the resolution and against the majority of NAM states which abstained, because it felt obligated after having pressured the EU-3 to omit reference to immediate referral to the U.N. Security Council.[22] Moreover, India explained its vote this way:

> In our Explanation of Vote, we have clearly expressed our opposition to Iran being declared as noncompliant with its safeguards agreements. Nor do we agree that the current situation could constitute a threat to international peace and security. Nevertheless, the resolution does not refer the matter to the Security Council and has agreed that outstanding issues be dealt with under the aegis of the IAEA itself. This is in line with our position and therefore, we have extended our support.[23]

On February 4, 2006, following Iran's resumption of some uranium enrichment research and development, the IAEA Board of Governors met in an emergency session and voted to report Iran's noncompliance to the U.N. Security Council.[24] India voted with the United States to report Iran, although this followed a controversial remark to the press the previous week by Mulford that India would have to support the United States on Iran in Vienna or the U.S. Congress would not support the peaceful nuclear cooperation agreement.[25]

Iran may also test India's support for curtailing peaceful nuclear programs. India has always been an advocate of states' rights to develop the peaceful uses of nuclear energy and for thirty years has derided the NPT and nonproliferation policies as discriminatory. The official Iranian press agency reported Prime Minister Singh as telling President Ahmadinejad on September 22, 2005, that solutions to Iran's nuclear problem should be based on the principle that Iran as an NPT member should retain its lawful rights.[26] On September 26, 2005, Foreign Secretary Saran told the press that "With respect to Iran's right to peaceful uses of nuclear energy, that is something which we have ourselves no reservations about."[27] In September 2006, India joined in the 118-nation Nonaligned Movement (NAM) summit statement that expressed support for Iran's "choices and decisions in the field of peaceful uses of nuclear technology and its fuel cycle policies."[28]

Reported Indian Transfers of WMD-related items to Iran.[29] Concerns about India's relationship with Iran extend, for some, to the transfer of Weapons of Mass Destruction (WMD)-related items. Entities in India and Iran appear to have engaged in very limited nuclear, chemical and missile-related transfers over the years. There are no publicly available indications of activities related to biological weapons. In the early 1990s, when Iran actively sought nuclear-related assistance and technology from many foreign sources, India appears to have played only a minor role in contrast to other states. India signed an agreement in November 1991 to provide a 10 megawatt research reactor to Tehran, but cancelled under pressure from the United States. Nonetheless, India reportedly trained Iranian nuclear scientists in the 1990s.[30] More recently, India's Foreign Minister Jaswant Singh stated in December 2003 that India "has and would continue to help Iran in its controversial bid to generate nuclear energy."[31]

In September 2004, the United States imposed sanctions on two Indian nuclear scientists, Dr. Y.S.R. Prasad and Dr. C. Surendar, under the Iran Nonproliferation Act. Indian officials protested, stating that cooperation had taken place under the auspices of the IAEA Technical Cooperation program. Other reports suggest that the scientists, who had served as Chairman and Managing Director of the Nuclear Power Corporation of India, Ltd. (NPCIL), which runs India's power reactors, passed information to Iran on tritium extraction from heavy water reactors.[32] Sanctions were lifted on Dr. Surendar in 2005.

In the chemical area, there is one confirmed transfer of 60 tons of thionyl chloride, a chemical that can be used in the production of mustard gas, from India to Iran in March

1989.[33] Other shipments in that time-frame reportedly were halted under U.S. pressure. India does not appear in the CIA's unclassified nonproliferation report to Congress as a supplier of chemical-weapons-related exports to Iran since the report began publication in 1997. India signed the Chemical Weapons Convention in 1993 and deposited its instrument of ratification until 1996. However, in December 2005, the United States imposed sanctions on Sabero Organic Chemicals Gujarat Ltd and Sandhya Organic Chemicals Pvt. Ltd, pursuant to the Iran Nonproliferation Act of 2000. In July 2006, the United States imposed sanctions on Balaji Amines and Prachi Poly Products, chemical manufacturers, pursuant to the Iran and Syrian Nonproliferation Act.[34]

Restricting Enrichment and Reprocessing

One of India's commitments in the July 18 statement was to refrain from transferring enrichment and reprocessing technologies to states that do not already have those technologies and to support international efforts to limit their spread. To some observers, U.S. efforts to restrict development of those aspects of the nuclear fuel cycle (enrichment and reprocessing) that are most useful in a nuclear weapons development program are seen as creating a new category of "have-nots" — those states that can have some peaceful nuclear technology but cannot be trusted with it all. In other words, states like Japan, Germany, and Brazil might be trusted with sensitive technologies, but states like Iran and North Korea cannot be trusted. Historically, India has supported states' inalienable right to all peaceful uses of nuclear energy.

India's External Affairs Minister Shri Pranab Mukherjee stated September 5 that:

> India will not be the source of proliferation of sensitive technologies, including enrichment and reprocessing transfers. We stand for the strengthening of the nonproliferation regime. We support international efforts to limit the spread of ENR equipment or technologies to states that do not have them.[35]

David Albright, president of the Institute for Science and International Security (ISIS), published a report on March 10, 2006, that asserted that India had potentially exported centrifuge enrichment-related technology by virtue of tendering public offers and providing blueprints for technology to interested parties.[36] ISIS followed up with a September 18, 2008, report that described Indian sales of documents related to centrifuges, as well as illicit Indian procurement of a chemical used in reprocessing.[37] It is not clear whether Indian procurement practices facilitate transfer of technology, but the U.S. nuclear cooperation agreement will have no impact on those procurement practices. Although the State Department asserted in responses to questions for the record from Senator Lugar that the United States will not engage in reprocessing or enrichment technology cooperation with India,[38] other NSG members may transfer such technology.

The NPAS notes that India, by concluding an Additional Protocol to its IAEA safeguards agreement, "will commit to reporting to the IAEA on exports of all NSG Trigger List items."

Other Priorities

In his February 11, 2004, speech, President Bush outlined several counterproliferation priorities, including expanding the Proliferation Security Initiative; strengthening laws and international controls against WMD and missile proliferation (ultimately resulting in adoption of UNSCR 1540); expanding the G8 Global Partnership; and strengthening IAEA safeguards through universal adoption of the Additional Protocol. Ambassador Joseph has noted that India's adherence to NSG and MTCR guidelines would help ensure that WMD and missile-related technologies would not be transferred. Although India's adoption of the Additional Protocol would contribute to its universalization, there are few proliferation benefits to be realized from the adoption of such a protocol in a nuclear weapons state. Finally, although the United States reportedly has asked India to endorse PSI, that endorsement has not been forthcoming.

Impact on the Nonproliferation Regime

India's status outside the nonproliferation regime raises possible concerns that the nuclear agreement could negativelyaffect nuclear nonproliferation efforts. Some considerations include cohesion within the NSG, effect on non-nuclear weapon member states of the NPT, potential missed opportunities to strengthen the nuclear nonproliferation regime, and whether U.S. nuclear cooperation might in any way assist, encourage, or induce India to manufacture nuclear weapons, in possible violation of our Article I obligation under the NPT.

NSG Cohesion

Cohesion within the NSG is critical to effective implementation of export controls. As noted earlier, the NSG has followed the U.S. lead on requiring full-scope safeguards as a condition of nuclear supply. During the September 8, 2005 hearing, House International Relations Committee Chairman Henry Hyde noted that "Many of us are strong supporters of the NSG and would not want to see it weakened or destroyed." Chairman Hyde asked whether the administration could assure the Committee that

> ... no matter what else happens, that the administration will continue to abide by NSG guidelines, and if you are unable to gain consensus within the NSG for the amendments you need, you will not implement the new India policy in violation of NSG guidelines.

Ambassador Joseph told the Committee that "we intend to take no action that would undercut the effectiveness of the NSG," and further, that the Administration did not intend to change the consensus procedure or even change the NSG full-scope safeguards condition of nuclear supply.[39] P.L. 109-401 states that the NSG should decide "by consensus to permit supply to India of nuclear items covered by" the NSG guidelines.

Dissent within the NSG could be counterproductive to achieving other objectives the United States is pursuing in nuclear nonproliferation, such as restricting the fuel cycle, disarming North Korea, and restraining Iran, all of which rely on the considerable support of friends and allies. Moreover, harmonizing export controls has played a key role in Bush counter- and non-proliferation policies in the last few years and is particularly important for interdiction efforts. U.S.-India cooperation could prompt other suppliers, like China, to justify supplying other nonnuclear-weapon states, like Pakistan. China, which joined the NSG in

2004, has reportedly favored an NSG decision based on criteria, not just an exception for India.[40] Indeed, Pakistani Foreign Secretary Shah Mahmood Qureshi said that Islamabad is interested in similar nuclear cooperation with nuclear supplier states, the Press Trust of India reported July 24, 2008. A July 18, 2008, letter from Pakistan's Permanent Representative to the IAEA similarly reflected such an interest.[41]

Russia, which only halted fuel supplies to the Indian Tarapur reactors in December 2004 at the insistence of the NSG, resumed fuel supplies to Tarapur under the guise of the safety exception, reportedly to the dismay of many NSG members.[42]

Effect on NPT Member States

India has complained for years that it has been excluded from regular nuclear commerce because of its status outside the NPT. Some observers believe this is a good thing and shows that the policy works. Others believe that a new paradigm is needed for India because it will not join the NPT as a non-nuclear weapon state. One observer argued in a 2005 law review journal that India could join the NPT as a non-nuclear weapon state and not give up its nuclear weapons, primarily because the NPT defines "nuclear weapon states" but does not define non-nuclear weapon states and because the treaty does not expressly prohibit non-nuclear weapon states from possessing nuclear weapons, just from acquiring, manufacturing, receiving transfers of or control of nuclear weapons and not to seek or receive any assistance in manufacturing nuclear weapons.[43] However, that approach would require India to stop producing fissile material for nuclear weapons and place all nuclear material (except that which is in its nuclear weapons) under IAEA safeguards.

The NPT is basically a two-way bargain. Non-nuclear-weapon states under the NPT give up the option of developing nuclear weapons in exchange for the promise of peaceful nuclear cooperation. Nuclear weapon states under the treaty commit to eventual disarmament. India, as a state outside the NPT, is bound by neither of these commitments. Some observers may see the offer of nuclear cooperation previously reserved for states under the NPT with full-scope safeguards not only as undermining the agreements made by non-nuclear weapon states, but also the commitments made by nuclear weapon states to eventually disarm. In this view, India's continued unilateral testing moratorium is insufficient, compared with signing the Comprehensive Test Ban Treaty (CTBT) and its support for FMCT negotiations is insufficient compared with capping its nuclear weapons fissile material production now, as four of the five nuclear weapon states formally have done. Some have suggested that the absence of an Indian cap on fissile material production for weapons may make it difficult for China to declare it has halted fissile material production for weapons. Others have suggested that, absent a cap on fissile material production, it would be difficult to ensure that peaceful nuclear cooperation was not indirectly assisting or encouraging India's nuclear weapons program.

The proliferation shocks of the 1990s, when the Iraqi and North Korean clandestine nuclear weapons programs surfaced, led to the strengthening of the NPT and export control regimes. At the 1995 NPT Review and Extension Conference, NPT parties affirmed the NSG's decision to require full-scope safeguards for nuclear exports, supporting the principle that non-NPT parties should not be eligible for the same kinds of assistance as NPT parties in good standing. At the 2000 conference, NPT parties again supported that principle. According to the U.S. ambassador to the conference at that time, "Reinforcement of this guideline is important given some who have questioned whether this principle should be relaxed for India and Pakistan, which have not accepted full-scope IAEA safeguards. The answer from NPT parties is clearly no."[44]

In the past 10 years, virtually all states agreed to strengthen the nonproliferation regime, sacrificing some sovereignty by allowing additional, intrusive inspections under the Additional Protocol. In the wake of revelations in 2004 about Pakistani scientist A.Q. Khan's nuclear black market sales, non-nuclear weapon states under the NPT are also being asked to consider further restrictions on their sovereignty by voluntarily restricting their access to sensitive nuclear technologies like uranium enrichment and reprocessing. If some states view the U.S.-Indian nuclear cooperation agreement as a breach of faith in the basic bargain of the NPT, they might be less inclined to accept additional sacrifices, to the detriment of the nonproliferation regime.

Missed Opportunities

Ambassador Joseph described the nuclear initiative as representing "a substantial net gain for nonproliferation. It is a win for our strategic relationship, a win for energy security, and a win for nonproliferation." Ambassador Joseph said he was "convinced that the nonproliferation regime will emerge stronger as a result."[45]

However, some observers have suggested the United States asked for too little. For example, Fred McGoldrick, Harold Bengelsdorf and Lawrence Scheinman, argued in the October 2005 issue of *Arms Control Today* that

> It is open to serious doubt whether the proposed Indian concessions were significant enough to justify the accommodations promised by the United States and whether the steps the United States and India agreed to take in the civil nuclear area will, on balance, be supportive of global nonproliferation efforts... If the Bush Administration is able to implement the joint declaration without significant modification, it will have given the Indians a great deal — acknowledgment as a de facto nuclear weapon state and access to the international nuclear energy market — in return for largely symbolic concessions in the nonproliferation area.[46]

Robert Einhorn of the Center for Strategic and International Studies told members of the House International Relations Committee on October 26, 2005, that several of the steps pledged by India are "simply reaffirmations of existing positions."[47] The Indian embassy itself has downplayed the depth and breadth of its nonproliferation commitments, describing all but its safeguards commitments under the July 2005 statement in the following way:

> A number of existing policies were also reiterated by India, among them a unilateral moratorium on nuclear testing, working towards conclusion of a multilateral Fissile Material Cut-off Treaty, non-transfer of enrichment and reprocessing technologies, securing nuclear materials and technology through export control, and harmonisation with MTCR and NSG guidelines.[48]

India has had a self-imposed nuclear test moratorium for years, although supporters of this agreement note that this agreement would bind India bilaterally to honoring that pledge. If the NSG used a similar criterion in approving exports, it could further strengthen that pledge. India has supported FMCT negotiations for years, despite continuing to produce fissile material for use in nuclear weapons. Since the pace of FMCT negotiations has been glacial, support for negotiations could allow India to continue producing fissile material indefinitely. Moreover, the draft treaty on FMCT tabled by the United States in Geneva on May 18, 2006, would not require India's accession for the treaty to enter into force, thus lessening the pressure on India to join. Prime Minister Singh told his Parliament on August 17, 2006 that "India is willing to join only a non discriminatory, multilaterally negotiated and internationally verifiable FMCT."[49] Unfortunately, this conflicts with the U.S. draft proposal, which contains no verification measures.

The most far-reaching of the commitments is to separate civilian and military facilities, declare civilian facilities, and place them under safeguards. Administration officials have pointed to this aspect of the agreement as a nonproliferation "plus." Yet, allowing India broad latitude in determining which of its facilities to put under international safeguards is a privilege accorded currently only to nuclear weapon states under the NPT. Although the United States "in no way recognizes India as an NPT nuclear weapons state," excluding military facilities from inspections is a tacit recognition of their legitimacy.

IAEA Director General Dr. Mohamed ElBaradei said that he has "always advocated concrete and practical steps towards the universal application of IAEA safeguards."[50] In remarks to the Carnegie Endowment's Nonproliferation Conference in November 2005, Dr. ElBaradei cited additional safety benefits of putting more Indian facilities under safeguards. However, it should be noted that the NSG already has an exception to its full-scope safeguards requirement for safety-related items.

The Administration has asserted that India has an "exceptional" record of nonproliferation and despite a few isolated sanctions, most of the evidence supports the view that India has exercised restraint in export controls.[51] As such, however, New Delhi's promise to refrain from transferring enrichment and reprocessing technologies to states that do not have them, as well as its promise to adhere to NSG guidelines, may be little more than a formality.

Many observers have noted that there are no measures in this global partnership to restrain India's nuclear weapons program. Many have suggested that the United States should have asked New Delhi to halt fissile material production for weapons. Ambassador Joseph stated that the United States remains "committed to achieving Indian curtailment of fissile material production, and we have strongly encouraged a move in this direction. We stand willing to explore options that might serve this objective, but we will not insist on it for purposes of this civil nuclear initiative."[52] Indian officials, on the other hand, have taken pains to point out that "There is no commitment at all to cease production of fissile material ahead of the conclusion of such a multilateral [FMCT] treaty."[53] Prime Minister Singh told the parliament in August 2006 that "Our position on this matter is unambiguous. We are not willing to accept a moratorium on the production of fissile material."[54] Other observers have noted that although India committed to a test ban, it did not commit to signing the CTBT. Still other observers have suggested that if India insists on being treated as a nuclear weapon state, it should undertake responsibilities similar to those of the other nuclear weapon states, for example, placing fissile material excess to defense needs under safeguards. Many believe that real limits on India's nuclear weapons program would constitute a "win" for nonproliferation.

U.S. NPT Article I Obligations/Aiding India's Nuclear Arsenal

Article I of the NPT states that

> each nuclear-weapon State Party to the Treaty undertakes not to transfer to any recipient whatsoever nuclear weapons or other nuclear explosive devices or control over such weapons or explosive devices directly, or indirectly; and not in any way to assist, encourage, or induce any non-nuclear-weapon State to manufacture or otherwise acquire nuclear weapons or other nuclear explosive devices, or control over such weapons or explosive devices.

Given that India will continue to make nuclear weapons, but is considered under the NPT to be a non-nuclear weapon state, the question arises as to whether U.S. assistance might in any way violate Article I.[55] In testimony before the House International Relations Committee, David Albright of ISIS stated that "Without India halting production of fissile material for its nuclear weapons programs, nuclear assistance, particularly any in the areas involving the fuel cycle, would likely spill over to India's nuclear weapons program."[56]

Three areas raise potential concerns: whether the separation plan is adequate to ensure that cooperation does not in any way assist in the development or production of nuclear weapons; whether cooperation confers nuclear weapons state status on India, with an unintended consequence of encouraging the Indian nuclear weapons program; and whether opening up the international uranium market frees up India's domestic uranium for use in its weapons program.

Separation Plan Credibility

Administration officials have defended the separation plan as credible and defensible because it covers more than just a token number of Indian facilities, provides for safeguards in perpetuity, and includes upstream and downstream facilities.[57] However, although IAEA safeguards ensure that nuclear material is not diverted, there are no procedures or measures in place to ensure that information, technology and know-how are not transferred from the civil sector to the military sector. This issue, which the September 2008 NPAS does not appear to address, could become a key loophole. For example, U.S. assistance to one of the eight indigenous power reactors, whether focused on nuclear safety, improving operational efficiency, or extending its lifetime, could easily be applied by Indian personnel to one of the similar, but unsafeguarded indigenous power reactors. Some Indian commentators have suggested that the United States has little technology to offer India, and others have doubted whether U.S. assistance would be provided to those indigenous power reactors.

Conferring Nuclear Weapon-State Status

A second area that raises concerns is whether nuclear cooperation confers nuclear weapon state status on India, which could encourage its weapons program. Senator Lugar noted in a hearing on November 2, 2005 that "Prior to the July 18 joint statement India had repeatedly sought unsuccessfully to be recognized as an official nuclear weapons state, a status the NPT reserves only for the United States, China, France, Russia and the United

Kingdom. Opponents argue that granting India such status will undermine the essential bargain that is at the core of NPT, namely, that only by foregoing nuclear weapons can a country gain civilian nuclear assistance." Dr. Ashton Carter, testifying at that SFRC hearing, stated that:

> India obtained *de-facto* recognition of its nuclear weapons status. The United States will behave, and urge others to behave, as if India were a nuclear weapons state under the NPT. We won't deny it most civil nuclear technology or commerce. We won't require it to put all of its nuclear facilities under IAEA safeguards — only those it declares to be civil. Beyond these technicalities, nuclear recognition confers an enormous political benefit on India.

Secretary Rice, in response to a question for the record in April 2006 on India's nuclear weapon state status, stated that "While India has nuclear weapons and we must deal with this fact in a realistic, pragmatic manner, we do not recognize India as a nuclear weapon state or seek to legitimize India's nuclear weapons program." However, other officials' statements appear to lend more support to India. Under Secretary of State Nicholas Burns told reporters on March 2, 2006, that "... India is a nuclear weapons power, and India will preserve part of its nuclear industry to service its nuclear weapons program."[58]

IAEA Director-General ElBaradei argues that the U.S.-India deal is "neutral" because "it does not confer any 'status,' legal or otherwise, on India as a possessor of nuclear weapons."[59] Nonetheless, the successful U.S. effort to create an exemption in its nuclear cooperation law for New Delhi has placed India in the company of only four other nations — the United Kingdom, France, China, and Russia — all *de jure* nuclear weapon states. Many observers believe that this legitimizes India's nuclear weapons program by providing *de facto* recognition. Indian official statements repeatedly have used the term "advanced nuclear states" as synonymous with nuclear weapon states; Prime Minister Singh told the Parliament in August 2006 that

> The July Statement did not refer to India as a Nuclear Weapons State because that has a particular connotation in the NPT, but it explicitly acknowledged the existence of India's military nuclear facilities. It also meant that India would not attract full-scope safeguards such as those applied to non-nuclear weapon states that are signatories to the NPT and there would be no curbs on continuation of India's nuclear weapon related activities. In these important respects, India would be very much on par with the five Nuclear Weapon States who are signatories to the NPT. Similarly, the Separation Plan provided for an India specific safeguards agreement with the IAEA with assurances of uninterrupted supply of fuel to reactors together with India's right to take corrective measures in the event fuel supplies are interrupted. We have made clear to the US that India's strategic programme is totally outside the purview of the July Statement, and we oppose any legislative provisions that mandate scrutiny of our nuclear weapons programme or our unsafeguarded nuclear facilities.

Offsetting India's Uranium Shortage

Finally, critics of U.S.-Indian civil nuclear cooperation have argued that giving India access to the international uranium market would free up New Delhi's domestic uranium resources for use in its weapons program.[60] India has limited indigenous uranium reserves and apparently has difficulty producing reactor fuel from these reserves. New Delhi has reportedly reduced its power reactors' electricity output because of fuel shortages.[61] Since the NSG's 1992 adoption of the full-scope safeguards condition for exports, New Delhi has not had access to the international uranium market.[62] Foreign Secretary Saran pointed out on February 18, 2008, that "a major expansion in nuclear power in the medium term" would require India to import "higher capacity reactors and uranium fuel."[63] Similarly, the NPAS states that "India must import fuel, reactors, and other technologies...to meet its nuclear electricity-generating targets."

India's current fuel situation means that New Delhi cannot produce sufficient fuel for both its nuclear weapons program and its projected civil nuclear program. A panel of nuclear experts concluded in 2006 that

> India's production of weapon grade plutonium is currently constrained by the competing demands of India's nuclear-power reactors for its limited domestic supply of natural uranium. If India could import fuel for its civilian nuclear reactors, it could use more domestic uranium for the production of weapon materials.[64]

Acknowledging the country's uranium limitations, India's leading nuclear strategist K. Subrahmanyam suggested December 12, 2005, in *The Times of India*, that New Delhi should use imported nuclear fuel to preserve its domestic uranium reserves for nuclear weapons:

> Given India's uranium ore crunch and the need to build up our minimum credible nuclear deterrent arsenal as fast as possible, it is to India's advantage to categorize as many power reactors as possible as civilian ones to be refueled by imported uranium and conserve our native uranium fuel for weapon-grade plutonium production."[65]

Proponents of U.S.-Indian nuclear cooperation have made several arguments regarding the Article I issue. None of these claims, however, refute the fact that India's access to the international uranium market will result in more indigenous Indian uranium available for weapons, because it will not be consumed by New Delhi's newly safeguarded reactors.[66]

For example, proponents of the deal argue that India already has sufficient uranium to increase its nuclear arsenal and that New Delhi does not plan to increase that arsenal. For example, the NPAS states that "India is capable of maintaining and expanding its existing nuclear arsenal within the limit of its indigenous resources and capabilities." Secretary Rice made a similar argument during an April 5, 2006, House International Relations Committee hearing. But these arguments do not address the constraints India faces in pursuing its civilian and military nuclear programs using only indigenous uranium.

The NPAS also addresses New Delhi's intentions regarding its future nuclear arsenal. First, the statement says that Washington has "no evidence indicating that India plans to use additional domestic uranium reserves in its nuclear weapons programs as a consequence of implementing" the nuclear cooperation agreement. Second, the NPAS argues that New Delhi has "a posture of nuclear restraint," citing India's stated no-first-use nuclear weapon policy and need for only a "credible minimum deterrent." India, however, has never defined what it means by such a deterrent; Saran stated during an April 2006 television interview that "there is no responsibility on part of India to declare what its minimum deterrent is."[67] Moreover,

New Delhi's intentions are irrelevant to determining U.S. compliance with its Article I obligations.

Furthermore, the NPAS appears to argue that the agreement may reduce India's potential to produce additional fissile material for weapons, because the additional indigenous Indian reactors placed under safeguards "will no longer be available for this purpose." However, the statement characterizes the reactors' potential to serve this purpose as "theoretical." And, as noted above, India is not obligated to place future reactors under safeguards.

The State Department report submitted with the agreement notes that IAEA safeguards will prevent India from using its civil nuclear facilities for its nuclear weapons program. It also describes the ways in which U.S. export control policies prevent exported U.S. dual-use nuclear technologies from being used for military purposes.[68]

In the view of many nonproliferation analysts, the key to ensuring that civilian nuclear cooperation does not assist India's weapons program is to insist on New Delhi halting its fissile material production for weapons. That would narrow the area of concern to technology transfer to the weapons and delivery systems themselves, rather than fissile material production in reactors, enrichment facilities, and reprocessing plants. Among others, Henry Sokolski suggested in the Wall Street Journal that "If we want to keep this aid from freeing up India's domestic nuclear resources to make more bombs ... we have to get serious about India capping its nuclear weapons program."

STEPS REQUIRED BY P.L. 109-401

As noted above, P.L. 109-401 allows the President to exempt a U.S. nuclear cooperation agreement with India from several AEA requirements. Before such an agreement can enter into force, however, the President must first certify that several steps have been completed. President Bush did so September 10. After the President signs H.R. 7081, which both the House and Senate have passed, Washington and New Delhi must, according to the agreement's text, "exchange diplomatic notes informing each other that they have completed all applicable requirements" in order for the agreement to enter into force.

Separation Plan and Safeguards[69]

U.S. and Indian officials agreed on India's separation plan in March 2006. The key elements of that plan are:[70]

- 8 indigenous Indian power reactors will be placed under an India-specific safeguards agreement, bringing the total number of power reactors under safeguards to 14 of 22 (6 are already under safeguards)[71]
- Future power reactors may also be placed under safeguards, if India declares them as civilian
- Some facilities in the Nuclear Fuel Complex (e.g., fuel fabrication) will be specified as civilian in 2008

9 research facilities and 3 heavy water plants would be declared as civilian, but are "safeguards-irrelevant."

The following facilities and activities were not on the separation list:

8 indigenous Indian power reactors
Fast Breeder test Reactor (FTBR) and Prototype Fast Breeder Reactors (PFBR) under construction
Enrichment facilities
Spent fuel reprocessing facilities (except for the existing safeguards on the Power Reactor Fuel Reprocessing (PREFRE) plant)
Research reactors: CIRUS (which will be shut down in 2010), Dhruva, Advanced Heavy Water Reactor
3 heavy water plants
Various military-related plants (e.g., prototype naval reactor).

The separation plan stated that India would begin placing facilities under safeguards in 2006 and complete the process in 2014. However, since the IAEA did not approve New Delhi's safeguards agreement until 2008, India will need to update that timeline. Acting Deputy Assistant Secretary of State for International Security And Nonproliferation Richard Stratford told the Senate Foreign Relations Committee September 18, that New Delhi stands by its initial plan to bring its facilities under safeguards by 2014.

India's Implementation Document noted that facilities were excluded from the civilian list if they were located in a larger hub of strategic significance, even if the facilities themselves were not normally engaged in activities of strategic significance, calling into question whether the plan really will result in a "separation" of civilian and military facilities. Moreover, the plan stated that electricity grid connectivity is not relevant to the separation exercise and that grid connectivity would be necessary "irrespective of whether the reactor concerned is civilian or not civilian." This means that "military" reactors will continue to provide civilian electricity.

Another question that arises is whether India, in the absence of full-scope safeguards, can provide sufficient confidence that U.S. peaceful nuclear technology will not be diverted to nuclear weapons purposes, as many believe it was in 1974.[72] In response to a question for the record submitted by Senator Lugar on April 5, 2006 on whether exports of nuclear material or reactors from the United States would in any way assist India's nuclear weapons program, the Administration noted that "Any items sent to India would be subject to safeguards, and implementation of the Additional Protocol would provide further assurances of the non-diversion of such items or material."[73] However, the Additional Protocol provides assurances of absence of undeclared activities, rather than of the non-diversion of safeguarded items, contrary to Secretary Rice's assertions.

Administration officials repeatedly have stressed that India's separation plan must be credible, transparent, and defensible from a nonproliferation standpoint,[74] and that "the resultant safeguards must contribute to our nonproliferation goals."[75] To those observers who interpreted that statement to mean that a separation plan would need to take into account India's past commitments (e.g., use of purportedly "peaceful" nuclear reactors like CIRUS to produce plutonium for nuclear weapons) and the impact on its nuclear weapons program (e.g., capping India's fissile material production), the separation plan may not appear credible. To those observers who interpreted "credible" to mean that all power reactors that supplied electricity would be declared civilian because they have a civilian use, the separation plan also may not appear credible. Secretary Rice has stressed, however, that more reactors under safeguards means more transparency, more physical security, better nuclear safety, and therefore increased safety for the United States.[76] Even so, some observers may argue that types of facilities safeguarded are critical in assessing whether the plan is defensible from a nonproliferation standpoint. For example, in terms of preventing terrorist access to fissile material, safeguarding facilities like reprocessing and enrichment plants and breeder reactors could be viewed as providing a significant nonproliferation benefit because the materials produced by these plants are a few steps closer to potential use in a bomb. In addition, safeguards on enrichment, reprocessing plants, and breeder reactors would support the 2002 U.S. National Strategy to Combat Weapons of Mass Destruction, in which the United States pledged to "continue to discourage the worldwide accumulation of separated plutonium and to minimize the use of highly-enriched uranium."[77]

India-IAEA Discussions/Domestic Opposition[78]

After the United States and India concluded the nuclear agreement last July, New Delhi delayed beginning talks with the IAEA about a safeguards agreement because of domestic opposition from Communist and other leftist parties, known as the Left Front.[79] Until recently, the United Progressive Alliance government, led by Prime Minister Singh, depended on those parties' support in order to stay in power. In India, the executive can enter into international agreements without parliamentary approval, but the Left Front threatened to withdraw its support if the government went ahead with the safeguards discussion. Indian officials had indicated multiple times that the government would not risk prompting early elections in order to push the deal through. In November 2007, the Left Front agreed to allow the government to engage in discussions with the IAEA. The talks were announced November 21, and the two parties subsequently met five times.

New Delhi had indicated that, once a safeguards text has been agreed upon with the IAEA Secretariat, the government would seek approval from an ad hoc political committee (which includes the Communists) before proceeding further with the agreement. Speaking before a Calcutta audience February 3, External Affairs Minister Mukherjee said that when "the draft agreement [with the IAEA] is ready it will be brought back to the United Progressive Alliance (UPA)-Left Coalition committee for its approval and suggestion."[80] Similarly, Communist Party of India (Marxist) General Secretary Prakash Karat stated November 16 that "we have come to an understanding that the government can go to the IAEA secretariat. But the outcome of the talks should be brought to the committee before moving to the IAEA board of governors."[81] The committee last met June 25. The government, however, never presented the text of the safeguards agreement to the committee, and at New Delhi's request, the IAEA Secretariat circulated the draft text (GOV/2008/30) [82] July 9 to the agency's board.

Pakistan, along with several unidentified board members, had "voiced strong reservations" about the safeguards agreement, according to a July 24 *Nucleonics Week* article, which added that no members have indicated that they would vote against the agreement.[83] But the Board of Governors approved the agreement by consensus August 1.

Four Left Front parties withdrew their support for the coalition government July 9, shortly after Singh announced that India would approach the IAEA board. However, the coalition government won a July 22 vote of confidence, staving off the threat of early elections. Karat stated September 7 that the Left Front will only support a government that would terminate the nuclear agreement with the United States.[84] The opposition Bharatiya Janata Party has also continued to express its opposition to the deal and has stated that it would attempt to renegotiate it if the party regains power.[85]

India's Safeguards Agreement[86]

IAEA Director-General ElBaradei described India's safeguards agreement as an "umbrella agreement" that allows for any facility identified by New Delhi in the future to become subject to safeguards. According to its text, the agreement will enter into force when the IAEA "receives from India written notification that India's statutory and/or constitutional requirements for entry into force have been met." ElBaradei also explained that, since New Delhi has committed to place additional reactors under safeguards, concluding an umbrella agreement was more efficient than negotiating different agreements for each facility.

According to the safeguards agreement, India is to provide the IAEA with a declaration of its nuclear facilities "based on [New Delhi's] sovereign decision to place voluntarily its civilian nuclear facilities under Agency safeguards in a phased manner." India will implement this provision in a two-step process. First, New Delhi will provide a list of nuclear facilities that it intends to place under safeguards in the future. On July 25, India provided to the IAEA a document — a copy of New Delhi's 2006 separation plan — containing a list of its nuclear facilities.[87] The IAEA anticipates that these facilities will be those listed in India's declaration. Later, New Delhi will notify the IAEA when specific facilities are to be safeguarded. Those facilities will be placed on an Annex to the agreement. The IAEA expects to begin safeguarding new facilities in 2009. India will also have to notify the agency of imported items that are required to be safeguarded. These will not be listed in the Annex.

A State Department official said that the India's submission of this plan does not constitute submission of the declaration required by the safeguards agreement, but does satisfy P.L. 109-401's requirement regarding New Delhi's declaration.[88] India is not required to submit its IAEA declaration until the safeguards agreement enters into force.

India's placement of nuclear facilities under safeguards appears to be contingent on its conclusion of nuclear supply agreements with other countries. Anil Kakodkar, Chairman of India's Atomic Energy Commission, said in a July 20 interview that India's identification of "any facility as civilian is conditional on that facility benefitting from full civil nuclear cooperation" with other countries.[89]

Some observers have expressed concerns about the agreement's preamble, which contains language suggesting that India could withdraw nuclear facilities or fuel from safeguards if New Delhi so chooses. For example, the preamble states that India "may take corrective measures to ensure uninterrupted operation of its civilian nuclear reactors in the event of disruption of foreign fuel supplies." New Delhi has not defined "corrective measures," although Kakodkar described them as "unspecified sovereign actions."[90]

The preamble also states that

> [a]n essential basis of India's concurrence to accept Agency safeguards is… support for an Indian effort to develop a strategic reserve of nuclear fuel to guard against any disruption of supply over the lifetime of India's reactors.

New Delhi may want such a stockpile to hedge against a cut-off of fuel supplies in the event that, for example, India tests a nuclear weapon.

However, ElBaradei stated August 1 that the agreement's specific termination clauses "override any general clauses in the agreement." Additionally, the State Department stated in January 2008 responses to Questions for the Record submitted by the House Committee on Foreign Affairs that New Delhi "has expressed its view that for purposes of implementing the U.S.-India Agreement," IAEA safeguards "can and should be regarded as being 'in perpetuity.'"[91]

It is also worth noting that, if India were to terminate IAEA safeguards on U.S. nuclear exports (or special nuclear material produced from or with such exports), section 123 a. (1) of the AEA requires that fall-back safeguards be maintained on those exports. The nuclear cooperation agreement states that

> safeguards will be maintained with respect to all nuclear materials and equipment transferred pursuant to this Agreement, and with respect to all special fissionable material used in or produced through the use of such nuclear materials and equipment, so long as the material or equipment remains under the jurisdiction or control of the cooperating Party.

The State Department noted that if IAEA safeguards "fail to be applied," the two countries "must enter into arrangements for alternative measures to fulfill" the above requirement.[92] The Department's January responses also stated that "it would not be consistent with the proposed agreement text for ... corrective measures to detract from the applicability" of safeguards to the relevant nuclear items "including after termination or expiration of the agreement."[93]

NSG Support

Following formal and informal U.S. consultations with NSG members, the United States presented during a March 2006 Consultative Group meeting a draft decision for potential discussion during the NSG plenary in May 2006.[94] That draft sought an exception for India to the NSG requirements of full-scope safeguards, notwithstanding the exceptions for safety assistance and for those agreements signed before the full-scope safeguards requirement came into effect in 1992. It did not contain any restrictions on enrichment or reprocessing cooperation, nor on heavy water or HEU or plutonium sales.[95]

The United States subsequently developed a second draft decision, which incorporated the suggestions of supporting NSG members.[96] After revising that draft following consultations with New Delhi, Washington submitted it to Germany, the current NSG chair, in early August.[97] The second version did not contain any additional restrictions on India. Indeed, it weakened one section of the 2006 draft which stated that NSG members could engage in nuclear trade with New Delhi if "the participating Government intending to make the transfer is satisfied that India continues to fully meet all" of its nonproliferation and safeguards commitments. The new draft stated only that

> Participating Governments shall maintain contact and consult through regular channels on matters connected with the implementation of the Guidelines, taking into account relevant international commitments and bilateral agreements with India.

The NSG considered the new draft decision during an August 21-22 Extraordinary Plenary meeting and decided during a similar meeting held September 4-6 to exempt India from some of its export guidelines. This decision means that members' decisions to export previously restricted nuclear items to India are now governed by individual governments' policies.[98]

Although several countries advocated that certain conditions (such as an explicit ban on the transfer of enrichment and reprocessing technology, as well as a provision that nuclear supplies to India would end if New Delhi were to test a nuclear weapon) be placed on an exemption for India, the final language contains no such explicit conditions.[99] Instead, it states that the exemption is "based on" Indian commitments and actions, which are essentially the same as the requirements in P.L. 109-401. The NSG statement also notes that the India has agreed to continue its "unilateral moratorium on nuclear testing."

The NSG agreed to exempt India from the portions of its guidelines that require India to have full-scope IAEA safeguards "provided that transfers of sensitive exports [enrichment and reprocessing technology] remain subject to paragraphs 6 and 7 of the Guidelines."

The relevant portions of those paragraphs state that

> suppliers should exercise restraint in the transfer of sensitive facilities, technology and material usable for nuclear weapons or other nuclear explosive devices. If enrichment or reprocessing facilities, equipment or technology are to be transferred, suppliers should encourage recipients to accept, as an alternative to national plants, supplier involvement and/or other appropriate multinational participation in resulting facilities ... [and]

> For a transfer of an enrichment facility, or technology therefor, the recipient nation should agree that neither the transferred facility, nor any facility based on such technology, will be designed or operated for the production of greater than 20% enriched uranium without the consent of the supplier nation, of which the IAEA should be advised.

Ireland reportedly stated after the NSG decision that, "on the basis of consultations during the meeting, it 'understands that no [NSG member] currently intends to transfer to India any facilities, equipment, materials, or technology related to the enrichment of uranium, or the reprocessing of spent fuel.'"[100] Under Secretary of State for Arms Control and International Security John Rood made a similar assertion during a September 18, 2008, Senate Foreign Relations Committee hearing.

Berman explained September 26 that he chose to support H.R. 7081 partly because Secretary Rice "made a personal commitment" to him that "the United States will make its 'highest priority' at the November meeting of the Nuclear Suppliers Group the achievement of a decision by all of the nuclear suppliers to prohibit the export of enrichment and reprocessing equipment and technology" to non-NPT states. Asked the same day about Berman's statement, Rice told Reuters that the United States would advocate for "strict limits" on the export of such technology.

The NSG is considering adopting criteria for exporting enrichment and reprocessing technology. President Bush stated in February 2004 that NSG members should refuse to sell "enrichment and reprocessing equipment and technologies to any state that does not already possess full-scale, functioning enrichment and reprocessing plants." The administration has since shifted its position and proposed export criteria of its own. France first introduced such criteria in 2004.[101]

The September 2008 NSG statement also says that participating governments will meet "and act in accordance with paragraph 16 of the [group's] Guidelines" if one or more members "consider that circumstances have arisen which require consultations." Paragraph 16 provides a list of potential steps for NSG members to take if

> one or more suppliers believe that there has been a violation of supplier/recipient understanding resulting from these Guidelines, particularly in the case of an explosion of a nuclear device, or illegal termination or violation of IAEA safeguards by a recipient.

Under such circumstances, NSG members could agree to cut off nuclear supplies; indeed, New Zealand stated September 6 that "in the event of a nuclear test by India, this exemption will become null and void." However, the NSG would have to agree by consensus to cut off nuclear exports.

Several NSG governments indicated in statements after the vote that a September 5, 2008, statement from Mukherjee describing India's "stand on disarmament and nonproliferation" played a decisive role in persuading them to agree to the exemption.[102] However, he simply reiterated previous Indian policies and articulated no new commitments. For example, Mukherjee stated that India "remain[s] committed to a voluntary, unilateral moratorium on nuclear testing." But New Delhi is already committed to such a moratorium. Furthermore, Congress party spokesperson Manis Tiwari stated September 4 that "[i]f the need arises and if it is in our national interest, we are ready to test not once, not twice but a hundred times."[103]

India's Nuclear Cooperation with Other Countries

India is now free to engage in nuclear cooperation with NSG countries other than the United States. Indeed, a spokesperson for India's Ministry of External Affairs stated September 11, 2008, that New Delhi is "moving towards finalizing bilateral agreements with other friendly partner countries such as France and Russia." India and France signed a civil nuclear cooperation agreement on September 30, 2008. That agreement, however, does not include the transfer of enrichment or reprocessing technology, according to French Ambassador to India Jerome Bonnafort.[104]

Prime Minister Singh stated February 12, 2008, that New Delhi and Moscow had "finalized negotiations in regard to reaching an agreement on cooperation in the construction of additional nuclear power plants in India." The two countries have not yet signed the agreement. Asked when they would do so, Kakodkar stated September 30 that "we cannot fix a time-line" to such an event.[105] But Mukherjee stated October 20 that India hopes to sign the agreement in December.

Foreign Secretary Saran reportedly identified Kazakhstan, Niger, and Uzbekistan October 21 as other potential candidates for nuclear cooperation.[106] During an October 30 speech, Singh added Canada and the United Kingdom to that list.

New Delhi is reportedly waiting for Congress to approve the nuclear cooperation agreement before implementing similar agreements with other countries.[107] A September 10 letter from Indian Foreign Secretary Shivshankar Menon states that

> it is the intention of the Government of India and its entities to commence discussions with U.S. nuclear energy firms and conclude agreements after entry into force of the [U.S.-India] Agreement for cooperation in the construction of nuclear power units at least at two sites approved by the Government of India, which would be capable of generating a minimum of 10,000 MW.[108]

However, Menon appeared to qualify this claim, adding that such deals would be concluded

> on the basis of mutually acceptable technical and commercial terms and conditions that enable a viable tariff regime for electricity generated. It is the expectation of the Government of India that this partnership will contribute towards providing energy to India's population in a manner that takes into account affordability, sustainability of nuclear fuel resources and credibility of nuclear waste management."

Moreover, Under Secretary of State for Political Affairs William Burns indicated during the September 18 hearing that India will not wait indefinitely for Congressional approval.

Convention on Supplementary Compensation for Nuclear Damage.

Menon's September 10 letter also stated that "it is the intention of the Indian Government to take all steps necessary to adhere to the Convention on Supplementary Compensation for Nuclear Damage [CSC] prior to the commencement of international civil nuclear cooperation under" the U.S.-India agreement." India's decision to become a party to the CSC is, according to the State Department, "an important step in ensuring that U.S. nuclear firms can compete on a level playing field with other international competitors" because many other countries' nuclear firms "have other liability protections afforded to them by their governments."[109] U.S. firms could engage in nuclear trade with India without the CSC's protections, but would likely be very reluctant to do so. The convention has not yet entered into force.

Other Required Steps

Additional Protocol

Section 104 (b) (3) of P.L. 109-401 requires a Presidential determination that "India and the IAEA are making substantial progress toward concluding an Additional Protocol consistent with IAEA principles, practices, and policies that would apply to India's civil nuclear program." ElBaradei told the IAEA Board of Governors August 1 that New Delhi and the agency have already begun discussions on an additional protocol to the draft safeguards agreement. Additionally, India has submitted a letter outlining a proposed Additional Protocol, which the agency is currently reviewing. According to the State Department, ElBaradei concluded September 10 that India has made substantial progress toward concluding such a protocol. Indian and IAEA officials held another round of talks September 17, according to the State Department.[110]

As previously noted, Additional Protocols, which are based on a Model Additional Protocol, are designed to augment the IAEA's ability to detect undeclared nuclear activities in a member-state. Since New Delhi has nuclear weapons and is keeping some of its nuclear facilities outside of safeguards, "there are bound to be important differences between" India's Additional Protocol and the Model Protocol, according to the NPAS.

Declaration of Nuclear Facilities

Section 104 (b) (1) requires that India file "a declaration regarding its civil facilities and materials with the IAEA." As noted above, a State Department official said that the India's submission of this plan does not constitute submission of the declaration required by the safeguards agreement, but does satisfy P.L.109-401's requirement.[111] New Delhi is neither required to place any new facilities under safeguards, nor to adhere to the separation plan. However, an Indian facility must be placed under safeguards in order for it to receive foreign assistance.

Harmonization with NSG/MTCR Guidelines and Adherence to NSG Guidelines

Section 104 (b) (6) (B) requires a presidential determination that India has harmonized "its export control laws, regulations, policies, and practices with the guidelines and practices" of the MTCR and the NSG. Section 104 (b) (6) (B) requires a determination that New Delhi adhere to the NSG guidelines.

The State Department report assesses that India has harmonized its export control laws with the NSG and MTCR guidelines "up through the 2005 revisions, and has the means in place to make future updates to its guidelines and control lists."[112] New Delhi stated its adherence to the NSG in a September 8 letter to the IAEA and its adherence to the MTCR in a September 9 letter to the MTCR point of contact.[113]

According to the September NSG statement, the group's chair (which rotates each year) "is requested to consult with India regarding changes to and implementation of" the group's guidelines. This provision gives New Delhi what is essentially a non-binding consultative role in formulating changes to the guidelines. India had been reluctant to adhere to the guidelines because they sometimes change and New Delhi, as a non-member, will not be able to participate in the Group's decisions regarding such changes.[114]

The Atomic Energy Act and Consultations with Congress

Under existing law (Atomic Energy Act of 1954; P.L. 95-242; 42 U.S.C. § 2153 et seq.) all significant nuclear cooperation requires an agreement for cooperation.[115] The Nuclear Non-Proliferation Act of 1978 (NNPA) amended the Atomic Energy Act of 1954 to include, among other things, a requirement for full-scope safeguards for significant nuclear exports to non-nuclear weapon states.[116]

At issue are the requirements for full-scope nuclear safeguards contained in Section 123 a. (2) for approval of an agreement for cooperation and in Section 128 for licensing nuclear exports. India, a non-party to the NPT, does not have full-scope safeguards, nor is it ever expected to adopt full-scope safeguards, since it has a nuclear weapons program that would preclude them. Also at issue is the requirement in Section 129 to stop exports if a non-nuclear weapon state has detonated a nuclear device after 1978, among other things. India detonated several nuclear devices in 1998.

These three sections of the AEA provide mechanisms for the President to waive those requirements and sanctions (in Section 129), which are spelled out in more detail below. The sections also provide legislative vetoes, in the form of concurrent resolutions, of the presidential determinations. In 1983, however, the Supreme Court decided in *INS v. Chadha* that legislative veto provisions that do not satisfy the bicameralism and presentment requirements of Article I of the Constitution were unconstitutional. In 1985, some parts of the AEA were amended to provide for joint resolutions of approval or disapproval (e.g., Section 123 d.). The *Chadha* decision affects how Congress would disapprove of such presidential determinations under existing law and therefore affects the impact of the Administration's proposed legislation.

Agreements for Cooperation

Section 123 of the AEA (42 U.S.C. 2153) specifies what must happen before nuclear cooperation can take place.

Section 123 a. states that the proposed agreement shall include the terms, conditions, duration, nature, and scope of cooperation and lists nine criteria that the agreement must meet. It also contains provisions for the President to exempt an agreement from any of the nine criteria, and includes details on the kinds of information the executive branch must provide to Congress;

Section 123 b. specifies the process for submitting the text of the agreement to Congress;

Section 123 c. specifies how Congress approves cooperation agreements that are limited in scope (e.g., do not transfer nuclear material or cover reactors larger than 5 MWe.).[117]

Section 123 d. specifies how Congress approves agreements that do cover significant nuclear cooperation (transfer of nuclear material or reactors larger than 5 MWe), including exempted agreements.

The United States has over 20 agreements for cooperation in place now, and had an agreement with India from 1963 to 1993. Such agreements for cooperation are "framework" agreements — they do not guarantee that cooperation will take place or that nuclear material will be transferred, but rather set the terms of reference and provide authorization for cooperation. The 1963 U.S.-India cooperation agreement is anomalous in that it did guarantee fuel for the Tarapur reactors, even though other U.S. nuclear cooperation agreements reportedly have not included any such guarantees.[118]

Section 123 a. lists nine criteria that an agreement must meet unless the President determines an exemption is necessary. These are listed in Section 123 a., paragraphs (1) through (9), 42 U.S.C. 2153. They are guarantees that (1) safeguards on nuclear material and equipment transferred continue in perpetuity; (2) full-scope safeguards are applied in non-nuclear weapon states; (3) nothing transferred is used for any nuclear explosive device or for any other military purpose; (4) the United States has the right of return if the cooperating state detonates a nuclear explosive device or terminates or abrogates an International Atomic Energy Agency (IAEA) safeguards agreement; (5) there is no transfer of material or classified data without U.S. consent; (6) physical security is maintained; (7) there is no enrichment or reprocessing by the recipient state without prior approval; (8) storage is approved by United States for plutonium and highly enriched uranium; and (9) anything produced through cooperation is subject to all of the above requirements.

In the case of India, the most difficult of these requirements to meet is the full-scope safeguards requirement for non-nuclear weapon states (Sec. 123 a. (2)). India is considered to be a non-nuclear weapon state because it did not, as defined by the nuclear Nonproliferation Treaty, explode a nuclear device before January 1, 1967.[119] The President may exempt an agreement for cooperation from any of the requirements in Section 123 a. if he determines that meeting the requirement would be "seriously prejudicial to the achievement of U.S. non-proliferation objectives or otherwise jeopardize the common defense and security." An exempted agreement would not become effective "unless the Congress adopts, and there is enacted, a joint resolution stating that the Congress does favor such agreement."[120] In other words, both chambers of Congress must approve the agreement if it does not contain all of the Section 123 a. requirements.

If Congress votes to approve an agreement for cooperation that was exempted because the recipient state did not have full-scope safeguards (Section 123 a. (2)), such approval would essentially waive the Nuclear Regulatory Commission's (NRC) obligation to consider full-scope safeguards as an export license authorization criterion under Section 128. However, Congress would still have the authority to review one export license authorization approximately every 12 months after the agreement for cooperation has entered into force. (See discussion below)

Section 123 d., in part, states the following:

> if Congress fails to disapprove a proposed agreement for cooperation which exempts the recipient nation from the requirement set forth in subsection 123 a. (2), such failure to act shall constitute a failure to adopt a resolution of disapproval pursuant to subsection 128 b. (3) for purposes of the Commission's consideration of applications and requests under section 126 a. (2) and there shall be no congressional review pursuant to section 128 of any subsequent license or authorization with respect to

that state until the first such license or authorization which is issued after twelve months from the elapse of the sixty-day period in which the agreement for cooperation in question is reviewed by the Congress.[121]

Export Licensing

In addition to specifying criteria for framework agreements, the AEA sets out procedures for licensing exports (Sections 126, 127, and 128 codified as amended at 42 U.S.C. 2155, 2156, 2157). The Nuclear Regulatory Commission (NRC) is required to meet criteria in Sections 127 and 128 in authorizing export licenses; Section 128 contains the requirement for full-scope safeguards for non-nuclear weapon states. Section 126 b. (2) contains a provision for the President to authorize an export in the event that the NRC deems that the export would not meet Section 127 and 128 criteria. The President must determine "that failure to approve an export would be seriously prejudicial to the achievement of U.S. nonproliferation objectives or otherwise jeopardize the common defense and security." The President would submit his executive order, along with a detailed assessment and other documentation, to Congress for 60 days of continuous session. After 60 days of continuous session, the export would go through unless Congress passes a concurrent resolution of disapproval.[122]

In the case of exports pursuant to an exempted agreement for cooperation (i.e., exempted from the full-scope safeguards requirement), as described above, the NRC would not have to meet the full-scope safeguards requirement in assessing whether it could issue export licenses (Section 128 b. (3)). Congress would review one license every 12 months. If Congress passed a resolution of disapproval, no further exports could be made during that Congress.[123]

In both cases, Section 128 contains a provision for the President to waive termination of exports by notifying the Congress that the state has adopted full-scope safeguards or that the state has made significant progress toward full-scope safeguards, or that U.S. foreign policy interests dictate reconsideration. Such a determination would become effective unless Congress disagrees with the President's determination.[124]

Termination of Cooperation

Section 129 of the AEA (42 U.S.C. 2158) requires ending exports of nuclear materials and equipment or sensitive nuclear technology to any non-nuclear-weapon state that, after March 10, 1978, the President determines to have

detonated a nuclear explosive device;
terminated or abrogated IAEA safeguards;
materially violated an IAEA safeguards agreement; or
engaged in activities involving source or special nuclear material and having "direct significance" for the manufacture or acquisition of nuclear explosive devices, and "has failed to take steps which, in the President's judgment, represent sufficient progress toward terminating such activities."

In addition, Section 129 would also halt exports to any nation the President determines

to have materially violated the terms of an agreement for cooperation with the United States, or assisted, encouraged, or induced anyother non-nuclear weapon state to obtain nuclear explosives or the materials and technologies needed to manufacture them; or re-transferred or entered into an agreement for exporting reprocessing equipment, materials or technology to another non-nuclear weapons state.

The President can waive termination if he determines that "cessation of such exports would be seriously prejudicial to the achievement of United States nonproliferation objectives or otherwise jeopardize the common defense and security." The President must submit his determination to Congress, which is then referred to the House International Relations Committee and the Senate Foreign Relations Committee for 60 days of continuous session. The determination becomes effective unless Congress opposes it.[125]

P.L. 109-401[126]

On March 9, 2006, the Administration submitted its proposed legislation to Representative Hyde and Senator Lugar, and on March 16, 2006, Representatives Hyde and Lantos introduced H.R. 4974, and Senator Lugar introduced S. 2429. Following public hearings and committee mark-ups, the House passed H.R. 5682 on July 26, 2006 by a vote of 359 to 68 and the Senate passed its version of H.R. 5682, substituting the text of the amended S. 3709, on November 16, 2006 by a vote of 85 to 12. One issue that held up the Senate bill was the inclusion, in Title II, of the implementing legislation for the U.S. Additional Protocol — an agreement between the United States and the IAEA to provide for enhanced information, access, and inspection tools for IAEA inspectors as they inspect U.S. nuclear and other facilities under the U.S. voluntary safeguards agreement.

The House and Senate version of the H.R. 5682 were remarkably similar, with four differences.[127] The Senate version contained an additional requirement for the President to execute his waiver authority, an amendment introduced by Senator Harkin and adopted by unanimous consent that the President determine that India is "fully and actively participating in U.S. and international efforts to dissuade, sanction and contain Iran for its nuclear program." This provision was changed to a reporting requirement in the conference report. The Senate version also had two unique sections related to the cooperation agreement, Sections 106 and 107, both of which appear in the conference report. Section 106 (now Section 104 (d) (4)) prohibits exports of equipment, material or technology related for uranium enrichment, spent fuel reprocessing or heavy water production unless conducted in a multinational facility participating in a project approved by the IAEA or in a facility participating in a bilateral or multilateral project to develop a proliferation-resistant fuel cycle. Section 107 (now Section 104 (d) (5)) would establish a program to monitor that U.S. technology is being used appropriately by Indian recipients. Finally, the Senate version also contained the implementing legislation for the U.S. Additional Protocol in Title II, which was retained in the conference report.

P.L. 109-401 allows the President to

exempt a proposed agreement for cooperation with India from the full-scope safeguards requirement of Section 123 a. (2) of the Atomic Energy Act;

exempt an agreement from any export review by the Congress under Section 128 of the AEA;

exempt the agreement from restrictions resulting from India's nuclear weapons activities under Section 129 a. (1) (D) of the AEA, and exempt the agreement from a cutoff in exports because of India's 1998 nuclear test.

It does not exempt the agreement from a future cutoff in exports if India tests a nuclear explosive device again. For the President to exercise his waiver authority, seven requirements, as outlined earlier, must be met. P.L. 109-401 contains numerous statements of policy and reporting requirements, as well as restrictions on certain kinds of transfers. There are specific prohibitions on (as outlined in Section 104 (d)): (1) transfers that would violate U.S. obligations under Article 1 of the NPT not to in any way assist any country to manufacture or otherwise acquire nuclear weapons; (2) transfers that would violate NSG guidelines in force at the time; (3) a cutoff in exports if India is found to have violated NSG or MTCR guidelines; (4) enrichment and reprocessing cooperation, except to "a multinational facility participating in an IAEA-approved program to provide alternatives to national fuel cycle capabilities; or ... a facility participating in, and the export, reexport, transfer, or retransfer is associated with, a bilateral or multinational program to develop a proliferation-resistant fuel cycle." Additionally, the law provides for a nuclear export accountability program (formerly Section 107 of the Senate version of H.R. 5682).

President's Signing Statement

In President Bush's signing statement, he noted that the act "will strengthen the strategic relationship between the United States and India."[128] With respect to particular provisions, President Bush stated that the executive branch would construe two sections of the bill as "advisory" only: policy statements in Section 103 and the restriction contained in Section 104 (d) (2) on transferring items to India that would not meet NSG guidelines. On the first, the President cited the Constitution's "commitment to the presidency of the authority to conduct the Nation's foreign affairs"; on the second, the President raised the question of whether the provision "unconstitutionally delegated legislative power to an international body." In other words, the President was questioning whether Congress were ceding authority to approve U.S. exports to the NSG. However, U.S. officials, including Secretary of State Rice, have formally told Congress multiple times that the United States government would abide by NSG guidelines. The President's signing statement also noted that the executive branch would construe "provisions of the Act that mandate, regulate, or prohibit submission of information to the Congress, an international organization, or the public, such as sections 104, 109, 261, 271, 272, 273, 274, and 275, in a manner consistent with the President's constitutional authority to protect and control information that could impair foreign relations, national security, the deliberative processes of the Executive, or the performance of the Executive's constitutional duties." This seems to suggest that the executive branch might limit the scope of reporting required by Congress in those sections, not just on national security grounds, but to protect executive branch processes or performance. The implications of the approach outlined in this signing statement will not be clear until the executive branch produces (or does not produce, as the case may be) required reports.

Issues for Congress

The Nuclear Cooperation Agreement

The agreement announced in July by the United States and India lists a variety of civilian nuclear projects on which the two countries "may pursue cooperation." Although the Bush administration argues that the agreement "is consistent with applicable U.S. law,"[129] some members of Congress have expressed concern that it may be inconsistent with parts of P.L. 109-401. For example, H.Res. 711, which was referred to the House Committee on Foreign Affairs October 4, 2007, states that "it is the sense of the House of Representatives" that the Bush administration should not propose changes to NSG guidelines until it has resolved "all differences of interpretation" of the agreement with New Delhi and "answered all outstanding questions raised by Congress regarding apparent inconsistencies between the nuclear cooperation agreement" and P.L. 109-401. Non-governmental experts have also raised questions about several aspects of the agreement, arguing that they may be inconsistent with P.L. 109-401.[130]

Sensitive Nuclear Technology

Despite restrictions in P.L. 109-401 regarding U.S. exports of equipment, material or technology related to uranium enrichment, spent fuel reprocessing or heavy water production, the agreement states that

> Sensitive nuclear technology, heavy water production technology, sensitive nuclear facilities, heavy water production facilities and major critical components of such facilities may be transferred under this Agreement pursuant to an amendment to this Agreement.

However, the agreement also states that "transfers of dual-use items that could be used in enrichment, reprocessing or heavy water production facilities will be subject to the Parties' respective applicable laws, regulations and license policies." Such transfers would, therefore, be subject to the same restrictions described in P.L. 109-401. Any other transfers of such technology would require changes to existing U.S. law. The State Department has said that Washington does not intend to negotiate an amendment to the agreement.[131] Furthermore, "as a matter of policy, the United States does not transfer dual-use items for use in sensitive nuclear facilities" and "will not assist India in the design, construction, or operation of sensitive nuclear technologies through the transfer of dual-use items, whether under the [123] Agreement or outside the Agreement," according to the State Department.[132]

Nuclear Testing/Right of Return

P.L. 109-401 does not exempt the agreement from a future cutoff in exports if India tests a nuclear explosive device again.[133] However, the agreement does not explicitly mention U.S. responses to such a test of such a device. Instead, the agreement states that "either Party shall have the right to terminate this Agreement prior to its expiration on one year's written notice to the other Party" — that is, the agreement does not limit the grounds upon which the agreement may be terminated.

Similarly, the agreement provides that the party seeking termination

> has the right to cease further cooperation under this Agreement if it determines that a mutually acceptable resolution of outstanding issues has not been possible or cannot be achieved through consultations.

This provision means that nuclear cooperation under the agreement may be terminated by a party *during* the one-year notice period for termination of the agreement.

The agreement also specifies that the two governments are to "hold consultations" prior to ceasing cooperation or terminating the agreement. The United States and India are to

> take into account whether the circumstances that may lead to termination or cessation resulted from a Party's serious concern about a changed security environment or as a response to similar actions by other States which could impact national security.

This provision suggests that, in the event that India conducts a nuclear explosive test, New Delhi may argue that the agreement should not be terminated (and nuclear cooperation should not cease) because geopolitical circumstances justified the test. However, in such cases, the U.S. right to terminate and cease cooperation under this provision would not be constrained by the results of the consultations.

With regard to the U.S. right of return, Section 123 a. (4) of the AEA requires that nuclear cooperation agreements include

> a stipulation that the United States shall have the right to require the return of any nuclear materials and equipment transferred pursuant thereto and any special nuclear material produced through the use thereof if the cooperating party detonates a nuclear explosive device or terminates or abrogates an agreement providing for IAEA safeguards.

The July agreement states that, following the cessation of cooperation under this agreement, either party has the right to require the return of "any nuclear material, equipment, non-nuclear material or components transferred under this Agreement and any special fissionable material produced through their use." However, the agreement does not say explicitly that a future Indian test of a nuclear explosive device would allow the United States to exercise its right of return. Rather, it provides for a right of return whenever a party has given notice of termination of the agreement and has ceased nuclear cooperation, which would include but not be limited to the circumstances specified in section 123.a(4) of the AEA. The agreement also provides that a "notice by a Party that is invoking the right of return shall be delivered to the other Party on or before the date of termination of this Agreement." This means that the right of return cannot be exercised after the one-year interval prior to the agreement's termination.

Fuel Supply

A closely related issue is the agreement's four assurances regarding India's future nuclear fuel supply:

> The United States is willing to incorporate assurances regarding fuel supply in the bilateral U.S.-India agreement on peaceful uses of nuclear energy under Section 123 of the U.S. AEA, which would be submitted to the U.S. Congress.
> The United States will join India in seeking to negotiate with the IAEA an India-specific fuel supply agreement.
> The United States will support an Indian effort to develop a strategic reserve of nuclear fuel to guard against any disruption of supply over the lifetime of India's reactors.
> If, despite these [above] arrangements, a disruption of fuel supplies to India occurs, the two governments would jointly convene a group of friendly supplier countries (including countries such as Russia, France, and the United Kingdom) to pursue such measures as would restore fuel supply to India.

The last two provisions are particularly controversial because they could potentially provide India a way to mitigate the effects of a U.S. cessation of nuclear exports (in the event that, for example, India tests a nuclear weapon).[134] Indeed, Indian Foreign Secretary Shyam Saran asserted in a February 18, 2008, statement that, under the 123 agreement, India is entitled to build a strategic fuel reserve "to last the lifetime of such reactors." And a spokesperson for India's ruling Congress Party indicated that reserve supplies of fuel would enable India to continue operating its reactors even if other countries halted cooperation in response to an Indian nuclear test.[135]

P.L. 109-401 contains several provisions that could be in tension with the July agreement. For example, Section 103 (b) (10) addresses the issue of a fuel reserve:

> Any nuclear power reactor fuel reserve provided to the Government of India for use in safeguarded civilian nuclear facilities should be commensurate with reasonable reactor operating requirements.

With regard to supplying India with nuclear fuel after a nuclear test, Section 103 a. (6)[136] says that the United States should

> Seek to prevent the transfer to a country of nuclear equipment, materials, or technology from other participating governments in the NSG or from any other source if nuclear transfers to that country are suspended or terminated...."

Similarly, Section 102 (13) expresses the sense of Congress that the United States "should not seek to facilitate or encourage the continuation of nuclear exports to India by any other party if such exports are terminated under United States law."

However, President Bush's September 10 message transmitting the agreement to Congress characterizes the agreement's fuel-supply assurances as "political commitments" that are not "legally binding" because the agreement is only a "framework agreement" that does not compel specific nuclear cooperation. Furthermore, according to the State

Department, the "disruption of fuel supplies" referred to in the agreement refers only to disruptions "that may result through no fault" of India's.[137]

Regarding the question of non-U.S. suppliers, Washington has not sought commitments from any other country to supply fuel to India. The "United States would be compelled to encourage transfers of nuclear fuel to India by other" NSG members if supply disruptions "occur through no fault of India's own," according to the State Department.[138] However, these assurances "are not ... meant to insulate India against the consequences of a nuclear explosive test or a violation of nonproliferation commitments." Indeed, such U.S. commitments "would no longer apply" if the United States were to terminate the agreement in response to an Indian nuclear test.

With respect to fuel reserves, the agreement does not define what it means to "support an Indian effort to develop a strategic reserve." Furthermore, the State Department suggests that the United States may not supply India with a fuel reserve sufficient for the lifetime of India's reactors, though the department's 2008 responses to Questions for the Record do not specify the size of any such reserve.[139]

P.L. 110-369- Key Provisions

As noted above, the House passed H.R. 7081, which approved the nuclear cooperation agreement, September 27, 2008.[140] The Senate Committee on Foreign Relations had, following a September 18 hearing and subsequent markup, approved identical legislation, S. 3548 (introduced by Senator Christopher Dodd), September 23. The Senate passed H.R. 7081 October 1. President Bush signed P.L. 110-369 into law October 8.

P.L. 110-369, the United States-India Nuclear Cooperation Approval and Nonproliferation Enhancement Act, obviated the 30-day consultative period, as well as other procedures cited in sections 123 b. and d. of the AEA. Section 101 of the bill states that "notwithstanding the provisions for congressional consideration and approval of a proposed agreement for cooperation" in those two sections, "Congress hereby approves the United States-India Agreement for Cooperation on Peaceful Uses of Nuclear Energy." It also states that the agreement "shall be subject to" applicable U.S. laws as if it had been approved according to section 123's provisions.

Declarations of Policy

P.L. 110-369 contains several declarations of U.S. policy. Section 102 (a) states that "it is the understanding of the United States" that the agreement's provisions

> have the meanings conveyed in the authoritative representations provided by the President and his representatives to the Congress and its committees prior to September 20, 2008, regarding the meaning and legal effect of the Agreement.

As noted above, some lawmakers had previously expressed concern about ambiguities in the agreement and whether it met the requirements of P.L. 109-401. During the debate over the bill, Berman stated September 26 that "I continue to have concerns about ambiguities in the agreement" and inserted the State Department's January 2008 responses to the committee's questions into the record in order to "clarify the meaning of these and other important issues." The documents "constitute key and dispositive parts of the 'authoritative representations' described in section 102," he added.

The law contains two other provisions apparently designed to clarify that the agreement's fuel reserve and fuel supply provisions are not intended to provide New Delhi a way to test nuclear weapons without fear of consequence. The first, section 102 (b) (1), states that "in the event that nuclear transfers to India are suspended or terminated" pursuant to U.S. law, "it is the policy of the United States to seek to prevent the transfer to India of nuclear equipment, materials, or technology" from other NSG participants "or from any other source." This provision is also contained in section 103 (a)(6) of P.L. 109-401.

The second, section 102 (b)(2), restates a provision contained in section 103 (b) (10) of P.L. 109-401 regarding the fuel reserve:

> Any nuclear power reactor fuel reserve provided to the Government of India for use in safeguarded civilian nuclear facilities should be commensurate with reasonable reactor operating requirements.

Certification Requirements

P.L. 110-369 contains two certification requirements that must be met before the United States exchanges diplomatic notes with India — a step which, as noted above, is necessary for the agreement to enter into force. Section 102 (c) requires the President to certify to Congress that the agreement is "consistent with" U.S. obligations under Article I of the NPT. Section 204 (a) requires the President to certify to the Senate Foreign Relations Committee and the House Foreign Affairs Committee that it is U.S. policy to work with NSG members "to agree to further restrict the transfers of equipment and technology related to the enrichment of uranium and reprocessing of spent nuclear fuel." President Bush transmitted the certifications, along with a Memorandum of Justification, October 20. The memorandum provided no reasoning underlying the determinations.

In addition, Section 204 (b) states that

> the President shall seek to achieve, by the earliest possible date, either within the NSG or with relevant NSG Participating Governments, the adoption of principles, reporting, and exchanges of information as may be appropriate to assure peaceful use and accounting of by-product material in a manner that is substantially equivalent to the relevant provisions [of the nuclear cooperation agreement.]

There is no certification requirement for this provision, although section 204(c) requires the President to submit a report every six months on U.S. efforts to achieve these changes.

Section 104 of P.L. 110-369 requires that, before the NRC can issue export licenses, the President must determine and certify to Congress that India's IAEA safeguards agreement has entered into force and that New Delhi's declaration of its nuclear facilities to the IAEA "is not materially inconsistent with the facilities and schedule" described in India's separation plan.

Reporting Requirements

P.L. 110-369 adds several reporting requirements to P.L. 109-401. It amends section 104 (g)(1) to require that the President inform the Senate Foreign Relations Committee and the House Foreign Affairs Committee of "any material inconsistencies" with respect to content or timing between India's separation plan and the notifications New Delhi is to provide to the IAEA pursuant to paragraph 14 of the safeguards agreement. P.L. 110-369 also amends section 104(g)(2) to require the President to report on a variety of activities that could be undertaken pursuant to the nuclear cooperation agreement.

Section 202 of P.L. 110-369 amends section 123 of the AEA to require the President to keep the Senate Foreign Relations Committee and the House Foreign Affairs Committee "fully and currently informed of any initiative or negotiations relating to a new or amended agreement for peaceful nuclear cooperation."[141]

Procedures for Subsequent Arrangements

The nuclear cooperation agreement grants New Delhi consent to reprocess nuclear material transferred pursuant to the agreement, as well as "nuclear material and by-product material used in or produced through the use of nuclear material, nonnuclear material, or equipment so transferred." However, India must first "establish a new national reprocessing facility dedicated to reprocessing safeguarded nuclear material under IAEA safeguards." In addition, the United States and India must "agree on arrangements and procedures under which such reprocessing or other alteration in form or content will take place in this new facility."

Section 201 of P.L. 110-369 specifies procedures to Congress to consider such a subsequent arrangement. First, the President must transmit to the Senate Foreign Relations Committee and the House Foreign Affairs Committee a report describing the reasons for the proposed arrangement, a description (including the text) of the arrangement, and a certification that the United States

> will pursue efforts to ensure that any other nation that permits India to reprocess or otherwise alter in form or content nuclear material that the nation has transferred to India or nuclear material and by-product material used in or produced through the use of nuclear material, non-nuclear material, or equipment that it has transferred to India requires India to do so under similar arrangements and procedures.

In addition, 30 days of continuous session must elapse after the President has submitted the report. The proposed arrangement shall not take effect if Congress adopts a joint resolution of disapproval within this 30-day period. Section 201 requires that such a resolution "be considered pursuant to the procedures set forth in section 130 i" of the AEA. Section 205, however, shortens from 45 to 15 days the amount of time that the Senate Foreign Relations Committee and the House Foreign Affairs Committee have to report the resolution.[142]

Appendix A : Frequently Asked Questions About U.S.-India Nuclear Cooperation

What was the Agreement Signed on March 2, 2006?

In July 2005, India committed to identifying and separating its civilian and military nuclear facilities and programs. On March 2, 2006, U.S. and Indian officials agreed upon a "separation" plan.

Is membership in the Nuclear Nonproliferation Treaty (NPT) Necessary to Sign a Peaceful Nuclear Cooperation Agreement?

No, but the Nuclear Nonproliferation Act of 1978 made comprehensive International Atomic Energy Agency (IAEA) safeguards a requirement for nuclear cooperation with non-nuclear weapon states.

What are Comprehensive IAEA Safeguards?

States that join the NPT as non-nuclear weapon states are obligated to sign an agreement with the IAEA to safeguard all the nuclear material in their state and under their jurisdiction. These are called "comprehensive" or "full-scope" nuclear safeguards, or INFCIRC/153-type safeguards.

Does India have IAEA Safeguards Now on Some Nuclear Facilities?

India has facility-specific (INFCIRC/66-type) safeguards on two U.S.-supplied reactors at Tarapur, two Canadian-supplied reactors at Rajasthan, and has concluded a safeguards agreement for two Russian-supplied reactors under construction at Kudankulam. India also applies intermittent safeguards at its reprocessing plant at Tarapur when safeguarded fuel is present.

If India has Nuclear Weapons, Why isn't it Considered a Nuclear Weapons State?

The Nuclear Nonproliferation Treaty (NPT) defined nuclear weapons states as those states that had detonated a nuclear explosive device before January 1, 1967. Those states are the United States, the United Kingdom, Russia, France, and China. U.S. law follows the NPT definition.

Which Laws did the Administration Seek to Adjust?

The Atomic Energy Act (P.L. 83-703) does not prohibit nuclear cooperation with India, but has three provisions that contain restrictions. The first is Section 123, which requires non-nuclear weapon state recipients of U.S. nuclear cooperation to have full-scope safeguards, among other requirements. The second is Section 128, which requires full-scope safeguards to license nuclear exports. The third is Section 129, which would terminate nuclear exports if a non-nuclear weapon state has conducted a nuclear test after 1978 or continues a nuclear weapons program without steps to terminate such activities.

What Facilities did India Designate as Civilian?

In a statement to the Indian Parliament on March 7, 2006, India identified 14 out of 22 power reactors to declare as civilian; some facilities at the fuel fabrication complex to be identified in the future; some spent fuel storage; 3 heavy water plants (which are not required to be safeguarded); and several research facilities (which are not required to be safeguarded). India has stated that the 14 plants equal 65% of its total nuclear electricity capacity (known as megawattage). However, six of those plants are already covered by existing IAEA safeguards agreements.

On May 11, 2006, Indian officials provided more details. The eight indigenous power reactors to be safeguarded include RAPS 3, 4, 5, & 6 (at Rajasthan); two at Uttar Pradesh (NAPS 1, 2); and two at Gujrat (KAPS 1, 2). The safeguards will be phased in beginning in 2008 or 2009 and completed by 2014. Other facilities (socalled "upstream") were also identified in May, to include a uranium oxide plant, two ceramic fuel fabrication plants, an enriched uranium oxide plant, an enriched fuel fabrication plant and the Gadolinia Facility.

What did P.L. 109-401 Accomplish?

P.L. 109-401, "The Henry J. Hyde United States-India Peaceful Atomic Energy Cooperation Act of 2006," was signed into law by President Bush on December 18, 2006. It allows the President to waive certain restrictions contained in the Atomic Energy Act, namely that non-nuclear weapon states, as defined by the NPT and U.S. law, must have full scope, or comprehensive safeguards on all nuclear material in their state before the United States can engage in nuclear cooperation with them. P.L. 109-401 sets out seven requirements that the President must determine to have happened before he can exercise his waiver authority. The President determined September 10, 2008, that these requirements discussed above have been met.

Appendix B : India's September 5, 2008 Statement on Disarmament and Nonproliferation

Statement by External Affairs Minister of India Shri Pranab Mukherjee on the Civil Nuclear Initiative

To reiterate India's stand on disarmament and nonproliferation, EAM has made the following statement:

A Plenary meeting of the Nuclear Suppliers Group to consider an exception for India from its guidelines to allow for full civil nuclear cooperation with India is being held in Vienna from September 4-5, 2008.

India has a long-standing and steadfast commitment to universal, non-discriminatory and total elimination of nuclear weapons. The vision of a world free of nuclear weapons which Shri Rajiv Gandhi put before the UN in 1988 still has universal resonance.

We approach our dialogue with the Nuclear Suppliers Group and all its members in a spirit of cooperation that allows for an ongoing frank exchange of views on subjects of mutual interest and concern. Such a dialogue will strengthen our relationship in the years to come.

Our civil nuclear initiative will strengthen the international non-proliferation regime. India believes that the opening of full civil nuclear cooperation will be good for India and for the world. It will have a profound positive impact on global energy security and international efforts to combat climate change.

India has recently submitted a Working Paper on Nuclear Disarmament to the UN General Assembly, containing initiatives on nuclear disarmament. These include the reaffirmation of the unequivocal commitment of all nuclear weapon States to the goal of complete elimination of nuclear weapons; negotiation of a Convention on the complete prohibition of the use or threat of use of nuclear weapons; and negotiation of a Nuclear Weapons Convention prohibiting the development, production, stockpiling and use of nuclear weapons and on their destruction, leading to the global, non-discriminatory and verifiable elimination of nuclear weapons within a specified timeframe.

We remain committed to a voluntary, unilateral moratorium on nuclear testing. We do not subscribe to any arms race, including a nuclear arms race. We have always tempered the exercise of our strategic autonomy with a sense of global responsibility. We affirm our policy of no-first-use of nuclear weapons.

We are committed to work with others towards the conclusion of a multilateral Fissile Material Cut-off Treaty in the Conference on Disarmament that is universal, non-discriminatory and verifiable.

India has an impeccable non-proliferation record. We have in place an effective and comprehensive system of national export controls, which has been constantly updated to meet the highest international standards. This is manifested in the enactment of the Weapons of Mass Destruction and their Delivery Systems Act in 2005. India has taken the necessary steps to secure nuclear materials and technology through comprehensive export control legislation and through harmonization and committing to adhere to Missile Technology Control Regime and Nuclear Suppliers Group guidelines.

India will not be the source of proliferation of sensitive technologies, including enrichment and reprocessing transfers. We stand for the strengthening of the non-proliferation regime. We support international efforts to limit the spread of ENR equipment or technologies to states that do not have them. We will work together with the international community to advance our common objective of nonproliferation. In this regard, India is interested in participating as a supplier nation, particularly for Thorium-based fuel and in establishment of international fuel banks, which also benefit India.

India places great value on the role played by the IAEA's nuclear safeguards system. We look forward to working with the IAEA in implementing the India-specific Safeguards Agreement concluded with the IAEA. In keeping with our commitment to sign and adhere to an Additional Protocol with respect to India's civil nuclear facilities, we are working closely with the IAEA to ensure early conclusion of an Additional Protocol to the Safeguards Agreement.

END NOTES

1 The full text of the agreement, which was released August 3, 2007, can be found at [http://www.state.gov/r/pa/prs/ps/2007/aug/90050.htm].

2 The relevant documents are available at [http://foreignaffairs.house.gov/press_display. asp?id=555].

3 For an analysis of the proliferation implications of U.S. nuclear exports to India, see Gary Milhollin, "Stopping the Indian Bomb," *The American Journal of International Law*, July 1987, 81 A.J.I.L. 593. See [http://www.wisconsinproject.org/pubs/articles/1987/ stoppingindianbomb.htm].

4 The NNPA, in part, amended the Atomic Energy Act of 1954. See 42 U.S.C. 2151 et seq. Prior to the 1970 NPT, safeguards (inspections, material protection, control and accounting) were applied to specific facilities or materials (known as INFCIRC/66-type agreements). The NPT required safeguards on all nuclear material in all peaceful nuclear activities for non-nuclear-weapon-state parties (those states not having detonated a nuclear explosive device prior to January 1, 1967).

5 IAEA Document INFCIRC/254, *Guidelines for Transfers of Nuclear-related Dual-use Equipment, Materials, Software, and Related Technology*. Part 1 covers "trigger list" items: those especially designed or prepared for nuclear use: (i) nuclear material; (ii) nuclear reactors and equipment; (iii) non-nuclear material for reactors; (iv) plant and equipment for reprocessing, enrichment and conversion of nuclear material and for fuel fabrication and heavy water production; and (v) associated technology. Part 2 covers dual-use items. Additional NSG criteria for dual-use exports include NPT membership and/or full-scope safeguards agreement; appropriate end-use; whether the technology would be used in a reprocessing or enrichment facility; the state's support for nonproliferation; and the risk of potential nuclear terrorism.

6 China was not a member of the NSG until 2004. Russia, an NSG member, exported fuel, citing a safety exception, but NSG members objected so strongly that Russia suspended supply in 2004. Russia agreed to resupply Tarapur in late February and informed the NSG on February 27, 2006, reportedly citing the NSG safety exception.

7 See also CRS Report RL33072, *U.S.-India Bilateral Agreements and "Global Partnership,"* and CRS Report RL33529, *India-U.S. Relations*, by K. Alan Kronstadt.

8 See fact sheet on the NSSP at [http://www.state.gov/r/pa/prs/ps/2004/36290.htm].

9 Joint Statement Between President George W. Bush and Prime Minister Manmohan Singh, White House Press Release, July 18, 2005, Washington, DC (hereafter cited as "July 18 Joint Statement") [http://www.whitehouse.gov/news/releases/2005/07/20050718-6.html].

10 July 18 Joint Statement.

11 See CRS Report RS22474, *Banning Fissile Material Production for Nuclear Weapons: Prospects for a Treaty (FMCT)*, by Sharon Squassoni, Andrew Demkee, and Jill Marie Parillo, for more detailed information about the issue and negotiations.

12 Opening Statement, Chairman Richard G. Lugar, Senate Foreign Relations Committee hearing on "Implications of U.S.-India Nuclear Energy Cooperation," November 2, 2005 (hereafter referred to as November 2, 2005 SFRC India hearing).

13 The House International Relations Committee held the following hearings: "The U.S. and India: An Emerging Entente?" (September 8, 2005); "The U.S.-India Global Partnership: The Impact on Nonproliferation" (October 26, 2005); and "U.S.-India Global Partnership: How Significant for American Interests?" (November 16, 2005); "The U.S.-India Global Partnership" (April 5, 2006); "U.S.-India Global Partnership: Legislative Options" (May 11, 2006). See [http://www.internationalrelations.house.gov/] for testimonies of witnesses. The

Senate Foreign Relations Committee held the following hearings: "Implications of U.S.India Nuclear Energy Cooperation" (November 2, 2005); "U.S.-India Atomic Energy Cooperation: The Indian Separation Plan and the Administration's Legislative Proposal" (April 5, 2006); and "U.S.-India Atomic Energy Cooperation: Strategic and Nonproliferation Implications" (April 26, 2006). See [http://foreign.senate.gov/hearing.html] for testimonies.

[14] Statement of Under Secretary of State for Political Affairs, R. Nicholas Burns, September 8, 2005, House Committee on International Relations, Hearing on "The U.S. and India: An Emerging Entente?" (hereafter cited as "September 8, 2005, HIRC US-India hearing") p. 1.

[15] Remarks by Congressman Jim Leach, September 8, 2005, House International Relations Committee U.S.-India Hearing.

[16] Henry Sokolski, "Implementing the Indian Nuclear Deal: What's at Risk, What Congress Should Require," Briefing to Congress, September 2005.

[17] See "India's Growth Target Unrealistic," *Financial Times*, January 23, 2003, which quotes the Asia Development Bank.

[18] Brahma Chellaney, "US Deal is a Bad Choice for Power Generation," *International Herald Tribune*, December 27, 2005.

[19] Statement of Under Secretary of State for Political Affairs, R. Nicholas Burns, November 2, 2005, Senate Foreign Relations Committee Hearing on Implications of U.S.-India Nuclear Energy Cooperation.

[20] See Miriam Rajkumar, "Indian Independence," Carnegie Analysis, September 20, 2005, at [http://www. carnegieendowment.org/npp/publications/index.cfm?fa=view&id=17486].

[21] Dr. Francine Frankel, Statement before the House International Relations Committee, November 16, 2005, "India's Potential Importance for Vital U.S. Geopolitical Objectives in Asia: A Hedge Against a Rising China?"

[22] "Press Briefing by Foreign Secretary on the events in UN and IAEA," New Delhi, September 26, 2005, available at [http://www.indianembassy.org/press_release/2005/ Sept/29.htm].

[23] Briefing by MEA Official Spokesperson on Draft Resolution on Iran in IAEA, New Delhi, September 24, 2005, available at [http://www.indianembassy.org/press_release/2005/Sept/ 16.htm].

[24] See CRS Report RL34544, *Iran's Nuclear Program: Status*, by Paul K. Kerr.

[25] "U.S.-India Nuclear Deal Could Die, Envoy Warns," *Washington Post*, January 26, 2006.

[26] "Ahmadinejad Thanks India for Positive Stands on Iran in IAEA," IRNA, September 23, 2005.

[27] September 26, 2005 press briefing, op. cit.

[28] Iran Republic News Agency, "118 countries back Iran's nuclear program" *Iran Times,* September 18, 2006.

[29] See CRS Report RS22530, *India and Iran: WMD Proliferation Activities*, by Sharon Squassoni, for more information related to sanctions imposed for Indian transfers to Iran.

[30] See [http://www.nti.org/e_research/profiles/Iran/2867.html].

[31] "India Denies Nuclear Cooperation with Iran," *Agence France Presse*, December 13, 2003.

[32] John Larkin and Jay Solomon, "As Ties Between India and Iran Rise, U.S. Grows Edgy," *Wall Street Journal*, March 24, 2005.

[33] Thionyl chloride is a Schedule 3 chemical under the Chemical Weapons Convention. It has military and civilian uses, and is widely used in the laboratory and in industry.

[34] See list of sanctions at [http://www.state.gov/t/isn/c15234.htm].

[35] The full text of Mukherjee's statement is in **Appendix B**.

[36] David Albright and Susan Basu, "India's Gas Centrifuge Program: Stopping Illicit Procurement and the Leakage of Technical Centrifuge Know-How." Available at [http://www.isis-online.org/publications/southasia/ indianprocurement.pdf].

[37] David Albright and Paul Brannan, "Indian Nuclear Export Controls and Information Security: Important Questions Remain." Available at [http://www.isis-online.org/publications/southasia/India_18September 2008.pdf].

[38] "Questions for the Record Submitted to Under Secretaries Nicholas Burns and Robert Joseph by Chairman Richard G. Lugar (#6), Senate Foreign Relations Committee, November 2, 2005."

[39] September 8, 2005, HIRC US-India hearing.

[40] See, for example, "Nuclear Nonproliferation System is Challenged," *People's Daily,* March 16, 2006.

[41] Available at [http://verificationthoughts.blogspot.com/2008/07/indian-separation-plan. html].

[42] "Concern over Russian Plan to Sell Nuclear Reactor Fuel," *Financial Times*, March 15, 2006.

[43] David S. Jonas, "Variations on Non-nuclear: May the 'Final Four' Join the Nuclear Nonproliferation Treaty as Non-nuclear Weapon States While Retaining Their Nuclear Weapons?" *Michigan State Law Review,* Summer 2005, p. 417 ff. Mr. Jonas is General Counsel of the National Nuclear Security Agency.

[44] Ambassador Norman Wulf, "Observations from the 2000 NPT Review Conference," *Arms Control Today*, November 2000.

[45] September 8, 2005, HIRC US-India hearing.

[46] Fred McGoldrick, Harold Bengelsdorf, Lawrence Scheinman, "The U.S.-India Nuclear Deal: Taking Stock," *Arms Control Today*, October 2005, pp. 6-12. See [http://www.armscontrol.org/act/2005_10/OCT-Cover.asp].

[47] Statement by Robert J. Einhorn, Center for Strategic and International Studies, "The U.S.-India Global Partnership: The Impact on Nonproliferation" October 26, 2005.

[48] "Backgrounder on India-U.S. Civilian Nuclear Energy Cooperation," Indian Embassy, July 29, 2005. See [http://www.indianembassy.org/press_release/2005/July/29.htm].

[49] Prime Minister Singh, "Excerpts from Prime Minister's Reply to Discussion in Raja Sabha on Civil Nuclear Energy Cooperation with the United States." Remarks are available at the Indian Ministry of External Affairs website, [http://mea.gov.in].

[50] "IAEA Director General Reacts to U.S.-India Cooperation Agreement," See [http://www.iaea.org/ NewsCenter/ PressReleases/2005/prn200504.html]. Critics of the IAEA point out that it is an organization that measures its success in part by how much nuclear material and how many facilities are under inspection.

[51] On September 29, 2004, the State Department published Public Notice 4845 in the Federal Register imposing sanctions pursuant to the Iran Nonproliferation Act of 2000. Two Indian scientists were named — Dr. Prasad and C. Surendar. The State Department has not revealed what technology or equipment was transferred, but both scientists have worked for the Nuclear Power Corporation of India, Ltd., a government-owned entity that runs India's nuclear power plants. The Indian embassy reported in December 2005 that sanctions on Dr. Surendar had been removed. See [http://www.indianembassy.org/press_release/5.asp]. In the December 30, 2005 Federal Register, Public Notice 5257 stated simply that sanctions on an Indian entity issued in Public Notice 4845 had been rescinded.

[52] September 8, 2005, HIRC US-India hearing.

[53] "Backgrounder on India-U.S. Nuclear Energy Cooperation," July 29, 2005.

[54] "Excerpts from Prime Minister's Reply," August 17, 2006, op. cit.

[55] See Zia Mian and M.V. Ramana, "Wrong Ends, Means, and Needs: Behind the U.S. Nuclear Deal with India," *Arms Control Today*, January/February 2006. See also Robert Einhorn, "Limiting the Damage," *The National Interest,* Winter 2005/2006.

[56] Statement of David Albright before the House International Relations Committee on October 26, 2005 (hereafter cited as "HIRC October 26, 2005 hearing").

[57] Questions for the Record Submitted to Secretary of State Condoleezza Rice by Senator Richard Lugar (#2) Senate Foreign Relations Committee, April 5, 2006.

[58] White House, Office of the Press Secretary, "Press Briefing by Under Secretary of State for Political Affairs Nick Burns," Maurya Sheraton Hotel and Towers, New Delhi, India, March 2, 2006.

[59] Mohamed ElBaradei, "Rethinking Nuclear Safeguards," *Washington Post*, June 14, 2006.

[60] See Henry Sokolski, "Fissile isn't Facile," *Wall Street Journal,* February 21, 2006.

[61] See Charles Ferguson, "Reshaping the U.S.-Indian Nuclear Deal to Lessen the Nonproliferation Losses," *Arms Control Today*, April 2008. Ferguson cites information from the Nuclear Power Corporation of India. See also "Uranium Shortage Hits Nuclear Power," *The Hindu Business Line*, May 21, 2008.

[62] Several countries have supplied low-enriched uranium to the U.S.-origin Tarapur reactors, including France, China and Russia.

[63] "India and the Nuclear Domain." Available at [http://mea.gov.in/].

[64] Zia Mian, A.H. Nayyar, R. Rajaraman and M.V. Ramana, *Fissile Materials in South Asia: The Implications of the U.S.-India Nuclear Deal*, September 2006. Available at [http://www.fissilematerials.org/ipfm/site_down/ rr01.pdf].

[65] K. Subrahmanyam, former head of the Institute for Defence Studies and Analysis, was appointed Head of the National Security Council Advisory Board (NSCAB) established by the first Vajpayee government to draft the Indian nuclear doctrine. He currently chairs PM Singh's Global Strategic Developments Task Force. See also Dr. A. Gopalakrishnan, "Civilian and Strategic Nuclear Facilities of India," January 5, 2006.

[66] It is worth noting that even before the NPT entered into force, negotiators recognized that a state outside the treaty could preserve its domestic uranium sources for a possible weapons program as long as it agreed to accept IAEA safeguards on the items it imported. In the late 1960s, however, Congress was more concerned about ensuring that the United States could supply its allies outside the treaty, such as Japan and Germany, with nuclear fuel. According to Mason Willrich's history of the NPT,

> As long as India does not become a party to the Non-Proliferation Treaty, it can continue to import from the parties nuclear materials and equipment subject to safeguards for use in its civil nuclear power program. This would free its indigenous resources, particularly its limited uranium supply, for possible concentration on a nuclear weapons program.

(Mason Willrich, *Non-proliferation Treaty: Framework for Nuclear Arms Control*, The Michie Company, Charlottesville, VA, 1969, p. 125.)

[67] "India Won't Define Minimum N-Deterrent: Saran," *Press Trust of India*, April 8, 2006.

[68] *Report Pursuant to Section 104 (c) of the Hyde Act Regarding Civil Nuclear Cooperation with India.* Submitted to Congress September 10, 2008. (Hereafter cited as, "2008 State Department Report.")

[69] See CRS Report RL33292, *India's Nuclear Separation Plan: Issues and Views*, by Sharon Squassoni, for details on the separation plan. See the previous section for additional issues concerning the separation plan.

[70] Prime Minister Singh presented "Implementation of the India-United States Joint Statement of July 18, 2005: India's Separation Plan," to Parliament on March 7, 2006. This is available at [http://indianembassy.org/ newsite/press_release/2006/Mar/sepplan.pdf]. The plan was updated on May 11, 2006 to include names of reactors and upstream facilities, as well as dates they would be submitted to safeguards.

[71] According to the May 11th update, the 8 indigenous reactors to be safeguarded are: 4 at Rajasthan (RAPS 3, 4, 5 & 6); 2 at Uttar Pradesh (NAPS 1, 2); and 2 at Gujrat (KAPS 1, 2).

[72] Although India maintained a certain ambiguity by calling its 1974 test a "peaceful nuclear explosion," the 1998 tests leave little doubt that the experience gained was put to use in a nuclear weapons program. Plutonium produced in the CIRUS reactor, which the United States supplied with heavy water, was used in the 1974 test. See Victor Gilinsky and Paul Leventhal, "India Cheated," *Washington Post*, June 15, 1998. U.S. documents from the early 1970s indicate that the United States interpreted its nuclear cooperation agreement with India to prohibit peaceful nuclear explosions. Washington communicated this position to New Delhi. The documents are available at [http://www.armscontrol.org/country/ india/Historic_Documents_India_Nuclear_Test.asp].

[73] The Additional Protocol is a measure to strengthen safeguards by providing for additional information, access and inspection tools. INFCIRC/540, concluded in 1997, is the model upon which states' protocols to their safeguards agreements are based.

[74] Statement of Dr. Joseph, November 2, 2005, SFRC India hearing.

[75] Ibid.

[76] Condoleezza Rice, "Our Opportunity With India," *Washington Post*, March 13, 2006.

[77] National Strategy to Combat Weapons of Mass Destruction, December 2002. Available at [http://www.whitehouse.gov/news/releases/2002/12/WMDStrategy.pdf].

[78] See also CRS Report RL33529, *India-U.S. Relations*, by K. Alan Kronstadt.

[79] Those parties argue that the agreement would compromise India's sovereignty by drawing New Delhi into a "strategic alliance" with Washington. See, for example, [http://www.cpim.org/] for a detailed account of objections from the Communist Party of India (Marxist).

[80] "N-deal strategic to India's progress: Pranab Mukherjee," *Indo Asian News Service*, February 3, 2008.

[81] "After Left Nod, Govt Decides To Go Ahead With IAEA Talks On N-Deal," *Financial Express*, November 16, 2007.

[82] Available at [http://pmindia.nic.in/IaeaIndiaSGADrft.pdf].

[83] Mark Hibbs and Daniel Horner, "Pakistan, Other States Not Satisfied After Indian Briefing on IAEA Pact," *Nucleonics Week*, July 24, 2008.

[84] "Will Support Govt That Scraps 123," *The Economic Times*, September 8, 2008.

[85] Interview with Leader of the Opposition (Lok Sabha) L.K. Advani, *The Hindu*, July 11, 2008; "BJP Will Renegotiate N-Deal If Comes To Power: Sushma Swaraj," *The Economic Times*, September 7, 2008.

[86] Unless otherwise noted, this section is based on ElBaradei's August 1, 2008 comments to the IAEA Board of Governors, as well as personal communications with IAEA officials, and current and former State Department officials.

[87] Available at [http://www.iaea.org/Publications/Documents/Infcircs/2008/infcirc731.pdf].

[88] Author interview, September 23, 2008.

[89] "Indian Daily Interviews Atomic Body Chairman on Nuclear Deal," *The Hindu*, July 20, 2008.

[90] Ibid.

[91] Questions for the Record Submitted to Jeffrey Bergner, Assistant Secretary for Legislative Affairs by Rep. Tom Lantos, House Committee on Foreign Affairs (#12), October 5, 2007. Available at [http://www.hcfa.house. gov/110/press090208.pdf]. (Hereafter, "Questions for the Record, 2007.")

[92] Ibid. (#11).

[93] Ibid. (#42).

[94] The Consultative Group is the NSG's "standing intersessional working body." See [http://www.nuclearsuppliers group.org/activities.htm].

[95] A copy of the proposal is available at [http://www.armscontrol.org/projects/india/20060327_Draft NSGProposal.asp].

[96] Author interviews with State Department official, February 4, 2008; August 14, 2008.

[97] The August 2008 draft is available at [http://www.armscontrol.org/node/3274].

[98] The text of the NSG statement is available at [http://www.nuclearsuppliersgroup.org/ PRESS/2008-09-Press-Vienna.pdf].

[99] Austria, Ireland, the Netherlands, New Zealand, Norway, and Switzerland issued a joint statement at the August meeting explaining that they had proposed amendments to the U.S. proposal in order to meet their "non-proliferation objectives." New Zealand's Disarmament and Arms Control Minister Phil Goff stated August 26 that approximately 50 amendments had been proposed to the U.S.-proposed text.

[100] Mark Hibbs and Daniel Horner, "Scope of NSG Exemption For India Yet to Be Defined by Member States," *Nucleonics Week*, September 11, 2008.

[101] Wade Boese, "Nuclear Export Criteria Lacks Consensus," *Arms Control Today*, June 2008.

[102] See Appendix B.

[103] Rama Lakshmi, "U.S. Letter Puts India's Premier On Defensive Over Nuclear Deal," *Washington Post*, September 5, 2008.

[104] "Indo-French Pact Not to Cover Nuclear Enrichment Technology Sale - Envoy," *Press Trust of India*, September 19, 2008.

[105] "Indian Official Indicates French Firms May Have To Wait For Nuclear Trade," *Press Trust of India*, October 1, 2008.

[106] "India Needs to Tap Atomic Opportunity as Crisis May Slow Orders," *Bloomberg*, October 21, 2008.

[107] "India Tells U.S.: Can't Hold up N-Deals With Other Nations For Long," *Indo-Asian News Service*, September 17, 2008.

[108] Text Available at [http://svaradarajan.blogspot.com/2008/10/dear-bill-foreign-secretarysletter.html].

[109] "Questions for the Record Submitted to Under Secretary William Burns and Acting Under Secretary John Rood by Senator Robert P. Casey, Senate Foreign Relations Committee, September 18, 2008."

[110] Ibid.

[111] Author interview, September 23, 2008.

[112] State Department Report 2008.

[113] Ibid.

[114] Author interviews with State Department official August 11, 2008; August 14, 2008.

[115] Nuclear cooperation includes the distribution of special nuclear material, source material, and byproduct material, to licensing for commercial, medical, and industrial purposes. These terms, "special nuclear material," "source material,"and "byproduct material," as well as other terms used in the statute, are defined in 42 U.S.C. § 2014.

[116] P.L. 83-703, 42 U.S.C. §§ 2153 et seq.

[117] In the 1954 Act, the provisions in Section 123 c. covered all agreements for cooperation. Section 123 d. was added in 1958 (P.L. 85-479) to cover military-related agreements. In 1974, P.L. 93-485 amended Section 123 d. to include agreements that covered reactors producing more than 5 MW thermal or special nuclear material connected therewith.

[118] United States General Accounting Office, "Nuclear Agreement: Cooperation Between the United States and the People's Republic of China," GAO/NSIAD-86-21BR, November 1985, Appendix I-1.

[119] 42 U.S.C. 2153 a.(2). Section 4 (b) of the NNPA specifies that all other terms used in the NNPA not defined in Section 4 "shall have the meanings ascribed to them by the 1954 Act, the Energy Reorganization Act of 1974 and the Treaty [NPT]." S.Rept. 95-467 further clarified that under the NPT, the five nuclear weapon states are the U.S., U.K., China, the Soviet Union, and France. U.S. Code Congressional and Administration News, 95th Cong., 2nd sess., 1978, vol. 3, p. 329.

[120] This new requirement was added by the Export Administration Amendments Act of 1985, P.L. 99-64, Section 301 (b) (2), 99 Stat. 120.

[121] The language "fails to disapprove" is an artifact of the 1978 Nuclear Nonproliferation Act, which used legislative vetoes in the form of concurrent resolutions of disapproval. In 1985, following the Supreme Court's *Chadha* decision invalidating the use of legislative vetoes, the Export Administration Amendments Act created a separate approval process for exempted agreements, which this part of Section 123 d. is referring to, that called for a joint resolution of approval. Thus, "fails to disapprove" could be interpreted as "approves" in the form of a joint resolution of approval.

[122] In light of the *Chadha* decision, passing a concurrent resolution could invite a legal challenge. Although this is not provided for in the AEA, Congress could choose to pass a joint resolution of disapproval or a bill stating in substance it did not approve.

[123] Section 128 b. (3) refers to a "resolution of disapproval," and this would likely be a joint resolution of disapproval, in light of the *Chadha* decision.

[124] Section 128 b. (2) refers to a "concurrent resolution." In light of the *Chadha* decision, Congress could pass a joint resolution disagreeing with the President's determination, or pass a bill barring nuclear exports for a certain period of time to that country.

[125] Section 129 specified that the President's determination "shall not become effective if during such sixty-day period the Congress adopts a concurrent resolution stating in substance that it does not favor the determination." However, P.L. 110-369 amended that section to change the "concurrent resolution" provision to a "joint resolution," presumably to overcome potential issues raised by the *Chadha* decision..

[126] See CRS Report RL33561, *U.S.-India Nuclear Cooperation: A Side-By-Side Comparison of Current Legislation*, by Sharon Squassoni and Jill Marie Parillo (hereafter cited as CRS Report RL33561) for more detail on the bills.

[127] See H.Rept. 109-590 and for S.Rept. 109-288, dated July 20, 2006, background on the bill.

[128] See [http://www.whitehouse.gov/news/releases/2006/12/20061218-12.html]

[129] Department of State Fact Sheet July 27, 2007, at [http://www.state.gov/r/pa/prs/ps/2007/ 89552.htm].

[130] See, for example, Sharon Squassoni, "Issues in U.S.-India Nuclear Cooperation," November 7, 2007 [http://www.carnegieendowment.org/publications/index.cfm?fa=view& id=19697&prog=zgp&proj=znpp,zsa],

and Daryl G. Kimball and Fred McGoldrick "U.S.-Indian Nuclear Agreement: A Bad Deal Gets Worse," August 3, 2007, at [http://www.armscontrol.org/pressroom/2007/20070803_IndiaUS.asp?print].

131 Questions for the Record, 2007 (#8).

132 Ibid. (#s 4 and 5).

133 As noted above, the President retains the right to waive the termination of nuclear exports.

134 In a February 18, 2008 statement, Saran asserted that, under the 123 agreement, India is entitled to build a strategic fuel reserve "to last the lifetime of such reactors."

135 "BJP, Left On 'Unholy Alliance' To Oppose N-Deal: Congress," *Press Trust of India*, September 5, 2008.

136 As noted above, the President's signing statement says that he "shall construe" Section 103 as "advisory."

137 Questions for the Record, 2007 (#16).

138 Ibid. (#18).

139 Ibid. (#19-20).

140 H.R. 7039, a bill identical to H.R. 7081, was introduced by Representative Alana Ros-Lehtinen September 24. The next day, Representative Howard Berman introduced H.R. 7061, a bill very similar to H.R. 7081.

141 H.R. 7061 required the President to consult with the House Foreign Affairs Committee and the Senate Foreign Relations Committee regarding any such initiative or negotiations.

142 See CRS Report RS22937, *Nuclear Cooperation with Other Countries: A Primer*, by Paul K. Kerr and Mary Beth Nikitin.

In: India and the U.S: Future Relations...
Editor: Tim S. Macleod, pp.145-216

ISBN: 978-1-60741-197-0

Chapter 4

INDIA-U.S. RELATIONS

K. Alan Kronstadt
Specialist in South Asian Affairs
Foreign Affairs, Defense, and Trade Division

SUMMARY

Long considered a "strategic backwater" from Washington's perspective, South Asia has emerged in the 21st century as increasingly vital to core U.S. foreign policy interests. India, the region's dominant actor with more than one billion citizens, is often characterized as a nascent major power and "natural partner" of the United States, one that many analysts view as a potential counterweight to China's growing clout. Washington and New Delhi have since 2004 been pursuing a "strategic partnership" based on shared values such as democracy, pluralism, and rule of law. Numerous economic, security, and global initiatives, including plans for "full civilian nuclear energy cooperation," are underway. This latter initiative, launched by President Bush in July 2005 and provisionally endorsed by the 109th Congress in 2006 (P.L. 109-401, the "Hyde Act"), would reverse three decades of U.S. nonproliferation policy. It requires, among other steps, a Joint Resolution of Approval by Congress. Also in 2005, the United States and India signed a ten-year defense framework agreement that calls for expanding bilateral security cooperation. Since 2002, the two countries have engaged in numerous and unprecedented combined military exercises. Major U.S. arms sales to India are planned. The influence of a growing and relatively wealthy Indian-American community of more than two million is reflected in Congress's largest country-specific caucus.

Further U.S. interest in South Asia focuses on ongoing tensions between India and Pakistan rooted in unfinished business from the 1947 Partition, competing claims to the Kashmir region, and, in more recent years, "cross-border terrorism" in both Kashmir and major Indian cities. In the interests of regional stability, the United States strongly encourages an ongoing India-Pakistan peace initiative and remains concerned about the potential for conflict over Kashmiri sovereignty to cause open hostilities between these two nuclear-armed countries. The United States seeks to curtail the proliferation of nuclear weapons and ballistic missiles in South Asia. Both India and Pakistan have resisted external pressure to sign the major nonproliferation treaties. In 1998, the two countries conducted nuclear tests that evoked international condemnation. Proliferation-related restrictions on U.S. aid were triggered, then later lifted through congressional-executive cooperation from 1998 to 2000. Remaining sanctions on India (and Pakistan) were removed in late 2001.

India is in the midst of major and rapid economic expansion. Many U.S. business interests view India as a lucrative market and candidate for foreign investment. The United States supports India's efforts to transform its once quasi-socialist economy through fiscal reform and market opening. Since 1991, India has taken major steps in this direction and coalition governments have kept the country on a general path of reform, yet there is U.S. concern that such movement is slow and inconsistent. India is the world's fourth-largest emitter of greenhouse gases. Congress also continues to have concerns about abuses of human rights, including caste- and gender-based discrimination, and religious freedoms in India. Moreover, the spread of HIV/AIDS in India has been identified as a serious development. See also CRS Report RL34161, *India-U.S. Economic and Trade Relations*. This report will be updated regularly.

INTRODUCTION

Long considered a "strategic backwater" from Washington's perspective, South Asia has emerged in the 21st century as increasingly vital to core U.S. foreign policy interests. India, the region's dominant actor with more than one billion citizens, is often characterized as a nascent major power and "natural partner" of the United States, one that many analysts view as a potential counterweight to China's growing clout. Washington and New Delhi have since 2004 been pursuing a "strategic partnership" based on shared values such as democracy, pluralism, and rule of law. Numerous economic, security, and global initiatives, including plans for "full civilian nuclear energy cooperation," are underway. This latter initiative, launched by President Bush in July 2005 and provisionally endorsed by the 109th Congress in 2006 (P.L. 109-401, the "Hyde Act"), would reverse three decades of U.S. nonproliferation policy. It requires, among other steps, a Joint Resolution of Approval by Congress. Also in 2005, the United States and India signed a ten-year defense framework agreement that calls for expanding bilateral security cooperation. Since 2002, the two countries have engaged in numerous and unprecedented combined military exercises. Major U.S. arms sales to India are planned. The influence of a growing and relatively wealthy Indian-American community of more than two million is reflected in Congress's largest country-specific caucus.

Both leading U.S. presidential candidates express full-throated support for a deepened and expanded U.S.-India partnership. Senator Barak Obama would like to see U.S.-India ties strengthened "across the board," with a particular focus on energy issues. Senator John McCain claims the United States has a "vested interest in India's success" and he calls for improved military and counterterrorism cooperation, along with mutual efforts to strengthen democracy and energy security. Both Senators are explicit supporters of U.S.-India civil nuclear cooperation as proposed by the Bush Administration.[1]

INDIA IN BRIEF

Population	: 1.15 billion; *growth rate*: 1.6% (2008 est.)
Area	: 3,287,590 sq. km. (slightly more than one-third the size of the United States)
Capital	: New Delhi
Head of Government	: Prime Minister Manmohan Singh (Congress Party)
Ethnic Groups	: Indo-Aryan 72%; Dravidian 25%; other 3%
Languages	: 22 official, 13 of which are the primary tongue of at least 10 million people; Hindi is the primary tongue of about 30%; English widely used
Religions	: Hindu 81%; Muslim 13%; Christian 2%; Sikh 2%, other 2% (2001 census)
Life Expectancy at Birth	: female 72 years; male 67 years (2008 est.)
Literacy	: female 48%; male 73% (2001 census)
Gross Domestic Product (at PPP)	: $3.03 trillion; *per capita*: $2,784; *growth rate* 9% (2007)
Currency	: Rupee (100 = $2.37)
Inflation	: 6.4% (2007)
Defense Budget	: $28.5 billion (2.4% of GDP; 2007)
U.S. Trade	: exports to U.S. $24.0 billion; imports from U.S. $17.6 billion (2007)

Sources: CIA World Factbook; U.S. Department of Commerce; Economist Intelligence Unit; Global Insight; Military Balance

KEY CURRENT ISSUES AND DEVELOPMENTS

U.S.-India Civil Nuclear Cooperation[2]

Plans to initiate U.S.-India civil nuclear cooperation were long hampered by domestic political resistance in India, but are again underway in mid-2008. In a major policy shift by the United States, a July 2005 U.S.-India Joint Statement notably asserted that "as a responsible state with advanced nuclear technology, India should acquire the same benefits and advantages as other such states," and President Bush vowed to work on achieving "full civilian nuclear energy cooperation with India." As a reversal of three decades of U.S. nonproliferation policy, such proposed cooperation stirred controversy and required changes in both U.S. law and in international guidelines. Enabling U.S. legislation became public law in December 2006 (P.L. 109-401 or "the Hyde Act").

For nearly one year from mid-2007 to mid-2008, however, India's United Progressive Alliance (UPA) coalition government, led by the Congress Party of Prime Minister Manmohan Singh, was unable to overcome persistent and unrelenting resistance to the pact from communist party leaders who provide the ruling coalition with crucial parliamentary support. By threatening to withdraw such support if the UPA went forward with the initiative, the Left Front obstructed its potential consummation, leading many analysts to conclude that planned cooperation would not take place in the foreseeable future. A July 2008 political realignment in New Delhi, however, freed the UPA to continue its pursuit of the deal. On August 1, the International Atomic Energy Agency (IAEA) Board of Governors approved the safeguards accord with India. On August 21, the 45-member Nuclear Suppliers Group (NSG) is set to meet to discuss adjusting its guidelines to permit nuclear trade with India. If this step is taken, U.S.-India civil nuclear cooperation can commence only after Congress approves a Joint Resolution of Approval. The text of the 123 Agreement must be submitted for 30 days of continuous congressional session before any vote can take place. Thus, by nearly all accounts, the U.S. congressional calendar presents a major obstacle to the deal's consummation in 2008.[3]

Recent Background

In July 2007, the United States and India announced having concluded negotiations on a peaceful nuclear cooperation (or "123") agreement. Then-Under Secretary of State for Political Affairs Nicholas Burns, the lead U.S. negotiator, called the deal "perhaps the single most important initiative that India and the United States have agreed to in the 60 years of our relationship" and "the symbolic centerpiece of a growing global partnership between our two countries."[4] U.S. officials urged New Delhi to move rapidly toward completing remaining steps to consummation of the pact. These included finalizing arrangements for IAEA inspections of India's civilian nuclear facilities and winning the endorsement of the NSG for nuclear trade. Following these steps, the 123 Agreement can become operative only through a Joint Resolution of Approval from Congress. There have been significant apparent contradictions between the expectations of and public statements by U.S. and Indian officials on this issue.[5]

Many independent Indian commentators approved of the pact, seeing in it an end to "nuclear apartheid" that likely will "go down as one of the finest achievements of Indian diplomacy."[6] There also is evidence that the Indian business community supports the deal as a means of contributing to India's rise as a major power and of bolstering the country's energy security. In November 2007, 23 former Indian military chiefs, senior bureaucrats, and scientists signed an open letter to Parliament urging approval of the pact so as to remove the "crippling constraints" India suffers due to international regimes that deny it high-technology goods.[7] With multiple admonitions from senior U.S. government officials in 2008 that the time needed to consummate the deal was growing short, many Indian commentators joined in pressing their government to avoid an uncertain future by moving quickly to finalize the pact. Some see India's nuclear power industry in dire need of uranium supplies that can only come from the international market. Uranium shortages appear to be hampering India nuclear power sector, which is running at or below half capacity.[8]

In New Delhi, where the executive can enter international agreements without parliamentary approval, Prime Minister Singh's Congress Party-dominated cabinet endorsed the agreement text immediately upon its finalization. His UPA coalition government then set about assuring domestic skeptics that the autonomy of the country's nuclear weapons program would be maintained and that all key commitments previously made to parliament were being adhered to, including those related to plutonium reprocessing and nuclear weapons testing rights, as well as assured and uninterrupted supplies of nuclear fuel even if the agreement is terminated.[9] Later, in response to continued controversy over whether or not

India's freedom to conduct future nuclear weapons tests is restricted by the agreement, External Affairs Minister Pranab Mukherjee told Parliament, "There is nothing in the bilateral agreement that would tie the hands of a future government or legally constrain its options."[10]

Despite such assurances, ensuing debate over the deal divided the New Delhi establishment as much as any issue in the country's history. Prime Minister Singh may have underestimated the degree of anti-Americanism and anti-imperialism held by his coalition's communist Left Front allies, who provided his ruling coalition with crucial parliamentary support. In August 2007, senior leaders of the main opposition Bharatiya Janata Party (BJP) reiterated their party's "reservations" about the nuclear deal and its potentially negative impact on India's nuclear weapons program. Yet India's communist parties went much further in their criticisms, issuing a joint statement which called the 123 Agreement "flawed" and claiming that it "must be seen as a crucial step to lock India into the U.S. global strategic designs." Their view is not limited to those with communist sentiments: One former Indian national security advisor asserted that while a vast majority of the country's rising urban middle class firmly favors closer India-U.S. ties, it "will not tolerate a subservient relationship" and retains significant differences in approaches to third parties such as Iran and Pakistan.[11]

The political squabbling in New Delhi put the nuclear deal on lengthy hold. In October 2007, Prime Minister Singh informed President Bush that "certain difficulties have arisen with respect to the operationalization" of the deal.[12] Hopes for consummation were revived in November when the Left Front allowed the Indian government to begin talks with the IAEA. Yet, by year's end, the communist leadership was again threatening to withdraw support for the ruling coalition unless talks were halted. December negotiations with the IAEA reportedly were hampered by "technical glitches" related to India's demand for "unconditional" guarantees of fuel supplies in perpetuity. External Affairs Minister Mukherjee insisted in the first days of 2008 that New Delhi had not given up on the deal and was continuing with its efforts to resolve the face-off with the Left Front.[13]

Nonproliferation experts have been consistent in their opposition to the nuclear deal, believing it will significantly damage the global nonproliferation regime and facilitate an Asian nuclear arms race. Some have asserted that the text of the 123 Agreement disregards the legislative intent of the Hyde Act, especially in the area of continued supplies of nuclear fuel to India even if that country tests a nuclear weapons and the agreement is terminated. Others warn that NSG endorsement of an exception for India will "virtually ensure the demise of global nuclear export restraints."[14] A January 2008 letter to NSG officials endorsed by more than 130 nonproliferation experts and nongovernmental organizations argued that India's commitments thus far did not justify making "far-reaching" exceptions to international nonproliferation rules and norms. The document asked that NSG members consider the potential costs of granting to India any special safeguards exceptions and urged the body to make clear that all nuclear trade with India would cease upon that country's resumption of nuclear testing for any reason.[15] Opponents warn that the already weakened international nonproliferation regime may be mortally damaged by the proposed alteration of international norms. Particular criticism arises in the area of future nuclear testing, which nonproliferation advocates say is likely to be facilitated by the deal.[16]

At least one nonproliferation advocate in Congress concluded that the 123 Agreement "is not consistent with [congressional] requirements and restrictions" and would "deeply damage" the global nonproliferation regime. He identified the issues of nuclear testing, assurances of fuel supply, and the reprocessing of U.S.-origin nuclear material three core concerns.[17] During a February 2008 hearing, Secretary of State Condoleezza Rice assured the House Foreign Affairs Committee (HFAC) that the U.S. government will support India in the NSG only if any resulting exemptions are fully consistent with the provisions of the Hyde Act. Nonproliferation advocates say Secretary Rice's pledge will require a shift in U.S. policy, in particular by placing conditions on India's ability to engage in global nuclear trade.[18] Representative Howard Berman, the HFAC Chairman and a supporter of the initiative, finds it "incomprehensible" that the Administration would seek or accept an NSG exemption that omits many of the conditions contained in the Hyde Act. He says such an exemption would be inconsistent with U.S. law, be harmful to U.S. business interests, and undermine U.S. nonproliferation objectives. In line with previous Administration assurances to Congress, he expects U.S. negotiators to reject any NSG exemption "that does not faithfully reflect all of the Hyde Act conditions."[19]

Current Status

Left Front leaders maintained their adamant opposition to any "operationalization" of the nuclear deal, which for them meant the government should not seek IAEA Board of Governors approval for the draft agreement on safeguarding India's nuclear facilities. They saw Prime Minister Singh following a timeline set by the Bush Administration at the expense of India's national interests, and they threatened to withdraw support for the UPA coalition.[20] There were signs in May that the U.S. government had wound down its efforts to persuade NSG members to provide an exemption for India. In mid-May, U.S. officials were saying the window for completing the necessary steps had become "very narrow" and, by June, reports of the deal's outright failure were appearing.[21]

On July 8, the communist parties formally withdrew their support for the Congress-led ruling coalition, saying they opposed a "strategic embrace with the most aggressive power in the world today."[22] Days later, with his domestic political standing bolstered by a regional party that could partially compensate for the loss of Left Front support (see "Domestic Political Realignment" section below), Prime Minister Singh was able to attend a G8 summit meeting in Japan with renewed optimism about the nuclear deal's prospects. New Delhi moved quickly to obtain IAEA approval by submitting a draft safeguards accord and, in mid-July, Foreign Secretary Menon was joined in Vienna by Under Secretary of State William Burns for consultations with IAEA Secretary-General Mohammed ElBaradei, an avid proponent of the deal. Indian officials were then dispatched to numerous foreign capitals to lobby IAEA and NSG member governments for support.[23] President Bush agrees with Prime Minister Singh that the pact should be finalized "as expeditiously as possible." Some observers, already viewing the deal overly favoring of India, see little reason for the U.S. government to move precipitously to finalize it.[24]

On August 1, the IAEA Board of Governors approved the safeguards accord with India. The IAEA Secretary-General insisted that the accord met all of the body's legal requirements and was of "indefinite duration."[25] The next major step toward consummation is obtaining an adjustment of NSG guidelines so as to allow India to purchase nuclear fuel and technologies on the international market. Representatives from all 45 NSG member states are scheduled to gather in Vienna on August 21. New Delhi has been firm in demanding a "clean and unconditional exemption" from the NSG, one that would waive all guidelines normally applied to non-nuclear weapons states under the NPT.[26] Yet unconditional NSG approval may not be a given, as some member states may be hesitant to endorse nuclear trade with a country that is not signatory to the NPT and that has tested nuclear weapons. Japan, for example, recently has expressed such concerns. Some reports indicate that smaller member states may seek to add amendments (conditions) such as requests that India join the NPT and/or CTBT, or that safeguards be made permanent regardless of the status of fuel supply.[27]

The text of a draft U.S. proposal for the NSG, circulated on August 6, has come under fire from nonproliferation advocates for its alleged weakening of NSG credibility and its failure to include clear statements that would end all cooperation in the event of a future Indian nuclear weapons test; prohibit the transfer to India of sensitive processing, enrichment, or heavy water technologies; and call upon India to stop producing fissile materials. According to one analysis, the U.S. draft contains language contrary to the 2006 Hyde Act.[28]

While top U.S. officials withheld comment on India's internal political processes, there remains a sense of urgency in Washington, with the Bush Administration (and many in Congress) eager to see the deal consummated during its remaining term in office. Some analysts warned that a failure to submit the 123 Agreement to Congress by mid-summer would require starting the difficult negotiation process anew in 2009, perhaps involving a Democratic U.S. Administration and/or Congress that might be more favorable to arguments made by nonproliferation advocates. Former Under Secretary of State Burns has himself opined that a future U.S. presidential administration is highly unlikely to replicate the deal in its present form, meaning that "the only opportunity to realize the potential of this deal is with the administration of President Bush."[29]

Domestic Political Realignment

Domestic debate in India on the pending U.S.-India nuclear deal triggered the most serious crisis faced by the UPA government since it came to power in May 2004. In fact, the turmoil nearly led to a collapse of the ruling coalition and early elections as both Prime Minister Singh and the Left Front parties maintained staunch and mutually incompatible positions on the deal. The August 2007 release of the 123 Agreement text brought an uproar in the Indian Parliament — effectively shutting the body down at times — with numerous lawmakers complaining that the deal would restrict India's ability to test nuclear weapons in the future and threaten its foreign policy independence.[30] An urgent meeting between Singh and communist leader Prakash Karat ended without reconciliation, and the Left Front warned the central government of "serious consequences" if it moved forward with the plan.[31]

To facilitate what could onlybe an interim truce between the Congress partyand the Left Front, the government created a panel of government officials, politicians, and scientists to "study" the nuclear deal. Communist leaders agreed to join the 15member panel, which met for the first time in September 2007. Ten rounds of talks were held over ensuing months, but neither side budged from its strident position. With Prime Minister Singh and Congress Party chief Gandhi seeming to veer from strident support for the deal to an acceptance of its potentially permanent hibernation in only a matter of days during October, the New Delhi government's credibility came into question.[32] By March 2008, communist leaders again were openly threatening to withdraw support for the UPA coalition and so bring an early end to the government's term, which is scheduled to terminate in May 2009.

Indications arose in June that Prime Minister Singh would push for approval of U.S.-India civil nuclear cooperation despite Left Front opposition. Talk of early elections again increased. Yet, on July 8, the same day India's communist parties formally withdrew their support for the Congress-led ruling coalition, the regional powerhouse Samajwadi Party (SP) formally announced that its 39 parliamentarians would support — but not join — the UPA. It brushed off criticism by the Bahujan Samaj Party (BSP), its Uttar Pradesh political rivals, that the nuclear deal was "anti-Muslim."[33] (The SP and BSP are both reliant on the state's large Muslim electorate; Muslims account for about one-fifth of Uttar Pradesh's population.) As conveyed by SP leader Amar Singh, "For us, communalism is a bigger danger than imperialism. Advani is a bigger danger than Bush."[34] Some analysts view the Congress Party's embrace of the SP as evidence of a rightward shift in national politics.[35]

With a partial replacement for the Left Front secured, the government set a July 22 date for a confidence vote, which requires the 543-member Lok Sabha (lower house) to vote yes or no on a motion expressing confidence in the ruling coalition. The opposition-leading BJP mobilized for the perceived opportunity to topple the UPA government and trigger early elections in which it might prevail. As the date neared and the anticipated outcome remained unclear, the Congress Party used the advantages of incumbency to entice wavering parliamentarians. Such efforts reportedly included offering ministerships and other perquisites to gain the support of smaller regional parties, some of them comprised of but one Lok Sabhan.[36] On July 22, after two days of raucous parliamentary debate, the Singh government survived the vote by a wider-than-expected margin of 275-256, with 11 abstentions, thus averting early elections. Yet the victory may have come at some cost: bribery charges were immediate and included claims by BJP legislators that they had been offered huge sums of cash to abstain from voting. Moreover, the UPA may be haunted by deal-making with smaller parties of questionable reliability.[37]

Economic Woes

India's economy has in recent months been rocked by soaring inflation, and power shortages have sparked public outrage and protests. In June, the New Delhi government took a political risk in announcing a ten percent hike in fuel prices. The move triggered street protests in several states, including strikes that virtually shut down the Andhra Pradesh and West Bengal. Investor concerns about soaring gasoline costs likely contributed to a 3.3% one-day drop in the value of the Sensex index of the Bombay Stock Exchange. Indeed, a sharp increase in food and fuel costs may counterbalance recent growth in the Indian economy.[38] In mid-June, inflation rates reached a 13-year high of more than 11% and prices for basic foodstuffs reportedly rose by as much as 50% in some smaller Indian cities in less than six months. The Reserve Bank of India responded by raising its benchmark lending rate to the highest level in six years. Inflationary pressures continued throughout July and, in early August, breached 12%, due mainly to soaring food prices. The central government's deteriorating public finances, due mainly to rising subsidies, are threatening India's investment grade credit ratings. Power shortages have forced some key state governments, including Maharashtra, Andhra Pradesh, and Karnataka, to strictly ration commercial electricity supplies.[39]

Some observers have expressed optimism that, with the Left Front no longer a central factor for the central government's decision making, stalled economic reform efforts could move forward with the help of the pro-business Samajwadi Party, potentially boosting rates of foreign investment. In late July, Finance Minister P. Chidambaram pledged to revive reforms, especially in the banking and insurance sectors. Yet it is considered likely that more urgent economic problems and impending national elections will combine to keep such efforts on the back burner.[40] Despite serious difficulties, some more optimistic commentators offer that, because the shocks are largely external, and high investment rates persist, India's economy can be expected to continue to perform strongly.[41]

Terrorism and Deteriorating Relations with Pakistan

Among the top goals of Indian officials in 2008 has been gauging the new Pakistani government's commitment to the bilateral peace process. Within this modest context, the outcome of Pakistan's February national election was viewed as generally positive.[42] However, ensuing months have seen a deterioration of India-Pakistan relations, and some in New Delhi express frustration that the new civilian leaders in Islamabad have little influence over Pakistan's powerful military and intelligence agencies.[43] In August, the Indian national security advisor expressed worry at the possibly imminent removal from office of Pakistani President Pervez Musharraf, saying such a development would "leave radical extremist outfits with freedom to do what they like" in the region.[44]

In May, India accused Pakistan of committing multiple cease-fire and territorial violations along the Kashmiri Line of Control (LOC); one incident left an Indian soldier dead. June visits to Islamabad by External Affairs Minister Mukherjee, and later by Pakistan's foreign minister to New Delhi, were cordial and appeared to get the peace process back on track, but produced no new initiatives. Then, on July 7, a suicide car bomb killed 58 people, including four Indian nationals, at the Indian Embassy in Kabul, Afghanistan. Afghan and Indian officials later claimed to have evidence that Pakistan's intelligence agency was complicit in the attack, a charge reportedly echoed by the U.S. government. Late July serial bomb attacks in the cities of Bangalore and Ahmedabad killed scores of people and triggered heightened suspicions of foreign involvement in terrorist acts inside India.[45] Indian security officials also claim that Pakistan's Inter-Services Intelligence Directorate (ISI) is poised to send 800 religious militants into India.[46]

On July 21, Foreign Secretary Menon met with his Pakistani counterpart in New Delhi to launch the fifth round of the bilateral Composite Dialogue. Following the meeting, the Menon warned that recent events — culminating in embassy bombing had brought the peace process "under stress." Blunt language again followed a high-level meeting in Sri Lanka, where Menon suggested that India-Pakistan relations were at a four-year low ebb.[47] Along with the Kabul bombing, Indians widely suspect Pakistani complicity in recent terrorist attacks inside India. At the same time, further lethal shooting incidents along the LOC in July exacerbated bilateral tensions. When the Pakistani Senate passed a resolution on the situation in India's Jammu and Kashmir state (see below), an Indian official called the move "gross interference" in India's internal affairs. The exchange was soon repeated when the Pakistani foreign minister decried "excessive and unwarranted use of force" in Kashmir by the Indian government, a charge rejected as unhelpful by New Delhi. Moreover, New Delhi's progress in an initiative that would allow India to purchase nuclear materials and technologies on the international market spurred Islamabad to warn of a potential new nuclear arms race on the Asian subcontinent.[48]

Renewed Conflict in Kashmir

In late June, a state government decision to grant 99 acres of land to a trust for the popular Amarnath Hindu shrine in the Jammu and Kashmir state sparked violent protests by Muslims who say the move seeks to change the demographic balance in their Muslim-majoritystate. Public expressions of anger included a withdrawal from the state's coalition government by the influential regional People's Democratic Party and the subsequent resignation of Chief Minister Ghulam Nabi Azad, which placed the state under federal rule. Azad had responded to resistance by revoking the land grant decision, but protests did not subside and later spread to the Hindu-majority Jammu region. Dozens of people have been killed and hundreds wounded in clashes with police over more than one month of unrest.

Many of the state's Hindus were upset by the government's reversal; their efforts to block the sole road connecting the Kashmir Valley from the rest of India have left the capital of Srinagar short of food, fuel, and medical supplies. A high-level federal government meeting convened by Prime Minister Singh in early August concluded that a dialogue process was needed and would benefit from the active support of the opposition BJP, whose Hindu nationalist leanings may help to fuel the resentments the state's Hindu minority. Yet worsening strife, with at least 19 protesters killed and up to 300 security troops injured on August 11-12 alone, has led some to warn that the state could fall into "communal meltdown," squandering years of improvement.[49]

A July 2008 public opinion survey conducted in both India and Pakistan found a majority of respondents expressing an openness to a range of possible outcomes for Kashmir, including outright independence. While such an outcome was described as "unacceptable" by half of the Indians surveyed, the pollsters concluded that, "If a majority of all Kashmiris were to choose independence, a majority of Indians and Pakistanis would find such independence at least tolerable."[50]

Other Recent Developments

On August 12, at least 19 protesters were killed and up to 300 security troops injured in two days of clashes in Kashmir.

On July 26, some 53 people were killed and more than 120 wounded by 16 small bomb explosions in Ahmedabad, Gujarat.

On July 25, two people were killed by 7 small bomb explosions in Bangalore, Karnataka.

On July 24, suspected separatist militants killed nine people, including a woman and her four children, in Indian Kashmir.

On July 21, Foreign Secretary Menon met with his Pakistani counterpart in New Delhi to launch the fifth round of the bilateral Composite Dialogue.

On July 19, at least nine soldiers were killed by a landmine explosion near Srinagar, Kashmir.

On July 18, the India-Pakistan Working Group on confidence-building measures for Kashmir met in Islamabad.

On July 16, least 20 special commando police officers were killed when their vehicle struck a landmine planted by suspected Maoist militants in Orissa.

On July 9, President Bush met with Prime Minister Singh on the sidelines of the G8 Summit in Japan.

On July 7, a suicide car bomb killed 58 people, including four Indian nationals, at the Indian Embassy in Kabul, Afghanistan.

On July 2, 11 separatist militants and an army officer were killed in a gunbattle in Indian Kashmir.

On July 1, National Security Advisor Narayanan paid a visit to Tehran for talks with top Iranian leaders.

Also on July 1, at least six people were killed after suspected separatist militants exploded a bomb in a crowded Assam market.

On June 30, the New Delhi government unveiled India's first-ever national action plan to address climate change.

On June 29, at least 39 elite Indian anti-insurgency troops were feared drowned after their boat capsized following an attack by Maoist militants in Orissa.

On June 27, External Affairs Minister Mukherjee met with his Pakistani counterpart in New Delhi, where the two leaders agreed to launch the fifth round of the Composite Dialogue in July.

On June 24, Indian and Pakistan officials held a third meeting of their Joint Anti-Terrorism Mechanism in Islamabad.

On June 16, a Singaporean national was sentenced to three years in U.S. federal prison for conspiring with Indian government officials to illegally ship controlled U.S. computer technology to India for use in military missile systems.

Context of the U.S.-India Relationship

Background

U.S. and congressional interests in India cover a wide spectrum of issues, ranging from the militarized dispute with Pakistan and weapons proliferation to concerns about regional security, terrorism, human rights, health, energy, and trade and investment opportunities. In the 1990s, India-U.S. relations were particularly affected by the demise of the Soviet Union — India's main trading partner and most reliable source of economic and military assistance for most of the Cold War — and New Delhi's resulting need to diversify its international relationships. Also significant were India's adoption of significant economic policy reforms beginning in 1991, a deepening bitterness between India and Pakistan over Kashmir, and signs of a growing Indian preoccupation with China as a potential long-term strategic rival. With the fading of Cold War constraints, the United States and India began exploring the possibilities for a more normalized relationship between the world's two largest democracies. Throughout the 1990s, however, regional rivalries, separatist tendencies, and sectarian tensions continued to divert India's attention and resources from economic and social development. Fallout from these unresolved problems — particularly nuclear proliferation and human rights issues — presented major irritants in bilateral relations.

India's May 1998 nuclear tests were an unwelcome surprise and seen to be a policy failure in Washington, and they spurred then-Deputy Secretary of State Strobe Talbott to launch a series of meetings with Indian External Affairs Minister Jaswant Singh in an effort to bring New Delhi more in line with U.S. arms control and nonproliferation goals. While this proximate purpose went unfulfilled, the two officials soon engaged a broader agenda on the entire scope of U.S.-India relations, eventually meeting fourteen times in seven different countries over a two-year period. The Talbott-Singh talks were considered the most extensive U.S.-India engagement up to that time and likely enabled circumstances in which the United States could play a key role in defusing the 1999 Kargil crisis, as well as laying the groundwork for a landmark U.S. presidential visit in 2000.

President Bill Clinton's March 2000 visit to South Asia seemed a major U.S. initiative to improve relations with India. One outcome was a Joint Statement in which the two countries pledged to "deepen the India-American partnership in tangible ways."[51] A U.S.-India Joint Working Group on Counterterrorism was established that year and continues to meet regularly. During his subsequent visit to the United States later in 2000, Prime Minister Atal Bihari Vajpayee addressed a joint session of Congress and issued a second Joint Statement with President Clinton agreeing to cooperate on arms control, terrorism, and HIV/AIDS.[52]

In the wake of the September 2001 terrorist attacks on the United States, India took the immediate and unprecedented step of offering to the United States full cooperation and the use of India's bases for counterterrorism operations. Engagement was accelerated after a November 2001 meeting between President Bush and Prime Minister Vajpayee, when the two leaders agreed to greatly expand U.S.India cooperation on a wide range of issues, including regional security, space and scientific collaboration, civilian nuclear safety, and broadened economic ties.[53] Notable progress has come in the area of security cooperation, with an increasing focus on counterterrorism, joint military exercises, and arms sales. In late 2001, the U.S.-India Defense Policy Group met in New Delhi for the first time since India's 1998 nuclear tests and outlined a defense partnership based on regular and high-level policy dialogue.

Prime Minister Manmohan Singh paid a landmark July 2005 visit to Washington, where what may be the most significant joint U.S.-India statement to date was issued.[54] In March 2006, President Bush spent three days in India, discussed further strengthening a bilateral "global partnership," and issued another Joint Statement.[55] The Bush Administration has vowed to "help India become a major world power in the 21st century," and U.S.-India relations are today conducted under the rubric of three major "dialogue" areas: strategic (including global issues and defense), economic (including trade, finance, commerce, and environment), and energy. President Bush's 2002 *National Security Strategy of the United States* stated that "U.S. interests require a strong relationship with India." The 2006 version claims that "India now is poised to shoulder global obligations in cooperation with the United States in a way befitting a major power."[56] In the course of an annual assessment of global threats, Director of National Intelligence Mike McConnell said,

> We expect India's growing confidence on the world stage as a result of its sustained high rates of economic growth will make New Delhi a more effective partner of the United States but also a more formidable interlocutor in areas of disagreement, particularly in the WTO.[57]

In late 2007, Under Secretary of State Burns, who traveled to New Delhi at least eight times over a two-year period, penned an article lauding stronger U.S.-India relations while also identifying "considerable hurdles" to achieving an effective "global partnership." Foremost among these are terrorism, narcotics trafficking, and nuclear proliferation, which he avers must be dealt with through stronger bilateral security ties that will include defense sales.[58] At a 2007 U.S.-India business conference in Washington, Secretary of State Rice laid out the perspective that,

> We in America look to the rise of India as an opportunity, a chance to work with a great fellow democracy to share not only the benefits of the international system, but indeed, the burdens and the responsibilities of maintaining it, of strengthening it, and defending it. We are eager to continue charting a global partnership with India, one that addresses the global challenges upon which the safety and success of every nation now depends: stemming nuclear proliferation, fighting terrorism, combating disease, protecting the environment, supporting education and upward mobility, expanding economic development, and promoting freedom under the rule of law.[59]

Some analysts, however, see great potential but little likelihood of India becoming a major global power in the foreseeable future. Despite possession of a large, youthful, entrepreneurial population, a booming national economy, and growing power projection capabilities in the military realm, there remains much doubt about the capacity of India's leaders to engage in effective long-term strategic thinking and policy making. One senior Washington-based India-watcher has opined that, "The Indian strategic community is hopelessly unstrategic," and that its political community is "too domestically focused," thus precluding India's emergence as a substantive major power. Some Indian analysts agree that their national leaders lack a "coherent national grand strategy."[60]

Recognition of India's increasing stature and importance — and of the growing political influence some 2.3 million Indian-Americans — is found in the U.S. Congress, where the India and Indian-American Caucus is now the largest of all country-specific caucuses. Over the past seven years, legal Indian immigrants have come to the United States at a more rapid rate than any other group. In 2005 and 2006, the Indian-American community, relatively wealthy, geographically dispersed, and well-entrenched in several U.S. business sectors, conducted a major (and apparently successful) lobbying effort to encourage congressional passage of legislation to enable U.S.-India civil nuclear cooperation.[61]

India's Regional Relations

India is geographically dominant in both South Asia and the Indian Ocean region. While all of South Asia's smaller continental states (Pakistan, Bangladesh, Nepal, and Bhutan) share borders with India, none share borders with each other. The country possesses the region's largest economy and, with more than one billion inhabitants, is by far the most populous on the Asian Subcontinent. The United States has a keen interest in South Asian stability, perhaps especially with regard to the India-Pakistan conflict nexus and nuclear weapons dyad, and so closely monitors India's regional relationships.

Pakistan[62]

Decades of militarized tensions and territorial disputes between India and Pakistan arguably have hamstrung economic and social development in both countries while also precluding establishment of effective regional economic or security institutions. Seemingly incompatible national identities contributed to both wars and to the nuclearization of the Asian Subcontinent, with the nuclear weapons capabilities of both countries becoming overt in 1998. Since that time, a central aspect of U.S. policy in South Asia has been prevention of interstate conflict that could destabilize the region and lead to nuclear war. In 2004, New Delhi and Islamabad launched their most recent comprehensive effort to reduce tensions and resolve outstanding disputes, an effort that has to date resulted in modest, but still meaningful successes. New Delhi acknowledges that a stable Pakistan is in India's interests. At the same time, however, many top Indian leaders are convinced that Pakistan has long been and remains the main source India's significant domestic terrorism problems. They continue to blame Islamabad for maintaining an "infrastructure of terror" and for actively supporting terrorist groups such as Jaish-e-Mohammed and Laskar-e-Taiba that are held responsible for attacks inside India.[63]

Current Status. The halting India-Pakistan peace initiative was revived in mid-2008 after becoming moribund in the final months of 2007, when domestic political and security crises diverted the Pakistani government's attention away from its relations with India. New Delhi has watched the domestic turmoil of its neighbor and long-time rival with great interest, but little public comment. India takes pains to avoid even the perception of meddling in Pakistan's domestic political problems and so has been reticent and extremely cautious in its relevant public statements. A destabilized Pakistan represents a major security concern for New Delhi, but at the same time history shows that as Pakistan's internal difficulties grow, Pakistani interference in Indian affairs tends to decrease. Some view India's relatively muted response as strong evidence that the two countries have finally become "dehyphenated." Others call on New Delhi to reach out to the new Islamabad government with conciliatory gestures that could facilitate the consolidation of democratization in Pakistan.[64]

In 2006, India and Pakistan agreed to open a second Kashmiri bus route and to allow new truck service to facilitate trade in Kashmir (the new bus service began in June of that year). Subsequent "Composite Dialogue" talks were held to discuss militarized territorial disputes, terrorism and narcotics, and cultural exchanges, but high hopes for a settlement of differences over the Siachen Glacier have been dashed with repeated sessions ending without progress. Multiple sessions on the Tubal navigation project/Wullar barrage water dispute similarly have ended without forward movement.

The serial bombing of Bombay commuter trains in July 2006 killed nearly 200 people and injured many hundreds more. With suspicions regarding the involvement of Pakistan-based groups, New Delhi suspended talks with Islamabad pending an investigation. However, at a September meeting on the sidelines of a Nonaligned Movement summit in Cuba, Prime Minister Singh and Pakistani President Musharraf announced a resumption of formal peace negotiations and also decided to implement a new Joint Anti-Terrorism Mechanism. Soon after, however, Bombay's top police official said the 7/11 train bombings were planned byPakistan's intelligence services and, in October 2006, Prime Minister Singh himself said India had "credible evidence" of Pakistani involvement. (To date, India is not known to have gone public with or shared with Pakistan any incriminating evidence of Pakistani government involvement in the Bombay bombings.)

The Composite Dialogue resumed with a third round of foreign secretary-level talks when Foreign Secretary Shiv Shankar Menon hosted a New Delhi visit by his Pakistani counterpart in late 2006. No progress came on outstanding territorial disputes, but the two officials did give shape to the new anti-terrorism mechanism. Such a mechanism is controversial in India, where some analysts are skeptical about the efficacy of institutional engagement with Pakistan in this issue-area even as Islamabad is suspected of complicity in anti-India terrorism.

Indian External Affairs Minister Mukherjee met with his Pakistani counterpart in Islamabad in early 2007 for the first such visit in more than a year. The two men reviewed past progress and planned for a new round of talks. In February of that year, two bombs exploded on an Indian segment of the Samjhauta [Friendship] Express train linking Lahore, Pakistan, with Delhi. Resulting fires killed 68 people, most of them Pakistanis. Days later, Mukherjee hosted Kasuri in New Delhi, where the two men reaffirmed a bilateral commitment to the peace process despite the apparent effort to subvert it. While India refused a Pakistani request to undertake a joint investigation into that attack, the two countries did sign an agreement to reduce the risk of accidental nuclear war.

The new India-Pakistan anti-terrorism mechanism met for the first time in March 2007 and produced a joint statement in which both governments agreed to use the forum for exchanging information about investigations of and/or efforts to prevent terrorist acts on either side of the shared border, and to meet quarterly while immediately conveying urgent information. Hopes that the Samjhauta train bombing would provide a fitting "test case" apparently were dashed, however, when India declined to share relevant investigative information with Pakistan. Moreover, Indian officials were unhappy with Islamabad's insistence that the "freedom struggle" underway in Kashmir should not be treated as terrorism under this framework. Still, the continuing engagement even after a major terrorist attack was widely viewed as evidence that the bilateral peace process had gained a sturdy momentum.

A fourth round of the Composite Dialogue also was launched in March 2007, when the two foreign ministers met again in Islamabad. No new agreements were reached, but both officials lauded improved bilateral relations and held "the most sustained and intensive dialogue" ever on the Kashmir problem.[65] A fourth round of bilateral talks on economic and commercial cooperation held in August 2007 ended with agreements to facilitate importation of cement from Pakistan and tea from India, among others. Indian and Pakistani officials also held technical-level talks on the modalities of cross-border movement.

In September 2007, Pakistan issued a formal protest and expressed "deep concern" in response to the Indian government's announced intention to open the disputed territory of the Siachen Glacier to tourism, saying the region was "illegally occupied" by Indian troops in 1984 and its final status has yet to be determined due to an "inflexible Indian attitude."[66] October saw a second meeting of the Joint Anti-Terrorism Mechanism in New Delhi, where the two sides shared new information on terrorism and agreed to continue mutual investigatory cooperation.

Following a November 2007 imposition of emergency rule in Pakistan, political crisis in Islamabad is widely seen as having put what are at least temporary brakes on the bilateral peace process, and has also brought into question the efficacy of India's seeking to strike agreements with a Pakistani leader (Musharraf) whose political legitimacy and longevity in office are in doubt. New Delhi lauded Pakistan's February 2008 electoral processes and expressed preparedness to resume the Composite Dialogue once a new government is in place in Islamabad. The leader of Pakistan's leading political party, Asif Zardari, expressed hope that India-Pakistan economic ties should be strengthened even without a settlement of the Kashmir issue, saying Kashmir is a situation upon which Pakistan and India "can agree to disagree." Prime Minister Singh has invited Pakistan's new civilian leaders to put the past behind them and build a new cooperative relationship with India.[67]

In May 2008, External Affairs Minister Mukherjee met with his Pakistani counterpart in Islamabad for a review of the fourth round of the Composite Dialogue. The two leaders reaffirmed their determination to not let terrorism impede the bilateral peace process. A month later, the new Pakistani Foreign Minister, Shah Mehmood Qureshi, made his first official trip to New Delhi, where it was agreed that the fifth round of the Composite Dialogue would take place in July. June 2008 also saw the bilateral anti-terrorism mechanism meet for only the third time in nearly two years. Among the top goals of Indian officials has been gauging the new Pakistani government's commitment to the bilateral peace process. Within this modest context, the outcomes have been viewed as positive.[68]

Background. Three wars — in 1947-48, 1965, and 1971 — and a constant state of military preparedness on both sides of the border have marked six decades of bitter rivalry between India and Pakistan. The bloody and acrimonious nature of the 1947 partition of British India and continuing violence in Kashmir remain major sources of interstate tensions. Despite the existence of widespread poverty across South Asia, both India and Pakistan have built large defense establishments — including nuclear weapons capability and ballistic missile programs — at the cost of economic and social development. The two countries reportedly continue to stockpile a combined 11 million landmines and up to 2,000 square kilometers of India's Jammu and Kashmir state may remain mined.[69] The nuclear weapons capabilities of India and Pakistan became overt in May 1998, magnifying greatly the potential dangers of a fourth war. Although a bilateral peace process has been underway for more than four years, little substantive progress has been made toward resolving the Kashmir issue, and New Delhi continues to be rankled by what it calls Islamabad's insufficient effort to end Islamic militancy that affects India.

The Kashmir problem is itself rooted in claims by both countries to the former princely state, now divided by a military Line of Control (LOC) into the Indian state of Jammu and Kashmir and Pakistan-controlled Azad [Free] Kashmir (see "The Kashmir Issue," below). Normal relations between New Delhi and Islamabad were severed in December 2001 after a terrorist attack on the Indian Parliament was blamed on Pakistan-supported Islamic militants. Other lethal attacks on Indian civilians spurred Indian leaders to call for a "decisive war," but intense international diplomatic engagement, including multiple trips to the region by high-level U.S. officials, apparently persuaded India to refrain from attacking.[70] In October 2002, the two countries ended a tense, ten-month military standoff at their shared border, but there remained no high-level diplomatic dialogue between India and Pakistan (a July 2001 summit meeting in the Indian city of Agra had failed to produce any movement toward a settlement of the bilateral dispute).

In April 2003, Prime Minister Vajpayee extended a symbolic "hand of friendship" to Pakistan. The initiative resulted in slow, but perceptible progress in confidence-building, and within months full diplomatic relations between the two countries were restored. Islamabad responded positively and, in November, took its own initiatives, most significantly the offer of a cease-fire along the Kashmir LOC. A major breakthrough in bilateral relations came at the close of a January 2004 summit session of the South Asian Association for Regional Cooperation in Islamabad. After a meeting between Vajpayee and Pakistani President Musharraf — their first since July 2001 — the two leaders agreed to re-engage a "composite dialogue" to bring about "peaceful settlement of all bilateral issues, including Jammu and Kashmir, to the satisfaction of both sides." A May 2004 change of governments in New Delhi had no effect on the expressed commitment of both sides to carry on the process of mid- and high-level discussions. Some analysts believe that increased people-to-people contacts have significantly altered public perceptions in both countries and may have acquired permanent momentum. Others are less optimistic about the respective governments' long-term commitment to dispute resolution. Moreover, an apparent new U.S. embrace of India has fueled Pakistan's anxieties about the regional balance of power.

China

India and China together account for one-third of the world's population, and are seen to be rising 21st century powers and potential strategic rivals. The two countries fought a brief but intense border war in 1962 that left China in control of large swaths of territory still claimed by India. Today, India accuses China of illegitimately occupying nearly15,000 square miles of Indian territory in Kashmir, while China lays claim to 35,000 square miles in the northeastern Indian state of Arunachal Pradesh. The 1962 clash ended a previously friendly relationship between the two leaders of the Cold War "nonaligned movement" and left many Indians feeling shocked and betrayed. While Sino-Indian relations have warmed considerably in recent years, the two countries have yet to reach a final boundary agreement. Adding to New Delhi's sense of insecurity have been suspicions regarding China's long-term nuclear weapons capabilities and strategic intentions in South and Southeast Asia. A strategic orientation focused on China appears to have affected the course and scope of New Delhi's own nuclear weapons, ballistic missile, and other power projection programs.[71]

Beijing's military and economic support for Pakistan — support that is widely understood to have included nuclear weapons- and missile-related transfers — is a major and ongoing source of friction; past Chinese support for Pakistan's Kashmir position has added to the discomfort of Indian leaders. New Delhi takes note of Beijing's security relations with neighboring Burma and the construction of military and port facilities on the Indian Ocean.[72] The two countries also have competed for trade partners and energy resources to feed their rapidly growing economies; India's relative poverty puts New Delhi at a significant disadvantage in such competition.[73]

Analysts taking a realist political theory perspective view China as an external balancer in the South Asian subsystem, with Beijing's material support for Islamabad allowing Pakistan to challenge the aspiring regional hegemony of a more powerful India. More wary observers, especially in India, see Chinese support for Pakistan as a key aspect of Beijing's perceived policy of "encirclement," or constraint, of India as a means of preventing or delaying New Delhi's ability to challenge Beijing's region-wide influence.

Despite historic and strategic differences, high-level exchanges between India and China regularly include statements that there exists no fundamental conflict of interest between the two countries. During a landmark 1993 visit to Beijing, then-Prime Minister Narasimha Rao signed an agreement to reduce troops and maintain peace along the Line of Actual Control that divides the two countries' forces at the disputed border. Numerous rounds of border talks and joint working group meetings aimed at reaching a final settlement have been held since 1981 — a dozen of these since both countries appointed special representatives in 2003 — with New Delhi and Beijing agreeing to move forward in other issue-areas even as territorial claims remain unresolved. Some skeptical Indian analysts believe China is using the so far unavailing border dialogue as "diplomatic cover to be intractable and revanchist."[74]

A 2003 visit to Beijing by then-Prime Minister Vajpayee was viewed as marking a period of much improved relations. In 2004, India's army chief visited Beijing to discuss deepening bilateral defense cooperation and a first-ever India-China strategic dialogue was later held in New Delhi. Military-to-military contacts have included modest but unprecedented combined naval and army exercises. During Chinese Prime Minister Wen Jiabao's 2005 visit to New Delhi, India and China inked 11 new agreements and vowed to launch a "strategic partnership" to include broadened defense links and efforts to expand economic relations.[75] In a move that eased border tensions, China formally recognized Indian sovereignty over the former kingdom of Sikkim, and India reiterated its view that Tibet is a part of China.[76] Moreover, in 2006, dubbed the "Year of India-China Friendship," the two countries formally agreed to cooperate in securing overseas oil resources. In July of that year, India and China reopened the Nathu La border crossing for local trade (the Himalayan pass had been closed since the 1962 war). Sino-India trade relations are soaring — bilateral commerce was worth nearly $39 billion in 2007, a 15-fold increase over the 1999 value. In fact, China may soon supplant the United States as India's largest trading partner. Still, Indian leaders are concerned that trade with China is woefully unbalanced, with China enjoying a large surplus.

Indo-Chinese relations further warmed in late 2006, when Chinese President Hu Jintao made a trip to India, the first such visit by a Chinese president in a decade. There India and China issued a Joint Declaration outlining a "ten-pronged strategy" to boost bilateral socio-economic ties and defense cooperation, and to "reinforce their strategic partnership." The two countries, which declared themselves "partners for mutual benefit" rather than rivals or competitors, also signed 13 new pacts on a variety of bilateral initiatives. The Joint Declaration notably contained an agreement to "promote cooperation in the field of nuclear energy," although no details have been provided on what form such cooperation might take. India's army chief spent a week in China in mid-2007, providing fresh impetus to bilateral defense cooperation. A late 2007 visit to Beijing by Congress Party chief Sonia Gandhi may have been part of an effort to balance New Delhi's increasingly close relations with the United States, Japan, and other regional countries, relations that may be straining Indo-Chinese ties.

Prime Minister Singh's January 2008 visit to Beijing, his first as Prime Minister, saw India and China agreed to further strengthen trade and defense relations. Singh called on Beijing to expand market access for Indian goods so as to correct his country's growing trade imbalance with China. A number of significant unresolved bilateral issues, not least the conflicting territorial claims, had analysts foreseeing no major new initiatives growing from the summit. The resulting document, "A Shared Vision for the 21st Century," resolved to promote global peace and prosperitythrough an India-China relationship built on trust and based on equality. It included an unprecedented expression of Chinese support for a greater Indian in the U.N. Security Council, as well as calls for further regional economic integration and resolution of outstanding territorial disputes through peaceful negotiations.[77] External

Affairs Minister Mukherjee met with his Chinese counterpart in Beijing in June 2008; the two leaders pledged to maintain peace on the India-China border but offered no new approaches to resolving outstanding territorial disputes.[78]

Militarized bilateral frictions persist. Ahead of Prime Minister Singh's China trip, External Affairs Minister Mukherjee conceded that Chinese troops had sometimes intruded on Indian territory and that infrastructure development on the Chinese side of the border was "much superior" to that on the Indian side. Just two weeks after returning from China, Singh was in India's remote Arunachal Pradesh state for the first such prime ministerial trip in nearly a decade. The visit ostensibly was meant to assure the region's citizens that New Delhi remained mindful of their development needs. Indian officials have been clear in conveying to Beijing that they consider the state to be "an integral part of India."[79] Some Indian analysts, wary of China's territorial claims and military presence in the region, lauded what they saw as Singh's symbolic demonstration of Indian resolve in the face of Chinese provocations. In apparent response to China's rapid development of infrastructure on its side of the disputed border, the Indian army plans to deploy two new mountain divisions to the region within eight years.[80] In May 2008, reports that China was basing a nuclear submarine on Hainan Island in the South China Sea triggered alarm in New Delhi. Hainan is 1,200 miles from the strategically vital Malacca Straits. Indian concern was compounded by reports of apparent missile launch sites from which Chinese nuclear forces may target northern India. Moreover, India's pursuit of a military space program to defend its satellites may portend a regional arms race and exacerbate existing India-China tensions.[81]

Burma

India continues to pursue closer relations with the repressive regime in neighboring Burma, with an interest in energy cooperation and to counterbalance China's influence there. Such engagement seeks to achieve economic integration of India's northeast region and western Burma, as well as to bolster energy security. The Bush Administration urges India to be more active in pressing for democracy in Burma: in October 2007, Deputy Secretary of State John Negroponte said, "Now is the time for Beijing and New Delhi to forgo any energy deals that put money in the pockets of the junta and to suspend weapons sales to this regime." However, New Delhi calls democracy and human rights internal Burmese issues.[82]

During September 2007, major pro-democracy street protests in Burma grew in scale and the Rangoon military regime launched a violent crackdown to suppress the movement being led by Buddhist monks. In response, the United States announced new sanctions on Burma and urged other countries to follow suit. Following Rangoon's crackdown, New Delhi has continued to favor dialogue and is opposed to imposing sanctions on Rangoon. India is, in fact, moving ahead with plans to assist Rangoon in building a port in northwestern Burma as part of an effort develop that country's natural gas industry. This approach, justified by Indian leaders as being a pragmatic pursuit of their national interest, has elicited accusations of Indian complicity in Burmese repression.[83]

On October 1, 2007, **S.Res. 339**, expressing the sense of the Senate on the situation in Burma, was passed by the full Senate. The resolution includes a call for the United States and the United Nations to "strongly encourage China, India, and Russia to modify their position on Burma and use their influence to convince the Government of Burma to engage in dialogue with opposition leaders and ethnic minorities towards national reconciliation." On the same day, New Delhi reiterated its calls for political reform in Burma and urged Rangoon to launch a formal inquiry into recent use of force against pro-democracy protestors there, but New Delhi was not seen to be adjusting its Burma policy in any meaningful way.[84] In a justification of New Delhi's relatively uncritical approach to the Rangoon regime, some commentators call past and continued cooperation by the Burmese military vital in New Delhi's efforts to battle separatist militants in India's northeast.[85]

Press reports in late 2007 indicated that New Delhi was halting arms sales to Rangoon; however it appears that India's supply of military equipment to Burma has only been "slowed."[86] International human rights groups and some in Congress have criticized New Delhi's military interactions with Rangoon.[87] Burma's foreign affairs minister visited New Delhi in the first week of 2008 for wide-ranging discussions with his Indian counterpart. Prime Minister Singh expressed satisfaction with positive India-Burma relations while also stressing "the need for greater urgency in bringing about political reforms and national reconciliation" through a "broad-based" process.[88] When Burma's second-highest ranking military ruler visited New Delhi in April 2008, the two countries reached agreement on a $120 million-project that will see India upgrade numerous waterways and highways in Burma. An early May cyclone devastated Burma's coastal areas and left at least 78,000 people dead. The New Delhi government sought to keep with "India's close and good neighborly ties with the friendly people" of Burma by quickly rushing food, water, and medical supplies to its devastated neighbor.[89]

Iran[90]

India-Iran relations may complicate progress in New Delhi's nascent "strategic partnership" with Washington. India's relations with Iran traditionally have been positive and, in 2003, the two countries launched a bilateral "strategic partnership" of their own.[91] The Indian government and firms have invested a reported total of nearly $10 billion in Iran since 2000, placing India 10th on the list of international investors worldwide. Some in the U.S. Congress voiced past concerns that New Delhi's policies toward Tehran's controversial nuclear program were not congruent with those of Washington, although these concerns were eased when India voted with the United States (and the majority) at the IAEA sessions of September 2005 and February 2006. India urges the United States to refrain from unilaterally taking on the task of preventing Iran's potential development of nuclear weapons and leave the job to the IAEA. New Delhi believes there is no military solution to the issue and warns that any military strike on Iran "would have disastrous consequences for the entire region."[92]

During the period from 2004 to 2006, the United States sanctioned Indian scientists and chemical companies for transferring to Iran WMD-related equipment and/or technology (most sanctions were chemical-related, but one scientist was alleged to have aided Iran's nuclear program). New Delhi called the moves unjustified. Included in legislation to enable U.S.-India civil nuclear cooperation (P.L. 109-141, the "Hyde Act") was a non-binding assertion that U.S. policy should "secure India's full and active participation" in U.S. efforts to prevent Iran from acquiring weapons of mass destruction.[93] New Delhi firmly opposes the emergence of any new nuclear weapons powers in the region.

Many in Congress have voiced concern about India's relations with Iran and their relevance to U.S. interests. Some worry especially about New Delhi's defense ties with Tehran and have sought to link the issue with congressional approval of U.S.-India civil nuclear cooperation.[94] Expressions of these congressional concerns became more pointed in 2007.[95] New Delhi has offered assurances that all of India's dealings with Iran are permitted under U.N. Security Council Resolutions; one official expressed being "quite amazed" at reports of closer India-Iran military ties. In September 2007, Assistant Secretary of State Boucher conceded that some concerns about India-Iran military relations are "exaggerated," but that the onus is on New Delhi to "explain" its relations with Tehran.[96]

In April 2008, President Ahmadinejad arrived in New Delhi for a five-hour visit and met with top Indian leaders. It was the first such visit by an Iranian president since 2003. India's foreign secretary took the opportunity to express satisfaction with the course of the bilateral relationship and stressed his government's view that building a physically secure, economically and commercially viable natural gas pipeline from Iran to India would be in both countries' interests. When asked if India's relations with Iran could jeopardize warm relations with the Untied States, the foreign secretary said he did not think so, offering that deeper engagement with Iran would facilitate regional stability and that, "Everything we do with Iran is open, above-board, and quite clear to everybody."[97] In the run-up to the Iranian leader's visit, a State Department spokesman had expressed hope that New Delhi would call on Ahmadinejad to meet U.N. Security Council requirements that Iran suspend its uranium enrichment activities. The comment sparked outrage and indignation in New Delhi, where the External Affairs Ministry responded by saying India and Iran were "perfectly capable" of managing their own bilateral relations and needed no external guidance in this regard.[98]

There are further U.S. concerns that India will seek energy resources from Iran, thus benefitting financially a country the United States is seeking to isolate. Indian firms have in recent years taken long-term contracts for purchase of Iranian gas and oil. Natural gas purchases could be worth many billions of dollars, but thus far differences over pricing and transport have precluded sales. Building upon growing energy ties is the proposed construction of a pipeline to deliver Iranian natural gas to India through Pakistan. The Bush Administration repeatedly expresses strong opposition to any gas pipeline projects involving Iran, but top Indian officials insist the project is in India's national interest and they remain "fully committed" to the multi-billion-dollar venture. The Iran-Libya Sanctions Act (P.L. 107-24) required the President to impose sanctions on foreign companies that make an "investment" of more than $20 million in one year in Iran's energy sector. The 109th Congress extended this provision in the Iran Freedom Support Act (P.L. 109-293). To date, no firms have been sanctioned under these Acts.

The "IPI" Pipeline Project.[99] New Delhi insists it is going ahead with a proposed joint pipeline project to deliver Iranian natural gas to Pakistan and on to India. Despite positive signaling, New Delhi had in the latter months of 2007 maintained only low-profile participation in relevant negotiations, perhaps in part due to sensitivities surrounding the as-yet unconsummated U.S.-India civil nuclear cooperation agreement. Earlier in 2007, officials from the three countries resolved a long-running price-mechanism dispute, opening the way for a fourth meeting of the India-Pakistan Joint Working Group on the IPI (Iran-Pakistan-India) Pipeline in Islamabad, where the two countries agreed to split equally expected gas supplies. Indian leaders consistently describe the pipeline project as being in the nation's interest for greater energy security. As Iran and Pakistan move to finalize the pipeline project, India in April 2008 confirmed that it would rejoin talks. Beijing has expressed interest in Pakistani proposals that China participate in the IPI project, possibly spurring more energetic

Indian participation.[100] Ever-optimistic Iranian leaders anticipate a trilateral agreement to launch the project will be inked by midsummer 2008. Such a development could be considered a significant failure of U.S. policy that could convey a sobering message about America's allegedly declining international and regional clout.[101]

Some independent analysts and Members of Congress assert that completion of an IPI pipeline would represent a major confidence-building measure in the region and could bolster regional energy security while facilitating friendlier Pakistan-India ties (see, for example H.Res. 353 in the 109th Congress). Some Indian strategic analysts contend that New Delhi would risk alienating the Pakistani leadership if it were to withdraw from the project.[102] As part of its efforts to isolate Iran economically, the Bush Administration actively seeks to dissuade New Delhi from participation in this project, and a State Department official has suggested that current U.S. law dictates American opposition. Some independent analysts concur with this view and urge Washington to assist the Indian and Pakistani governments in developing alternative energy sources, including liquified natural gas and pursuit of a proposed pipeline that would deliver Turkmen natural gas to South Asia through Afghanistan.[103] In May 2007, Indian Oil Minister Murli Deora assured concerned Left Front parties that India "will not be cowed down by any threat" regarding its relations with Iran, saying that India's participation in the IPI pipeline project "is not the business of the United States."[104]

Other Countries

India takes an active role in assisting reconstruction efforts in **Afghanistan**, having committed some $1.2 billion to this cause, as well as contributing some 4,000 workers and opening numerous consulates there (much to the dismay of Pakistan, which fears strategic encirclement and takes note of India's past support for Afghan Tajik and Uzbek militias). Among Indian assistance to Afghanistan are funding for a new $111 million power station, an $84 million road-building project, a $77 million dam project, and construction of Kabul's new $67 Parliament building, to be completed in 2010. There are reported to be several hundred Indian commandos stationed in Afghanistan to provide protection for Indian reconstruction workers. The United States has welcomed India's role in Afghanistan. A July 2008 suicide bombing at India's Kabul Embassy was taken as a stark message to Indian leaders that Taliban militants and their allies want New Delhi to withdraw from Afghanistan. Prime Minster Singh instead responded by vowing $450 million in new Indian aid for Afghan reconstruction.[105]

Looking to the north, New Delhi supports consolidation of **Nepal**'s democratic and conflict resolution processes, in particular through continued political assimilation of the Maoists. India remains concerned by political instability in Kathmandu and by the cross-border infiltration of Maoist militants into India. In April 2008, Nepali Maoists won a surprise electoral victory in taking more than one-third of Kathmandu's Constituent Assembly seats to oversee a new coalition government. The new Kathmandu government has since threatened to abrogate the 1950 Indo-Nepal Peace and Friendship Treaty, which allows for unrestricted travel and residency across the shared border. While Indian officials are fairly sanguine about the development and vow openness to working with the new Nepali government, they are likely to have concerns about the potential for instability in Nepal to exacerbate India's own internal insecurities.[106]

To the east, and despite India's key role in the 1971 creation of neighboring **Bangladesh**, New Delhi's relations with Dhaka have been fraught with tensions related mainly to the cross-border infiltration of Islamic and separatist militants, and tens of millions of illegal migrants into India. New Delhi is undertaking a $1.2 billion project to fence India's entire 2,000-mile shared border with Bangladesh. The two countries' border forces engage in periodic gunbattles. Still, New Delhi and Dhaka have cooperated on counterterrorism efforts and talks on energy cooperation continue. The Bangladeshi faction of the Harakat ul-Jihad-I-Islami — an Islamist militant outfit that was designated as a Foreign Terrorist Organization under U.S. law in March 2008 and that has links to Pakistan-based terrorist groups — has been implicated in several terrorist attacks inside India, including May 2008 terrorist bombings that killed at least 63 people in Jaipur, Rajasthan. Bangladesh's military-backed interim government, which took power in 2007, may benefit India by reducing anti-India rhetoric and by addressing the apparently growing influence of Islamist forces that are seen as a threat to Indian interests.

In the island nation of **Sri Lanka** off India's southeastern coast, a Tamil Hindu minority has been fighting a separatist war against the Sinhalese Buddhist majority since 1983. A Norwegian-brokered cease-fire unraveled in 2006 and, after a series of military successes in 2007, the Colombo government abrogated the cease-fire in January 2008. More than 60 million Indian Tamils live in southern India and tens of thousands of Sri Lankan Tamil refugees have fled to India in recent months and years. India's armed 1987 intervention to assist in enforcing a peace accord resulted in the deaths of more than 1,200 Indian troops and led to the 1991 assassination of former Indian Prime Minister Rajiv Gandhi by Tamil militants. Since that time, New Delhi has maintained friendly relations with Colombo while refraining from any deep engagement in third-party peace efforts. New Delhi resists Colombo's push for more direct Indian involvement and insists there can be "no military solution" to the island's ethnic troubles. The Indian Navy played a key role in providing disaster relief to Sri Lanka following the catastrophic December 2004 Indian Ocean tsunami.

Moscow was New Delhi's main foreign benefactor for the first four decades of Indian independence. **Russia** continues to be "indispensable to India's foreign policy interests," according to Prime Minister Singh, who calls energy cooperation the core of the two countries' "strategic partnership."[107] India's single largest foreign investment is a $1 billion stake in a joint oil and gas venture on Russia's Sakhalin Island. Moreover, and despite some post-Cold War diversification of its defense suppliers, India continues to obtain the bulk of its imported military hardware from Russian firms. In 2007, Russian President Vladimir Putin paid a visit to New Delhi, where he met with top Indian officials; signed several bilateral agreements on energy, science, and space cooperation; and offered to sell four new 1,000-megawatt nuclear reactors to India. In November, Prime Minister Singh visited Moscow, where he and Putin discussed economic, energy, and defense ties. Agreement for the construction of four new nuclear reactors was deferred due to "technical hitches." Some commentators believe the U.S. government pressured New Delhi to avoid the deal. Russia's status as a main supplier of Indian defense equipment currently is threatened by several disputes, including over the refitting of an aircraft carrier (which has seen major delays and cost overruns), a spat over Russia's allegedly substandard upgradation of an Indian attack submarine, and other irritants.[108]

India's relations with **Japan** only began to blossom in the current decade after being significantly undermined by India's 1998 nuclear weapons tests. Today, leaders from both countries acknowledge numerous common values and interests. They are engaging a "strategic dialogue" formally launched with a 2007 visit to Tokyo by Foreign Minister Mukherjee, who spoke of Japan as a "natural partner in the quest to create an arc of advantage and prosperity" in Asia. Mukherjee emphasized India's desire for economic integration in Asia and cooperative efforts to secure vital sea lanes, especially in the Indian Ocean. Japan's support for the latter initiative has included plans for unprecedented joint naval exercises. New Delhi and Tokyo also share an interest in seeing membership of the U.N. Security Council expanded; both governments aspire to permanent seats. India seeks Japan's endorsement for proposed U.S.-India civil nuclear cooperation, which has not been forthcoming to date. A mid-2007 visit to New Delhi by Japanese Prime Minister Shinzo Abe, who was effusive in his praise of India as a "partner and friend," was seen by many as part of a long-term Japanese effort to hedge against China's growing regional influence. Abe and Prime Minister Singh issued a "Roadmap for New Dimensions to the Strategic and Global Partnership" outlining plans for security cooperation and comprehensive economic engagement.[109] Singh met with the new Japanese Prime Minister, Yasuo Fukada, in Singapore in November and reiterated a commitment to the India-Japan "strategic and global partnership."

The U.S. and Japanese governments have sought India's participation in a prospective **quadrilateral "axis of democracy"** that would include Australia and could conceivably have a security alliance dimension (Australian officials reportedly are skeptical of such a pact for fear of alienating China). In 2007, U.S., Indian, and Japanese naval vessels conducted unprecedented combined exercises off Japan's east coast. In September of that year, India hosted unprecedented five-country naval exercises in the Bay of Bengal (with Australian and Singaporean vessels also participating). Officials stressed that the exercises — which involved a total of 27 ships and submarines, among them two U.S. aircraft carriers — were not prompted by China's growing military strength. New Delhi favors greater trilateral India-U.S.Japan cooperation, especially in the areas of trade and energy security, but shies from anything that could be construed as a multilateral security alliance.

Political Setting

India is the world's most populous democracy and remains firmly committed to representative government and rule of law. As a nation-state, India presents a vast mosaic of hundreds of different ethnic groups, religious sects, and social castes. U.S. policymakers commonly identify in the Indian political system shared core values, and this has facilitated increasingly friendly relations between the U.S. and Indian governments. In 2008, the often-cited Freedom House again rated India as "free" in the areas of political rights and civil liberties.

National Elections[110]

With a robust and working democratic system, India is a federal republic where the bulk of executive power rests with the prime minister and his or her cabinet (the Indian president is a ceremonial chief of state with limited executive powers). Most of India's prime ministers have come from the country's Hindi-speaking northern regions and all but two have been upper-caste Hindus. The 543-seat Lok Sabha (People's House) is the locus of national power, with directly elected representatives from each of the country's 28 states and 7 union territories. A smaller upper house, the Rajya Sabha (Council of States), may review, but not veto, most legislation, and has no power over the prime minister or the cabinet. National and state legislators are elected to five-year terms. The most recent parliamentary elections were held in the spring of 2004.

National elections in October 1999 had secured ruling power for a Bharatiya Janata Party (BJP)-led coalition government headed by Prime Minister Vajpayee. That outcome decisively ended the historic dominance of the Nehru-Gandhi-led Congress Party, which was relegated to sitting in opposition at the national level (its members continued to lead many state governments). However, a surprise Congress resurgence under Sonia Gandhi in the 2004 elections brought to power a new left-leaning coalition government led by former finance minister and Oxford-educated economist Manmohan Singh, a Sikh and India's first-ever non-Hindu prime minister. Many analysts attributed Congress's 2004 resurgence to the resentment of rural and poverty-stricken urban voters who felt left out of the "India shining" campaign of a BJP more associated with urban, middle-class interests. Others saw in the results a rejection of the Hindu nationalism associated with the BJP.

The current Congress-led United Progressive Alliance (UPA) ruling coalition has marked nearly four years in power, exceeding the expectations of some observers. Opinion surveys suggest that both Prime Minister Singh and party chief Gandhi have remained fairly popular national figures. However, February 2007 state elections in Punjab and Uttaranchal saw Congress candidates decisively defeated by the BJP and its allies, causing some pundits to suggest that national economic policies and rising inflation may have damaged the ruling coalition's standing. Such arguments were forwarded when the Bahujan Samaj Party (BSP) won an outright majority in May 2007 state assembly elections in Uttar Pradesh, India's most populous state. During its four years overseeing a national ruling coalition, the Congress Party has lost 12 assembly elections and was dislodged by the main opposition BJP in four states, including Karnataka and Punjab. Meanwhile, under the party presidency of Rajnath Singh, the BJP has enjoyed seven consecutive election victories.[111] Congress's surprise May 2008 loss in Karnataka set the party on its heels in the run-up to national polls expected in early 2009, with many analysts concluding that national political momentum has shifted away from the party. Some observers saw in the Karnataka election dynamics signs that urban voters are exercising new-found muscle in ways that could weaken the country's traditionally pro-rural politicians.[112]

Prime Minister Singh, though widely admired as an honest and intelligent figure, has been unable to succeed in pushing through most of the UPA agenda, and his party's state-level electoral setbacks have most analysts predicting no bold policy initiatives before the next national election expected in 2009. This is especially so in the wake of the New Delhi government's inability to consummate a civil nuclear cooperation deal with the United States, an issue upon which the UPA leadership has staked considerable political capital. By most accounts, 2007 was a particularly unsuccessful year for the incumbent national government.[113]

The Congress Party[114]

Congress's electoral strength reached a nadir in 1999, when the party won only 110 Lok Sabha seats. Observers attributed the poor showing to a number of factors, including the failure of Congress to make strong preelection alliances (as had the BJP) and perceptions that party leader Sonia Gandhi lacked the experience to lead the country. Support for the Congress, which dominated Indian politics for decades, had been in fairly steady decline following the 1984 assassination of Prime Minister Indira Gandhi and the 1991 assassination of her son, Prime Minister Rajiv Gandhi.

Sonia Gandhi, Rajiv's Italian-born, Catholic widow, refrained from active politics until the 1998 elections. She later made efforts to revitalize the party by phasing out older leaders and attracting more women and lower castes — efforts that appear to have paid off in 2004. Today, Congress again occupies more parliamentary seats (145) than any other party and, through unprecedented alliances with powerful regional parties, it again leads India's government under the UPA coalition. As party chief and UPA chair, Gandhi is seen to wield considerable influence over the coalition's policy making process. Her foreign origins have presented an obstacle and likely were a major factor in her May 2004 decision to decline the prime ministership. As key Congress party figures express support for the future leadership of her son and new parliamentarian, Rahul Gandhi, Manmohan Singh's political authority is correspondingly undermined.[115]

The Bharatiya Janata Party (BJP)[116]

With the rise of Hindu nationalism, the BJP rapidly increased its parliamentary strength during the 1980s. In 1993, the party's image was tarnished among some, burnished for others, by its alleged complicity in serious communal violence in Bombay and elsewhere. Some hold elements of the BJP, as the political arm of extremist Hindu groups, responsible for the incidents (the party has advocated "Hindutva," or an India based on Hindu culture, and views this as key to nation-building).

While leading a national coalition from 1998-2004, the BJP worked — with only limited success — to change its image from right-wing Hindu fundamentalist to conservative and secular, although 2002 communal rioting in Gujarat again damaged the party's credentials as a moderate organization. The BJP-led National Democratic Alliance (NDA) was overseen by party notable Prime Minister Atal Vajpayee, whose widespread personal popularity helped to keep the BJP in power. After 2004, the BJP was weakened by leadership disputes, criticism from Hindu nationalists, and controversy involving party president Lal Advani (in 2005, Advani ceded his leadership post and Vajpayee announced his retirement from politics). The party did, however, take control of the Karnataka state government in November 2007, the first time the BJP has held power in southern India. In preparing for a new round of national elections, the party may adhere to its core Hindutva philosophy; it has nominated hardliner Advani to be its next prime ministerial candidate and may continue efforts to demonize India's Muslim minority as part of a long-standing electoral strategy.[117] Some observers, however, believe the party is looking beyond its traditional vote bank to appeal to urban, middle-class concerns such as governance and commerce, especially in the wake of party notable Narendra Modi's reelection as Chief Minister of the western Gujarat state in December 2007.[118]

Regional Parties

The influence of regional and caste-based parties has become an increasingly important variable in Indian politics; the 2004 national elections saw such parties receiving nearly half of all votes cast. Never before 2004 had the Congress Party entered into pre-poll alliances at the national level, and numerous analysts attributed Congress's success to precisely this new tack, especially thorough arrangements with the Bihar-based Rashtriya Janata Dal and Tamil Nadu's Dravida Munnetra Kazhagam. The newfound power of both large and smaller regional parties, alike, is seen to be reflected in the UPA's ministerial appointments, and in the Congress-led coalition's professed attention to rural issues and to relations between state governments and New Delhi.

Two significant regional parties currently independent of both the ruling coalition and the BJP-led opposition are the Samajwadi Party, a largely Muslim- and lower caste-based organization highly influential in Uttar Pradesh, and the Bahujan Samaj Party (BSP) of Bihar, which also represents mainly lower-caste constituents. State assembly elections in Uttar Pradesh — home to more than 170 million Indians and one of only four states where the Congress Party is not in power — concluded in May 2007 and saw a major victory for the BSP and its lower-caste, female leader Mayawati, who reached out to upper-caste and other groups to secure an outright majority, the first time in 14 years that a single party secured such status. Mayawati is believed to have national political aspirations and her party's success with caste-based politics may erode support for the Congress party in expected 2009 national elections.[119] The outcome may have been an important indicator of national political trends, especially in gauging satisfaction with the current center coalition. In June 2007, eight regional parties formally launched a new "Third Front" that might emerge as a national alternative to the UPA and NDA. Well-known Tamil Nadu politician Jayalalithaa is a notable leader.[120]

The Left Front[121]

Although the Communist Party of India (Marxist) seated the third largest number of parliamentarians in 2004, its vote bank is almost wholly limited to West Bengal and Kerala (the Left Front coalition holds about 11% of all Lok Sabha seats). Communist parties have in the past been bitter rivals of the Congress in these states, but a mutual commitment to secularism appears to have motivated their cooperation against the BJP in 2004.[122] Early alarm was sounded that the new influence of communists in New Delhi might derail India's economic reform efforts; Indian industrial leaders sought to assure foreign investors that Left Front members are not "Cuba-style communists," but could be expected to support the UPA reform agenda. The communist Chief Minister of West Bengal, Buddhadeb Bhattacharya, has himself actively sought corporate investment in his state. However, since coming to power, the Congress-led coalition has slowed most aspects of its economic reform program, including suspending major government disinvestment and special economic zone initiatives. These moves are widely viewed as gestures to the strongly opposed communists.[123] The Left Front also has been vocal in criticisms of closer India-U.S. relations, taking particular aim at proposed civil nuclear cooperation and any signs that the United States seeks to make India a "junior partner" in efforts to counter China.

BILATERAL ISSUES

"Next Steps in Strategic Partnership" and Beyond

The now-concluded Next Steps in Strategic Partnership (NSSP) initiative encompassed several major issues in U.S.-India relations. New Delhi has long pressed Washington to ease restrictions on the export to India of dual-use high-technology goods (those with military applications), as well as to increase civilian nuclear and civilian space cooperation. These three key issues came to be known as the "trinity," and top Indian officials insisted that progress in these areas was necessary to provide tangible evidence of a changed U.S.-India relationship. There were later references to a "quartet" when the issue of missile defense was included. In January 2004, President Bush and Prime Minister Vajpayee issued a joint statement declaring that the U.S.-India "strategic partnership" included expanding cooperation in the "trinity" areas, as well as expanding dialogue on missile defense.[124] This initiative was dubbed as the NSSP and involved a series of reciprocal steps.

In July 2005, the State Department announced successful completion of the NSSP, allowing for expanded bilateral commercial satellite cooperation, and removal/revision of some U.S. export license requirements for certain dual-use and civil nuclear items. Taken together, the July 2005 U.S.-India Joint Statement and a June 2005 U.S.-India Defense Framework Agreement include provisions for moving forward in all four NSSP issue-areas.[125] Many observers saw in the NSSP evidence of a major and positive shift in the U.S. strategic orientation toward India, a shift later illuminated more starkly with the Bush Administration's intention to initiate full civil nuclear cooperation with India.

Civil Nuclear Cooperation[126]

India's status as a non-signatory to the 1968 Nuclear Nonproliferation Treaty (NPT) has kept it from accessing most nuclear-related materials and fuels on the international market for more than three decades. New Delhi's 1974 "peaceful nuclear explosion" spurred the U.S.-led creation of the Nuclear Suppliers Group (NSG) — an international export control regime for nuclear-related trade — and Washington further tightened its own export laws with the Nuclear Nonproliferation Act of 1978 (P.L. 95-242). New Delhi has long railed at a "nuclear apartheid" created by an apparent double standard inherent in the NPT, which, they maintain, allows certain states to legitimately employ nuclear deterrents while other states cannot. Senior Indian officials reiterate the widely-held Indian perspective that reaching a civil nuclear deal with the United States remains crucial to the process of removing constraints placed on India by "an increasingly selective, rigorous, and continually expanding regime of technologydenial," claiming that only by "turning the nuclear key" will India be able to open the door to global trade in dual use and other sophisticated technologies.[127]

Under U.S. and international law, civil nuclear cooperation with India cannot commence until Washington and New Delhi finalize a peaceful nuclear cooperation agreement (and Congress endorses such an agreement), until New Delhi concludes its own safeguards agreement with the International Atomic Energy Agency, and until the NSG allows for such cooperation. At present, nuclear power accounts for less than 3% of India's total electricity generation, and an Indian government official has estimated that, even under optimistic scenarios, this percentage would likely no more than double over the next 25 years.[128]

The Bush Administration Policy Shift. Differences over nuclear policy bedeviled U.S.-India ties for decades and — given New Delhi's lingering resentments — have presented a serious psychological obstacle to more expansive bilateral relations. In a major policy shift, the July 2005 U.S.-India Joint Statement notably asserted that "as a responsible state with advanced nuclear technology, India should acquire the same benefits and advantages as other such states," and President Bush vowed to work on achieving "full civilian nuclear energy cooperation with India." As a reversal of three decades of U.S. nonproliferation policy, such proposed cooperation stirred controversy and required changes in both U.S. law and in NSG guidelines. India reciprocally agreed to take its own steps, including identifying and separating its civilian and military nuclear facilities in a phased manner and placing the former under international safeguards. Some in Congress express concern that civil nuclear cooperation with India might allow that country to advance its military nuclear projects and be harmful to broader U.S. nonproliferation efforts. While the Bush Administration previously had insisted that such cooperation would take place only within the limits set by multilateral nonproliferation regimes, it later actively sought adjustments to U.S. laws and policies, and has approached the NSG in an effort to adjust that regime's guidelines, which are set by member consensus.

In March 2006, President Bush and Prime Minister Singh issued a Joint Statement that included an announcement of "successful completion of India's [nuclear facility] separation plan."[129] After months of complex and difficult negotiations, the Indian government had presented a plan to separate its civilian and military nuclear facilities as per the July 2005 Joint Statement. The separation plan would require India to move 14 of its 22 reactors into permanent international oversight by the year 2014 and place all future civilian reactors under permanent safeguards. Shortly thereafter, legislation to waive the application of certain requirements under the Atomic Energy Act of 1954 with respect to India was, at the President's request, introduced in the U.S. Congress.

Potential Benefits and Costs. Secretary of State Rice appeared before key Senate and House committees in April 2006 to press the Bush Administration's case for civil nuclear cooperation with India. The Administration offered five main justifications for making changes in U.S. law to allow for such cooperation, contending that doing so would

- benefit U.S. security by bringing India "into the nonproliferation mainstream;"
- benefit U.S. consumers by reducing pressures on global energy markets, especially carbon-based fuels;
- benefit the environment by reducing carbon emissions/greenhouse gases;
- benefit U.S. business interests through sales to India of nuclear reactors, fuel, and support services; and
- benefit progress of the broader U.S.-India "global partnership."[130]

Many leading American experts on South Asian affairs joined the Administration in urging Congress to support the new policy, placing particular emphasis on the "necessary" role it would play in promoting a U.S.-India global partnership.[131]

The U.S. Chamber of Commerce — which, along with the U.S.-India Business Council, lobbied vigorously in favor of President Bush's initiative — speculated that civil nuclear cooperation with India could generate contracts for American businesses worth up to $100 billion, as well as generate up to 27,000 new American jobs each year for a decade. A more modest estimate foresees the deal generating as much as $40 billion in new foreign investment into India.[132] However, foreign companies such as Russia's Atomstroyexport and France's Areva may be better poised to take advantage of the Indian market. Moreover, U.S. nuclear suppliers will likely balk at entering the Indian market in the absence of nuclear liability protection, which New Delhi does not offer at present.

Further hearings in the Senate and House during mid-2006 saw a total of fifteen independent analysts weigh in on the potential benefits and/or problems that might accrue from such cooperation. Numerous nonproliferation experts, scientists, and former U.S. government officials warned that the Bush Administration's initiative was ill-considered, arguing that it would facilitate an increase in the size of India's nuclear arsenal, potentially leading to a nuclear arms race in Asia, and would undermine the global nonproliferation regime and cause significant damage to key U.S. security interests. Some experts opined that the Administration's optimism, perhaps especially as related to the potential effects on global energy markets and carbon emissions, could not be supported through realistic projections.[133]

Geopolitical Motives. In the realm of geopolitics, much of the Administration's argument for moving forward with the U.S.-India nuclear initiative appears rooted in an anticipation/expectation that New Delhi will in coming years and decades make policy choices that are more congruent with U.S. regional and global interests (a desire for such congruence is, in fact, written into the enabling legislation, P.L. 109-401). Proponents suggest that this U.S. "gesture" will have significant and lasting psychological and symbolic effects in addition to the material ones, and that Indian leaders require such a gesture in order to feel confident in the United States as a reliable partner on the world stage. Skeptics aver that the potential strategic benefits of the nuclear initiative are being over-sold. Indeed, centuries of Indian anti-colonial sentiments and oftentimes prickly, independent foreign policy choices are unlikely to be set aside in the short run, meaning that the anticipated geopolitical benefits of civil nuclear cooperation with India remain speculative and at least somewhat dependent upon unknowable global political developments.

Congressional Action. After months of consideration, key House and Senate committees took action on relevant legislation in June 2006, passing modified versions of the Administration's proposals by wide margins. The new bills (H.R. 5682 and S. 3709) made significant procedural changes to the Administration's original proposal, changes that sought to retain congressional oversight of the negotiation process, in part by requiring the Administration to gain future congressional approval of a completed peaceful nuclear cooperation agreement with India (this is often referred to as a "123 Agreement," as it is negotiated under the conditions set forth in Section 123 of the Atomic Energy Act). During the final months of its tenure, the 109th Congress passed enabling legislation with broad bipartisan support.[134] So-called "killer amendments" were rejected by both chambers (Indian government and Bush Administration officials had warned that certain proposed new provisions, such as those requiring that India halt its fissile material production or end its military relations with Iran, would trigger New Delhi's withdrawal from the entire negotiation).

In a December 2006 "lame duck" session, congressional conferees reconciled the House and Senate versions of the legislation and provided an explanatory statement (H.Rept. 109-721). President Bush then signed the Henry J. Hyde United States-India Peaceful Atomic Energy Cooperation Act of 2006 (P.L. 109-401 or the "Hyde Act") into law, calling it a "historic agreement" that would help the United States and India meet the energy and security challenges of the 21st century. The President also issued a signing statement asserting that his approval of the act "does not constitute [his] adoption of the statements of policy as U.S. foreign policy" and that he will construe such policy statements as "advisory." Some in Congress expressed concern that President Bush would seek to disregard Congress's will.[135]

In mid-2007, as negotiations on a 123 Agreement were underway,16 experts, scholars, and former U.S. government officials signed a letter urging Senators to hold the Bush Administration to the "set of core conditions and limitations" of the Hyde Act, including termination of assistance upon an Indian nuclear test, permanent and unconditional safeguards on civilian Indian facilities, and prohibitions on reprocessing and enrichment technologies.[136] A July letter to President Bush signed by 23 Members of the House stressed the need for any civil nuclear cooperation agreement with India to conform to "the legal boundaries set by Congress." The letter noted that the U.S. Constitution provides Congress with the sole authority to regulate foreign commerce, and it expressed ongoing concerns about "India's deepening military-to-military relationship with Iran ... [which] places congressional approval of the Agreement for Nuclear Cooperation in jeopardy."[137]

Indian Concerns. Almost immediately upon the release of the July 2005 Joint Statement, key Indian political figures and members of the country's insular nuclear scientific community issued strong criticisms of the bilateral civil nuclear initiative; some such criticisms continue to this day. Former Prime Minister Vajpayee, along with many leading figures in his opposition BJP party, insisted that the deal as envisioned would place unreasonable and unduly expensive demands on India, particularly with regard to the separation of nuclear facilities. In reaction to the U.S. Congress's passage of enabling legislation in late 2006, the BJP listed numerous continuing objections, and went so far as to call the deal "unacceptable" and aimed at "capping, rolling back, and eventually eliminating India's nuclear weapons capability."[138] Many analysts view the BJP's opposition as political rather than substantive, especially in light of the fact that the 2004 NSSP initiative was launched during the BJP's tenure.[139]

Some Indian analysts, wary of U.S. intentions in pursuing bilateral civil nuclear cooperation, believe the initiative may be cover for a broader effort to cement India's cooperation in a number of non-energy-related areas, such as defense trade and New Delhi's relations with Iran. From this perspective, the U.S. government repeatedly "shifted the goalposts" to forward its own (veiled) nonproliferation goals.[140] India's influential communist parties, whose Left Front provides crucial support to the Congress-led ruling coalition in New Delhi, have focused their ire on geopolitical aspects of the civil nuclear initiative. In late 2006, the leader of India's main communist party declared the U.S.-India civil nuclear deal "not acceptable" as it would "seriously undermine India's independent foreign policy." Previously, the Left Front had called India's two IAEA votes on Iran a "capitulation" to U.S.

pressure.[141] Indian leftists thus have been at the forefront of political resistance to India's becoming a "junior partner" of the United States.

Equally stinging and perhaps more substantive criticism came from several key Indian scientists, whose perspectives on the technical details of the civil nuclear initiative are considered highly credible. India's nuclear scientific community, mostly barred from collaboration with international civil nuclear enterprises as well as direct access to key technologies, has worked for decades in relative isolation, making its members both proud of their singular accomplishments and sensitive to any signs of foreign "interference." Many viewed the enabling legislation passed by the U.S. Congress as being more about nonproliferation and less about energy cooperation. They considered it both intrusive on and preclusive of their activities.

The major criticisms of existing plans for U.S.-India civil nuclear cooperation made by Indian commentators (and at times by the Indian government) are summarized as follows:

India's unilateral moratorium on nuclear tests was being codified into a bilateral obligation through a clause that would allow the United States to reclaim any supplied nuclear equipment if India were to test a nuclear device;

India was being denied nuclear reprocessing technologies warranted under "full cooperation;"

India was not being given prior authorization to reprocess spent fuel;

India was not being given assurances that it will receive uninterrupted fuel supplies in perpetuity; and

language on securing India's assistance with U.S. efforts to prevent Iran from obtaining weapons of mass destruction would limit New Delhi's foreign policy independence.[142]

Prime Minister Singh stood firm against such wide-ranging and high-profile criticisms, repeatedly assuring his Parliament that relevant negotiations with the United States have not altered basic Indian policies or affected New Delhi's independence on matters of national interest. Within this context, however, Singh expressed concern about some of the points listed above.[143] Regardless of the legally binding or non-binding nature of certain controversial sections of the U.S. legislation, New Delhi found many of them to be either "prescriptive" in ways incompatible with the provisions of the July 2005 and March 2006 Joint Statements, or "extraneous" and "inappropriate to engagements among friends."[144]

Bilateral Negotiations Completed. In July 2007, the United States and India announced having concluded negotiations on a peaceful nuclear cooperation ("123") agreement, calling it a "historic milestone" in the bilateral strategic partnership. The announcement came one week after a fifth round of formal bilateral negotiations had ended in Washington, where a high-level Indian delegation led by National Security Advisor M.K. Narayanan had met with numerous top U.S. officials, including Vice President Cheney and Secretary of State Rice. Under Secretary of State Burns, the lead U.S. negotiator, called the deal "perhaps the single most important initiative that India and the United States have agreed to in the 60 years of our relationship" and "the symbolic centerpiece of a growing global partnership between our two countries."[145] U.S. officials urged New Delhi to move rapidly toward completing remaining steps to consummation of the pact.

Among the text's more salient provisions are the following:

India is granted authorization to reprocess spent fuel at a national reprocessing facility that New Delhi plans to establish under International Atomic Energy Agency safeguards.

In the event of a future nuclear test by India, the two countries would launch immediate bilateral consultations to "consider carefully the circumstances" and take into account whether the circumstances resulted from "serious concern about a changed security environment or as a response to similar actions by other states which could impact national security." While the U.S. President would have a right to demand the return of all U.S.-supplied nuclear equipment and material in such a circumstance, the text recognizes that "exercising the right of return would have profound implications" for bilateral relations and calls for both parties to "take into account the potential negative consequences" of any termination of ongoing cooperation.

India is given assurances that supplies of fuel for its civilian reactors will not be interrupted — even if the United States terminates the 123 Agreement — through U.S. commitments to "work with friends and allies ... to create the necessary conditions for India to obtain full access to the international fuel market," and to "support an Indian effort to develop a strategic reserve of nuclear fuel."[146]

Press reports had indicated that U.S. granting of unambiguous reprocessing rights, along with an Indian insistence on U.S. guarantees of an uninterrupted fuel supply for all imported reactors, had become a central obstacle in the lead-up to the talks, and that Indian negotiators had taken uncompromising positions in both areas. Subsequent reports suggested that U.S. negotiators made considerable concessions to Indian demands and that the agreement could face resistance in Congress if its legal stipulations are seen to deviate from those found in the Hyde Act.[147] In early 2008, External Affairs Minister Mukherjee reassured the Indian Parliament of his government's view that the Hyde Act is relevant only to interaction between the legislative and executive branches of the U.S. government, and that only the provisions of the 123 Agreement will be binding upon New Delhi. This distinction was echoed by Assistant Secretary of State Boucher during his contemporaneous visit to New Delhi.[148]

Civil Space Cooperation

India has long sought access to American space technology; such access has since the 1980s been limited by U.S. and international "red lines" meant to prevent assistance that could benefit India's military missile programs. India's space-launch vehicle technology was obtained largely from foreign sources, including the United States, and forms the basis of its intermediate-range Agni ballistic missile booster, as well as its suspected Surya intercontinental ballistic missile program. India is today seen to maintain one of the world's most advanced space programs.[149]

The NSSP called for enhanced U.S.-India cooperation on the peaceful uses of space technology, and the July 2005 Joint Statement anticipated closer ties in space exploration, satellite navigation and launch, and in the commercial space arena. Major conferences on India-U.S. space science and commerce were held in Bangalore (headquarters of the Indian Space Research Organization) in both 2004 and 2005. During President Bush's 2006 visit to India, the two countries committed to move forward with agreements that will permit the launch of U.S. satellites and satellites containing U.S.

components by Indian space launch vehicles and they later agreed to include two U.S. scientific instruments on India's planned Chandrayaan lunar mission. In 2007, a meeting of the U.S.-India Joint Working Group on Civil Space Cooperation was held in Washington, where officials expressed satisfaction with growing bilateral ties in the aerospace field.

High-Technology Trade[150]

U.S. Commerce Department officials have sought to dispel "trade-deterring myths" about limits on dual-use trade by noting that less than 0.5% of total U.S. trade value with India is now subject to licensing requirements and that the great majority of dual-use licensing applications for India are approved (about 95% in 2007). July 2003 saw the inaugural session of the U.S.India High-Technology Cooperation Group (HTCG), where officials discussed a wide range of issues relevant to creating the conditions for more robust bilateral high technology commerce; the sixth HTCG meeting was held in New Delhi in February 2008 (at the 2007 session, U.S. Commerce Secretary Carlos Gutierrez had unveiled a new "Trusted Customer" program designed to facilitate greater high-tech trade with India). In 2005, the inaugural session of the U.S.-India High-Technology Defense Working Group was held under HTCG auspices.[151] Commerce's Bureau of Industry and Security formally designated India as an eligible country under its "Validated End-User" program in October 2007. This designation will allow certain trusted Indian buyers to purchase high-technology goods without an individual license.[152]

Since 1998, a number of Indian entities have been subjected to case-by-case licensing requirements and appear on the U.S. export control "Entity List" of foreign end users involved in weapons proliferation activities. In 2004, as part of NSSP implementation, the United States modified some export licensing policies and removed the Indian Space Research Organization (ISRO) headquarters from the Entity List. Further adjustments came in 2005 when six more subordinate entities were removed. Indian entities remaining on the Entity List are four subordinates of the ISRO, four subordinates of the Defense Research and Development Organization, three Department of Atomic Energy entities, and Bharat Dynamics Limited, a missile production agency.[153]

Security Issues

The Indian Militar[154]

With more than 1.3 million active personnel, India's is the world's third-largest military (after China and the United States). The country's defense budget grew by 11% to about $28 billion in 2007 and is up more than 30% since 2000 (adjusted for inflation). The army — more than one million strong and accounting for nearly half of the budget — has traditionally dominated, but the navy and air force are becoming more important as India seeks to project its power and protect an Exclusive Economic Zone of more than two million square kilometers. For 2007, the air force procurement budget of $3.75 billion was nearly 44% of the service-specific total, with the navy receiving another $2.56 billion.

The Indian army possesses more than 4,000 main battle tanks and some 4,500 towed artillery tubes. The navy has grown rapidly in recent years, currently operating

48 principal surface combatants (including one aircraft carrier) and 16 submarines. There also is a significant amphibious capacity: 17 landing ships (including one recently acquired from the United States) can carry nearly 5,000 troops or 100 tanks. The navyis developing an indigenous nuclear-powered attack submarine to be armed with nuclear-tipped cruise missiles and also plans to lease a Russian Akula-class submarine as part of its "sea-based strategic deterrence." The air force flies 565 combat-capable aircraft, the majority of them Russian-built MiGs, along with some late-model Sukhoi-30, as well as French-built Mirage and Anglo-French Jaguar aircraft. It also possesses modest airborne early warning and in-flight refueling capabilities provided by Russian-made platforms. A Strategic Forces Command oversees as many as 170 intermediate- and short-range ballistic missiles capable of delivering nuclear warheads, and has plans to field a new Agni-IV missile with a range that would give it inter-continental capabilities.

New Delhi increasingly seeks to shift advanced military imports from finished platforms to co-production with foreign suppliers. A 2005 deal with France provides for technology transfers and Indian construction of six Scorpene submarines to be delivered in 2012-2017. In seeking to replace its aging arsenal of MiG-21 fighters, India may purchase up to 186 new jets (126 for the air force and 60 for the navy) and has signaled a desire for technology sharing and co-production in this effort: only 18 of the new air force jets are to be manufactured abroad. In addition to the Scorpene submarines, other notable recent purchases for the Indian military include hundreds of the latest Russian T-90 tanks and upgrades on 600 existing T-72s; 3 new Russian-built missile frigates; 24 new MiG-29K naval jets for deployment on the *INS Vitramaditya* (formerly the Russian *Gorshkov*); 40 upgraded Su-30 MKI ground attack aircraft, major upgrades on existing MiG and Jaguar combat aircraft; and 66 jet trainers from Britain.

Russia continues to provide the bulk of India's imported defense wares. In recent years, however, Israel has roughly equaled Russia in the value of defense exports to India, with each country providing about $1.5 billion worth of defense supplies in 2006. Moreover, India and Israel are engaging in new joint development projects involving missile technology.[155] India was the leading developing world arms purchaser from 1999-2006, making arms transfer *agreements* totaling $22.4 billion during that period.[156] As India seeks to expand its power projection capabilities, it has come under fire from some for continuing to prepare for a conventional interstate war that may be unlikely to occur. According to one report, of the country's nearly two million persons in uniform, only about 5,000 have meaningful counterterrorism training.[157]

U.S.-India Security Cooperation

Defense cooperation between the United States and India is in the early stages of development (unlike U.S.-Pakistan military ties, which date back to the 1950s). Since September 2001, and despite a concurrent U.S. rapprochement with Pakistan, U.S.-India security cooperation has flourished; U.S. diplomats rate military cooperation among the most important aspects of transformed bilateral relations. The India-U.S. Defense Policy Group (DPG) — moribund since India's 1998 nuclear tests and ensuing U.S. sanctions — was revived in late 2001 and meets annually.

In June 2005, the United States and India signed a ten-year defense pact outlining planned collaboration in multilateral operations, expanded two-way defense trade, increasing opportunities for technology transfers and co-production, expanded collaboration related to missile defense, and establishment of a bilateral Defense Procurement and Production Group. The agreement may be the most ambitious such security pact ever engaged by New Delhi. A Maritime Security Cooperation Agreement, inked in 2006, commits both countries to "comprehensive cooperation" in protecting the free flow of commerce and addressing a wide array of threats to maritime security, including piracy and the illicit trafficking of weapons of mass destruction and related materials. In April 2007, the Commander of the U.S. Pacific Command, Adm. Tim Keating, told a Senate panel that the Pentagon intends to "aggressively" pursue expanding military-to-military relations with India. During his August 2007 visit to New Delhi, Adm. Keating lauded U.S.-India defense relations as "solid, good, and improving steadily."[158] The sentiment was echoed by Secretary of Defense Gates during his February 2008 visit to the Indian capital.

The United States views defense cooperation with India in the context of "common principles and shared national interests" such as defeating terrorism, preventing weapons proliferation, and maintaining regional stability. Many analysts view increased U.S.-India security ties as providing an alleged "hedge" against or "counterbalance" to growing Chinese influence in Asia, though both Washington and New Delhi repeatedly downplay such probable motives. Still, while a congruence of U.S. and Indian national security objectives is unlikely in the foreseeable future, convergences are being identified in areas such as shared values, the emergence of a new balance-of-power arrangement in the region, and on distinct challenges such as WMD proliferation, Islamist extremism, and energy security. There also remain indications that the perceptions and expectations of top U.S. and Indian strategic planners are divergent on several key issues, including the role of Pakistan, approaches to conflict resolution in Iraq and in Palestine, and Indian's relations with Iran, as well as with repressive governments in places such as Burma and Sudan.[159]

Combined Military Exercises. Since early 2002, the United States and India have held a series of unprecedented and increasingly substantive combined exercises involving all military services. "Cope India" air exercises have provided the U.S. military with its first look at advanced Russian-built Su-30MKIs; in 2004, mock air combat saw Indian pilots in late-model Russian-built fighters hold off American pilots flying older F-15Cs, and Indian successes were repeated versus U.S. F-16s in 2005. Indian pilots joined military aviators from South Korea and France to participate in August 2008 U.S. Air Force training exercises over Nevada. U.S. and Indian special forces soldiers have held at least five "Vajra Prahar" joint exercises, and at least 133 U.S. Special Forces soldiers have attended India's Counter-Insurgency Jungle Warfare School. Moreover, major annual "Malabar" joint naval exercises are held off the Indian coast. The seventh and most recent of these came in September 2007, when India hosted a total of 27 warships from five countries — including the United States, Japan, Australia, and Singapore — for maneuvers in the Bay of Bengal. It was the first time such exercises were conducted off India's east coast. U.S. and Indian officials tout ongoing joint maneuvers as improving interoperability and as evidence of an overall deepening of the bilateral defense relationship.[160]

Arms Sales.[161] Along with increasing military-to-military ties, the issue of U.S. arms sales to India has taken a higher profile, with some analysts anticipating that New Delhi will spend as much as $40 billion on weapons procurement over the next five years.[162] The first-ever major U.S. arms sale to India came in 2002, when the Pentagon negotiated delivery of 12 counter-battery radar sets (or "Firefinder" radars) worth a total of $190 million. India also purchased $29 million worth of counterterrorism equipment for its special forces and has received sophisticated U.S.made electronic ground sensors to help stem the tide of militant infiltration in the Kashmir region. In 2004, Congress was notified of a sale to India involving up to $40 million worth of aircraft self-protection systems for mounting on the Boeing 737s that carry India's head of government. Moreover, the State Department has authorized Israel to sell to India the jointly developed U.S.-Israeli Phalcon airborne early warning system, an expensive asset that some analysts believe may tilt the regional strategic balance even further in India's favor.

In 2006, Congress authorized and New Delhi approved the $44 million purchase of the *USS Trenton*, a decommissioned American amphibious transport dock. The ship, which became the second largest in the Indian navy when it was commissioned as the *INS Jalashwa* in June 2007, set sail for India carrying six surplus Sikorsky UH-3H Sea King helicopters purchased for another $39 million.[163] In May 2007, the Pentagon notified Congress of a possible sale to India of six C-130J Hercules military transport aircraft (along with related equipment, training, and services) in a deal that could be worth more than $1 billion to the manufacturer, Maryland-based Lockheed Martin. In January 2008, Washington and New Delhi signed an agreement to finalize the deal, which represents the largest-ever U.S. defense sale to India.

The Indian government reportedly possesses an extensive list of desired U.S.made weapons, including PAC-3 anti-missile systems, electronic warfare systems, and possibly even combat aircraft. The March 2005 unveiling of the Bush Administration's "new strategy for South Asia" included assertions that the United States welcomed Indian requests for information on the possible purchase of F-16 or F/A-18 fighters, and indicated that Washington is "ready to discuss the sale of transformative systems in areas such as command and control, early warning, and missile defense."[164] India in August 2007 invited foreign tenders for the sale of 126 new multi-role combat aircraft in a deal that could be worth more than $10 billion. Lockheed Martin's F-16 and Illinois-based Boeing's F/A-18 are competing with aircraft built in Russia, France, Sweden, and by a European consortium. Lockheed's pitch reportedly includes offering a "super-cruise" version of the F-16 that saves large amounts of fuel by achieving supersonic speeds without the use of afterburners. Boeing, for its part, has sought to establish multiple joint ventures that could better position the company to become India's preferred aerospace and defense partner.[165]

Some top Indian officials express concern that the United States is a "fickle" partner that may not always be relied upon to provide the reciprocity, sensitivity, and high-technology transfers sought byNew Delhi.[166] In 2006, the Indian Navydeclined an offer to lease two U.S. P-3C maritime reconnaissance aircraft, calling the arrangements too costly. Moreover, India's offset policy states that any defense purchases worth more that $76 million must include offset clauses amounting to at least 30% of the deal's total value. This policy, already described as "narrow" and "fairly restrictive" by the U.S. Ambassador to India, was altered to require that fully half of the value of any multi-role combat aircraft import be attached to offsets. U.S. laws requiring on-site verifications of exported defense equipment may represent a further irritant, as Indian officials reportedly have expressed discomfort with such physical inspections.[167]

Joint U.S.-India military exercises and arms sales negotiations can cause disquiet in Pakistan, where there is concern that induction of advanced weapons systems into the region could disrupt the "strategic balance" there. Islamabad worries that its already disadvantageous conventional military status vis-à-vis New Delhi will be further eroded by India's acquisition of sophisticated "force multipliers." In fact, numerous observers identify a pro-India drift in the U.S. government's strategic orientation in South Asia. Yet Washington regularly lauds Islamabad's role as a key ally in the U.S.-led counterterrorism coalition and assures Pakistan that it will take no actions to disrupt strategic balance on the subcontinent.

U.S.-India Counterterrorism Cooperation. One facet of the emerging "strategic partnership" between the United States and India is greatly increased counterterrorism cooperation. The U.S. State Department's *Country Reports on Terrorism 2007* identified India as being "among the world's most terror-afflicted countries" and counted more than 2,300 Indian deaths due to terrorism in 2007 alone. State finds numerous problems with New Delhi's capacity to combat terrorism:

> The Indian government's counterterrorism efforts remained hampered by outdated and overburdened law enforcement and legal systems. The Indian court system was slow, laborious, and prone to corruption; terrorism trials can take years to complete. Many of India's local police forces were poorly staffed, lacked training, and were ill-equipped to combat terrorism effectively.[168]

Some Indian analysts complain that the intelligence gathering capabilities of India's security forces remain woefully inadequate and preclude effective law enforcement and preventive action.[169]

In November 2001, President Bush and then-Indian Prime Minster Vajpayee agreed that "terrorism threatens not only the security of the United States and India, but also our efforts to build freedom, democracy and international security and stability around the world."[170] In 2002, India and the United States launched the Indo-U.S. Cyber Security Forum to safeguard critical infrastructures from cyber attack. The June 2005 "New Framework for the U.S.-India Defense Relationship" lists "defeating terrorism and violent religious extremism" as one of four key shared security interests, and it calls for a bolstering of mutual defense capabilities required for such a goal.[171] An April 2006 session of the U.S.-India Joint Working Group on Counterterrorism — the seventh such meeting since the group's founding in January 2000 — ended with a statement of determination from both countries to further advance bilateral cooperation and information sharing on such areas of common concern as bioterrorism, aviation security, advances in biometrics, cyber-security and terrorism, WMD terrorism, and terrorist financing.[172] Expanding military-to-military links have included company-level joint counterinsurgency training of army units.[173]

In October 2005, the United States and India concluded a treaty on criminal matters that would institutionalize law enforcement cooperation and create a regularized channel for mutual assistance. Among the hoped-for benefits has been more effective counterterrorism efforts.[174] It was reported in May 2006 that the United States had offered demining assistance, counterinsurgency training for police forces, and humanitarian relief for persons internally displaced by conflict related to the Maoist rebellion.[175] Moreover, three months after the July 2006 Bombay terrorist bombings, senior CIA officials reportedly traveled to New Delhi to discuss improving counterterrorism cooperation with Indian leaders, and an FBI official later called for closer law enforcement and intelligence coordination with India in light of terrorist attacks in that country's interior.[176] There have been signs that U.S. government agencies have taken greater notice of links apparent between Pakistan-based terrorist groups and wanted Indian criminal boss Dawood Ibrahim, who is suspected of residing in Karachi, Pakistan. In 2003, the U.S. Department of the Treasury formally designated Ibrahim as a terrorist supporter and accused him of collaborating with Al Qaeda in South Asia.[177]

Nuclear Weapons and Missile Proliferation[178]

Many policy analysts consider the apparent arms race between India and Pakistan as posing perhaps the most likely prospect for the future use of nuclear weapons by states. In May 1998, India conducted five underground nuclear tests, breaking a self-imposed, 24-year moratorium on such testing. Despite international efforts to dissuade it, Pakistan quickly followed. The tests created a global storm of criticism and represented a serious setback for two decades of U.S. nuclear nonproliferation efforts in South Asia. Following the tests, President Clinton imposed full restrictions on non-humanitarian aid to both India and Pakistan as mandated under Section 102 of the Arms Export Control Act. India currently is believed to have enough fissile material, mainly plutonium, for 55-115 nuclear weapons; Pakistan, with a program focused on enriched uranium, may be capable of building a similar number. Both countries have aircraft capable of delivering nuclear bombs. India's military has inducted short- and intermediate-range ballistic missiles, while Pakistan itself possesses short- and medium-range missiles (allegedly acquired from China and North Korea). All are assumed to be capable of delivering nuclear warheads over significant distances.

Proliferation in South Asia is part of a chain of rivalries — India seeking to achieve deterrence against China, and Pakistan seeking to gain an "equalizer" against a conventionally stronger India. In 1999, a quasi-governmental Indian body released a Draft Nuclear Doctrine for India calling for a "minimum credible deterrent" (MCD) based upon a triad of delivery systems and pledging that India will not be the first to use nuclear weapons in a conflict. In 2003, New Delhi announced creation of a Nuclear Command Authority. After the body's first session in September of that year, participants vowed to "consolidate India's nuclear deterrent." India thus appears to be taking the next steps toward operationalizing its nuclear weapons capability. According to the director of the U.S. Defense Intelligence Agency in a 2007 statement to a Senate panel, India is building its stockpile of fission weapons and is likely to continue work on advanced warhead and delivery systems.[179]

U.S. Nonproliferation Efforts and Congressional Action

Soon after the May 1998 nuclear tests in South Asia, Congress acted to ease aid sanctions through a series of legislative measures.[180] In September 2001, President Bush waived remaining sanctions on India pursuant to P.L. 106-79. During the 1990s, the U.S. security focus in South Asia sought to minimize damage to the nonproliferation regime, prevent escalation of an arms race, and promote Indo-Pakistani bilateral dialogue. In light of these goals, the Clinton Administration set out "benchmarks" for India and Pakistan based on the contents of U.N. Security Council Resolution 1172, which condemned the two countries' nuclear tests. These included signing and ratifying the Comprehensive Nuclear Test Ban Treaty (CTBT); halting all further production of fissile material and participating in Fissile Material Cutoff Treaty negotiations; limiting development and deployment of WMD delivery vehicles; and implementing strict export controls on sensitive WMD materials and technologies.

Progress in each of these areas has been limited, at best, and the Bush Administration quickly set aside the benchmark framework. Along with security concerns, the governments of both India and Pakistan face the prestige factor attached to their nuclear programs and domestic resistance to relinquishing what are perceived to be potent symbols of national power. Neither has signed the CTBT, and both appear to be producing weapons-grade fissile materials. (India has consistently rejected the CTBT, as well as the Nuclear Nonproliferation Treaty, as discriminatory, calling instead for a global nuclear disarmament regime. Although both India and Pakistan currently observe self-imposed moratoria on nuclear testing, they continue to resist signing the CTBT — a position made more tenable by U.S. Senate's rejection of the treaty in 1999.) The status of weaponization and deployment is unclear, though there are indications that this is occurring at a slow but steady pace. Section 1601 of P.L. 107-228 outlined U.S. nonproliferation objectives for South Asia. Some in Congress identify "contradictions" in U.S. nonproliferation policy toward South Asia, particularly as related to the Senate's rejection of the CTBT and U.S. plans to build new nuclear weapons. In May 2006, the United States presented in Geneva a draft global treaty to ban future production of fissile material (a Fissile Material Cutoff Treaty) that it hopes will be supported by India. Some analysts speculated that the move was meant to bolster U.S. congressional support for proposed U.S.-India civil nuclear cooperation.

India's Economy and U.S. Interests[181]

Overview

India is in the midst of a major and rapid economic expansion, with an economy projected to soon be the world's third largest. Although there is widespread and serious poverty in the country, observers believe long-term economic potential is tremendous, and recent strides in the technology sector have brought international attention to such new global high-tech centers as Bangalore and Hyderabad. However, many analysts and business leaders, along with U.S. government officials, point to excessive regulatory and bureaucratic structures as a hindrance to the realization of India's full economic potential. The high cost of capital (rooted in large government budget deficits) and an "abysmal" infrastructure also draw negative appraisals as obstacles to growth. Constant comparisons with the progress of the Chinese economy show India lagging in rates of growth and foreign investment, and in the removal of trade barriers. Just prior to his March 2006 visit to New Delhi, President Bush noted India's "dramatic progress" in economic reform while insisting "there's more work to be done," especially in lifting caps on foreign investment, making regulations more transparent, and continuing to lower tariffs.[182]

According to the Economist Intelligence Unit, India's per capita GDP was only about $824 in 2007. The highly-touted information technology and business processing industries employ only about one-third of one percent of India's work force and, while optimists vaunt an Indian "middle class" of some 300 million people, a larger number of Indians subsists on less than $1 per day.[183] Yet, even with the existence of ongoing problems, the current growth rate of India's increasingly service-driven economy is among the highest in the world and has brought the benefits of development to many millions of citizens. The U.N. Development Program ranked India 128th out of 177 countries on its 2007/2008 human development index (between Morocco and Laos), down from 126th in 2006.[184]

After enjoying an average growth rate above 6% for the 1990s, India's economy cooled with the global economic downturn after 2000. Yet sluggish, Cold War-era "Hindu rates of growth" had become a thing of the past. For the fiscal year ending March 2006, real change in GDP was 8.5%, the second-fastest rate of growth among the world's 20 largest economies. During FY2006/2007, India's economy expanded by a blistering 9.2% and nearly matched this rate again in FY2007/2008 with a 9% expansion. Robust growth in the services, manufacturing, and industry sectors continues, but is moderated by a weak agricultural sector (low productivity levels in this sector, which accounts for nearly one-fifth of the country's GDP, are a drag on overall growth).[185] Short-term estimates are encouraging, predicting expansion well above 7% for the next two years. A major upswing in services is expected to lead; this sector now accounts for more than half of India's GDP.

India's central bank warned in early 2007 that rising inflation and surging stock and property markets were "signs of overheating" in the country's economy. Some analysts criticize the bank for being too timid in reining in domestic demand.[186] Consumer price inflation rose somewhat in mid-2007, then appeared to level off at a lower rate toward year's end (with a year-on-year rate of 5.5% in January), but may rise again in 2008. The soaring Bombay Stock Exchange tripled in value from 20012006, then apparently overheated with the worst-ever daily decline of its benchmark Sensex index on May 22, 2006, when almost 11% of its total value was lost (related also to political developments). The market subsequently stabilized and then recovered mightily, reaching new highs in the closing months of 2006. More new record highs became even more frequent in the latter half of 2007 and the Sensex was up nearly 40% for the year. India now boasts more billionaires than any other Asian country and has the fourth most in the world, trailing only the United States, Germany, and Russia. The bounty of India's newly-super-wealthy is traced largely to phenomenal gains in the country's stock market, but, in a further indicator of serious income disparity, only about 2% of the country's working-age population hold any stock at all.[187]

A major U.S. concern with regard to India is the scope and pace of reforms in what has been that country's quasi-socialist economy. Reforms begun in 1991, under the Congress-led government of Prime Minister Rao and his finance minister, current Prime Minister Singh, boosted growth and led to major new inbound foreign investment in the mid-1990s. Reform efforts stagnated, however, under weak coalition governments later in the decade, and combined with the 1997 Asian financial crisis and international sanctions on India (as a result of its 1998 nuclear tests) to further dampen the economic outlook. Following the 1999 parliamentary elections, the BJP-led government launched second-generation economic reforms, including major deregulation, privatization, and tariff-reducing measures.

Once seen as favoring domestic business and diffident about foreign involvement, New Delhi appears to gradually be embracing globalization and has sought to reassure foreign investors with promises of transparent and nondiscriminatory policies. A January 2007 report from global investment banking and securities firm Goldman Sachs called India's recent high growth rates a result of structural rather than cyclical increases and projected a sustainable growth rate of about 8% through 2020. It identified political developments — including a rise in protectionism; supply-side restraints, including business climate, education, and labor market reforms; and environmental degradation — as representing major risks to future growth.[188] An October 2007 country survey from the Paris-based Organization for Economic Cooperation and Development (OECD) traced India's economic successes to reforms that reduced the role of the state in economic affairs and claimed that New Delhi's pursuit of further "ambitious and wide-ranging reforms" could push India's growth rate to a sustainable 10% annually.[189] Other analyses identify water shortages, urban woes, and pollution as further potential threats to Indian prosperity.[190]

Trade and Investment

As India's largest trade and investment partner, the United States strongly supports New Delhi's continuing economic reform policies. A U.S.-India Trade Policy Forum was created in November 2005 to expand bilateral economic engagement and provide a venue for discussing multilateral trade issues. The United States currently accounts for about one-sixth of all Indian exports. India was the 16th largest export market for U.S. goods in 2007 (up from 21st the previous year). Levels of U.S.-India trade, while relatively low, are blossoming; the total value of bilateral trade has doubled since 2001 and the two governments intend to see it doubled again by 2009. U.S. imports from India in 2007 were valued at $24 billion (up 10% over 2006). Leading imports included cotton apparel; textiles; and pearls, gemstones, and jewelry. Exports to India in 2007 totaled $17.6 billion (up 75% over 2006), with civilian aircraft; telecommunications equipment; finished pearls, gemstones, and jewelry; and chemical fertilizers as leading categories. Bilateral trade in private commercial services was worth more than $13 billion more, split evenly between imports and exports.[191]

Annual inward direct investment to India from all countries rose from a mere $74 million in 1991 to $5.5 billion in 2001 and $17.5 billion in 2006.[192] Net portfolio investment added another $7.1 billion in FY2006/2007. According to Indian officials, about one-seventh of foreign direct investment in India since 1991 has come from U.S. firms; in recent years, the major U.S.-based companies Microsoft, Dell, Oracle, and IBM have made multi-billion-dollar investments in India (U.S. firms invested about $2 billion in India in 2006; Indian companies invested roughly the same amount in the United States). The stock of U.S. foreign direct investment in India was just below $9 billion for 2006. India's foreign exchange reserves were at a record $300 billion in August 2008. India has moved to raise limits on foreign investment in several key sectors, although U.S. officials prod New Delhi to make more rapid and more substantial changes to foreign investment ceilings, especially in the retail, financial services, and banking sectors. In March 2006, the U.S.-India CEO Forum — composed of ten chief executives from each country representing a cross-section of key industrial sectors — issued a report identifying India's poor infrastructure and dense bureaucracy as key impediments to increased bilateral trade and investment relations.[193]

In a May 2007 speech on U.S.-India relations, Under Secretary of State Burns captured all the major U.S. concerns (and advice) with regard to bilateral economic issues with India, saying New Delhi must insure that

> new regulations or old red tape don't impeded growth, and that foreign companies have a clear path to settling commercial disputes when they arise. The Indian

government should also continue economic reforms and liberalizations that have been the basis of India's economic boom so far. ... In order to achieve higher growth rates as well as broad rural development, India requires world-class airports, irrigation, and communications networks. It needs modern power grids, ports, and highways, and many other infrastructural improvements that could be vastly accelerated by greater investment, both public and private. ... Our focus is on facilitating and promoting foreign direct investment, enhancing bilateral consultations on reducing tariff and non-tariff barriers to trade in industrial goods, services, and agriculture, preventing the illicit use of the financial system, and strengthening India's regime for intellectual property rights.[194]

In September 2007, U.S. Ambassador Mulford opined that, "Continued reform and liberalization will help further boost ... and spread the benefits of rapid economic growth to more recipients across India."[195] During his October 2007 visit to India, U.S. Treasury Secretary Paulson told a Mumbai audience,

In the long term, India can take a number of steps to become even more competitive, such as reducing requirements that financial institutions hold large amounts of government debt, reducing requirements for banks to provide credit to certain priority sectors, and removing various restrictions and caps on foreign investment. Limits on debt and equity financing, and asset allocation restrictions on financial institutions, are impediments to putting resources to their most productive use.[196]

Barriers to Trade and Investment

Despite significant tariff reductions and other measures taken by India to improve market access, according to the 2008 report of the United States Trade Representative (USTR), a number of foreign trade barriers remain, including high tariffs, especially in the agricultural sector. The USTR asserts that "continued reduction of the bilateral trade deficit will depend on significant additional Indian liberalization of the trade and investment regime."[197] The Commerce Department likewise encourages New Delhi to continue lowering tariffs as a means of fostering trade and development. Indian Finance Minister Chidambaram agrees that high rates of investment must be maintained to sustain the country's economic growth. In 2007, India regained full investment-grade status after a 15-year hiatus when Standard & Poor's upgraded India's sovereign rating, but the country's public finances remain much weaker than comparable states: India has a public debt-to-GDP ratio (85%) more than three times higher than China's, and interest consumes nearly one-third of total revenue.[198]

India's extensive trade and investment barriers have been criticized by U.S. government officials and business leaders as an impediment to its own economic development, as well as to stronger U.S.-India ties. For example, in 2004, then-U.S. Under Secretary of State Alan Larson opined that "trade and investment flows between the U.S. and India are far below where they should and can be," adding that "the picture for U.S. investment is also lackluster." He identified the primary reason for the suboptimal situation as "the slow pace of economic reform in India." In 2007, Under Secretary of the Treasury Tim Adams urged India to further reduce trade and investment barriers, liberalize its financial sector, and improve its business climate as key means to "compete effectively in the global economy."[199]

Inadequate intellectual property rights protection is another long-standing issue between the United States and India. The USTR places India on its Special 301 Priority Watch List for "inadequate laws and ineffective enforcement" in this area. The International Intellectual Property Alliance (IIPA), a coalition of U.S. copyright-based industries, estimated U.S. losses of $913 million due to copyright piracy in India in 2007, with some 95% of this in the categories of business and entertainment software (estimated loss amounts do not include motion picture piracy, which in 2004 was estimated to have cost some $80 million). The IIPA expresses frustration that "little significant progress" is being made in more effectively enforcing copyright protection in India.[200] In December 2006, Under Secretary of Commerce and Director of the U.S. Patent and Trademark Office Jon Dudas told a New Delhi audience that "further modifications are necessary" in India's intellectual property rights protection regime and that India's copyright laws are "insufficient in many aspects." He also warned that "piracy and counterfeiting rates will continue to rise without effective enforcement."[201]

While the past two decades have seen a major transformation of the Indian economy, it remains relatively closed in many aspects. The Heritage Foundation's *2008 Index of Economic Freedom* — which some say may overemphasize the value of absolute growth and downplay broader quality-of-life measurements — rated India's economy as being "54% free" and ranked it 115th out of 162 countries. The index highlights restrictive trade policies, heavy government involvement in the banking and finance sectors, rigorous investment caps, demanding regulatory structures, and a high incidence of corruption.[202] Berlin-based Transparency International placed India 72nd out of 179 countries in its 2007 "corruption perceptions index." The group's 2006 "bribery index" found India to be the worst offender among the world's top 30 exporting countries.[203] The Vancouver-based Fraser Institute provides a more positive assessment of economic freedom in India, while also faulting excessive restrictions on capital markets.[204]

Special Economic Zones (SEZs)

In 2005, New Delhi announced plans to allow Indian states to establish Chinese-style special economic zones that would encourage foreign investment and boost employment by bypassing the country's strict labor and tax laws. Parliament soon approved implementation and, in early 2006, the SEZ Act went into effect. With well over 200 such zones approved and hundreds more planned, SEZs became a matter of significant controversy. Proponents view them as sensible means of growing the economy through greatly increased investment, as well as improving infrastructure. Yet the policy has elicited energetic opposition from interest groups representing the political left and right, alike. Some critics say building SEZs on fertile agricultural land will impoverish farmers without adequate compensation. Even Congress Party chief Sonia Gandhi openly opposed exposing farmers to "unscrupulous developers." Other detractors, including India's finance minister, warn that the government will be denied billions of dollars in tax revenues lost due to special concessions offered to participating firms. In early 2007, after Left Front parties demanded extensive curbs on the initiative, New Delhi suspended approval of 304 more SEZs pending decisions on issues including compensation for displaced farmers.[205] In March of that year, police in Nandigram, West Bengal, opened fire on a group of protesters who were demonstrating against state land appropriations for a planned SEZ. At least 14 people were killed and the incident led to days of violent protests against the state government's action. Soon after, the West Bengal government dropped its plans and the federal government vowed to "refine" its SEZ policy to make it more equitable.[206]

Multilateral Trade Negotiations[207]

In 2006, the World Trade Organization's "Doha Round" of multilateral trade negotiations were suspended due to disagreement among the WTO's six core group members — which include the United States and India — over methods to reduce trade-distorting domestic subsidies, eliminate export subsidies, and increase market access for agricultural products. The United States and other developed countries seek substantial tariff reductions in the developing world. India, like other members of the "G-20" group of developing states, has sought more market access for its goods and services in the developed countries, while claiming that developing countries should be given additional time to liberalize their own markets. In particular, India is resistant to opening its markets to subsidized agricultural products from developed countries, claiming this would be detrimental to tens of millions of Indian farmers and result in further depopulation of the countryside. According to Indian officials, the WTO's narrow focus on economic issues excludes political and social variables which are equally sensitive for New Delhi and which constrain the options available to the Indian government. They seek greater U.S. understanding of this dynamic. The Indian economy could benefit significantly from lowered farm subsidies in developed countries and expanded trade in services, but indigenous industries could also be harmed if New Delhi were to reduce tariffs that currently protect India's exporting sectors, especially in textiles and garments.[208]

Indian Commerce Minister Nath has blamed U.S. intransigence for the Doha Round's collapse. In mid-2007, Indian officials rejoined the negotiations, then claimed the talks had again "collapsed" due to lack of convergence among the major actors. U.S. Trade Representative Schwab later expressed surprise at how "rigid and inflexible" India (and Brazil) were during the negotiations, and she suggested that "some countries ... really don't want a Doha round outcome." In September, however, Nath again expressed optimism in identifying a new and "greater comprehension of India's sensitivities" on the effects of U.S. farm subsidies.[209]

Indian leaders were reported to be especially dissatisfied with draft documents they believe are too restrictive of their domestic policies meant to protect Indian farmers from a flood of foreign imports. The U.S. government, for its part, continues to insist that it can only cut its own domestic farm subsidies if advanced developing states such as India (and China and Brazil) do more to open their own markets to foreign goods. In June 2008, a Commerce Department official called India a "roadblock to success" in the negotiations by treating them as a "donor's conference" and resisting all reasonable liberalization proposals, even those being offered by other developing countries.[210] When dialogue was rejoined in July, Commerce Minister Nath assumed the mantle of unofficial spokesman for the world's developing economies, frustrating many Western negotiators by creating what seemed an intractable obstacle to progress. The potentially final collapse of talks came when U.S. negotiators could not agree with their Indian and Chinese counterparts on levels for a "safeguard clause" meant to protect developing states from unrestricted imports, which the Americans believed were being set too low. Some commentators said the Doha Round's failure marked a conclusive end to an era in which free trade was organized around rules set in the West.[211]

The Energy Sector and Climate Change

India's continued economic growth and security are intimately linked to the supply of energy resources. Indeed, Indian leaders insist that energy security is an essential component of the country's development agenda, calling for an integrated national energy policy, diversification of energy supplies, greater energy efficiency, and rationalization of pricing mechanisms. The country's relatively poor natural energy resource endowment and poorly functioning energy market are widely viewed as major constraints on continued economic growth. Estimates indicate that maintaining recent rates of growth will require that India increase its commercial energy supplies by 4%-6% annually in coming years.[212] The U.S. government has committed to assist India in promoting the development of stable and efficient energy markets there; a U.S.-India Energy Dialogue was launched in July 2005 to provide a forum for bolstering bilateral energy cooperation, meeting most recently in New Delhi in April 2008.[213]

Increasing Energy Consumption. India is the world's fifth largest energy consumer and may become third by the middle of this century. Overall power generation in the country more than doubled from 1991 to 2005.[214] Coal is the country's leading commercial energy source, accounting for more than half of national demand. India is the world's third most productive coal producer, and domestic supplies satisfy most demand (however, most of India's coal is an inefficient low-grade, high-ash variety). Oil consumption accounts for some one-third of India's total energy consumption; about 70% of this oil is imported (at a rate of 1.7 million barrels per day in 2006), mostly from the West Asia/Middle East region. India's domestic natural gas supply is not likely to keep pace with demand, and the country will have to import much of its natural gas, either via pipeline or as liquefied natural gas. Hydropower, especially abundant in the country's northeast and near the border with Nepal, supplies about 5% of energy needs. Nuclear power, which Indian government officials and some experts say is a sector in dire need of expansion, currently accounts for only 1% of the country's energy supplies and less than 3% of total electricity generation.[215] Even optimistic projections suggest that nuclear power will provide less than 10% of India's generation capacity in 25 years and there are doubts about New Delhi's projected goal of generating 20 gigawatts of nuclear power by 2020.[216]

Roughly one-fifth of the India's power is consumed by farmers' irrigation systems, making the farm lobby a powerful obstacle to curtailing subsidies provided by State Electricity Boards, which collectively lose billions of dollars annually. Moreover, from one-quarter to one-half of India's electricity is said to disappear though "transmission losses," i.e., theft. In the summer of 2007, worsening shortfalls were causing electrical outages of up to nine hours per day in the industrial and agricultural belts of Punjab, Gujarat, and Maharashtra; the capital of Delhi often has power for only 14 hours each day. A burgeoning electricity crisis may be severely hampering India's continued economic security and growth.[217]

During a March 2007 visit to New Delhi, U.S. Energy Secretary Sam Bodman held wide-ranging talks with numerous Indian officials and business leaders to discuss India's energy needs and strategies for relevant bilateral cooperation. Secretary Bodman stressed "the absolute necessity of substantial and sustained investment in innovation on a global scale" and listed five major global goals for all countries, including the United States and India: 1) diversifying the available supply of conventional fuels and expanding their production; 2) diversifying energy portfolios through expanded use of alternative and renewable sources, including nuclear energy; 3) promoting increased energy efficiency and conservation; 4) reducing pollution and energy intensity in the global economy; and 5) protecting critical energy infrastructure.[218]

Climate Change Policies. With emissions of more than 500 million tons of carbon dioxide per year, India is the world's fourth-largest producer of greenhouse gases (GHGs) (after the United States, China, and Russia). Per capita emissions are, however, only about one-sixteenth those of the United States. The negative impact of climate change likely will be seen across India's broad range of ecosystems, with agriculture, infrastructure, and water resources most affected. Indian officials, who note that India accounts for 17% of the earth's population but only 4% of its GHG emissions, thus far reject any policies or international agreements that would set limits on their own national emissions while calling it "imperative" that developed countries commit themselves to reducing their own emissions. New Delhi criticizes Washington for failing to take "historical responsibility for cumulative emissions" and for bringing "extraneous considerations of industrial competitiveness and employment" to bear on the debate. India asserts that its own continued economic development and poverty reduction efforts preclude capping its GHG emissions and claim there has been a "persistent attempt" by some developed countries to "avoid their legal obligations" under international treaties.[219]

In June 2008, the New Delhi government unveiled India's first-ever "national action plan" to address climate change, with Prime Minister Singh acknowledging that the country faced a "dangerous problem" and vowing to devote greater attention to renewable energy, water conservation, and preserving natural resources. The plan sets forth eight "national missions" for sustainable development: (1) solar energy; (2) enhanced energy efficiency; (3) sustainable habitat; (4) conserving water; (5) sustaining the Himalayan ecosystem; (6) a "Green India;" (7) sustainable agriculture; and (8) a Strategic Knowledge Platform for Climate Change."[220]

Collaborative Efforts. India is a party to both the U.N. Framework Convention on Climate Change and the Kyoto protocol. According to the principles in both these treaties of "common but differentiated responsibility," India is a developing country not required to set legally binding emissions limits under these agreements. In July 2005, the United States joined with India, China, Japan, Australia, and South Korea in the Asia-Pacific Partnership (APP) on Clean Development and Climate, a U.S.-led effort to accelerate the development and deployment of clean energy technologies through a voluntary public-private partnership among six major Asia-Pacific nations. Sydney, Australia, hosted the inaugural meeting in January 2006 and the body's second ministerial meeting was held in October 2007 in New Delhi, where the United States announced providing grant funds for 23 clean technology projects in India under the Partnership's aegis.[221] However, funding shortfalls have hampered the APP initiative since its inception. India also participates in the Major Economies Meeting (MEM) on Energy Security and Climate Change, initiated by President Bush in 2007. The process involves 16 nations (plus the EU) that are major greenhouse gas emitters. Its third session was held in Paris in April 2008.[222]

Some in Congress have sought to increase international cooperation on energy-related matters, including with India. The Energy Diplomacy and Security Act of 2007 (**S. 193**) was reported out of the Senate Foreign Relations Committee in April 2007. The bill includes provisions for establishing energy crisis response mechanisms in cooperation with the governments of India and China. In February, **H.R. 1186**, to promote global energy security through increased U.S.-India cooperation, was introduced in the House. The International Climate Cooperation Re-engagement Act of 2007 (**H.R. 2420**) was reported out of the House Foreign Affairs Committee in June. The bill contains provisions for expanding efforts to promote U.S. exports in clean and efficient energy technologies to India and China. The Clean Energy Partnership With India Act of 2008 (**H.R. 5705**), referred to House committee in April 2008, would establish a commission for improving and promoting bilateral renewable energy cooperation with India.

The Kashmir Issue

Although India suffers from several militant regional separatist movements, the Kashmir issue has proven the most lethal and intractable. Gunbattles and bomb blasts in India's Jammu and Kashmir state reportedly killed an average of 5 or 6 people every day over the period 1989-2006.[223] Conflict over Kashmiri sovereignty also has brought global attention to a potential "flashpoint" for interstate war between nuclear-armed powers. The problem is rooted in competing claims to the former princely state, divided since 1948 by a military Line of Control (LOC) separating India's Muslim-majority Jammu and Kashmir state and Pakistan-controlled Azad [Free] Kashmir. The dispute relates to the national identities of both countries: India has long sought to maintain its secular, multi-religious credentials, in part by successfully incorporating a Muslim-majority region, while Pakistan has since independence been conceived as a homeland for the subcontinent's Muslims. India and Pakistan fought full-scale wars over Kashmir in 1947-1948 and 1965. Some Kashmiris seek independence from both countries. Spurred by a perception of rigged state elections in 1989, an ongoing separatist war between Islamic militants (and their supporters) and Indian security forces in Indian-held Kashmir is ongoing and has claimed tens of thousands of lives.[224]

India blames Pakistan for supporting "cross-border terrorism" and for fueling a separatist rebellion in the Muslim-majority Kashmir Valley with arms, training, and militants. Islamabad, for its part, claims to provide only diplomatic and moral support to what it calls "freedom fighters" who resist Indian rule and suffer alleged human rights abuses in the region. New Delhi insists that the dispute should not be "internationalized" through involvement bythird-party mediators and India is widely believed to be content with the territorial status quo. In 1999, a bloody, six-weeklong battle in the mountains near the LOC at Kargil cost more than one thousand lives and included Pakistani army troops crossing into Indian-controlled territory. Islamabad has sought to bring external major power persuasion to bear on India, especially from the United States. The longstanding U.S. position on Kashmir is that the issue must be resolved through negotiations between India and Pakistan while taking into account the wishes of the Kashmiri people.

During the early years of the Kashmir insurgency, hundreds of thousands of indigenous Hindu "Pandits" were driven from the region in what amounted to a form of "ethnic cleansing." Up to half a million Kashmiri Pandits, accounting for the vast majority of Hindus then living in the area around Srinagar, fled their homes after coming under threat from Muslim militants. For many Indians, the Kashmir dispute cannot be resolved without arrangements for the return of these refugees, more than 100,000 of whom continue to live in camps with government support. Resolutions in the 110th Congress (**H.Con.Res. 55** and **S.Con.Res. 38**) call for the safeguarding of the physical, political, and economic security of the Kashmiri pandits.

Some separatist groups, such as the Jammu and Kashmir Liberation Front (JKLF), continue to seek an independent or autonomous Kashmir. Others, including the militant Hizbul Mujahideen (HuM), seek union with Pakistan.[225] In 1993, the All Parties Hurriyat [Freedom] Conference was formed as an umbrella organization for groups opposed to Indian rule in Kashmir. The Hurriyat membership of more than 20 political and religious groups has included the JKLF (originally a leading militant force, now a political group) and Jamaat-e-Islami (the political wing of the HuM). The Hurriyat Conference, which states that it is committed to seeking dialogue with the Indian government on a broad range of issues, calls for a tripartite conference on Kashmir, including Pakistan, India, and representatives of the Kashmiri people. Hurriyat leaders demand Kashmiri representation at any talks between India and Pakistan on Kashmir. The Hurriyat formally split in 2003 after a dispute between hardliners allied with Islamabad and moderates favoring negotiation with New Delhi. Subsequent efforts to reunify the group failed. In 2005, the Congress Party-led government renewed high-level contact with moderate Hurriyat leaders begun by the previous BJP-led coalition. Two years later, however, Hurriyat leader and noted Kashmiri cleric Mirwaiz Umar Farooq said talks between the Indian government and moderate Kashmiri separatists had suffered a "complete breakdown of communication," and he accused New Delhi of lacking the will needed to find a political solution to the problem.[226]

In December 2006, Pakistani President Musharraf issued a newly-modified version of his "out-of-the-box" thinking on resolution to the Kashmir problem, saying Pakistan is "against independence" for Kashmir, and offering instead a four-point proposal that would lead to "self-governance," defined as "falling between autonomy and independence." Many analysts saw the proposal as being roughly in line with New Delhi's Kashmir position. Some Kashmiri separatist groups rejected the proposal as an abandonment of Islamabad's long-held policy, but Indian leaders welcomed Musharraf's statements; in February 2007, Prime Minister Singh said the Pakistani government was "saying the right thing" in rejecting armed militancy as a solution to the Kashmir problem. Still, a lack of consensus among Kashmiri leaders and political parties has hampered progress. Even Kashmiri political figures who accept the principle of a solution within the framework of the Indian Constitution cannot agree on what such a solution may look like, and the Hurriyat Conference — which may have contributed to its own marginalization by boycotting the state's 2002 elections — remains rife with its own divisions. Some analysts urge greater U.S. efforts to prod the New Delhi and Islamabad governments along in the ongoing search for a final resolution.[227]

At least 8,000 Kashmiris have "disappeared" during the conflict; some of these may occupy the nearly 1,000 unmarked graves discovered near the LOC in early 2008.[228] When measured in terms of human deaths, levels of violence in Kashmir were high and steady through the mid- and late 1990s, peaked in 2001, and have been in decline since. Despite waning rates of infiltration and separatist-related violence, the issue continues to rankle leaders in New Delhi and remains a serious impediment to progress in the current India-Pakistan peace initiative. Even as the normalization of India-Pakistan relations moves forward — and to some extent in reaction to their apparent marginalization in the face of this development — separatist militants continue their attacks on both civilians and Indian security forces, and many observers in both India and the United States believe that active support for Kashmiri militants remains Pakistani policy. The militants, seeing their relevance and goals threatened by movement toward peaceful resolution, regularly lash out with bloody attacks meant to derail the process.

Figure 1 indicates that levels of violence in Kashmir were high and steady through the mid- and late 1990s, peaked in 2001, and have been in decline since. The long-term reduction in violence has allowed for a rebirth of the region's major tourist industry.[229] Yet, despite waning rates of infiltration and separatist-related violence, the issue continues to rankle leaders in New Delhi and remains a serious impediment to progress in the current India-Pakistan peace initiative. Even as the normalization of India-Pakistan relations moves forward — and to some extent in reaction to their apparent marginalization in the face of this development — separatist militants continue their attacks on both civilians and Indian security forces, and many observers in both India and the United States believe that active support for Kashmiri militants remains Pakistani policy. The militants, seeing their relevance and goals threatened by movement toward peaceful resolution, still lash out with bloody attacks likely meant to derail the process.

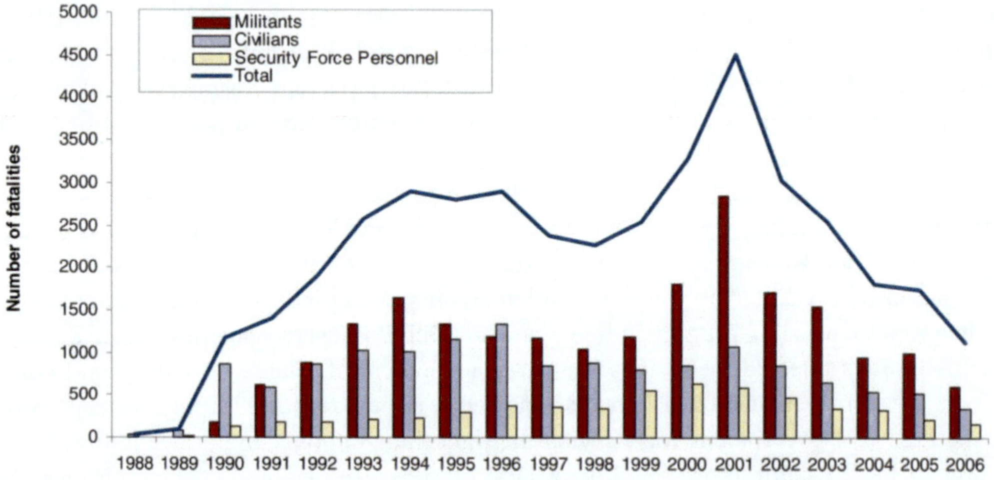

Figure 1. Deaths Related to Kashmiri Separatism, 1988-2006

Source: Adapted by CRS. Data from the Institute for Conflict Management, New Delhi, India.

Despite some ongoing violence, many indicators point to positive long-term trends. The steadily reduced rates of infiltration may be attributed to the endurance of India-Pakistan dialogue and, with a flurry of diplomatic exchanges in late 2006, many analysts saw prospects for a meeting of minds between New Delhi and Islamabad as being better than ever before (determining and incorporating the desires of the Kashmiri people remain highly problematic).[230] In 2006, India's army chief credited much of a 20% drop in levels of violence in the region to the surrender of more and more "disillusioned" militants. At the same time, the state's political leadership has lauded a major decline in reported human rights abuses by security forces, attributing the improvement to policies of restraint launched by the Peoples Democratic Party-Congress Party coalition which took power in 2002.[231] New Delhi has more recently vowed to pull troops out of Kashmir if militant infiltrations and violence there cease, but to date only nominal troop withdrawals have come in response to a somewhat improved security situation in the region. In late 2007, India's Home Ministry stated that the "overall stable security situation in the [Jammu and Kashmir] State is indicative of transition to normalcy."[232] There appears to be widespread public support among Kashmir Valleycitizens for demilitarization of the region and a major reduction in the number of India troops stationed there.[233]

While those responsible for Kashmir's security remain vigilant and convinced that the Islamabad government still "controls the tap" of cross-LOC infiltration, the people of the Muslim-majority Kashmir Valley have been widely approving of the "flexibility" exhibited by Pakistan's president and hopeful that such flexibility will be mirrored in New Delhi so as to create a resolution that works for all stakeholders.[234]

Other Regional Dissidence

The United States maintains an ongoing interest in India's domestic stability and the respect for internationally recognized human rights there. The U.S. Congress has held hearings in which such issues are discussed. As a vast mosaic of ethnicities, languages, cultures, and religions, India can be difficult to govern. Internal instability resulting from diversity is further complicated by colonial legacies such as international borders that separate members of the same ethnic groups, creating flashpoints for regional dissidence and separatism. Beyond the Kashmir problem, separatist insurgents in remote and underdeveloped northeast regions confound New Delhi and create international tensions by operating out of neighboring Bangladesh, Burma, Bhutan, and Nepal. New Delhi has at times blamed the governments of those countries for "sheltering" separatist groups beyond the reach of Indian security forces, and New Delhi has launched joint counter-insurgency operations with some of these neighbors. At the same time, Maoist rebels continue to operate in numerous states and represent a growing threat to internal sovereignty. India also has suffered outbreaks of serious communal violence between Hindus and Muslims, especially in the western Gujarat state.

The Northeast

Since the time of India's foundation, numerous militant groups have fought for greater ethnic autonomy, tribal rights, or independence in the country's northeast region. Some of the tribal struggles in the small states known as the Seven Sisters are centuries old. It is estimated that more than 50,000 people have been killed in such fighting since 1948, including about 20,000 killed in a 28-yearold Naga insurgency and another 10,000 deaths in 15 years of fighting in the Assam state. In the small state of Manipur alone there are said to be more than 20 separatists groups fighting the Indian army at a cost of more than 8,000 lives over two decades, and the writ of the central government there is tenuous, at best.[235] As militant groups are seen to benefit from highly profitable criminal activities such as informal taxation, kidnaping, and smuggling, many observers conclude that only more effective economic development and integration of India's northeast will allow for the resolution of myriad ethnic conflicts there.[236]

The United Liberation Front of Assam (ULFA), the National Liberation Front of Tripura, the National Democratic Front of Bodoland (NDFB), and the United National Liberation Front (seeking an independent Manipur) are among the approximately 40 militant groups at war with the central government. These groups reportedly field a total of no more than 20,000 trained cadres. ULFA, like other groups, accuses New Delhi of exploiting their state's resources while doing little to forward development and allowing thousands of non-indigenous people (often Hindi-speakers from Bihar) to flood the local job markets. In 2005, the U.S. State Department's Counterterrorism Office listed ULFA among its "other groups of concern," the first time an Indian separatist group outside Kashmir was so named.[237] In June 2008, six ULFA field commanders abjured violence and vowed to seek peaceful resolution through negotiation.

Maoist Insurgency

Also operating in India are "Naxalites" — Maoist insurgents ostensibly engaged in violent struggle on behalf of landless laborers and tribals. These groups, most active in inland areas of east-central India, claim to be battling oppression and exploitation in order to create a classless society. Their opponents call them terrorists and extortionists. The groups get their name from Naxalbari, a West Bengal village and site of a militant peasant uprising in 1967. In 2006, Prime Minister Singh identified a worsening Maoist insurgency as "the single biggest internal security challenge" ever faced by India, saying it threatened India's democracy and "way of life."[238] Some of these groups may be growing poppy and extorting farmers and opium traders to fund their activities. Further reports indicate the rebels are placing new emphasis on recruiting child soldiers. Some analysts warn that, by blocking access to raw materials vital to India's manufacturing sector, the Naxalite movement could deter investors and so thwart India's long-term economic success.[239] Naxalites now operate in about half of India's 28 states; related violence has killed more than 6,000 people over the past two decades, including some 650 deaths in 2007. Indian government officials seek to downplay the threat by pointing out that only 2% of the country's 650,000 villages are affected and only 2% of the country's 14,000 police stations report Naxalite activity.[240]

The most notable of India's Maoist militant outfits are the People's War Group (PWG), mainly active in the southern Andhra Pradesh state, and the Maoist Communist Center of West Bengal and Bihar. In 2004, the two groups merged to form the Communist Party of India (Maoist). Both appear on the U.S. State Department Counterterrorism Office's list of "groups of concern" and both are designated as terrorist groups by New Delhi, which claims there are nearly 10,000 Maoist militants active in the country. Other estimates see some 20,000 such fighters in India, including up to 5,000 in the central Chhattisgarh state alone. Such militants possess sophisticated weapons and communications equipment. PWG cadres were behind a 2003 landmine attack that nearly killed the chief minster of Andhra Pradesh. In 2004, that state's government lifted an 11-year-old ban on the PWG, but the Maoists soon withdrew from ensuing peace talks, accusing the state government of breaking a cease-fire agreement. Violent attacks on government forces then escalated in 2005 and have continued with even greater frequency since.

The Chhattisgarh state government has since 2005 sponsored a grassroots anti-Maoist effort. This "Salwa Judum" ("Campaign for Peace" or, literally, "collective hunt") militia — comprised of about 5,000 lightly-armed tribal people who are paid about $1 per day — is viewed by some as an effective countervailing people's movement. Others label it a vigilante group that has engaged in its own coercive and violent tactics against innocent tribals, one that only serves to accentuate the conflict as "a cure that is worse than the disease."[241] Following a March 2007 raid on a Chhattisgarh police camp by up to 600 armed rebels in which 55 people, including 19 policemen, were killed, Maoist leaders threatened further attacks if the Salwa Jundum was not dismantled. A May 2008 report for India's Planning Commission recommended that the Salwa Jundum campaign represented "an abdication of the state itself" and should immediately be ended.[242] New York-based Human Rights Watch later called on the New Delhi and Chhattisgarh governments to end all official support for the campaign, including provision of weapons, and to launch"serious and independent investigations" of related human rights abuses.[243]

Analysts warn that Naxalite activity — including swarming attacks on government facilities and coordinated, multi-state economic blockades — is spreading and becoming more audacious in the face of incoherent and insufficient Indian government policies to halt it. A shortage of police personnel appears to be a key problem. In late 2007, Prime Minister Singh asked India's states to establish specialized, dedicated forces to address Maoist militancy. In mid-2008, the federal government announced plans to create a new 10,000-strong force trained specifically to fight the rebels. However, these efforts do not address the "intellectual appeal" of the Maoists, which India's national security advisor says remains a key problem.[244]

Hindu-Muslim Tensions

Some elements of India's Hindu majority have at times engaged in violent communal conflict with the country's Muslim minority. In 1992, a huge mob of Hindu activists in the western city of Ayodhya demolished a 16th century mosque said to have been built at the birth site of the Hindu god Rama. Ensuing communal riots in cities across India left many hundreds dead. Bombay was especially hard hit and was the site of coordinated 1993 terrorist bombings believed to have been a retaliatory strike by Muslims. In 2002, another group of Hindu activists returning by train to the western state of Gujarat after a visit to the Ayodhya site of the now razed Babri Mosque (and a proposed Hindu temple) were attacked by a Muslim mob in the town of Godhra; 58 were killed. Up to 2,000 people died in the fearsome communal rioting that followed, most of them Muslims. The BJP-led state and national governments came under fire for inaction; some observers saw evidence of state government complicity in anti-Muslim attacks.

The U.S. State Department and human rights groups have been critical of New Delhi's largely ineffectual efforts to bring those responsible to justice; some of these criticisms were echoed by the Indian Supreme Court in 2003. In 2005, the State Department made a controversial decision to deny a U.S. visa to Gujarat Chief Minster Narendra Modi under a U.S. law barring entry for foreign government officials found to be complicit in severe violations of religious freedom.[245] The decision was strongly criticized in India. More than five years after the Gujarat riots, international human rights groups express serious concerns about obstacles faced by victims seeking justice, the continuing internal displacement of thousands of families who lack basic necessities, and large numbers of uninvestigated related criminal cases (despite the Indian Supreme Court's 2004 order to reopen nearly 1,600 such cases). A 2006 central government report found deep communal divisions continuing to haunt Gujarat, concretelyexpressed through ghettoization and religious segregation. In 2008, a U.N. envoy said such divisions combine with a culture of impunity to raise the risk of future violence.[246] Sporadic communal violence continues to affect several Indian states.

Human Rights Issues

Many of India's more than one billion citizens suffer from numerous and oftentimes serious human rights abuses. Some analysts are concerned that, as Washington pursues a new "strategic partnership" with New Delhi, U.S. government attention to such abuses has waned. According to the U.S. State Department's *Country Report on Human Rights Practices, 2007*, the Indian government "generally respected the human rights of its citizens; however, numerous serious problems remained." These included extensive societal violence against women; extrajudicial killings, including faked encounter killings; excessive use of force by security forces, arbitrary arrests, and incommunicado detentions in Kashmir and several northeastern states; torture and rape by agents of the government; "harsh, life-threatening" prison conditions and lengthy pretrial detentions without charge; "pervasive" police corruption; forced prostitution; child prostitution and female infanticide; forced child labor; human trafficking; and "ubiquitous" caste-based discrimination and violence, among others. Terrorist attacks and kidnapings also remained grievous problems, especially in Kashmir and the northeastern states. Indian law provides for extensive human rights protections, but enforcement is "lax" and convictions rare.[247]

The 2007 annual report from New York-based Human Rights Watch noted that India has a vibrant press and civil society, but also suffers from a number of chronic human rights problems. It called impunity a "critical issue" involving officials and members of the security services abusing their power and who are "rarely if ever brought to justice for torture, arbitrary detentions and extrajudicial killings ...." Listed among other human rights concerns in India is the alleged "failure to implement policies that protect the rights of children, religious minorities, those living with HIV/AIDS or those belonging to vulnerable communities such as tribal groups, Dalits and other 'backward' castes." London-based Amnesty International's 2007 annual report also claims that perpetrators of human rights violations in India, in particular those related to 2002 communal rioting in Gujarat, continued to enjoy impunity, and it asserts that concerns over protection of economic, social, and cultural rights of already marginalized communities grew in 2006.[248] The State Department itself recognizes impunity as a major human rights problem in India, asserting in an April 2007 report that "A widespread culture of impunity among police and security forces and pervasive corruption continued to be the principal obstacles to improving human rights" there.[249]

The State Department's Bureau of Democracy, Human Rights, and Labor has claimed that India's human right abuses "are generated by a traditionally hierarchical social structure, deeply rooted tensions among the country's many ethnic and religious communities, violent secessionist movements and the authorities' attempts to repress them, and deficient police methods and training."[250] India's 1958 Armed Forces Special Powers Act, which gives security forces wide leeway to act with impunity in conflict zones, has been called a facilitator of "grave human rights abuses" in several Indian states (in December 2006, Prime Minister Singh said he would seek to amend the controversial Act). In 2007, the problem of "staged encounters" in which police officers kill suspects in faked shootouts came to the fore.[251] India generally denies international human rights groups official access to Kashmir and other sensitive areas.

Human Trafficking

The State Department's latest annual report on trafficking in persons (issued June 2008) said, "India is a source, destination, and transit country for men, women, and children trafficked for the purposes of forced labor and commercial sexual exploitation." It placed India on the "Tier 2 Watch List" for the fifth consecutive year for "failure to provide evidence of increasing efforts to combat trafficking in persons" and for "making no progress" in efforts to address the problem of bonded labor, which affects an estimated 20-65 million Indians. Moreover, State criticized the India's federal and state governments for largely ignoring "the pervasive problem of government complicity in trafficking." Upon the report's release, the head of State's trafficking office, Ambassador Mark Lagan, said "India still doesn't recognize the degree to which bonded labor is a substantial human trafficking problem in its country. It has weak anti-corruption efforts and prosecutions are too few."[252]

Religious Freedom

An officially secular nation, India has a long tradition of religious tolerance (with periodic lapses), which is protected under its constitution. The population includes a Hindu majority of 82% as well as a large Muslim minority of some 150 million (14%). Christians, Sikhs, Buddhists, Jains, and others total less than 4%. Although freedom of religion is protected by the Indian government, human rights groups have noted that India's religious tolerance is susceptible to attack by religious extremists. In its annual report on international religious freedom released in September 2007, the State Department found "no change in the status of respect for religious freedom" by India's national government:

> [G]overnment policy continued to contribute to the generally free practice of religion; however, problems remained in some areas. Some state governments enacted and amended "anti-conversion" laws and police and enforcement agencies often did not act swiftly enough to effectively counter societal attacks, including attacks against religious minorities. Despite Government efforts to foster communal harmony, some extremists continued to view ineffective investigation and prosecution of attacks on religious minorities, particularly at the state and local level, as a signal that they could commit such violence with impunity, although numerous cases were in the courts at the end of the reporting period. The National Government, led by the United Progressive Alliance (UPA), continued to implement an inclusive and secular platform that included respect for the right to religious freedom.

The report added that a "Hindutva" — or Hindu nationalist — ideology continued to influence some government policies and actions at the state and local levels over the previous year.[253]

A May 2008 report of the U.S. Commission on International Religious Freedom noted continued improvements since the 2004 election of the Congress-led coalition, but warned that concerns about religious freedom in India remain. These include ongoing attacks against religious minorities, perpetrated mainly by Hindu activists and most often in states with BJP-led governments. The Commission also continued to criticize allegedly insufficient state efforts to pursue justice in cases related to 2002 communal rioting in Gujarat. More than five years after those riots, the victims are said to still face serious challenges and obstacles in securing justice, and a large number of related criminal cases remain uninvestigated and unresolved.[254]

Caste-Based Discrimination

The millennia-old Hindu caste system reflects Indian occupational and socially-defined hierarchies. Sanskrit sources refer to four social categories: priests (Brahmin), warriors (Kshatriya), traders (Vayisha) and farmers (Shudra). Tribals and lower castes were long known as "untouchables" — a term now officially banned but still widely used — or Dalits.[255] Although these categories are understood throughout India, they describe reality only in the most general terms. National-level legislation exists to protect India's lower castes, yet, according to the U.S. State Department, "The Scheduled Castes and Scheduled Tribes (Prevention of Atrocities) Act lists offenses against disadvantaged persons and prescribes stiff penalties for offenders; however, this act had only a modest effect in curbing abuse and there were very few convictions."[256] In July 2007, **H.Con.Res. 139**, expressing the sense of Congress that the United States should address the ongoing problem of untouchability in India, was passed by the full House.

Female Infanticide and Feticide

Given traditional societal discrimination against females, uneven female-to-male ratios are a matter of concern for India. The incidence of female infanticide and gender-selective abortions is identified as a growing human rights problem in India. The diffusion of enabling medical technology and the existence of unethical doctors have made sex-selective abortions more common there. Prime Minister Singh has called female feticide in India a "national shame" and said the government has a responsibility to curtail the widespread practice. The country's most recent census (in 2001) found only 927 girls aged 0-6 for every 1,000 boys nationwide. Wealthier states, such as Delhi, Punjab, and Gujarat, have the lowest ratios (Punjab's was the lowest at 798).[257] A 2006 study in the British medical journal *Lancet* estimated that up to 10 million Indian females are "missing" due to sex-selective abortions and infanticide over the past two decades, and that some 500,000 girls are being "lost" annually.[258] According to a June 2008 nongovernmental report, the incidence of female feticide is only increasing.[259] The most recent U.S. State Department *Country Report on Human Rights* for India (released March 2008), claims that, in many Indian states,

Baby girls were either aborted or, after birth, left in the cold to contract pneumonia and perish. NGOs alleged that medical practitioners and government workers often were complicit in pushing or persuading women to abort their girl children. Sex determination tests are illegal under the 1994 Pre-Natal Diagnostic Techniques Act. However, NGOs reported that some family planning centers continued to reveal the sex of fetuses. According to the NGO IFES, feticide is a $116 million industry.[260]

In 2007, the New Delhi announced the establishment of a series of orphanages to raise unwanted baby girls in an effort to reduce the incidence of female infanticide.[261]

HIV/AIDS

The United Nations has estimated that 5.7 million Indians are infected with HIV/AIDS, giving India the largest such population worldwide (India overtook South Africa in this category in 2006). However, a July 2007 U.N.-backed study found that India's infected population was about 2.5 million and the U.S. government estimate rises only to 3.1 million.[262] Due to the country's large population, prevalence rates among adults remain below 1%. India's AIDS epidemic has become generalized in four states in the country's south (Andhra Pradesh, Tamil Nadu, Karnataka, and Maharashtra) and two in the northeast (Manipur and Nagaland). According to USAID, these six states account for 80% of the country's reported AIDS cases.[263] India first launched its AIDS control program in 1992; New Delhi boosted related funding to about $120 million in the most recent fiscal year and in July 2007 launched a new $2.8-billion National AIDS Control Program that will expand free treatment for HIV-positive persons, as well as boost the number of awareness and prevention campaigns. Stigma, gender inequalities, and discrimination present major obstacles to controlling India's HIV/AIDS epidemic. In the country's traditional society, open discussion of sexuality and risk of infection is rare, making education difficult: one Indian government survey found that nearly half of Indian women had not even heard of the disease. Analysts opine that substantially greater resources are needed to address HIV/AIDS in India than are currently available.[264]

As part of its foreign assistance program in India, the U.S. government supports integrated HIV/AIDS prevention, treatment, and support services in high prevalence states. India received nearly $30 million in direct U.S. assistance for such programs in FY2007 under the President's Plan for AIDS Relief (PEPFAR), for a projected total of some $136 million for FY2004-FY2008.[265] In January 2007, **H.R. 175**, to provide assistance to combat HIV/AIDS in India, and for other purposes, was introduced in the House, but has not moved out of committee to date.

U.S. Assistance

A total of more than $15 billion in direct U.S. aid went to India from 1947 through 2007, nearly all of it in the form of economic grants and loans, more than half as food aid. In February 2007, in response to several years of rapid Indian economic expansion and New Delhi's new status as a donor government, the State Department announced a 35% reduction in assistance programs for India. The bulk of the cuts are to come from development assistance and food aid programs. Another smaller decrease came in 2008 "in recognition of the continuing growth of the Indian economy and the ability of the government to fund more"development programs.[266]

Economic

According to the U.S. Agency for International Development (USAID), India has more people living in abject poverty (some 385 million) than do Latin America and Africa combined. USAID programs in India, budgeted at about $69 million in FY2008, concentrate on six areas: (1) *health* (improved overall health with a greater integration of food assistance, reproductive services, and the prevention of HIV/AIDS and other infectious diseases); (2) *environment* (improved access to clean energy and water); (3) *education* (improved literacy and teacher capacity); (4) *economic opportunity* (agricultural reform and improved financial markets); (5) *disaster response*; and (6) *tsunami recovery*.[267]

Security

The United States has provided about $169 million in military assistance to India since 1947, more than 90% of this distributed from 1962-1966. In recent years, modest security-related assistance has emphasized export control enhancements, counterterrorism and counternarcotics programs, and military training. Early Bush Administration requests for Foreign Military Financing were later withdrawn, with the two countries agreeing to pursue commercial sales programs. The Pentagon reports military sales agreements with India worth $429 million in FY2002-FY2007.

Selected Relevant Legislation in the 110th Congress

The Tom Lantos Block Burmese JADE (Junta's Anti-Democratic Efforts) Act of 2008 (**H.Res. 1341**) was passed by the House in July 2008.

The Clean Energy Partnership With India Act of 2008 (**H.R. 5705**), was referred to House committee in April 2008.

H.Res 928, expressing the sense of the House that the United States should initiate negotiations to enter into a free trade agreement with India, was referred to House committee in January 2008.

The Clean Energy Act of 2007 became P.L. 110-140 in December 2007. The bill contains provisions for promoting U.S. exports in clean and efficient energy technologies to India and China.

H.Res. 711, expressing the sense of the House concerning the U.S.India nuclear cooperation agreement, was referred to House committee in October 2007.

H.R. 3730, to establish a U.S.-India interparliamentary exchange group, was referred to House committee in October 2007.

S.Res. 339, expressing the sense of the Senate on the situation in Burma, was passed by the full Senate in October 2007.

H.Res. 638, expressing the sense of the House that the U.N. Charter should be amended to establish India as a permanent member of the U.N. Security Council, was referred to House committee in September 2007.

H.Con.Res. 139, expressing the sense of Congress that the United States should address the ongoing problem of untouchability in India, was passed bythe full House and referred to Senate committee in July 2007.

S.Con.Res. 38, calling for the safeguarding of the physical, political, and economic security of the Kashmiri pandits, was referred to Senate committee in June 2007 (a House version, **H.Con.Res. 55**, was referred to House subcommittee in April).

H.R. 1186, to promote global energy security through increased U.S.-India cooperation, was referred to House committee in February 2007.

H.R. 175, to provide assistance to combat HIV/AIDS in India and for other purposes was referred to House committee in January 2007.

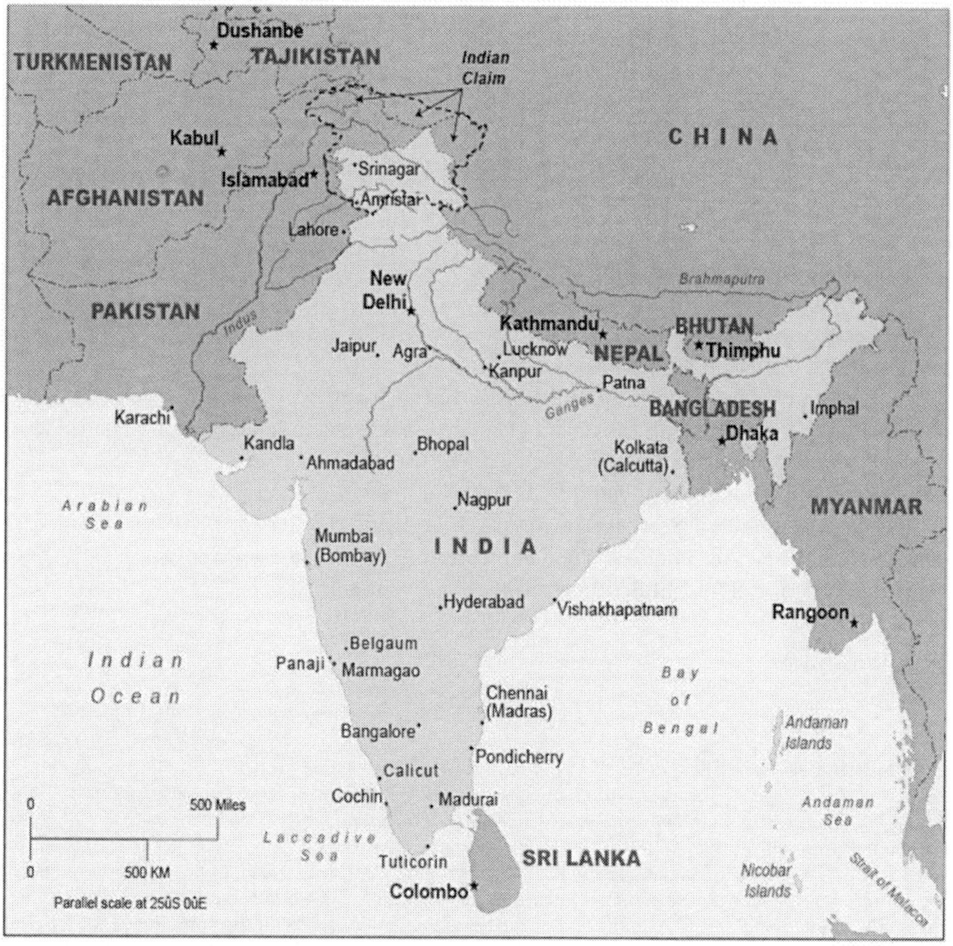

Figure 2. Map of India

Source: Map Resources. Adapted by CRS. (2/2007).

Table 1. Direct U.S. Assistance to India, FY2001-FY2009 (in millions of dollars)

Program or Account	FY 2001	FY 2002	FY 2003	FY 2004	FY 2005	FY 2006	FY 2007	FY 2008 (est.)	FY 2009 (req.)
CSH	24.6	41.7	47.4	47.8	53.2	52.8	53.4	58.9	60.1
DA	28.8	29.2	34.5	22.5	24.9	19.7	15.7	10.5	0.9
ESF	5.0	7.0	10.5	14.9	14.9	5.0	4.9	—	—
IMET	0.5	1.0	1.0	1.4	1.5	1.3	1.5	1.2	1.2
INCLE	—	—	—	—	—	—	—	—	0.4
NADR	0.9	0.9	1.0	0.7	4.2	2.7	1.1	2.7	1.7
PEPFAR	—	—	—	20.4	26.6	29.6	29.9	29.8	[b]
Subtotal	**59.8**	**79.8**	**94.4**	**126.6**	**125.3**	**111.1**	**106.5**	**103.1**	**64.3**
Food Aid[a]	50.4	77.5	35.7	30.8	26.1	30.7	31.0	13.5	13.5
Total	**110.2**	**157.3**	**130.1**	**157.4**	**151.4**	**141.8**	**137.5**	**116.6**	**77.8**

Sources: U.S. Departments of State and Agriculture; U.S. Agency for International Development. FY2008 amounts are estimates; FY2009 amounts are requested. Columns may not add up due to rounding.

Abbreviations:

CSH: Child Survival and Health
DA: Development Assistance
ESF: Economic Support Fund
IMET: International Military Education and Training
INCLE: International Narcotics Control and Law Enforcement
NADR: Nonproliferation, Anti-Terrorism, Demining, and Related (mainly export control assistance, but includes anti-terrorism assistance for FY2007)
PEPFAR: President's Emergency Plan for AIDS Relief

a. P.L. 480 Title II (grants), Section 416(b) of the Agricultural Act of 1949, as amended (surplus donations), and Food for Progress. Food aid totals do not include freight costs.

b. Country sub-allocations for PEPFAR are released later in the fiscal year.

END NOTES

[1] "'I Am Reluctant To Seek Changes In The N-Deal'" (interview), *Outlook* (Delhi), July 21, 2008; John McCain, "America Has a Vested Interest in India's Success" (op-ed), *Indian Express* (Mumbai), August 8, 2008.

[2] See also CRS Report RL33016, *U.S. Nuclear Cooperation With India*, and "Next Steps in Strategic Partnership" section below.

[3] "Congress May Not Pass U.S.-India Nuclear Pact," *Washington Post*, July 9, 2008. According to Section 123b of the Atomic Energy Act, the President is to submit the text to the Senate Foreign Relations Committee and the House Committee on Foreign Affairs. The President is then to consult with the committees for a period of not less than thirty days of continuous session." According to Section 123d, the two committees shall, after that time, "each hold hearings on the proposed agreement for cooperation and submit a report to their respective bodies recommending whether it should be approved or disapproved." Therefore, the minimum amount of time that must elapse before Congress can vote on a joint resolution of approval is 30 days of continuous session, in addition to the amount of time Congress would take to hold hearings.

[4] See [http://www.state.gov/p/us/rm/2007/89559.htm].

[5] A useful table is at [http://www.carnegieendowment.org/files/123agreementchart.pdf].

[6] "End of Nuke Apartheid Against India," *Times of India* (Delhi), August 4, 2007; C. Raja Mohan, "India Gains, US Doesn't Lose" (op-ed), *Indian Express* (Delhi), August 4, 2007.

[7] See [http://www.indianexpress.com/story/239308.html].

[8] G. Parthasarathy, "We Won't Get a Better Deal" (op-ed), *Times of India* (Delhi); "Don't Wait for Obama"(editorial), *Indian Express* (Mumbai), both February 22, 2008; M.R. Srinavasan, "Nuclear Ground Realities" (op-ed), *Indian Express* (Mumbai), March 29, 2008; K. Subramanyam, "Why the Nuke Deal is Crucial" (op-ed), *Times of India* (Delhi), April 7, 2008; "Govt Admits Lack of Fuel Delayed Start-Up of Two N-Power Plants," *Indian Express* (Mumbai), May 8, 2008.

[9] See [http://www.indianembassy.org/newsite/press_release/2007/Aug/4.asp].

[10] See [http://www.indianembassy.org/newsite/press_release/2007/Aug/7.asp].

[11] "Indian Communists Reject U.S. Nuclear Pact," *Reuters*, August 7, 2007; Brajesh Mishra, "No to Subservient Relations," *India Today* (Delhi), September 24, 2007.

[12] See [http://www.indianembassy.org/newsite/press_release/2007/Oct/12.asp].

[13] "India Says Not Given Up on U.S. Nuclear Deal," *Reuters*, January 4, 2008.

[14] See, for example, William Potter and Jayantha Dhanapala, "The Perils of Non-Proliferation Amnesia," *Hindu* (Chennai), September 1, 2007.

[15] See "Fix the Proposal for Renewed Cooperation With India," January 7, 2008, at [http://www.armscontrol.org/pressroom/2008/NSGappeal.asp].

[16] "Indo-US N-Deal 'Nonproliferation Disaster': Critics," *Press Trust of India*, July 11, 2008" Michael Krepon, "Faits Accompli, Complicity, and Nuclear Proliferation," July 30, 2008, at [http://www.stimson.org/pub.cfm?ID=654].

[17] "Courses of Action for Congress and the Nuclear Suppliers Group: A Conversation with the Hon. Edward J. Markey on Nuclear Cooperation Between the United States and India," Council on Foreign Relations, September 13, 2007.

[18] Transcript: House Foreign Affairs Committee Holds Hearing on the Fiscal 2009 International Relations Budget, February 13, 2008; Arms Control Association press release at [http://www.armscontrol.org/pressroom/2008/20080214_Rice_India.asp].

[19] See [http://www.armscontrol.org/node/3240].

[20] Prakash Karat, "Left Will Not Compromise," *People's Democracy* (New Delhi), June 29, 2008; "India's Left-Wing to Reconsider Support for Gov't: Officials," *Agence France Presse*, July 1, 2008.

[21] "Zilchonium Bomb," *Outlook* (Delhi), May 12, 2008; "Nuclear Deal Is Not Dead But Down to Last Days: Mulford," *Hindu* (Chennai), May 20, 2008; "US-India Nuclear Deal Dead," *Financial Times* (London), June 10, 2008.

[22] "India Left Ends Coalition Support," *BBC News*, July 8, 2008

[23] "India Begins Lobbying With IAEA, NSG for Nuclear Deal," *Hindu* (Chennai), July 25, 2008.

[24] "Bush, Singh Agree to Forge Ahead on Nuclear Pact," *Agence France Presse*, July 24, 2008; "No Rush, Please" (editorial), *New York Times*, July 5, 2008.

[25] "India Inspections Deal Meets IAEA Standards: ElBaradei," *Agence France Presse*, August 1, 2008.

[26] "Kakodkar: India is Firm on Unconditional Waiver," *Hindu* (Chennai), August 3, 2008; "India Firm on 'Unconditional' Exemption," *Hindu* (Chennai), August 12, 2008.

[27] "Japan Has 'Concerns' on US-India Nuclear Deal," *Associated Press*, August 5, 2008; "Smaller NSG Nations for Changes in N-Deal?," *Times of India* (Delhi), August 13, 2008. See also "Nuclear Trade Exemption for India Won't Come Easy," *Reuters*, August 8, 2008.

[28] See [http://armscontrol.org/node/3274].

[29] "Post-Bush, India May Have to Start From Scratch," *Hindustan Times* (Delhi), October 23, 2007; [http://www.state.gov/p/us/rm/2008/101628.htm].

[30] In September, India's leading communist party issued an open letter to Parliament expressing the Left Front's strong opposition to the proposed nuclear deal, calling the alleged creation of a "strategic alliance with America" an unacceptable departure from the Common Minimum Program and rejecting a perceived "military alliance with America" (see [http://www.cpim.org/statement/statements_2007.htm]).

[31] "India's Left Issues Blunt Threat Over Nuclear Deal," *Reuters*, September 13, 2007.

[32] According to a U.S.-based analyst, "The abrupt halt ... casts a serious doubt about the willingness and ability of any government in New Delhi to act in a responsible, predictable, and reliable fashion" (Sumit Ganguly, "Save the Nuclear Deal," *Times of India* (Delhi), October 26, 2007).

[33] SP chief Mulayam Singh is viewed as a secular and liberal figure, but he has faced corruption probes and accusations of incompetence as three-time past chief minister of India's most populous state. His key rival is BSP leader and current state Chief Minister Mayawati, whose party won an outright majority in May 2007 state assembly elections. Mayawati, the most important low-caste politician in India's history, has aspirations to become the country's Prime Minister, but also suffers from accusations of corruption ("As Communists Fade, India's New Kingmaker Emerges," *Reuters*, July 12, 2008; "Mayawati Plans to Seek India's Premier Post," *Wall Street Journal*, August 11, 2008).

[34] "SP Says It Will Back Congress in Trust Vote," *Economic Times* (Delhi), July 6, 2008.

[35] Praful Bidwai, "Rightward Turn" (op-ed), *Frontline* (Chennai), August 1, 2008.
[36] "Cong Ready to Open Bag of Bounties," *Telegraph* (Kolkata), July 18, 2008.
[37] "Bribery — and Charges of It — Run Rampant in India," *Wall Street Journal*, July 24, 2008; "Indian Government's Unstable Win," *Christian Science Monitor*, July 24, 2008; "What Price Victory?," *Frontline* (Chennai), August 15, 2008.
[38] "India Wobbles on Fuel Hikes After Anger, Malaysia Firm," *Reuters*, June 6, 2008; "India's Fiscal Gains Offset by Rising Prices," *New York Times*, June 11, 2008.
[39] "Scale of India's Inflation Revealed," *BBC News*, June23, 2008; "India's Ratings Under Cloud as Govt Finances Sour," *Reuters*, July 15, 2008; "Power Crisis Hits Indian states," *BBC News*, July 25, 2008.
[40] "India Inc: Reforms May Get Impetus," *Financial Express* (Mumbai), July 23, 2008; "India Vows to Revive Economic Reforms," *Financial Times* (London), July 23, 208; "Despite Left Exit, India Shackled Over Reforms," *Reuters*, July 7, 2008.
[41] Kaushik Basu, "India's Economy - Reasons to Be Cheerful" (op-ed), *BBC News*, June 18, 2008.
[42] "Quietly Forward," *Frontline* (Chennai), June 20, 2008.
[43] "India Frustrated by a Rudderless Pakistan," *New York Times*, August 12, 2008; "India Yearns for Pakistan's Musharraf Amid Turmoil," *Associated Press*, August 12, 2008.
[44] "Q&A With Indian National Security Advisor MK Narayanan," *Straits Times* (Singapore), August 12, 2008.
[45] July's terrorist attacks may represent the "Indianization of the jihad," according to some analysts. The violence spurred many commentators to lament what they describe as an incompetent national security apparatus ("Sophisticated Attacks Catch Indian Agencies Napping," *Reuters*, July 29, 2008; "Hello, Anybody There?" (editorial), *Times of India* (Delhi), July 29, 2008).
[46] "India to Protest to Pakistan Over Border Shooting," *Reuters*, May 19, 2008; "Pakistan 'Behind Afghan Attacks,'" *BBC News*, July 14, 2008; "India Blames Pakistan in Embassy Bombing," *Associated Press*, July 21, 2008; "Pakistanis Aided Attack in Kabul, U.S. Officials Say," *New York Times*, August 1, 2008; "Bombings May Threaten India-Pakistan Relations,"*Christian Science Monitor*, July 28, 2008; "ISI Looking to Push 800 Militants Into India: BSF," *Indian Express* (Mumbai), August 4, 2008.
[47] "Briefing by Foreign Secretary After India-Pakistan Foreign Secretary-Level Talks," Indian Ministry of External Affairs, July 21, 2008; "India Official Sees Sinking Relations With Pakistan," *New York Times*, August 1, 2008.
[48] "Bombings May Threaten India-Pakistan Relations,"*Christian Science Monitor*, July 28, 2008; "Skirmishes Can Hurt India-Pakistan Peace Process," *Reuters*, July 30, 2008; Indian Ministry of External Affairs Press Briefing, August 7, 2008; "India Reacts 'Strongly' to Pakistan Comments on Kashmir Violence," *BBC Monitoring South Asia*, August 12, 2008; "Pakistan Warns of New Nuclear Arms Race With India," *Associated Press*, July 23, 2008.
[49] "Kashmir Strike as Tensions Rise," *BBC News*, August 7, 2008; "Kashmir Short of Essentials After Highway Blockade," *Reuters*, August 5, 2008; "Indian Leaders Urge Kashmir Talks," *BBC News*, August 6, 2008"; "Violence Threatens Kashmir Peace," *BBC News*, August 11, 2008.
[50] See [http://www.worldpublicopinion.org/pipa/pdf/jul08/Kashmir_Jul08_rpt.pdf].
[51] See [http://www.usindiafriendship.net/archives/usindiavision/delhideclaration.htm].
[52] See [http://clinton4.nara.gov/WH/new/html/Wed_Oct_4_105959_2000.html].
[53] See [http://www.state.gov/p/sca/rls/rm/6057.htm].
[54] [http://www.whitehouse.gov/news/releases/2005/07/20050718-6.html].
[55] [http://www.whitehouse.gov/news/releases/2006/03/20060302-5.html].
[56] See [http://www.comw.org/qdr/fulltext/nss2002.pdf] and [http://www.comw.org/qdr/fulltext/nss2006.pdf].
[57] [http://armed-services.senate.gov/statemnt/2007/February/McConnell%2002-27-07.pdf].
[58] Nicholas Burns, "America's New Strategic Opportunity With India," *Foreign Affairs*, November/December 2007.
[59] See [http://www.state.gov/secretary/rm/2007/06/87487.htm].
[60] Stephen Cohen cited in "Look Before You Hop" (interview); Harsh Pant, "'Adamant for Drift, Solid for Fluidity,'" both in *Pragati: The Indian National Interest Review*, June 2008 and July 2008, respectively.
[61] See "Indian Community Burgeoning in America," *Associated Press*, October 22, 2006; "Forget the Israel Lobby, the Hill's Next Big Player is Made in India," *Washington Post*, September 30, 2007.
[62] See also CRS Report RL33498, *Pakistan-U.S. Relations*.
[63] While levels of violence in Kashmir declined significantly in 2007 as compared to the previous year, some Indian analysts see signs that Islamist militants will seek to reverse this trend, perhaps with the urging and even support of Pakistani government elements. According to Indian National Security Advisor M.K. Narayanan, a former chief of the country's domestic intelligence agency, very few Indian Muslims have played major roles in domestic terrorism. He has asserted that, "Mostly, the [terrorist] activity has been generated from outside" and "the overwhelming majority" of India's terrorism problems emanates from the Pakistan-Afghanistan border region. Internal Indian government documents reportedly conclude that Pakistan's main intelligence agency has not changed its central objectives, which, according to these sources, include supporting anti-Indian militancy in Kashmir, Punjab, Assam, and along the India-Nepal and India-Bangladesh borders ("Negotiating War," *Outlook* (Delhi), May 28, 2008; "MK Narayanan" (interview), *India Abroad*, September

21, 2007; "ISI Still Helping Terror Groups Against India: Narayanan," *Times of India* (Delhi), March 26, 2008; "No Let Up in ISI Operations: Report," *Times of India* (Delhi), June 9, 2008).

[64] "As Pakistan Boils, India Watches," *Chicago Tribune*, December 30, 2007; "Pakistan Turmoil Draws Muted Concern in India," *Washington Post*, January 19, 2008; Praful Bidwai, "Changing Pakistan" (op-ed), *Frontline* (Chennai), July 4, 2008.

[65] See Pakistan Foreign Ministry Press Release No. 81/2007 at [http://www.mofa.gov.pk/ Press Releases/2007/March/PR_81_07.htm].

[66] See [http://www.mofa.gov.pk/Spokesperson/2007/Sep/Spokes_17_09_07.htm].

[67] See [http://www.indianembassy.org/newsite/press_release/2008/Mar/1.asp]; "Benazir Bhutto's Widow Wants Improved Relations With India,"*Associated Press*, March 1, 2008; "India PM Wants to Meet Pakistan's Leaders Halfway," *Reuters*, March 5, 2008.

[68] "India, Pakistan Say Satisfied With Peace Process," *Agence France Presse*, May 20, 2008; "Quietly Forward," *Frontline* (Chennai), June 20, 2008.

[69] See a 2007 International Campaign to Ban Landmines report at [http://www.icbl.org/ lm/2007/india.html].

[70] See Polly Nayak and Michael Krepon, "US Crisis Management in South Asia's Twin Peaks Crisis" at [http://www.stimson.org/southasia/pdf/USCrisisManagement.pdf].

[71] See, for example, "Wary of China, India to Boost Eastern Naval Fleet," *Reuters*, November 14, 2007; "Indian Army Wants Military Space Program," *Associated Press*, June17, 2008.

[72] For example, China is developing a billion dollar commercial port on the southern tip of Sri Lanka. Some Indian analysts fear the port could be used to support Chinese naval activity in the India Ocean ("India, China Jostle for Influence in Indian Ocean," *Associated Press*, June 7, 2008).

[73] An example is found in relations with Africa, where India's historical advantage has been eroded by Beijing's deeper pockets. The value of China's two-way trade with African countries is now more than double that of India's ("On China's Heels, India Vies for Its Old Edge in Africa," *Christian Science Monitor*, May 5, 2008).

[74] Brahma Chellaney, "Don't Get Cowed Down" (op-ed), *Times of India* (Delhi), October 2, 2007.

[75] See "India, China Hoping to 'Reshape the World Order' Together," *Washington Post*, April 12, 2005.

[76] March 2008 saw growing violence and instability in the disputed Tibet region when pro-independence protesters there took to the streets of Lhasa and Chinese government forces were deployed to suppress the agitators. While India recognizes Chinese sovereignty in Tibet, for 50 years the Indian city of Dharamasala has been home to the exiled Dalai Lama — a Tibetan spiritual leader and focus of the pro-independence movement — as well as to some 180,000 other Tibetan exiles who are given refuge but who are not allowed to engage in political activities on Indian soil. Discord in Tibet creates a dilemma for New Delhi, where officials seek to balance human rights concerns with a desire to maintain warm relations with Beijing. Many large Indian rivers originate in Tibet. Both India and the United States support Chinese dialogue with the Dalai Lama, even as New Delhi warns that figure to refrain from political activity. Some analysts criticize New Delhi's perceived timidity on the issue and assert that India's aspired great power status requires standing up to China on human rights issues. During her March visit to India, Speaker of the House Rep. Nancy Pelosi met with and expressed support for the Dalai Lama, and called on the Chinese government to end its violent crackdown in Lhasa (see [http://www.house.gov/ pelosi/press/releases/March08/dalai-lama.html]).

[77] "Aiming Low at China-India Summit," *BBC News*, January 13, 2008; "Shared Vision" at [http://meaindia.nic.in].

[78] "India, China Pledge Stronger Ties on Foreign Minister's Visit Amid Tensions," *Associated Press*, June 6, 2008.

[79] See [http://www.indianembassy.org/newsite/press_release/2008/Mar/1.asp].

[80] "Belated Awakening," *India Today* (Delhi), February 18, 2008; "India to Counter China With Strengthened Border Presence," *Jane's Defense Weekly*, February 20, 2008.

[81] "China Does Intrude Into India, Admits India," *Indian Express* (Delhi), January 12, 2008; "China's New N-Submarine Base Sets Off Alarm Bells," *Indian Express* (Mumbai),May 3, 2008; "India in China's Nuke Crosshairs," *Times of India* (Delhi), May 17, 2008; "Indian Army Wants Military Space Program," Associated Press, June 17, 2008; "India Army Chief Wary of Growing China Military," Reuters, July 3, 2008.

[82] See [http://www.state.gov/s/d/2007/94077.htm]and [http://meaindia.nic.in/pbhome.htm].

[83] "India to Push On With Myanmar Port Despite Unrest," *Reuters*, October 10, 2007; "India Silent on Myanmar Crackdown," *Associated Press*, October 23, 2007. One observer called New Delhi's policy a "reprehensively passive and callous posture" toward Burma's pro-democracy forces (Praful Bidwai, "Failing the Foreign Policy Test" (op-ed), *Frontline* (Chennai), October 19, 2007).

[84] "India Renews Pressure on Myanmar, Suggests Probe," *Reuters*, October 1, 2007; "India Silent on Myanmar Crackdown," *Associated Press*, October 23, 2007.

[85] See, for example, Shishir Gupta, "Rangoon Isn't Kathmandu" (op-ed), *Indian Express* (Delhi), October 2, 2007.

[86] "India's Halt to Burma Arms Sales May Pressure Junta," *Washington Post*, December 30, 2007; "Indian arms Sales to Myanmar Remain Under Scrutiny," *Jane's Defence Weekly*, January 16, 2008. In 2006, India transferred to Burma two maritime surveillance aircraft and a number of air defense guns, and the Indian defense minister announced the sale to Burma of more defense equipment — including tanks and heavy artillery — in exchange for Rangoon's counterterrorism cooperation and assistance in neutralizing Indian

separatists operating near their shared border ("Why India is Selling Weapons to Burma" *Christian Science Monitor*, July 23, 2007).

[87] Since 1988, the United States has imposed a wide range of sanctions against Burma, including passage of the Burma Freedom and Democracy Act of 2003 (P.L. 108-61) banning imports from Burma (renewed by Congress in 2007). In a 2007 floor statement, the Chairman of the House Foreign Affairs Committee criticized India (and China) for propping up the Rangoon government "through shockingly direct, blatant deals, including arms trading with this cruel junta in Burma." New York-based Human Rights Watch has lambasted India (among other countries) for "supplying Burma with weapons that the military uses to commit human rights abuses and to bolster its ability to maintain power" (see [http://hrw.org/english/docs/2007/10/10/burma17066.htm]).

[88] See the External Affairs Ministry January 2, 2008, press briefing at [http://meaindia.nic.in/pbhome.htm].

[89] "India Rushes Aid to Myanmar, Helping Warming Ties," *Reuters*, May 5, 2008.

[90] See also CRS Report RS22486, *India-Iran Relations and U.S. Interests*, and CRS Report RS20871, *The Iran-Libya Sanctions Act*.

[91] See text of the January 2003 "New Delhi Declaration" at [http://meaindia.nic.in/ declarestatement/2003/01/25jd1.htm]. In December 2007, Indian Foreign Secretary Menon visited Iran, where he held several high-level meetings and reiterated New Delhi's interest in establishing a strategic partnership with Tehran.

[92] Indian Ministry of External Affairs Press Briefing, July 14, 2008.

[93] Although President Bush indicated he has not adopted the law's statements of policy as U.S. foreign policy, this provision rankled many in New Delhi who view it as an "extraneous" constraint on India's foreign policy independence. In their explanatory statement accompanying P.L. 109-401, congressional conferees repeatedly emphasized their belief that securing India's assistance on this matter was "critical" (H.Rept. 109-721).

[94] See, for example,"Indian Navy Trains Iranian Sailors," *Defense News*, March 27, 2006; C. Christine Fair, "India and Iran: New Delhi's Balancing Act," *Washington Quarterly*, Summer 2007; "India Trains Iranian Navy Despite US Pressure," *Hindustan Times* (Delhi), September 4, 2007.

[95] In April, eight U.S. Senators sent a letter to Prime Minister Singh requesting that New Delhi "suspend its military cooperation" with Iran, asserting that "India's own interests are damaged by its support for the Iranian military" and that "India's principles are also poorly served by deepening its military relationship with Iran." In May, eight U.S. Representatives — including the Chair and Ranking Member of the House Foreign Affairs Committee — sent Singh a letter expressing "grave concern" at India's "increasing cooperation" with Iran. In July, a letter to President Bush by 23 House Members expressed concern with "India's deepening military-to-military relationship with Iran ... [which] places congressional approval of the Agreement for Nuclear Cooperation in jeopardy." In September, two Senators wrote to Secretary of State Rice to express their concern about India-Iran military-to-military relations, saying that, as supporters of the U.S.-India civil nuclear deal, they are "apprehensive that the [123] agreement could be sidetracked by what appears to be a growing relationship between Iran and India."

[96] "India Official Dismisses Iran Reports," *Washington Post*, May 2, 2007; "US Asks India to Come Clean On Ties With Iran," *Press Trust India*, September 19, 2007. See also "India's Long-Standing Ties With Iran Straining Alliance With U.S.," *Washington Post*, September 20, 2007.

[97] "Briefing by Foreign Secretary Shri Shivshankar Menon on Visit of President Ahmadinejad of Iran to India," Indian Ministry of External Affairs, April 29, 2008.

[98] See [http://www.state.gov/r/pa/prs/dpb/2008/apr/103842.htm]; "India Bristles at US Comments on Ahmadinejad Visit," *Agence France Presse*, May 22, 2008.

[99] See also CRS Report RS22486, *India-Iran Relations and U.S. Interests*, and CRS Report RS20871, *The Iran Sanctions Act (ISA)*.

[100] "China Shows Interest in Iran-Pakistan-India Gas Pipeline Project," *BBC Monitoring South Asia*, April 26, 2008.

[101] "Iran Sees Pipeline Deal With India, Pakistan by Mid-Year: Report," *Agence France Presse*, May 28, 2008; "India's Iran Pipeline Deal," *Forbes*, July 1, 2008.

[102] See, for example, K. Subrahmanyam, "Pipeline Dreams" (op-ed), *Indian Express* (Mumbai), July 3, 2008.

[103] Ariel Cohen, Lisa Curtis, and Owen Graham, "The Proposed Iran-Pakistan-India Gas Pipeline: An Unacceptable Risk to Regional Security," Heritage Foundation Backgrounder No. 2139, May 30, 2008.

[104] "India Won't Be Cowed Down: Deora" *Hindu* (Chennai), May 9, 2007.

[105] "Afghan Bombing Sends Stark Message to India," *New York Times*, July 9, 2008; "India Announces $450 Million Aid to Afghanistan," *Reuters*, August 4, 2008.

[106] "Maoists Scrap 1950 Indo-Nepal Treaty," *Indian Express* (Mumbai), April 24, 2008; "Elections in Nepal: Maoists Offer an Uncharted Course," CSIS *South Asia Monitor* 118, May 2, 2008.

[107] "Russia, India Cement Nuclear Ties With Offer of 4 New Reactors," *Associated Press*, January 25, 2007.

[108] "Are India and Russia No Longer Comrades?," *BBC News*, March 12, 2008.

[109] See [http://www.mofa.go.jp/region/asia-paci/pmv0708/joint-2.html].

[110] See also CRS Report RL32465, *India's 2004 National Elections*.

[111] "BJP on a Roll, Congress on the Ropes," *India Today* (Delhi), June 9, 2008.

[112] "Wake-Up Call for the Congress," *Hindustan Times* (Delhi), May 25, 2008; "Cracks of Doom for India's Ruling Party," *Reuters*, May 26, 2008; "BJP on a Roll, Congress on the Ropes," *India Today* (Delhi), June 9, 2008; "India's Silicon Valley Eyes Political Change," *Reuters*, May 19, 2008.

[113] "Unfinished Progressive Agenda," *India Today* (Delhi), June 11, 2007; "Weak India PM Battered by Allies and Enemies," *Reuters*, October 23, 2007; "The Nuclear Shadow," *India Today* (Delhi), January 14, 2008.

[114] See the Indian National Congress at [http://www.congress.org.in].

[115] "Ruling Party Wonders if India Needs Another Gandhi," *Reuters*, April 15, 2008; "Downsizing Manmohan," *India Today* (Delhi), April 28, 2008.

[116] See the Bharatiya Janata Party at [http://www.bjp.org].

[117] See, for example, A.G. Noorani, "Merchants of Hate" (op-ed), *Frontline* (Chennai), June 21, 2008.

[118] "BJP Goes Back to Hindutva," *Telegraph* (Kolkata), September 2, 2007; "Finally Number One," *India Today* (Delhi), February 11, 2008. In mid-2008, a fanatic Hindu nationalist party and regional ally of the BJP appeared to issue a call for "Hindu suicide squads" as a response to Islamist terrorism, spurring widespread public outrage and embarrassment for the NDA alliance ("Call for Hindu Suicide Squads Sparks Anger in India," *Reuters*, June 1, 2008).

[119] See, for example, "India's 'Untouchables Queen' Gains Power, Enemies," *Reuters*, January 21, 2008.

[120] The new front includes such regional powerhouses as the Telugu Desam of Andhra Pradesh, the AIADMK of Tamil Nadu, and the Samajwadi of Uttar Pradesh.

[121] See the Communist Party of India (Marxist) at [http://www.cpim.org].

[122] In 2008, Congress Party officials have warned Left Front leaders that any effort by communists to forge a "third front" could leave the electoral field open to Hindu nationalist forces found mainly in the BJP and its allies ("India's Ruling Congress Slams Left Ally's 'Third Front,'" *Reuters*, January 21, 2008).

[123] "India Gets Populist Pre-Election Budget," *BBC News*, February 29, 2008.

[124] See [http://www.whitehouse.gov/news/releases/2004/01/20040112-1.html].

[125] See [http://www.whitehouse.gov/news/releases/2005/07/20050718-6.html] and [http://www.indianembassy.org/press_release/2005/June/31.htm].

[126] See also CRS Report RL33016, *U.S. Nuclear Cooperation With India.*

[127] See, for example, a February 2008 speech by Indian Special Envoy and former Foreign Secretary Shyam Saran at [http://www.ndtv.com/convergence/ndtv/popups/shyamsaran.pdf].

[128] Cited in "U.S. Nuclear Deal Won't Power India's Boom," *Reuters*, March 13, 2007.

[129] See [http://www.whitehouse.gov/news/releases/2006/03/20060302-5.html].

[130] See "U.S.-India Civil Nuclear Cooperation Initiative Fact Sheet," U.S. Department of State, at [http://www.state.gov/r/pa/scp/2006/62904.htm]; Condoleezza Rice, "Our Opportunity With India" (op-ed), *Washington Post*, March 13, 2006.

[131] See, for example, an open letter Congress at [http://www.indianembassy.org/newsite/ press_release/ 2006/Mar/30.asp].

[132] See Sridhar Krishnaswami, "Indo-US N-Deal a Historic Opportunity" (op-ed), *India Abroad*, March 22, 2006; "US Nuclear Deal Likely to Get India 40bn Dollars Business," *BBC Monitoring South Asia*, August 13, 2007.

[133] See, for example, open letters to Congress at [http://fas.org/intt2006/ X3e_FDC01218.pdf]; [http://www.armscontrol.org/pdf/20060912_India_Ltr_Congress.pdf]; and [http://www.armscontrol.org/pdf/20051118_India_Ltr_Congress.pdf].

[134] In July 2006, the House passed H.R. 5682 by a vote of 359-68. In November, the Senate passed an amended version of the same bill by a vote of 85-12.

[135] See [http://www.whitehouse.gov/news/releases/2006/12/20061218-1.html]; [http://www.whitehouse.gov/news/ releases/2006/12/20061218-12.html]; "Bush India Statement Raises Congress Concerns," *Reuters*, December 21, 2006.

[136] See [http://www.armscontrol.org/pdf/20070515letteronUSIndia123House.pdf]. The Chairman of the Senate Foreign Relations Committee reportedly has said it would be unlikely that Congress would be willing to further amend U.S. law on nuclear testing and reprocessing ("Biden Cool to US Compromise on India Deal," *Reuters*, May 2, 2007).

[137] [http://markey.house.gov/index.php?option=com_content&task=view&id=3003&Itemid= 141].

[138] See "Press Statement of the BJP on the Indo-US Nuclear Deal," December 10, 2006, at [http://www.bjp.org].

[139] See, for example, "Politics of BJP's Nuclear Tantrum," *Telegraph* (Kolkata), August 7, 2007. Strobe Talbott, a Deputy Secretary of State in the Clinton Administration and a key interlocutor with India, has opined that the BJP government of the 1990s "would have astonished" at and eager to accept a similar deal, had it been offered then ("Buzz of the Week," *India Today* (Delhi), March 17, 2008).

[140] Siddharth Varadarajan, "This Has Nothing To Do With Energy" (op-ed), *Hindu* (Chennai), May 2, 2007; Brahma Chellaney, "Nuclear Non-Starter" (op-ed), *Wall Street Journal*, May 9, 2007.

[141] In February 2007, a former U.S. Assistant Secretary of Defense reportedly said that India's two IAEA votes on Iran had been "coerced" and paved the way for congressional approval of proposed U.S.-India civil nuclear cooperation. U.S. Ambassador to India David Mulford later called the attributed statement "inaccurate" ("'Rademaker is Not a U.S. Official,'" *Hindu* (Chennai), February 17, 2007).

[142] "Major Obstacles Persist in Nuclear Deal," *Hindu* (Chennai), April 25, 2007; A. Gopalakrishnan, "Hyde-Bound N-Deal Cannot Be Accepted" (op-ed), *Asian Age* (Mumbai), May 15, 2007.

[143] See "Excerpts from PM's Reply to Discussion in Rajya Sabha on Civil Nuclear Energy Cooperation with the United States," August 17, 2006, at [http://www.carnegie endowment.org/static/npp/Singh_speech_Aug_ 2006.pdf].

[144] Author interview with Indian government official, New Delhi, September 2006.

[145] See [http://www.state.gov/p/us/rm/2007/89559.htm].

[146] See text of the 123 Agreement at [http://www.state.gov/r/pa/prs/ps/2007/aug/90050.htm].

[147] "In Its Nuclear Deal With India, Washington Appears to Make More Concessions," *New York Times*, July 28, 2007; "India Nuclear Deal Said Complies With US Law," *Reuters*, July 25, 2007; "US Congress to Scrutinize Nuclear Pact With India," *Agence France Presse*, August 3, 2007. H.Res. 711, introduced in the House in October 2007, would seek the Bush Administration clarifications on the 123 Agreement's compliance with U.S. law.

[148] See [http://www.indianembassy.org/newsite/press_release/2008/Mar/1.asp]; "We Can Move Forward With Hyde Act and 123 Agreement: Boucher," *Hindu* (Chennai), March 4, 2008. In a move that angered many nonproliferation advocates who oppose the deal, the State Department requested that congressional staff adhere to unusually strict confidentiality restrictions and not share the answers to congressional inquiries with the general public. Some observers called this "virtual gag order" a strong indication that the answers contained information harmful to the deal's prospects ("State Department Asks Congress to Keep Quiet About Details of Deal," *Washington Post*, May 9, 2008).

[149] In April 2008, India's space agency set a world record by successfully launching ten satellites at one time in what was viewed as an impressive achievement and further sign that Indian scientists had made great and largely indigenous strides in mastering complex aerospace technologies ("India's Growing Strides in Space," *BBC News*, April 30, 2008).

[150] See also CRS Report RL34161, *India-U.S. Economic and Trade Relations.*

[151] See U.S. Department of Commerce, Bureau of Industry and Security, fact sheets at [http://www.bis.doc.gov/ InternationalPrograms/IndiaCooperation.htm] and [http://www.bis.doc.gov/InternationalPrograms/IndialCoop Presentation.htm].

[152] "US Streamlines High-Tech Export Controls on India," *Reuters*, October 2, 2007.

[153] See Commerce's Entity List at [http://www.bis.doc.gov/Entities].

[154] Much information in this section comes from *The Military Balance 2008* (Institute for International and Strategic Studies, London, 2008).

[155] India's January 2008 space launch of an Israeli military satellite elicited a formal complaint from Tehran, especially due to Iranian concerns that the satellite's sophisticated imaging systems will be used to monitor Iran's controversial nuclear program ("Iran Angered Over India's Launch of Israeli Spy Satellite," *Agence France Presse*, February 5, 2008).

[156] See CRS Report RL34187, *Conventional Arms Transfers to Developing Nations, 19992006.*

[157] Ajai Sukla, "Dysfunctional Defense" (op-ed), *Wall Street Journal Asia*, July 19, 2007.

[158] Senate Armed Services Committee Hearing on U.S. Military Command Budgets, April 24, 2007; "US Admiral Says Military Cooperation With India Improving Steadily," *Associated Press*, August 23, 2007.

[159] See also Vibhuti Hate and Teresita Schaffer, "U.S.-India Defense Relations: Strategic Perspectives," CSIS *South Asia Monitor*, April 4, 2007.

[160] "US-India Joint Exercises Growing in Sophistication, Scope," *Inside the Pentagon*, January 31, 2008.

[161] See also CRS Report RL33515, *Combat Aircraft Sales to South Asia.*

[162] "Building a Modern Arsenal in India," *New York Times*, August 31, 2007; US Aims to Edge Out Russia in big Arms Sales to India," *Reuters*, December 26, 2007. In December 2007, Boeing agreed in principle to send up to $1 billion in aerospace manufacturing work to India's state-owned Hindustan Aeronautics over the next decade. In January 2008, Lockheed Martin announced the opening of a subsidiary in New Delhi.

[163] India's comptroller later issued a report critical of the government for purchasing an "ageing ship" in a "hasty manner" without proper assessment of the ship's sea-worthiness, prompting communists in Parliament to demand an investigation. Indian navy officials reject the criticism and say the inexpensive ship will provide significant sea-lift capabilities ("US-Made *Jalashwa* a Lemon: CAG," *Times of India* (Delhi), Marc h 15, 2008).

[164] See [http://www.state.gov/r/pa/prs/ps/2005/43853.htm].

[165] "US Contenders Enhance Their MRCA Offerings to India," *Jane's Defence Weekly*, January 30, 2008; "Boeing Seeks Leverage on Indian Fighter Order,"*Aviation International News*, February 19, 2008; "Boeing Keen to Develop India's Aerospace Industry," Reuters, July 16, 2008.

[166] "Defense Firms Seek Sales in India," *Chicago Tribune*, December 21, 2006.

[167] "India Realigns Its Offset Policy," *Jane's Defense Weekly*, February 6, 2008; "Delhi to US: No Arms-Site Scan," *Telegraph* (Kolkata), February 28, 2008.

[168] See [http://www.state.gov/s/ct/rls/crt/2007/103709.htm].

[169] See, for example, Ajai Sahni, "Get to the Basics," *Outlook* (Delhi), May 21, 2008.

[170] "Joint Statement of U.S., India on Terrorism, Bilateral Ties," U.S. Department of State Washington File, November 9, 2001.

[171] See [http://www.indianembassy.org/press_release/2005/June/31.htm].

[172] See [http://usinfo.state.gov/is/Archive/2006/Apr/24-821244.html]. The most recent meeting of the Working Group was held in Washington in November 2007.

[173] "U.S. Troops on Front Line of Expanding India Ties," *Washington Post*, January 25, 2006.

[174] "U.S.-India Treaty on Mutual Legal Assistance in Criminal Matters Ratified," U.S. Embassy New Delhi Press Release, October 3, 2005.

[175] "US Offers India Help to Fight Maoists: Official," *Reuters*, May 26, 2006.

[176] "CIA Big Guns in Huddle," *Telegraph* (Calcutta), October 24, 2006; "FBI Looks to Boost Intelligence Ties With India," *Reuters*, November 27, 2006.

[177] "Hunting for India's 'Most Wanted,'" *Jane's Intelligence Digest*, December 9, 2005; Treasury notification at [http://www.ustreas.gov/press/releases/js909.htm].

[178] See also CRS Report RL32115, *Missile Proliferation and the Strategic Balance in South Asia*, and CRS Report RS21237, *Indian and Pakistani Nuclear Weapons.*

[179] Statement of Lt. Gen. Michael Maples before the Senate Select Committee on Intelligence, January 11, 2007, at [http://intelligence.senate.gov/070111/maples.pdf].

[180] The India-Pakistan Relief Act of 1998 (in P.L. 105-277) authorized a one-year sanctions waiver exercised by President Clinton in November 1998. The Department of Defense Appropriations Act, 2000 (P.L. 106-79) gave the President permanent authority after October 1999 to waive nuclear test-related sanctions applied against India and Pakistan. On October 27, 1999, President Clinton waived economic sanctions on India (Pakistan remained under sanctions as a result of an October 1999 military coup). (See CRS Report RS20995, *India and Pakistan: U.S. Economic Sanctions*.)

[181] See also CRS Report RL34161, *India-U.S. Economic and Trade Relations*. Most of the economic data in these sections come from the Economist Intelligence Unit and Global Insight, as well as from U.S. and Indian government sources.

[182] See [http://www.whitehouse.gov/news/releases/2006/02/20060222-2.html].

[183] India's official poverty line for 2004-2005 was an income of 356 rupees (about $9) per person per month. By this measure, the national poverty rate was about 28%. Yet estimates indicate that some 400 million Indians subsist on less than 40 rupees per day. One British medical study found that more than half of all Indian children under the age of five are "stunted" by lack of proper nutrition. More than two million Indian children died in 2006— more than in any other country — and studies indicate that better delivery of healthcare for India's poorest children is necessary for meeting international millennium development goals ("Economic Boom Fails to Generate Optimism in India," *New York Times*, August 16, 2007; "51% of Indian Children Stunted by Undernutrition," *Hindu* (Chennai), May 15, 2008; "UN Warning on India Child Health," *BBC News*, August 5, 2008).

[184] See [http://hdr.undp.org/en/reports/global/hdr2007-2008].

[185] Despite a series of expensive programs meant to bring relief to India's beleaguered farmers, the government has failed to stem the incidence of farmer suicides, which are estimated to number some 10,000 each year ("No Let Up in India Farm Suicides," *BBC News*, May 5, 2008).

[186] "India Overheats," *Economist* (London), February 3, 2007.

[187] "India's Superrich Get Even Richer," *Christian Science Monitor*, December 18, 2007.

[188] [http://www.usindiafriendship.net/viewpoints1/Indias_Rising_Growth_Potential.pdf].

[189] See [http://www.oecd.org/eco/surveys/India].

[190] Pramit Mitra, "Running on Empty," CSIS South Asia Monitor 103, February 3, 2007, at [http://www.csis.org/media/csis/pubs/sam103.pdf]; World Bank, "Urban Challenges in India," February 5, 2007. One study found that 70% of Kolkata's population suffers from respiratory disorders caused by air pollution ("Air Pollution Suffocates Calcutta," *BBC News*, May 3, 2007).

[191] See [http://www.census.gov/foreign-trade/statistics/country/index.html].

[192] International Monetary Fund, *International Financial Statistics*.

[193] See "U.S.-India Strategic Economic Partnership," U.S.-India CEO Forum, March 2006 at [http://planningcommission.nic.in/reports/genrep/USIndia.pdf]. One 2008 news report criticized "India's astonishing inability to plan for its future and fix its sagging infrastructure" ("An Indian Airport Hurries to Make the First Flight," *New York Times*, May 22, 2008).

[194] See [http://www.state.gov/p/us/rm/2007/85424.htm].

[195] See [http://newdelhi.usembassy.gov/pr91907.html].

[196] See [http://www.ustreas.gov/press/releases/hp648.htm].

[197] See [http://www.ustr.gov/Document_Library/Reports_Publications/Section_Index.html].

[198] "India's Sovereign Credit Rating Upgraded," *Financial Times* (London), January 30, 2007.

[199] See [http://www.state.gov/e/rls/rm/2004/36345.htm] and [http://newdelhi.usembassy.gov/pr022007.html].

[200] See [http://www.iipa.com/rbc/2008/2008SPEC301INDIA.pdf].

201 See [http://newdelhi.usembassy.gov/pr120706.html]. Bush Administration policy is at [http://mumbai.usconsulate.gov/chris_israel.html].

202 See [http://www.heritage.org/research/features/index/country.cfm?id=India].

203 See [http://www.transparency.org]. According to Transparency's findings , one in three Indian families living below the poverty line paid a bribe in 2007 for basic public services.

204 See [http://www.fraserinstitute.ca/admin/books/chapterfiles/3aEFW2006ch3A-K.pdf#].

205 "India Puts Brakes on Tax-Break Zones," *Financial Times* (London), January 23, 2007; "India's Farmers Grumbling as SEZs Eat Up Land," *Financial Times* (London), March 12, 2007; "India to 'Refine' Economic Zone Policy After Shooting Deaths," *Agence France Presse*, March 19, 2007.

206 SEZ-related troubles continued in late 2007 with an upsurge in political violence in West Bengal and reports that state officials may have been complicit in attacks on farmers.

207 See also CRS Report RL32060, *World Trade Organization Negotiations*, and CRS Report RL33144, *WTO Doha Round*.

208 "India Sees Gains in WTO Deal, But Has Reservations," *Reuters*, July 16, 2008.

209 "India Blames U.S. for Failure of WTO Talks," *Hindu* (Chennai), July 26, 2006; "U.S. Says Doha Risks Being Delayed for Several Years," *Reuters*, July 5, 2007; "World Leaders Express New Optimism on Doha Deal," *Reuters*, September 25, 2007. American business interests also have been critical of the New Delhi government for failing to offer positive proposals for broaching the Doha impasse ("U.S. Business Presses India for More WTO Concessions," *New York Times*, May 6, 2008).

210 "India Unhappy With Fresh WTO Negotiating Texts," *Hindu* (Chennai), May 21, 2008; "U.S. Concerned About Direction of Doha Talks," *New York Times*, May 28, 2008; "US Accuses India of Trying to Wreck WTO Talks," *Agence France Presse*, June 9, 2008.

211 "Indian Minister Frustrates West at Trade Talks," *Wall Street Journal*, July 25, 2008; "Dismay at Collapse of Trade Talks," *BBC News*, July 30, 2008; "Beyond the Trade Pact Collapse," *New York Times*, August 3, 2008.

212 See Vibhuti Hate, "India's Energy Dilemma," Center for Strategic and International Studies, September 7, 2006, at [http://www.csis.org/media/csis/pubs/sam98.pdf].

213 See U.S. Department of State fact sheet at [http://www.state.gov/p/sca/rls/fs/2005/ 49724.htm]. In May 2006, the Senate Foreign Relations Committee passed S. 1950, to promote global energy security through increased cooperation between the United States and India on non-nuclear energy-related issues, but the full Senate took no action on the bill.

214 See a Ministry of Power report at [http://powermin.nic.in/reports/pdf/ar05_06.pdf].

215 Energy data from U.S. Department of Energy, Energy Information Administration, January 2007, at [http://www.eia.doe.gov/emeu/cabs/india.html]; Tanvi Madan, "India," Brookings Institution Energy Security Series Report, November 2006 at [http://www.brookings.edu/fp/research/energy/2006india.pdf].

216 John Stephenson and Peter Tynan, "Will the U.S.-India Civil Nuclear Cooperation Initiative Light India?," November 13, 2006, at [http://www.npec-web.org]; "Top Scientist Questions India's N-Energy Dream," *Times of India* (Delhi), September 9, 2007.

217 "India Struggles With Power Theft," BBC News, March 15, 2006; "Electricity Crisis Hobbles an India Eager to Ascend," New York Times, May 21, 2007; "Power Outages disrupt Life in India," *Associated Press*, March 10, 2008.

218 See [http://newdelhi.usembassy.gov/pr032007a.html].

219 "Talk by Special Envoy of Prime Minister, Shri Shyam Saran in Mumbai on Climate Change," Indian Ministry of External Affairs, April 21, 2008.

220 June 30, 2008 press release at [http://pmindia.gov.in/pressrel.htm]; "India Offers 8 Ideals on a Climate Change Policy, but Few Details," *New York Times*, July 1, 2008.

221 See remarks by James Connaughton, Chairman of President Bush's Council on Environmental Quality, at [http://newdelhi.usembassy.gov/pr101507a.html]. See also [http://www.asiapacificpartnership.org].

222 See [http://www.state.gov/g/oes/climate/mem] and [http://www.whitehouse.gov/news/releases/2008/04/20080418-20.html].

223 "India Says Kashmir Toll Over 41,000, Others Differ," *Reuters*, December 7, 2006.

224 Most estimates list from 41,000 to 66,000 related deaths. The Pakistan-based Kashmir Media Service claims that more than 92,000 Kashmiris have been "martyred" in the fighting.

225 An August 2007 opinion survey found nearly 90% of the residents of Srinagar, Kashmir's most populous and Muslim-majority city, desiring Kashmiri independence from both India and Pakistan. In the largely Hindu city of Jammu, however, 95% of respondents said Kashmir should be part of India (see [http://www.indianexpress.com/story/210147.html]).

226 "Kashmiri Separatist Says India Talks Break Down," *Reuters*, August 30, 2007.

227 See, for example, Lisa Curtis, "India and Pakistan Poised to Make Progress on Kashmir," Heritage Backgrounder No. 1997, January 12, 2007, at [http://www.heritage.org/Research/ AsiaandthePacific/bg1997.cfm].

228 "Clinging to Hope in Kashmir," *Chicago Tribune*, June 1, 2008.

229 "Tourists Flock Back to Kashmir," *BBC News*, June 24, 2008.

[230] "Army Chief Confirms Reduced Infiltration in Kashmir," *Hindustan Times* (Delhi), October 7, 2005; "A Step Closer to Consensus," *Frontline* (Chennai), December 15, 2006.

[231] "India's Army Says Tide Turning in Restive Kashmir," *Reuters*, October 1, 2006; "Kashmiri Leader Lauds Drop in Custodial Killings, Disappearances," *Agence France Presse*, October 30, 2006.

[232] See [http://mha.nic.in/internal%20security/ISS(E)-050208.pdf]. See also "After Brutal Years, Kashmiris Embrace New Calm," *Christian Science Monitor*, March 20, 2008.

[233] "Kashmir's Demilitarization Debate," *Jane's Intelligence Digest*, June 23, 2008.

[234] Author interviews, Srinagar, Kashmir, September 2006.

[235] In 2008, the Manipur government reportedly launched an initiative to arm and outfight villagers to facilitate the fight against separatist rebels there, a policy opposed by human rights groups ("India's Manipur Arms Civilians to Fight Rebels," *Reuters*, May 6, 2008).

[236] "India's Forgotten War," *BBC News*, August 8, 2007; "Militants' Hold Over Manipur Total," *Hindustan Times* (Delhi), September 9, 2007; "Militant Mire -Battling Insurgency in Northeast India," *Jane's Intelligence Review*, February 1, 2008.

[237] See [http://www.state.gov/s/ct/rls/crt/2005/65275.htm].

[238] "Indian PM Says Maoist Rebellion Gravest Threat," *Reuters*, April 13, 2006.

[239] "Indian Maoists Step Up Recruitment of Child Soldiers," *Reuters*, May 22, 2008; "In India, Death to Global Business," *Business Week*, May 7, 2008.

[240] See [http://www.satp.org/satporgtp/countries/india/database/fatalitiesnaxal.htm]; "Naxal Problem Should Not Be Exaggerated: Govt," *Indian Express* (Mumbai), March 19, 2008. According to India's Home Ministry, the states of Chhattisgarh and Jharkhand account for two-thirds of the country's Naxalite incidents and three-quarters of related casualties.

[241] Asian Center for Human Rights press release at [http://www.achrweb.org/ press/2007/IND0307.htm]. See also "Strategy Gone Awry," *Frontline* (Chennai), September 21, 2007.

[242] "Scrap Sulwa Jundum: Planning Commission Panel," *Hindu* (Chennai), May 21, 2008.

[243] See [http://hrw.org/reports/2008/india0708].

[244] Ajai Sahni, "Fighting the Maoists With Mantras," *Outlook* (Delhi), July 25, 2008; "In Heart of India, a Little-Known Civil War," *Christian Science Monitor*, May 1, 2007; "Orissa Losing War Against Naxalite Violence," *Hindu* (Chennai), February 18, 2008; "Manmohan Wants Naxal Forces Crippled," *Hindu* (Chennai), December 20, 2007; "Center to Raise Anti-Naxalite Force," *Hindu* (Chenai), July 1, 2008; "Q&A With Indian National Security Advisor MK Narayanan," *Straits Times* (Singapore), August 12, 2008.

[245] In November 2007, Human Rights Watch called on the Indian government to launch an investigation of Modi after he made statements apparently endorsing the extrajudicial execution of a terrorism suspect by police. In July 2008, 27 Members of Congress joined the U.S. Commission on International Religious Freedom in urging the State Department to reaffirm its past decision to block Modi's entry to the United States (see [http://hrw.org/ english/docs/2007/12/07/india17510.htm] and [http://www.uscirf.gov/ index.php?option=com_content&task=view&id=2219&Itemid=46]).

[246] See [http://web.amnesty.org/library/Index/ENGASA200072007?open&of=ENG-IND]; "Hindu, Muslim Ghettos Arise in Gujarat," *Christian Science Monitor*, July 5, 2007; "UN Envoy Says India Risks Religious Violence," *Reuters*, March 2008.

[247] See [http://www.state.gov/g/drl/rls/hrrpt/2007/100614.htm].

[248] See [http://hrw.org/englishwr2k7/docs/2007/01/10/global15039.htm] and [http://report2007.amnesty.org/ eng/Homepage].

[249] See [http://www.state.gov/g/drl/rls/shrd/2006/80590.htm].

[250] *Supporting Human Rights and Democracy: The U.S. Record 2002 -2003*," U.S. Department of State, at [http://www.state.gov/g/drl/rls/shrd/2002/21760.htm].

[251] See "Faked Deaths Show Ills of India's Police," *Associated Press*, June 7, 2007.

[252] See [http://www.state.gov/g/tip/rls/tiprpt/2008/105388.htm] and [http://www.state.gov/ g/tip/rls/rm/ 2008/ 105572.htm].

[253] See [http://www.state.gov/g/drl/rls/irf/2007/90228.htm].

[254] See [http://www.uscirf.gov].

[255] See [http://www.state.gov/r/pa/ei/bgn/3454.htm].

[256] See [http://www.state.gov/g/drl/rls/hrrpt/2006/78871.htm].

[257] "Indian Prime Minister Denounces Abortion of Females," *New York Times*, April 29, 2008; census data at [http://www.censusindia.net/t_00_004.html]. See also "Missing Girl Child," *India Today* (Delhi), November 11, 2003.

[258] Cited in "India Loses 10m Female Births," *BBC News*, January 9, 2006. A 2006 report from the U.N. Children's Fund found that about 7,000 fewer girls than expected are born each day in India due to female feticide ("Feticide Means 7,000 fewer Girls a Day in India," *Reuters*, December 12, 2006).

[259] "India Baby Girl Deaths 'Increase,'" *BBC News*, June 21, 2008.

[260] See [http://www.state.gov/g/drl/rls/hrrpt/2007/100614.htm].

[261] "Indian Govt to Raise Abandoned Girls," *Associated Press*, February 18, 2007.

[262] "India's HIV Cases Highly Overestimated, Survey Shows," *Reuters*, July 6, 2007; U.S. Embassy Fact Sheet on Indo-US Cooperation in Public Health, April 2, 2008.

[263] See [http://www.usaid.gov/our_work/global_health/aids/Countries/ane/india_05.pdf].

[264] See, for example, Pramit Mitra and Teresita Schaffer, "Public Health and International Security: The Case of India," July 2006, at [http://www.csis.org/media/csis/pubs/ 060731_aids_india.pdf].

[265] See [http://www.pepfar.gov/pepfar/press/81851.htm].

[266] See [http://www.state.gov/p/sca/rls/2008/104699.htm].

[267] See [http://www.usaid.gov/locations/asia/countries/india/india.html].

In: India and the U.S: Future Relations…
Editor: Tim S. Macleod, pp.215-232

ISBN: 978-1-60741-197-0

Chapter 5

EMERGING TRENDS IN THE SECURITY ARCHITECTURE IN ASIA: BILATERAL AND MULTILATERAL TIES AMONG THE UNITED STATES, JAPAN, AUSTRALIA, AND INDIA

Emma Chanlett-Avery and Bruce Vaughn
Analyst in Asian Affairs, Foreign Affairs, Defense, and Trade Division

SUMMARY

Some analysts have questioned whether U.S. security interests in the Asia Pacific region are best served by its existing framework of bilateral alliances. The region is now facing an array of changes: deepening trade links, the formation of new regional institutions, and increased attention to the threat of Islamic terrorism. Against this backdrop, China's rise represents the key driver in the evolving security landscape in Asia. China is now attracting regional states with its economic power and is offering competing vision to the U.S.-centric "hub and spoke" system of alliances. In essence, China's increasing economic, diplomatic, and military strength is compelling countries to rethink existing security arrangements and take initial steps that may lead to the formation of regional groupings of nations with common interests and values. At the same time, the Bush Administration has pursued stronger defense relations with Australia, Japan, and India.

Bilateral defense ties have also developed between Canberra, Tokyo, and New Delhi, with varying degrees of engagement. Fledgling initiatives for trilateral efforts among the nations have emerged; some defense planners see these efforts as building on existing security cooperation to further U.S. goals in the region by combining forces among partners and allies. As trilateral initiatives have taken shape, some officials have begun promoting a quadrilateral grouping, which would tie together the United States, Japan, Australia, and India. Although no formal quadrilateral groupings exist, the *Malabar 07* military exercises among the four countries in September 2007 provided an opportunity to test naval cooperation. Some observers caution that moving forward too fast with such a grouping could trigger a negative response from China.

Pursuit of multilateral security arrangements holds a number of potential challenges and opportunities for the United States. Of the four leaders who championed the trilateral and quadrilateral groupings, two left office in 2007 and two face significant political challenges. Japan's constitutional restraints on military involvement may limit the scope of its cooperation, and both Australia and India have some degree of reluctance to fully engage in any forum that might alienate Beijing. Increasing capabilities among like-minded nations could enhance stability and provide a platform for responding to natural disasters and humanitarian emergencies in the region, or to potential aggression by other countries, but it also risks threatening China, potentially spurring dangerous countermeasures. Finally, there is the risk that other Asian allies, such as South Korea, Thailand, and the Philippines, could feel excluded from multilateral initiatives among the United States, Japan, Australia, and/or India. This report may not be updated.

INTRODUCTION

Is the U.S. strategic architecture in Asia well-suited to adjust to the evolving correlates of power in Asia? The region is now facing an array of changes: deepening trade links, the formation of new regional institutions, and increased attention to the threat of Islamic terrorism. Some analysts have questioned whether U.S. security interests are best served by the existing framework ofbilateral alliances, while others believe the basic architecture is sound and may only require some relatively minor changes and/or additions to meet emerging challenges. Calls for a revision of America's security architecture in Asia may be a reaction to the development of new regional groups that exclude the United States. The goals of America's strategic architecture in Asia have traditionally included preventing the dominance of Asia by any single power or coalition of powers; maintaining a system of alliances to facilitate the projection of American power when needed; and securing sea lanes of communication to facilitate American commercial access and the free flow of trade in the region.[1] American power can also be used to promote American values such as democratic governments or provision of humanitarian and disaster assistance.

China's Rise

China's rise represents the key driver in the changing security landscape in Asia. China is now attracting regional states with its economic power and is offering a competing vision to the U.S.-centric "hub and spoke" system of alliances that was largely established in the post-World War II period. China's alternative is largely being constructed around trade relationships and diplomatic initiatives manifest in the East Asia Summit, the Association of Southeast Asian Nations (ASEAN) + 3 forum, various Chinese bilateral free trade initiatives, and China's "charm offensive."[2] Some also interpret China's more active involvement in the Shanghai Cooperation Organization (SCO), which conducted substantial military exercises in 2007, as China's attempt to develop an alternative security group to America's security partnerships in the region.[3] China's announced defense spending rose by 17.8% to approximately $45 billion 2007, following a 14.7% increase in 2006. Some analysts estimate real Chinese defense expenditure to be up to three times this amount.[4] In many ways, the emerging regional security groupings evoke heartlandrimland geopolitical debates along the lines drawn by Sir Halford Mackinder and Alfred Thayer Mahan a century ago.[5] While such geopolitical writers' theories have conceptional value, there is a danger that such paradigms can lead to needless confrontation. Though the rise of new great powers on the world stage historically has been destabilizing, if not a source of open conflict, many believe that China's rise (or resurgence) can be accommodated in a way that preserves U.S. interests and values in the region.

In essence, China's increasing economic, diplomatic, and military strength is compelling countries to rethink existing security arrangements and take initial steps that may lead to the formation of regional groupings of nations with common interests and values. The impetus behind these initiatives stems from three sources. First, economic forces of trade and investment in Asia have largely been generated by private business interests in an increasingly globalized world. National governments have widened the paths already established by trade and investment flows by concluding free-trade and other regional economic agreements. Second, diplomatic initiatives to increase political cooperation among states are generated by national governments seeking to protect their national interests and achieve national goals. The resulting regional organizations have provided a venue for face-to-face meetings and dialogue, but harmonizing political interests among Asian nations has been considerably more complicated than reducing trade and investment barriers through free-trade agreements. Third, security and military cooperation stems primarily from national perceptions of security threats — both current and future. Much of this military cooperation can be conducted "under the radar" using the guise of military exercises to test interoperability and communications.

There are signs that regional states anticipate a fading of American influence in the region relative to the rise of China.[6] This is partially driven by negative opinions of U.S. foreign policy. Despite recent American initiatives, some analysts believe that Asia is turning away from the United States and that, while the U.S. retains great influence in the region, this will not last given current trends.[7] A fundamental restructuring of American foreign policy priorities and mechanisms may, in the view of some, be necessary in order for America's poor public perception in the region to be changed.

Other Geopolitical Challenges

Beyond rising competition between the United States and China, other key geopolitical developments or potential conflict scenarios in Asia include rivalry between China and Japan, renewed tensions between India and China, the North Korea nuclear program, increasing competition for energy resources, resurgent Islamist challenges to Western interests and to moderate Muslim governments, renewed Russian focus on its security interests in Asia, instability and unrest in Burma and Thailand, and security challenges resulting from climate change. In addition, existing challenges remain, such as ongoing tension between India and Pakistan, and potential for military conflict on the Korean Peninsula or in the Taiwan Strait. An assessment of U.S. security interests in Asia must consider such challenges and shifts in the correlates of power in Asia.[8]

U.S. Response

The United States has begun to respond to these shifts and challenges in several ways. The United States has sought to reinvigorate its bilateral alliances and security ties with regional states such as Australia, Japan, and Singapore; launched an ASEAN-U.S. Enhanced Partnership Agreement; reopened military-to-military ties with Indonesia; and raised the profile of the Trilateral Security Dialogue with Japan and Australia. It also has embarked on a major initiative to develop a strategic security relationship with India. Currently, the Pentagon seems to be out in front of the rest of the U.S. government in fostering actual multi-national security cooperation among the major democratic states of Asia.

In early 2007, Vice President Dick Cheney proposed the idea that India join the trilateral group to make a quadrilateral group of like-minded democratic states.[9] In May 2007, representatives from the United States, India, Japan, and Australia reportedly met on the margins of the ASEAN Regional Forum meeting in the first exploratory meeting to discuss quadrilateral ties.[10] Beijing is thought to be suspicious of such developments and fears that they are aimed at the containment of China. China issued formal diplomatic protests to Australia, Japan, and India out of concern that they were forming a security alliance with the United States against China.[11]

The U.S. force structure is shifting to adapt to regional developments in the Asia Pacific. U.S. forces have been shifted to Guam as plans have moved forward to reposition and reduce the U.S. military posture in Japan and in South Korea.[12] The U.S. military buildup on Guam can serve to maintain U S military deterrence and warfighting capabilities for a number of potential conflict scenarios in the Asia-Pacific region.

Congressional Role

Currently, the congressional role is primarily in oversight and monitoring of developments in Asia and in ensuring that U.S. interests are protected as the new Asian security architecture evolves. The policy questions revolve mainly around intensity (how much effort and budget to devote to Asia compared with that going to other regions of the world) and inclusiveness (which countries to include). The intensity question seems particularly pertinent now since much of Asia perceives that U.S. attention is overly focused on Iraq and terrorism while China is quietly using its economic muscle and diplomatic charm to draw Asian nations more into its sphere of influence. The inclusiveness issue also seems pertinent given the historical U.S. reliance on the "hub and spoke" system of military alliances, the fear by China of "encirclement," and the widely held precept that more democratic nations are less likely to pose a security threat to the United States.

Other relevant congressional involvement includes the passage of a bill in 2006 that calls for the appointment of an overall U.S. ambassador to ASEAN, as well as the need for Senate ratification of the U.S.-Australia Treaty on Defense Trade Cooperation.

Democratic Values

The Bush Administration has consistently advocated that U.S. interests are best served by partnering with nations that share democratic values. In September 2007, President Bush proposed the creation of a new Asia Pacific Democracy Partnership to "provide a venue in which free nations will work together to support democratic values, strengthen democratic institutions, and assist those who are working to build and sustain free societies across the Asia Pacific region."[13] Some critics of the policy argue that "values-based diplomacy" may be simply a code word for excluding China and that it may feed Beijing's fear of Washington's strategic encirclement.[14] Few in the region would support a development that would threaten regional economic prosperity that is to a large extent dependent on rapidly expanding trade with China.

Bilateral Defense Relationships

China's rise has had a clear impact on existing and nascent defense relationships in the Asia-Pacific region. This section provides a brief assessment of the state of bilateral relationships among the United States, Australia, Japan, and India. Some defense ties are well-established and multi-layered, while others are embryonic. Each section examines the history of ties, current political climate, rationales for engagement, and challenges to cooperation.

U.S.-Australia[15]

The United States-Australia strategic and defense relationship under the rubric of the Australia-New Zealand-United States (ANZUS) alliance remains extremely close.[16] Australian access to intelligence and American arms is a key aspect of the bilateral relationship. A long-standing treaty ally, Australia has fought alongside the United States in most of America's wars and established a Free Trade Agreement with the United States in 2005. In September 2007, the nations signed the Australia- United States Treaty on Defense Trade Cooperation, which would ease restrictions associated with the International Trade in Arms Regulations (ITAR) by creating a comprehensive framework within which most defense trade can be carried out without prior government approval.[17] Only the United Kingdom has signed a similar agreement with the United States. Despite these ties, the relationship faces diplomatic recalibration. Prime Minister John Howard, a staunch supporter of Bush Administration policies, was defeated in parliamentary elections in November 2007. His replacement, Kevin Rudd of the Labor Party, while recognizing the constructive role that the United States plays in underpinning security in the Asia Pacific as well as the centrality of the ANZUS alliance to Australian security interests, has distanced himself from aspects of U.S. policy.

Australia looks to prudently position itself in evolving Asian power dynamics [18] Rudd, a former diplomat to China who is fluent in Mandarin, is likely to avoid policies that could be interpreted by the Chinese as being part of a containment strategy. Although there is a range of debate on the correct path that Australia should take on regional security developments in Asia, it appears that Australia will not pursue security linkages that could jeopardize its economic relationship with China. Some in Australia seek to define a position for Australia more equidistant between the United States and China to resist being drawn into a club of

Asian states based on democratic values that hints of attempting to contain Beijing. Australia's key defense policy document, *Defence Update 2007,* discusses the importance of Australia's strategic relationship not only with the United States but also with Japan, Indonesia, and India. Australia's 47% increase in defense spending since Howard assumed office in 1996 also reflects growing uncertainty in Australia with the evolving strategic environment in Asia.[19] This uncertainty was a driver in Australia's pursuit of a security agreement with Japan.

While Canberra is eager to maintain lucrative trade ties with Beijing, it is concerned over China's military build-up. Former Prime Minister Howard stated "the pace and scope of its (China's) military modernization, particularly the development of new and disruptive capabilities such as the anti-satellite missile, could create misunderstandings and instability in the region."[20] The 2007 *Defence Update* also states that the China-U.S. relationship "must be managed carefully."[21] On the other hand, at times Canberra appears anxious not to antagonize Beijing: in 2004, former Australian Foreign Minister Alexander Downer commented that the ANZUS treaty did not necessarily bind Australia to enter a conflict over Taiwan.[22]

United States-Japan[23]

For the United States, its alliance with Japan provides a platform for U.S. military readiness in Asia. About 53,000 U.S. troops are stationed in Japan and have the exclusive use of 89 facilities throughout the archipelago. Okinawa, hosting 37 of the facilities, is the major U.S. forward logistics base in the Asia-Pacific region. Since roughly 2001, Japan has developed a more muscular foreign policy and forward defense posture, including bolstering its military alliance with the United States. High-level U.S.-Japan bilateral statements have declared an expanded commitment to security cooperation by establishing common strategic objectives, outlining major command changes, and calling for greater interoperability between the two militaries. Japan's contributions to operations in Afghanistan and Iraq reinforced the notion of the alliance as one of the central partnerships of U.S. foreign policy in Asia.

Led by former Prime Ministers Junichiro Koizumi and Shinzo Abe, Japan has moved to re-tool its pacifist post-World War II stance. In December 2006, Japan's Defense Agency was formally upgraded to a ministry for the first time since World War II, and the ruling party has approved a referendum process to amend the constitution, including the war-renouncing Article 9. Although Article 9 states that "land, sea, and air forces, as well as other war potential, will never be maintained," the Japanese Self-Defense Forces (SDF) are in practice a well-funded and well-equipped military. U.S. officials have consistently voiced support for Japanese steps to "normalize" its defense posture.

As part of its effort to improve its own capability, as well as work more closely with U.S. forces, Japan has created a new joint staff office that puts all the ground, maritime, and air self-defense forces under a single command. A bilateral coordination center at Yokota Air Base will focus on missile defense cooperation, while a new SDF "Central Readiness Force Command" will be established at Camp Zama to create a joint operations facility with the U.S. Army command. The co-located headquarters, due to be completed by 2012, are anticipated to facilitate both greater U.S.-Japan cooperation as well as overall SDF "jointness." SDF participation in U.S.-led military operations has led to substantial interaction and cooperation with U.S. forces, from logistics training in Kuwait before dispatching to Iraq to working together on disaster relief operations following the December 2004 tsunami in the Indian Ocean. Bilateral interoperability was also tested in June-July 2006 as North Korea was preparing to test-launch a missile; ballistic missile defense coordination was carried out under real threat circumstances.

Recent events and political uncertainty in Japan may have slowed some of the increased cooperation in the U.S.-Japan alliance. Although ties remain strong fundamentally, the Bush Administration shift on North Korean nuclear negotiations, the July 2007 House resolution criticizing the Japanese government for past "comfort women" policies, and the apparent decision not to consider exporting the F-22 to Japan may have undermined to some degree Japanese confidence in the robustness of the alliance. Koizumi and Abe's platform of enhancing Japan's role in global affairs had been encouraged by U.S. officials who saw Japan's strategic interests aligning with their own. While Abe's successor Fukuda remains committed to the alliance relationship, he is considered to be more cautious in terms of adjusting Japan's security stance. Further, implementation of U.S. force realignment agreements depends on Tokyo providing the necessary resources and political capital. Because the realignment and transformation initiatives involve elements that are unpopular in the localities affected, successful implementation depends on leadership from the central government. If Fukuda's party continues to struggle to re-establish itself, details of the hard-fought agreements designed to sustain the alliance politically may falter.

United States-India[24]

The Bush Administration has pursed a strategic partnership with India since 2004, leading to a fundamental reorientation of the bilateral relationship. Many have viewed India and the United States as natural partners given that they are the world's two most populous democracies. Efforts by Washington and New Delhi, and bipartisan congressional support for U.S.-India civilian nuclear legislation, has made U.S.-India relations arguably "closer than ever before."[25] In July of 2005, President Bush and Prime Minister Manmohan Singh issued a joint statement to establish a "global partnership." Congress then endorsed the United States and India Nuclear Cooperation Promotion Act of 2006 (P.L. 109-401). The United States and India also signed a new Defense Framework Agreement in 2005.

U.S. policymakers appear now to perceive India as a key geopolitical actor in Asia rather than viewing the country through the lens of nuclear non proliferation. During the Cold War, India was more closely aligned with the Soviet Union despite being a democracy. In the post-Cold War period, India and the United States remained distant as a result of continuing U.S. emphasis on non proliferation and on Pakistan. At the same time, the prevailing Indian philosophy continued to view the world to a large extent through the prism of the Non-Aligned Movement, which India helped to create. The rise of China, energy issues, radical Islam, and a de-linking of the U.S.-Pakistan relationship from the U.S.-India relationship all have contributed to a perception of India as a desirable strategic partner in Asia.

China plays a prominent, though nuanced, role in the recent U.S. -India strategic convergence. An older generation of Indian security officials still resent China for the 1962 Sino-Indian border war, while a new generation is more amenable to India- China cooperation. India has potential areas of concern with China, such as competition for energy resources and unresolved border disputes, yet India is resistant to playing a subordinate role in any U.S. strategy to contain China. Some in India reportedly are concerned over rising competition with China and what some see as a potential strategic encirclement of India through China's relationships with countries such as Pakistan and Burma.[26] India's efforts to extend the strategic reach of its navy and attain broader blue water capabilities, including outside the Indian Ocean, may be motivated by China as well as protection of surrounding sea lanes.[27] The development of India's longer range missile capabilities also reflects concerns with China. U.S. interest in India may have led to increased Chinese interest in developing ties with India. Over the past four years, India-China trade has quadrupled to more than $20 billion per year.[28]

While the U.S.-India civil nuclear agreement has, at least for the present, been derailed by Prime Minister Manmohan Singh's left wing allies in parliament, sufficient momentum in the bilateral relationship appears to have been created to keep the goal of developing closer ties between New Delhi and Washington on track. Others fears that the collapse of the civilian nuclear deal could severely hamper the expansion of bilateral relations. The challenge for the next Administration will, according to some, be to build on the achievements of both the Clinton and Bush Administrations. This can be done by adding "ballast" to the relationship through expanded trade and defense ties including an announced goal of doubling bilateral trade in three years, a move toward greater defense technology sharing, strengthened U.S.-India military cooperation and possible co-production of weapons systems, and expanded counterterrorism cooperation.[29] India's standing in American strategic calculations also may rise should Pakistan devolve into further political unrest.

Japan-Australia

Fortified by a vibrant trade relationship, Tokyo and Canberra recently moved to upgrade defense ties. The impetus from both capitals to establish security cooperation may be a combination of fears of China's military modernization and a drive to further expand the capabilities of the Japanese military by working with another stalwart U.S. ally. In addition to annual bilateral trade of about $60 billion, Japan and Australia began negotiations for a free trade agreement (FTA) in April 2007. Cultural and educational exchanges are also extensive.

In March 2007, the countries concluded a security agreement, the first formal defense relationship for Japan outside of the U.S.-Japan alliance. Prime Ministers Howard and Abe released a statement affirming a "strategic partnership" based on shared democratic values and common security interests in the Asia-Pacific and beyond. Specific areas of cooperation outlined included counterterrorism, peace operations, disaster response, international law enforcement, and counter- proliferation of weapons of mass destruction. The agreement stems from some successful cooperation in the past, most notably the protection of the Japanese Self- Defense Forces by Australian troops during their reconstruction mission in Samawah, Iraq. Analysts have labeled the arrangement as somewhere between a formalized alliance and a more project-based "coalition of the willing!"[30]

Australia, like the United States, has an interest in encouraging Japan to "normalize" its defense posture and contribute more actively to regional stability. The defense establishment in Australia generally views Japanese willingness to shed its self-imposed restraints as a positive development. In the past, Japan had been more cautious in considering any security arrangements with Australia, despite encouragement from Canberra.[31] Many defense planners in Australia consider Japan to be a crucial component of the U.S. commitment to security in East Asia; strengthening the third leg of the trilateral security arrangement is seen as likely to have benefits for the U.S.-Australia alliance as well.[32] Relaxation of the Japanese ban on collective self-defense, which would allow Japan to participate in regional contingencies, would likely also be welcomed by Australian defense planners. On the other hand, some voices in Canberra stress the need for Australia to develop itself as an Asian power, independent from the U.S. position. From this vantage, Japan-Australia security cooperation could point to a new order no longer based entirely on a hub and spoke system with Washington at the center.[33]

Tokyo and Canberra share a wariness of Beijing's increasing military and political strength, a factor driving their cooperative initiatives. Despite a recent warming of relations, however, Sino-Japanese rivalry is far stronger and historically rooted than any tension in the Australia-China relationship. Australia has consistently emphasized the importance of the economic relationship with China and avoided offending Beijing, including not taking sides on any Asian historical issues. Drawing closer to Tokyo may risk Australia's ability to play the role of honest broker in Asian power relations.

Japan-India

Japan and India's bilateral relationship is relatively undeveloped, but both capitals have signaled an intention to significantly upgrade their economic and strategic ties. Japan and India have found common ground in their quests to gain permanent membership on the United Nations Security Council, joining with Brazil and Germany in a formal campaign in 2004. Although overall bilateral trade remains very modest (under $7 billion in 2006), India has been the largest recipient of Japanese foreign assistance for the past four years, displacing China. Japanese foreign direct investment (FDI) in India has soared as Japanese companies look to hedge their risks after investing heavily in China for the past several years.[34] The most ambitious project is a $90 billion Delhi-Mumbai industrial corridor, for which Japan is expected to provide billions in loans and private investments.

Reciprocal visits between Prime Ministers Singh and Abe in December 2006 and August 2007 advanced the fledgling partnership. In addition to a series of economic cooperation agreements, including a feasibility study for an FTA, the leaders looked to enhance the military-to-military relationship. All three SDF chiefs visited India in 2006-2007, and Indian vessels visited Yokosuka Naval Base outside of Tokyo. Other defense initiatives include sea-lane security cooperation, military exchanges, and regular meetings of both navies. Although support for bilateral ties remains, Abe has stepped down and Singh has struggled politically, leaving some question as to whether the leadership in both Tokyo and New Delhi intends to maintain the momentum of the signed agreements.

Both Japan and India have a strategic interest in balancing China's power in the region. Japan was a strong advocate of admitting India as a member of the East Asia Summit (EAS) as a way to dilute China's dominance of the meeting. As India's economic strength has grown, it has stretched itself strategically as well, increasingly entering the arena of Pacific powers. For both India and Japan, partnering with other Pacific militaries, particularly navies, provides a maritime balance to China, although India is more reluctant to adopt a stance that could be perceived as confrontational by Beijing. For Japan, cooperating with India's navy provides a valuable chance to train in the Indian Ocean; training and exercises elsewhere in East Asia raise uncomfortable issues because of many countries' lingering memories of Japan's wartime aggression.

Japan's and India's nascent strategic partnership represents a reversal from the harsh criticism and economic sanctions that Tokyo imposed on India following its 1998 nuclear tests. The issue of nuclear proliferation could be an area of potential contention between Japan and India. After the United States and India agreed to cooperate on civilian nuclear power, Japan voiced its reservations that this move would damage the Nuclear Non-Proliferation Treaty (NPT). Despite Japan's traditionally strict observance of international non proliferation principles, Tokyo appears to have decided not to oppose the proposed U.S.-India civilian nuclear deal if it reaches the Nuclear Suppliers Group for approval. The leaders' joint statement in August 2007 noted that they "shared the view that nuclear energy can play an important role as a safe, sustainable and nonpolluting source of energy."

Australia-India

The Australia-India relationship has long been underdeveloped. This is somewhat surprising given that the two nations share a number of traits: democratic government, the English language, membership in the British Commonwealth, complimentary economies, a love for cricket, location in the Indian Ocean region, and a common cause against Islamist terrorism.[35] Australia has periodically rediscovered India and sought to develop more substantial ties, with limited success. Once again, Australia and India appear to be seeking a closer relationship.

Australia-India defense ties were reestablished in 2000, after a hiatus due to differences over India's nuclear test in 1998. These ties have been largely limited to senior level visits and staff college exchanges.[36] In July 2007, Australia and India signed an Information Sharing Arrangement to facilitate the sharing of classified information between the defense departments, particularly in areas such as counterterrorism, peacekeeping, and maritime security. The arrangement facilitates practical cooperation and provides substance to a Memorandum of Understanding on Defence Cooperation signed during Prime Minister Howard's visit to India in 2006.[37] Such an initiative can be viewed as part of India's desire to play a larger role in Asian affairs beyond South Asia and the northern reaches of the Indian Ocean and to begin to shape its geopolitical environment within a larger Asian context.[38] It also appears to be part of an Indian strategy to balance the rise of China in Asia by drawing others in.[39] While Australia has sought greater cooperation with New Delhi, it has placed limits on that apparently for fear of antagonizing the Chinese.

Newly elected Prime Minister Rudd has identified India as a key emerging power in Asia, but his reservations about uranium sales to India may stall the bilateral relationship. Howard had been willing to consider the sales if the U.S. -India civilian nuclear deal went through, a deal which he supported. Some in New Delhi view a uranium deal for India as "something of a litmus test of the Australian government's wish for a genuine partnership."[40] According to one leading Australian analyst on India, "underlying many of Canberra's decisions about its relationship with India will be an awareness that the Asian regional security order is entering a difficult phase. The regional great powers are all hoping to shape the emerging regional architecture" and India will have a key role in that.[41]

Developing Trilateral Fora

As the Bush Administration has pursued stronger defense relations with Australia, Japan, and India, initiatives for trilateral efforts among the nations has emerged. Nascent three-way cooperation has built on existing bilateral alliances to further U.S. goals in the region by combining forces among partners and allies.

U.S.-Japan-Australia

Washington, Tokyo, and Canberra have pursued a formalized trilateral strategic grouping through leaders' meetings and naval exercises. On the sidelines of the Asia Pacific Economic Cooperation (APEC) forum in September 2007, President Bush, Prime Minister Howard, and Prime Minister Abe met to reaffirm the three-way strategic dialogue. Australian and Japanese officials strived to reassure Beijing about the meeting, saying that the focus of the talks were not "directed at any country." In October 2007, navies from the three countries conducted a drill in the Pacific west of Japan's southern Kyushu island that involved two destroyers and two P-3C anti-submarine patrol planes from the Japan MSDF and one P-3C patrol plane each from the U.S. Navy and the Australian air force. The joint exercise simulated search and rescue activities as well as an attack on a Japanese escort ship.[42]

An integrated missile defense system, currently under consideration, may be among the most advanced of potential trilateral arrangements. After North Korea tested ballistic missiles in July 2006 and then a nuclear device in October 2006, Japan and the United States accelerated the development of a joint missile defense system that employs both land and sea-based capabilities. Australia, a long-time U.S. intelligence partner, already has expressed a willingness to share information from its satellite tracking system.[43] Equipment compatibility would allow Canberra to join a trilateral arrangement; the government is in the process of acquiring three destroyers equipped with the Aegis combat system, the same system used by the U.S. and Japanese militaries.[44] Although development of a missile defense shield has been cast in terms of the threat from North Korea by officials from all three countries, many analysts see China as the longer-term threat and rationale for developing a sophisticated, multi-nation system. This goal remains challenging, however, particularly given that a strict interpretation of Japan's constitution may forbid Japan to shoot down missiles that are not headed for its territory.[45]

U.S.-Japan-India

The United States and Japan have sought similar trilateral arrangements with India. Compared with their respective relationships with Australia, U.S. defense cooperation and Japanese economic ties are far more modest with India. The significant strategic benefits of partnering with India, given its size and geographical location, have driven the aggressive pursuit of a more formalized security relationship. Although the three nations have not held a formal meeting, key bilateral statements have indicated support for a trilateral fora from all three capitals. In the May 2007 "2+2" meeting joint statement, the U.S. and Japanese foreign and defense ministers affirmed the shared strategic objective of "continuing to build upon partnerships with India to advance areas of common interests and increase cooperation." When Prime Minister Singh visited Tokyo in December 2006, he publicly welcomed the idea of consultation with "like-minded nations." Navies of the three countries operationalized the initiative with joint naval drills in the Pacific off Japan's east coast in April 2007. The exercise featured two U.S. destroyers, four Japanese escort vessels, and three Indian warships and focused on cooperation in the event of a major natural disaster.[46]

Evolving Multilateral Dynamics

As trilateral initiatives have taken shape, talk of a quadrilateral grouping which would tie together the United States, Japan, Australia, and India — has emerged. Advocates for expanding quadrilateral cooperation have pointed to the "Regional Core Group" that formed in the aftermath of the 2004 Indian Ocean tsunami as a model.[47] Former Japanese Prime Minister Abe was perhaps the most vocal supporter of the four-way forum. Incoming Prime Minister Rudd, however, may have doubts about a quadrilateral grouping. Because of the fall from power or declining political fortunes of the leaders who supported the quad, it is uncertain that enthusiasm will remain for building a stronger arrangement.

Malabar Multilateral Exercises

Although no formal quadrilateral groupings exist, the *Malabar 07* military exercises provided an opportunity to test naval cooperation. The Malabar exercises have traditionally been U.S.-India bilateral exercises, begun in 1994. The April 2007 exercises featured the United States, India, and Japan, and were held off the coast of Okinawa. A second round of exercises held in September was expanded to include the navies of Australia and Singapore. The five-nation exercise in the Bay of Bengal, a strategically significant location because of the approach to the Singapore and Malacca Straits, featured over 20,000 personnel, 28 ships, 150 aircraft, and 3 aircraft carriers.[48] The navies together practiced maritime interdiction, surface and antisubmarine warfare, and air combat exercises. Military officials leading the exercises emphasized the value of practicing interoperability, for use in both high-level warfighting and future humanitarian responses.[49]

China bristled at the exercises, questioning whether the grouping may form what some analysts have dubbed an "Asian NATO." U S military officials insisted the exercises were not directed at any particular country, but one officer claimed that the demonstration "provides a message to other militaries, and our own, that we are capable of operating together and that we work together with our regional partners to ensure stability in the region!"[50]

The naval exercises took place less than a month after the Shanghai Cooperation Organization (SCO) staged its own joint military exercises, with member states Russia, China, Kazakhstan, Kyrgyzstan, Tajikistan, and Uzbekistan all contributing troops. Dubbed *Peace Mission 2007,* the exercise featured over 4,000 ground troops and over 1,000 pieces of equipment, including 500 combat and special vehicles and 70 fixed-wing airplanes and helicopters.[51] After multiple rehearsals, the anti-terrorist drill was staged in front of the SCO member states' leaders in conjunction with the annual meeting in Kyrgyzstan. Although both *Malabar* and *Peace Mission* officials emphasized that their exercises were not aimed at any particular other states, the proximity both geographically and temporally led many observers to point out a potentially destabilizing competition between two military blocs.

POTENTIAL CHALLENGES AND OPPORTUNITIES FOR THE UNITED STATES

Political Changes

Despite initial enthusiasm for forming trilateral and/or quadrilateral security arrangements, the conservative leaders who originally supported the idea have all been compromised by their own domestic political situations. Abe left office precipitously in September 2007 after his party suffered a major parliamentary defeat; Howard was soundly defeated in November 2007 in the Australian parliamentarian elections; Singh's ruling coalition has struggled to stay intact; and President Bush faces political challenges and low public approval ratings. Maintaining the momentum for the multilateral initiatives may be challenging, depending on the inclinations of incoming administrations. Currently, the quadrilateral grouping appears to be on hold, and it remains to be seen if geopolitical forces will push cooperation forward.

Japan's Restraints

Despite Abe's strong support for expanding security ties with India and Australia, Japan's involvement in any multilateral security fora will be restricted, both legally because of Article 9 and socially because of the public's pacifist sentiments which — while declining — still remain strong. Japan's approach to the principle of "collective self-defense" has in the past been considered an obstacle to close defense cooperation. The term comes from Article 51 of the U.N. Charter, which provides that member nations may exercise the rights of both individual and collective self-defense if an armed attack occurs. A 1960 decision by Japan's Cabinet Legislation Bureau interpreted the constitution to forbid collective actions because it would require considering the defense of other countries, not just the safety of Japan itself. Abe convened a special commission to study whether the constitutional interpretation should be changed, and the members were widely expected to recommend that collective self-defense be allowed. As a result of Abe's resignation in 2007, the campaign to adjust the constitutional interpretation will likely stall, as new Prime Minister Yasuo Fukuda is considered unsupportive of the move. U.S. officials have pressured the Japanese government to allow collective self-defense, particularly in terms of allowing Japan to intercept missiles aimed at U.S. targets. Military engagement with other regional powers is likely to meet with more public and bureaucratic resistance than furthering cooperation with the United States.

Australia's Posture

America's key policy challenge in its alliance relationship with Australia will, according to some analysts, be to keep this staunch ally from shifting to a position where Canberra sees its role as a mediator between the United States and China rather than focused on working unambiguously with the United States.[52] This may involve countering Chinese attempts to drive a wedge between the United States and Australia. The unpopularity of the Bush Administration in Australia and its perceived unilateralist policies, including in Iraq, and the degree to which Australia's economy is benefitting from exports to China are key factors in this calculus. Australia may increasingly seek to develop its own independent ties with Asian powers, without appearing to be simply an American ally in the region. Australia's desire for a more independent foreign and strategic policy may be part of its efforts to reach out to other states such as Japan, Singapore, and India.[53] Canberra is also reluctant to offend China, which may place limits on its relationship with the United States. In July 2007, Australian Minister for Defence Brendon Nelson stated that "we do not wish to have formal quadrilateral strategic dialogue in defence and security matters.... We do not want to do anything which ... may otherwise cause concern in some countries, particularly China."[54]

India's Ambivalence

India's rising economic and political power makes it an increasingly appealing partner for the United States, in terms of both its democratic values and its geostrategic location. Obstacles to a closer bilateral relationship — most recently, the apparent faltering of the civilian nuclear deal in the Indian parliament — remain prominent. Further, some see India as somewhat mired in its identity as a member of the Non-Aligned Movement (NAM), a Cold-War era organization of states resisting great power politics. Through various statements, officials in New Delhi have indicated their desire to balance powers and create a "multipolar" Asia, suggesting that it may not agree with the U.S. goal of remaining the pre-eminent power in East Asia. Though India is wary of China's increasing strength, and therefore more open to cooperation with other powers, it has been insistent that it does not intend to "choose sides," and is opposed to any formal regional defense alliance. In addition, India has participated as an observer in the Shanghai Cooperation Organization (SCO) meetings.

China: Engagement vs. Isolation

For U.S. policymakers, the key challenge is to develop a strategic posture in the region that can accommodate China's peaceful economic rise while sending the signal that the United States is not leaving a geopolitical vacuum for China to fill. Developing joint capabilities through enhanced defense partnerships with like- minded states may discourage China from asserting itself in ways that harm U.S. interests. On the other hand, it risks creating a dangerous cycle of mutual hedging, in which Beijing is tempted to exhibit more aggressive behavior. This atmosphere would not be conducive to engaging China more fully as a "responsible stakeholder" in the international system. Developing multilateral groupings poses its own challenges, as all states must harmonize their approach to Beijing: at times, it may be difficult to reconcile a more conciliatory New Delhi or Canberra with a potentially more threatened Tokyo. Washington must carefully calibrate its diplomatic and military approach as it adjusts its Asia-Pacific presence to accommodate a range of competing interests.

U.S. Ties with Other Asian States

Many observers concur that the United States needs to be forward thinking and open to active and engaged partnerships and cooperation with key regional states while not pushing such cooperation to the point that it is destabilizing or unattractive to regional states. Such cooperation could better position the United States and like- minded countries to look after their shared interests through a focus on capacity building while not being formalized in a way that such cooperation appears to be aimed at containing China. An agenda aimed at the containment of China is not likely to attract regional states and could create a hostile security environment in Asia that would likely undermine U.S. and others' interests. The United States must be particularly careful not to isolate other existing allies, such as South Korea, the Philippines, and Thailand, as it pursues new partnerships in Asia. Some observers think that the election of Lee Myung-bak as South Korean president, who is considered likely to improve relations with both the United States and Japan, could provide an opening for drawing Seoul in a multilateral regional framework.

END NOTES

[1] Gerald Curtis, "The U.S. in East Asia: Not Architecture, But Action," *Global Asia,* Fall 2007. See also CRS Report RL33821, *U.S. Strategic and Defense Relations in the Asia Pacific Region,* by Bruce Vaughn.

[2] The East Asia Summit, begun in 2005, is a pan-Asian forum that includes Brunei, Burma, Cambodia, Indonesia, Laos, Malaysia, Philippines, Singapore, Thailand, Vietnam, China, South Korea, Japan, Australia, New Zealand, and India. ASEAN + 3 includes ASEAN (Brunei, Burma, Cambodia, Indonesia, Laos, Malaysia, Philippines, Singapore, Thailand, and Vietnam) and China, South Korea, and Japan. For a more detailed and comprehensive discussion of these, see CRS Report RL33653, *East Asia Regional Architecture: New Economic and Security Arrangements and U.S. Policy,* by Dick Nanto.

[3] The Shanghai Cooperation Organization is an intergovernmental mutual-security organization founded in 2001 that includes China, Russia, Kazakhstan, Kyrgyzstan, Tajikistan, and Uzbekistan.

[4] Mary-Anne Toy, "China's Defence Budget Set to Unnerve West," *The Age,* March 5, 2007.

[5] Sir Halford Mackinder, "The Geographical Pivot of History," Royal Geographical Society, 1904 and Captain Alfred Thayer Mahan, *The Influence of Seapower Upon History: 16601783* (Boston: Little, Brown and Company, 1890).

[6] W. Minick, "China Rising: East Asia Braces as American Influence *Fades,"Defense News,* March 19, 2007.

[7] Charles Morrison and Peter A. Petri, "Renewing the Pacific Partnership," *East West Wire,* November 8, 2007.

[8] William Tow, "America's Asia-Pacific Strategy is Out of Kilter," *Current History,* September 2007.

[9] William Tow, "America's Asia-Pacific Strategy is Out of Kilter," *Current History,* September 2007.

[10] C. Raja Mohan, "East Asian Security: India's Rising Profile," *RSIS Commentaries,* July 30, 2007.

[11] Brendon Nelson, "China Warns Canberra on Security Pact," *The Age,* June 15, 2007.

[12] See CRS Report RS22570, *Guam: U.S. Defense Deployments,* by Shirley A. Kan and Larry A. Niksch.

[13] The White House, Office of the Press Secretary, "U.S. Commitment to Strengthen Forces of Freedom, Prosperity in Region," September 7, 2007.

[14] Alan Dupont, "Not the Time to Deal Out Beijing," *The Australian,* March 26, 2007.

[15] For background information, see CRS Report RL33010, *Australia: Background and U.S. Relations,* by Bruce Vaughn.

[16] The New Zealand leg of what was originally a trilateral alliance has been suspended since the mid-1980s.

[17] For more information, see CRS Report RS22772, *The U.S. Australia Treaty on Defense Trade Cooperation,* by Bruce Vaughn.

[18] Robert Ayson, "Rudd and Asia's Security," *PacNet Newsletter.* November 28, 2007.

[19] The Hon. Dr. Brendan Nelson MP, Minister for Defence, "Defence Update 2007 - Protecting Our People, Interests and Values," July 5, 2007.

[20] "China Causing Uncertainty and Unease?" *Singapore Institute of International Affairs,* July 10, 2007. This text was also echoed in the Defence Update 2007.

[21] Department of Defence, The Australian Government, *Australia's National Security: A Defence Update 2007.*

[22] "Australian Govt Under Fire For Minister's Taiwan Comments," *OsterDowJones Commodity Wire,* August 20, 2004.

[23] See CRS Report RL33436, *Japan-US. Relations: Issues for Congress,* by Emma Chanlett-Avery, Mark E. Manyin, and William H Cooper and CRS Report RL33740, *The Changing U.S.-Japan Alliance: Implications for U.S. Interests,* by Emma Chanlett-Avery.

[24] For detailed information see CRS Report RL33529, *India-U.S. Relations,* by K. Alan Kronstadt and CRS Report RL33072, *U.S.-India Bilateral Arrangements and "Global Partnership,"* by K. Alan Kronstadt.

[25] President George W. Bush as quoted in "Bush Hails Partnership with India," *BBC News,* March 3, 2006.

[26] Brhama Chellaney, "Forestalling Strategic Conflict in Asia," *Far Eastern Economic Review,* November 2006.

[27] Gupreet Singh Khurana, "Interpreting India's Naval Strategy," *The Straits Times,* July 16, 2007.

[28] Lisa Curtis, The Triangular Dynamic in Asia: The U.S., India, and China," *Heritage Lectures,* April 26, 2007.

[29] Karl Inderfurth and Bruce Riedel, "A Rare, Stable Partnership," *The Baltimore Sun,* November 18, 2007.

[30] Yoshinobu Yamamoto, "Strengthening Security Cooperation with Australia: A New Security Means for Japan," *Policy Forum Online 07-083A.* November 1st, 2007.

[31] Aurelia George Mulgan, "New Directions in Australia-Japan Relations," University of New South Wales, Australian Defence Force Academy, June 2007.

[32] "Australia-Japan Relations: New Directions," *Strategic Insights,* Australia Strategic Policy Institute. July 2007.

[33] Rory Metcalf, "The Changing Asia-Pacific Security Web," *The Age,* March 16, 2007.

[34] "From Japan with Love," *Business Today,* September 23, 2007.

[35] Rory Medcalf, "Uranium Thom," *Times of India,* April 20, 2007.

[36] Mark Dodd, "India Defence Ties to be Tightened," *The Australian,* June 4, 2007.

[37] "Australia, India Sign Information Sharing Arrangement," *C41 News,* July 19, 2007.

[38] C. Raja Mohan, "East Asian Security: India's Rising Profile," *RSIS Commentaries,* July 30, 2007.

[39] C. Raja Mohan, "China and Japan Set to Redefine South Asian Geopolitics," *RSIS Commentaries,* March 30, 2007.

[40] Ron Walker, "Uranium for India: Avoiding the Pitfalls," *Lowy Institute,* May 2007.

[41] Sandy Gordon, Widening Horizons: Australia's New Relationship with India," Australian Strategic Policy Institute, May 2007.

[42] Japan, US, Australia to Conduct Patrol Plane Drill," *Nikkei.* (Translation from Japanese Morning Press Highlights, US Embassy in Tokyo), October 10, 2007.

[43] "Missile Defense Spreading East," *Kommersant International.* May 24, 2007.

[44] "Australia Studies Joint Missile Defense With US, Japan," *Dow Jones International News.* June 5, 2007.

[45] "Land of the Rising Gun-Japan's Shifting Security Identity," *Jane 's Intelligence Review,* September 1, 2007.

[46] Indian Navy Holds Joint Drills with Top Naval Powers," *Organisation of Asia-Pacific News Agencies,* April 17, 2007.

[47] U.S.-Japan-India Report, *Center for Strategic and International Studies,* August 16, 2007.

[48] "Kitty Hawk, Allies Complete Malabar Exercise," U.S. Navy press release, September 10, 2007.

[49] "Personal Relationships Key to Malabar," U.S. Navy press release, September 7, 2007.

[50] "KittyHawk, Allies Participate in Malabar Photo," U.S. Navy press release, September 10, 2007.

[51] "China-Russia Relations: Between Cooperation and Competition," *Comparative Connections*, October 2007.

[52] Dan Blumenthal, "Strengthening the U.S. - Australian Alliance. Progress and Pitfalls," *Asian Outlook,* April-May 2005.

[53] Craig Skehan, "Nelson Seeks New Friends if U.S. Falters," *The Sydney Morning Herald,* June 15, 2007.

[54] "Australia Allays Chinese Concerns," *BBC News,* July 12, 2007.

In: India and the U.S: Future Relations…
Editor: Tim S. Macleod, pp.231-280 ISBN: 978-1-60741-197-0

Chapter 6

MORE THAN JUST THE 123 AGREEMENT: THE FUTURE OF U.S.-INDO RELATIONS: HEARING BEFORE THE SUBCOMMITTEE ON THE MIDDLE EAST AND SOUTH ASIA OF THE COMMITTEE ON FOREIGN AFFAIRS HOUSE OF REPRESENTATIVES

United States Government Printing Office

The subcommittee met, pursuant to notice, at 2:33 p.m., in room 2172, Rayburn House Office Building, Hon. Gary L. Ackerman (chairman of the subcommittee) presiding.

Mr. ACKERMAN. The subcommittee will come to order.

Over the past year and a half, this subcommittee has examined a variety of issues and has, at least on our side, been very critical of the President, his administration and the state of affairs that the next President will inherit across the Middle East and South Asia as a result of the current President's policies. So today will be a change of pace, because, if there is one area in the subcommittee's jurisdiction where President Bush got the policy right, it is toward India.

But it isn't just this administration that they got India right. The Clinton administration moved from ostracizing India after the 1998 nuclear tests to embracing India as an emerging global power, a view cemented by President Clinton's historic trip to India in 2000, on which I was pleased and very proud to accompany the President on that mission.

The bipartisan recognition of India's importance in the 21st century underscored the need and provided the support for a broader, deeper and closer and warmer relationship between two countries and that required moving a particular irritant involving civil nuclear technology.

The July 2005 joint statement by Prime Minister Singh and President Bush proved the key to unlocking the door of a range of issues in which India and the United States not only could cooperate but should cooperate.

I believed then and I believe now that the case for civil nuclear cooperation between the United States and India is clear and compelling. I strongly support the 123 Agreement, and I look forward to the Government of India completing its internal process so that the U.S. Congress can give final approval to this historic deal.

As the title of this hearing indicates, however, there was much more to the July 2005 joint statement than civil nuclear cooperation, and there is much more to United States-India relations than just the 123 Agreement. In fact, the 2005 statement covered a broad range of issues, among which civil nuclear cooperation was just one.

That agreement revitalized the United States-India economic dialogue and launched a CEO forum to deepen our bilateral economic partnership. It committed both nations to accelerating trade, investment and technology collaboration, and launched the U.S.India Knowledge Initiative on Agriculture. And, in order to strengthen the foundations that make democracies credible and effective, the U.S.-India Global Democracy Initiative was launched.

The 2005 agreement also called for greater efforts in the arena of commercial civil space cooperation, more trade and high-technology items, and welcomed increased Indian efforts to prevent the proliferation of weapons of mass destruction.

Alongside the joint statement, the United States and India had earlier signed a 10-year defense pact, outlining planned global collaboration in multilateral operations, expanded two-way defense trade, increased opportunities for technology transfers and coproduction, as well as increased collaboration on missile defense, and the list goes on.

I enumerate these things because the details illuminate how far the relationship has come in just the last 3 years. The breadth and pace at which all these initiatives have expanded would boggle the mind of even the most optimistic supporter of United States-India relations.

All of these various initiatives are not just pronouncements made by heads of government and forgotten. They have been matched by follow-up and demonstrable success. I will cite just a couple of examples.

In the area of trade and investment, the United States is India's largest trading partner and accounts for about $^{1}/7$ of all foreign direct investment in India since 1991.

In the area of defense cooperation, the U.S.-India Defense Policy Group meets annually, and since 2002 the United States and India have held an unprecedented number and increased substantive combined exercises involving all military services. In addition, the amount and sophistication of defense sales to India has increased exponentially, and the Government of India has opened the door for United States firms to compete in the sale of multi-role fighters to India.

One area of longstanding cooperation I haven't mentioned is counterterrorism. India has been a victim of terrorism far longer than we have. Their experience with terrorism is deep and is as recent as the bombings last month in Jaipur, in which a series of seven blasts occurred in 20 minutes at crowded markets and their Hindu temples. Sixty-five people were killed, 150 wounded, according to official estimates. Our thoughts and prayers are with the families of the dead, and we wish the injured swift recovery.

This terrible attack serves as another gruesome reminder of how much in common the United States and India have when it comes to the global fight against terror and how we must redouble our efforts to develop effective tools to defeat terrorism and violent religious extremism.

But before anyone leaves this hearing with the idea that the United States and India will go riding off into the sunset and live happily ever after, if I can mix movie endings, there are some areas of disagreement that need to be mentioned and, if left to fester, could cut off our burgeoning relationship at the pass.

The one I have particularly in mind is India's relationship with Iran. I have heard about and understood from a wide variety of Indian Government officials India's historic ties to Iran and its domestic political need not to alienate hundreds of millions of its Muslim citizens. I have also heard and understood the arguments about India's ever-increasing needs for energy.

But I hope that India's officials will hear and understand the United States view of Iran: That Iran's pursuit of nuclear weapons and regional hegemony is a serious threat posed to international peace and stability in the Middle East and the vital national security interests of the United States.

I believe Indian officials understand the United States perspective on Iran, and I know that India shares United States opposition to Iran possessing nuclear weapons. Their courageous IAEA vote demonstrates that.

So I have a very difficult time understanding why the Government of India continues to pursue a pipeline with Iran and Pakistan at a time when other nations in the world are just not implementing U.N.-approved sanctions, which is India's historic position, but are going further by cutting off access to banking services and discouraging other economic interactions with Iran.

If the international community, India included, wants a peaceful resolution to the Iranian nuclear question, then joining the growing international efforts to isolate Iran that extend beyond the U.N. Security Council sanctions is the way to go forward. Continued pursuit of the IPI pipeline or other investments in Iran's energy sector, as was hinted a few weeks ago by unnamed officials at India's state-run Oil and Natural Gas Corporation, will halt and potentially even roll back the progress made in bilateral relations over the last several years.

I want to be clear that I am not suggesting that India abandon its historic independent foreign policy, though I am sure that there are those in India who will accuse me of just that. What I am suggesting is that India join the other nations who are doing more than just implementing U.N. sanctions in an effort to economically isolate Iran. It is an effort that I believe is fully consistent with India's historic support of multilateral institutions and cooperation.

There has been tremendous progress in United States-India relations over the last decade and particularly over the last 3 years. There is every opportunity and very good reasons to advance relations even further, and future generations would consider us fools if we were to squander them.

Mr. Wilson?

[The prepared statement of Mr. Ackerman follows:]

Prepared Statement of the Honorable Gary L. Ackerman, a Representative in Congress from the State of New York, and Chairman, Subcommittee on the Middle East and South Asia

The Subcommittee will come to order. Over the past year and a half, this subcommittee has examined a variety of issues and has, at least on our side, been very critical of the President, his Administration, and the state of affairs that the next President will inherit across the Middle East and South Asia as a result of the current president's policies. So today will be a change of pace, because if there is one area in the subcommittee's jurisdiction where President Bush got the policy right, it is towards India.

But it isn't just this Administration that got India right. The Clinton Administration moved from ostracizing India after the 1998 nuclear tests to embracing India as an emerging global power: a view cemented by President Clinton's historic trip to India in 2000 and I was pleased and proud to accompany President Clinton on that journey.

The bipartisan recognition of India's importance in the 21st century underscored the need and provided the support for a broader, deeper, closer and warmer relationship between the two countries and that required removing a particular irritant involving *civil* nuclear technology. The July 2005 joint statement by Prime Minister Singh and President Bush proved the key to unlocking the door to a range of issues on which India and the United States not only *could* cooperate but *should* cooperate.

I believed then and believe now that the case for civil nuclear cooperation between the United States and India is clear and compelling. I strongly support the 123 agreement and I look forward to the Government of India completing its internal processes so that the U.S. Congress can give final approval to this historic deal

As the title of this hearing indicates, however, there was much more to the July 2005 joint statement than civil nuclear cooperation and there is much more to U.S.India relations than just the 123 agreement. In fact the 2005 statement covered a broad range of issues among which civil nuclear cooperation was just one. That agreement revitalized the U.S.-India Economic Dialogue and launched a CEO Forum to deepen our bilateral economic partnership; it committed both nations to accelerating trade, investment and technology collaboration and launched the U.S.India Knowledge Initiative on Agriculture; and in order to strengthen the foundations that make democracies credible and effective the U.S.-India Global Democracy Initiative was launched. The 2005 agreement also called for greater efforts in the arena of commercial civil space cooperation, more trade in high technology items and welcomed increased Indian efforts to prevent the proliferation of weapons of mass destruction. Alongside the joint statement, the United States and India had earlier signed a ten year defense pact outlining planned collaboration in multilateral operations, expanded two-way defense trade, increased opportunities for technology transfers and co-production as well as increased collaboration on missile defense. And the list goes on.

I enumerate these things because the details illuminate how far the relationship has come in just the last three years. The breadth and pace at which all these initiatives have expanded would boggle the mind of even the most optimistic supporter of U.S.-India relations. All of these various initiatives are not just pronouncements made by heads of government and forgotten. They've been matched by follow-up and demonstrable success. I'll cite just a couple examples. In the area of trade and investment, the United States is India's largest trading partner and accounts for about one-seventh of all foreign direct investment in India since 1991. In the area of defense cooperation, the India-U.S. Defense Policy Group meets annually, and since 2002 the United States and India have held an unprecedented number, and increasingly substantive, combined exercises involving all military services. In addition, the amount and sophistication of defense sales to India has increased exponentially and the Government of India has opened the door for U.S. firms to compete for the sale of multi-role fighters to India.

One area of long-standing cooperation I haven't mentioned is counter-terrorism. India has been victims of terrorism for far longer than have we. Their experience with terrorism is deep and is as recent as the bombings last month in Jaipur, in which a series of seven blasts occurred in twenty minutes at crowded markets and near Hindu temples. 65 people were killed and 150 wounded according to official estimates. Our thoughts and prayers are with the families of the dead and we wish the injured swift recovery. This terrible attack serves as another gruesome reminder of how much in common the United States and India have when it comes to the global fight against terror and how we must redouble our efforts to develop effective tools to defeat terrorism and violent religious extremism.

But before anyone leaves this hearing with the idea that the United States and India will go riding off into the sunset and live happily ever after, if I can mix movie endings, there are some areas of disagreement that need to be mentioned and if left to fester could cut off our burgeoning relationship at the pass.

The one I have particularly in mind is India's relationship with Iran. I have heard about and understood from a wide variety of Indian government officials, India's historic ties to Iran and its domestic political need not to alienate hundreds of millions of its Muslim citizens. I have also heard and understood the arguments about India's ever increasing needs for energy. But I hope that India's officials will hear and understand the U.S. view of Iran: that Iran's pursuit of nuclear weapons and regional hegemony is a serious threat posed to international peace and stability in the Middle East and the vital national security interests of the United States. I believe Indian officials understand the U.S. perspective on Iran and I know that India shares U.S. opposition to Iran possessing nuclear weapons. Their courageous IAEA votes demonstrate that.

So I have a very difficult time understanding why the Government of India continues to pursue a pipeline with Iran and Pakistan at a time when other nations in the world are not just implementing UN approved sanctions, which is India's historic position, but are going further by cutting off access to banking services and discouraging other economic interactions with Iran. If the international community, India included, wants a peaceful resolution to the Iranian nuclear question, then joining the growing international efforts to isolate Iran that extend beyond the UN Security Council sanctions, is the way to go forward. Continued pursuit of the IPI pipeline or other investments in Iran's energy sector as was hinted at a few weeks ago by unnamed officials at India's state-run Oil and Natural Gas Corporation will halt and potentially even roll back the progress made in bilateral relations over the last several years. I want to be clear that I am not suggesting that India abandon its historically independent foreign policy, although I am sure there are those in India who will accuse me of just that. What I am suggesting is that India join the other nations who are doing more than just implementing UN sanctions in an effort to economically isolate Iran. It is an effort that I believe is fully consistent with India's historic support of multilateral institutions and cooperation.

There has been tremendous progress in U.S.-India relations over the last decade and particularly over the last three years. There is every opportunity and very good reasons to advance relations even further, and future generations will consider us fools if we squander them.

Mr. Wilson. Thank you, Mr. Chairman.

Thank you, Chairman Ackerman, for holding this hearing today on United States-India relations.

As a long-time supporter of strengthening the partnership between the United States and India, I believe it is important that we discuss and recognize that United States-Indo relations is indeed more than the 123 Agreement.

As a young child, I remember my father telling me about his time serving in India as a member of the Flying Tigers during World War II. His stories about entrepreneurial and hard-working people taught me valuable lessons about the culture and the people of India.

Since those days, our relationship with India has become a growing alliance that partners our dedication to democracy. After all, America is the world's oldest democracy and India is the world's largest democracy. And our willingness to be active participants in the global economy and marketplace, as well as our strategic responsibilities, in a rapidly changing world.

The United States and India need to continue to be fair and willing partners on economic, energy, and national security issues. I hope the political difficulties that have stalled movement on the Civilian Nuclear Agreement can be overcome.

I also hope that we cooperate with India on advancing research into new energy sources. With their rapidly expanding economy, the people of India will increasingly need access to affordable energy, as will the people of the United States. This will be mutually beneficial.

And, lastly, the security of both nations is the ultimate responsibility of our respective governments and surely the primary concern of all of our citizens. In the global war on terrorism, we have common enemies. And we can learn from our Indian partners how to defeat terrorists who have attacked India for 60 years and killed over 60,000 citizens.

Moving forward, there needs to be a robust and respectful debate about our strategic defense relationship, and, without a doubt, the discussions over energy and economic growth will contribute to that debate.

No relationship between any two nations will be without disagreements or competing interest at times. There are tremendous national, regional and global concerns that the people of India must address, but I have confidence they can and will. It is, in my estimate, vital that the United States continue to seek a fair and mutually respectful partnership with the people of India, as indicated by the past 3 years of tremendous progress.

America has been enriched by the immigration of 2.2 million citizens from India who have been vital to business, the medical and hospitality industries in America. With my personal experience as co-chair of the India Caucus, the largest country caucus in Washington, reflecting appreciation for the Republic of India, and through my many years of friendship with Indian-American community leaders, I value today's hearing and look forward to the testimony.

Again, I wish to thank Chairman Ackerman and my fellow committee members for this opportunity.

Mr. Ackerman. Mr. Scott?

Mr. Scott. Thank you, Mr. Chairman.

It is clear that the relationship between the United States and India is experiencing an extensive and groundbreaking transformation. This administration has already pledged to help India become a major world power in the 21st century.

India, as the most populous democracy in the world, shares our commitment to democracy and the fight against terror. From these shared interests, the manifestations of a strengthened India-American relationship are quite evident.

Economically, India and the United States will mutually benefit from this strengthening of our ties. The United States represents India's largest trading and investment partner. And, overall, India is the United States second-largest trading partner, after China. In light of these strong economic ties, a renewed relationship will yield not only an increase in bilateral trade but also an increased flow of investments.

In terms of nuclear power and energy, the signing of the 123 Agreement and the Hyde Act signals our confidence to the world to give India increased access to civilian nuclear technology for peaceful purposes such as energy security.

And while this robust relationship will prove largely positive for both parties, it is imperative that we analyze all the implications of this relationship. And I hope the panelists today will speak to the repercussions the United States will face from China as a result of strengthening ties with India. Insights into existing nuclear and economic policies regarding India will be very, very relevant.

Additionally, I would like to hear from our witnesses this afternoon of how this relationship may create a new dynamic in the upcoming Presidential elections, as we will have a new administration in just a very few months.

Recently, there have been talks surrounding India's desire to gain a permanent seat on the U.N. Security Council. I think it is important that we discuss how likely it is within the next 5 years that India will be successful in gaining such a seat and what strategies we might apply to see that that happens.

India has always had quite a rocky relationship with Pakistan. I would like to have some discussion this afternoon on Pakistan and India's relationship, and how will the United States balance its commitment to both these nations in such a competitive atmosphere.

And both the United States and India have faced terrorist attacks stemming from religious extremism. I think we need to discuss the question of how can each country help the other in the global war on terror.

There is much that we need to discuss, but also today, if it hasn't happened already given the time zones, India will meet with their left-wing allies concerning the nuclear deal between India and the United States. I think that this is a very momentous occasion, to say the least, and it would be very important to have some discussion on those implications, as far as the future of the coalition, the risks that are being run, and also what the International Atomic Energy is saying about this endeavor.

So needless to say, the topic is right. The future of the United States and India's relations will yield much to determine, quite honestly, the future of peace in the world.

Thank you, Mr. Chairman.

Mr. Ackerman. Thank you.

There being no further members of which to speak, we now turn to our very distinguished panel.

Dr. Stephen Cohen is a senior fellow in foreign policy at The Brookings Institution, which he joined in 1998 after a career as a professor of political science and history at the University of Illinois. He is the author, co-author or editor of 12 books, mostly on South Asian security issues, the most recent being "Four Crises and a Peace Process: American Engagement in South Asia" and "The Idea of Pakistan."

Dr. Cohen was a visiting professor at Lee Kuan Yew School of Public Policy in Singapore and taught at Keio University in Japan and Andhra University in India. He has also consulted with various foundations and government agencies and was a member of the State Department's policy planning staff from 1985 to 1987. He received his undergraduate degree from the University of Chicago and his doctorate from the University of Wisconsin.

Ambassador Teresita Schaffer is the director of the South Asia Program at the Center for Strategic and International Studies, which she joined in 1998 after a 30-year career in the Foreign Service.

Ambassador Schaffer served as Ambassador to Sri Lanka from 1992 to 1995 and has also served as Deputy Assistant Secretary of State for South Asia and director of the Foreign Service Institute. Over the course of her Foreign Service career, Ambassador Schaffer served in Tel Aviv, Islamabad, New Delhi and Dhaka.

Ambassador Schaffer has published widely on diverse South Asian topics. Most recently, she wrote "Kashmir The Economics of Peace-Building" and "Pakistan's Future and U.S. Policy Options." Ambassador Schaffer taught both at Georgetown and American Universities. And, if I count correctly, she speaks seven languages, including Urdu, Hebrew and Hindi.

Dr. Walter Andersen is associate director of the Southeast Asia Studies Program at Johns Hopkins School of Advanced International Studies. Dr. Andersen has served in a variety of positions in the State Department, which he joined in 1970 to work on India and Indian Ocean affairs.

After that, Dr. Andersen had assignments to Pakistan and Moscow. Dr. Andersen also served in New Delhi as special assistant to the U.S. Ambassador from 1988 to 1991. And when he returned to the United States, he headed the State Department's South Asia Division in the Office of Analysis for the Near East and South Asia.

Dr. Andersen has also worked on Indian Ocean security issues with Dr. Robert Scalapino at University of California-Berkley and, while at The Brookings Institute, wrote "The Brotherhood of Saffron" about the rise of Hindu nationalism in India. Dr. Andersen received a BA from Concordia College and his Ph.D. from the University of Chicago.

Welcome to all of you.

Your full statements will be placed in the record in its entireties. And if you could summarize in about 5 minutes or so, that with leave ample time for the members to ask questions.

Dr. Cohen, we will start with you.

STATEMENT OF STEPHEN P. COHEN, PH.D., SENIOR FELLOW, FOREIGN POLICY STUDIES, THE BROOKINGS INSTITUTION

Mr. Cohen. Thank you, sir.

Thank you, Congressman Ackerman and members of the subcommittee. I am pleased to share my expertise on the important question of the future of Indian-American relations.

Fifteen years ago, Indians and Americans both failed to anticipate or understand the events that were to transform the relationship along many dimensions. Mistakes were made on both sides, and the recent difficulties in consummating the nuclear agreement might have been avoided had we thought more clearly and realistically about the overall relationship and the developments within each country that affects our ties.

I will devote my time now to some of the areas of greatest promise and those areas where clear thinking and considered action may improve the relationship so that important Indian and American interests are advanced.

Good relations is often a euphemism for feeling good about the other country. This is not a useful criteria for developing policies that benefit both sides in specific and meaningful ways.

First, on the economy: Expanded two-way trade and new economic ties now constitute the ballast of the United States-India relationship. We need not worry over much about a return to the dark days of the 1970s when India saw the United States as a hostile, encircling power and Washington simply ignored India. Yet, government policy can facilitate or hamper economic ties.

In this case, the reforms have to be largely on the Indian side, but American business should be sensitive to Indian concerns and Indian practices and should endeavor to strengthen Indian capacities, especially in such areas as education. American operations in India should not be seen as exploitive, just as Indian operations in the United States will be judged as to whether they take away American jobs.

On strategic relations, the motto should be, "Look before you hop." It would be wrong to expect a close strategic relationship between the two countries on the basis of a hypothetical threat from China. A relationship should be seen and presented as reinsurance against a malevolent China, a future that may never happen.

In the meantime, both sides will be worried of being involved in the other's conflicts with third parties: India with American concerns about Iran; the United States with India's continuing conflict with Pakistan. In both cases, the root cause is political instability in Iran and Pakistan, which makes their policies unpredictable and potentially harmful. We should not demand Indian support for all of our Iranian policies any more than we should allow India to dictate our policy toward Pakistan.

There will, however, be many opportunities for second-tier military cooperation, notably in disaster relief, anti-piracy efforts, and in helping to stabilize countries that are unable to maintain their integrity.

Naval cooperation is likely to be the most fruitful area, as the Indian navy performs at a very high level of professionalism and now has a doctrine that encourages such cooperation. India should be invited to join the Task Force 150 in the Gulf, and India's navy, in its capacity for power projection, should be strengthened.

We should, of course, conclude the United States-India nuclear agreement. The bulk of work to enable the deal has already been accomplished, although the implementation will be very difficult. While it would be imprudent to renegotiate the entire agreement, I do see the possibility of concessions on both sides that make the agreement more attractive.

On our part, we can reduce some of the limits on India's use of reactor byproducts, because I do not believe that India intends to build a vast arsenal, and accept India as a nuclear-weapons state.

On India's part, the commitment to no more testing could be formalized, preferably by signing the CTBT. And they could stabilize their arsenal designs so no new testing was necessary and renew earlier commitments to arms control, starting with the revival of the Rajiv Gandhi Action Plan. They could also sign on to the Proliferation Security Initiative and join other arms control regimes.

The criteria should be: Does the agreement not only provide India with enhanced energy resources, which I think it does, but does it, on balance, enhance global arms control and restraints on the development and deployment of nuclear weapons? The United States should also translate the Indian agreement into a criteria- based format, potentially allowing Pakistan and even Israel to enter into a similar arrangement.

We should also give greater priority to bilateral cooperation on education, agriculture, which was part of the 2005 agreement, and regional water and environmental issues.

In my written testimony, I make the point that there is one area where I think, looking ahead 4, 5, 6, years, you could have a major, even catastrophic development, and that is the disposition of the water that falls in the Himalayas. This directly affects the livelihood and security of about 1 billion people in South Asia, plus China. So China, Nepal, India, Pakistan and Bangladesh are vitally affected by that water. And if the monsoon pattern should change, or one or another of the countries should attempt to manipulate or change the flow of that water, this would be a cause for war.

So I think this is an area where the U.S. should get involved, should learn about it, and possibly facilitate a regional arrangement which could manage this development over time. We need to recognize that this will be the big issue over the next decade and work toward collaborative mechanisms that include India in the resolution or amelioration.

Finally, we should build our intellectual resource base. For a long time, India was defined as an irritant. It did not count economically or strategically. Now that it does count, we need to better understand such changes as the caste and class revolutions, the shift of power from the center to the states, and as India has entered into an era of coalition governments.

Dealing with democracies always requires an extra effort. We must invest in the long-neglected research and scholarly base, a necessary but not sufficient foundation stone for wise policy.

With that, I conclude my testimony. Thank you.

[The prepared statement of Mr. Cohen follows:]

Prepared Statement of Stephen P. Cohen, Ph.D., Senior Fellow, Foreign Policy Studies, the Brookings Institution

Congressman Ackerman, and members of the Subcommittee, I am pleased to share my expertise on the important question of the future of American relations with India. Fifteen years ago, both Indians and Americans failed to anticipate or understand the events that were to transform the relationship along many dimensions. Mistakes were made on both sides, and the recent difficulties of consummating the nuclear agreement might have been avoided had we thought more clearly and realistically about the overall relationship and the developments *within* each country that affects our ties.

Therefore, I will only briefly summarize the past and devote most of my testimony to the future: those areas of greatest promise, those areas where little can (or should) be done, and those areas where clear thinking and concerted action may improve the relationship so that important Indian and American interests are advanced. "Good relations" is often a euphemism for feeling good about the other country. I've never regarded this as a useful criteria for developing policies that benefit both sides in specific and meaningful ways.

Changes in U.S.-India Relations

As I noted in *India: Emerging Power,* India is undergoing several revolutions, simultaneously. There is the federal revolution, a changed relationship between the state and the center, there are caste and class revolutions, as Indian society undergoes rapid change akin to our own civil-rights movement, and there is an economic revolution brought about by India's reasonably successful accommodation of the forces of globalization, which was facilitated by a change of economic policy in the early 1990s—a change that was fostered by

Prime Minister Manmohan Singh when he was Finance Minister. At about the same time, India's foreign policy underwent revolutionary change, as it slowly and painfully adjusted to the fact that the Soviet Union, a close friend and major military supplier, had disappeared. Coupled with other internal transformations, India is, in my judgment, one of the most revolutionary societies in the world, and with several important exceptions, these revolutions are proceeding peacefully.

In 1978, I published *India: Emergent Power?* It pointed to India's rise, but noted its failure to address the economy and its persistent conflict with Pakistan as factors that held India back. Twenty-three years later, my book on India did not have a question mark in its title. India's rise as a global power in the 21st century is all but certain. However significant questions remain concerning the speed, ease and uniformity of India's rise, and regarding the kind of power into which India will evolve. All of this will have a considerable impact on the U.S.-India bilateral relationship.

The most significant factor of the new U.S.-India relationship is that it is not based on relations between the two governments, but rather the relationship between their two societies and their economies. Indian-Americans are among the most successful of the recent immigrant groups to the United States. The U.S. remains immensely popular in India, particularly in the cities.[1] India is emerging as a cultural superpower, and just as Hollywood's influence is evident in Bollywood, the latter has established a position in the U.S. (as well as the rest of the world), and we now all consume Indian food in large quantities.

There remains an older generation in India that learned its anti-Americanism from the British, but they are less vehement, especially after they visit their children and relatives in the United States, returning with a somewhat more accurate picture of our virtues as well as our faults. There is also a somewhat younger generation of leftists who are ideologically anti-American They look to China and Russia to help balance American hegemony. While small in numbers, they are effective enough to block the U.S.-India nuclear agreement. I always had lingering doubts about the political viability of the "deal," hence the sub-title of a long paper I wrote several years ago: "A Deal Too Far?"

Indians clearly want closer economic ties with America, continue to see our country as a land of opportunity, and look to American practices for models and examples. We certainly could benefit from the Indian example in several spheres, notably in running free elections without controversy. Every time India goes to the polls, it is the world's largest organized human activity. The trade relationship still leaves much to be desired, due in large part to the underdevelopment of large-scale manu- facturing in India, but it is only a matter of time before the country makes greater headway in that sector. However, India is far behind China in that regard, and some of the recent books on "Chindia" that equate the two do a disservice to the truth.

Let me now focus on four areas: (1) bilateral defense cooperation, (2) the nuclear relationship, (3) key areas for greater cooperation and (4) areas of disagreement. I will conclude with some policy recommendations for the next U S administration and Congress.

Defense Cooperation, Exercises and Sales

The U.S.-India defense relationship has been unsettled since the end of the Cold War. Many American policymakers of the Clinton and Bush administrations harbored high hopes of India's evolution as a key U.S. strategic partner in South Asia, often a euphemism for a strategy of containing China, but which I would view as reinsurance for both the U.S. and India against the rise of a malevolent or hostile China.

Developments have not proceeded at the pace many had envisioned. Military-tomilitary ties have been among the more successful areas, with regular joint naval and air exercises between the U.S. and Indian militaries, but both India and the U.S. conduct exercises with many, many other countries, so this is not something extraordinary except in the context of a total absence of such exercises after 1963 (when American fighter aircraft trained alongside the Indian Air Force after the 1962 India-China war). Cooperation on counterinsurgency, an important aspect of security for both countries, has not been satisfactory, and more can certainly be done by both governments to exchange relevant ideas and training practices. That said, India and the Soviet Union never had military-to-military ties during the Cold War of the kind that India and the United States enjoy today. U.S.-India cooperation during the 2004-05 tsunami relief efforts was instructive and groundbreaking, but that remains the standout example of military cooperation.

Military sales have not yet risen to the level that U.S. defense corporations expected. India will be one of the largest markets for defense equipment in the coming two decades, but the United States has barely established a toehold there. There are a few promising signs. India recently agreed to purchase six C-130J aircraft, the biggest ever Indian purchase of American equipment in dollar terms. It also bought an amphibious transport ship, the *U.S.S. Trenton,* renamed the *I.N.S. Jalashwa,* which is now the second largest ship in the Indian fleet. These two purchases greatly expand India's power projection capacity, but I don't see a guiding strategic hand behind these decisions.

American corporations are today favored in a number of major defense tenders, but the Indian acquisition process is extraordinarily slow, and results will almost undoubtedly take some time. U.S. defense corporations would be wise to take some lessons from Israel's entry into the Indian market, as Israel is today India's second largest defense supplier Joint defense production and R&D remain many years off, although there may be greater room for cooperation with private Indian defense companies, who are only now coming into their own. India's stringent offsets mean that this route will be complex and difficult to negotiate.

There are two factors usually overlooked by American policymakers with regard to India's strategic evolution. The first is the domestic security threat facing India today. India's greatest national security challenge is no longer Pakistan or China or even terrorism, which has been responsible for more deaths in India than in any country other than Iraq in recent years. Its biggest threat is a leftist revolutionary movement termed the Naxalites (named after a Bengali village where a Maoist uprising took place in the 1970s). They have been in existence to a greater or lesser degree for decades. The movement—active today in a large swath of resource-rich central, eastern and north-eastern India, especially among tribals, low-caste Hindus, and ethnic minorities—is treated as a law and order problem. But it has the potential of becoming much more virulent and destabilizing should there be greater co-operation among Naxal groups in different Indian states, or should the Nepal communists turn out to be interested in supporting their Indian counterparts.

The second important factor is India's default preference for strategic caution, which is a major theme in my forthcoming book. India has traditionally refrained from employing its military muscle. It fought Pakistan to two stalemates in 19471948 and 1965, and its military involvement in the Sri Lankan civil war in the late 1980s proved a disaster. Today its engagement with its neighbors—including Pakistan, Sri Lanka, Nepal, Burma and

Bangladesh—is essentially non-military in nature. Two apparent exceptions to its strategic restraint were the 1971 war with Pakistan, which resulted in a decisive Indian victory, and the nuclear tests of 1998.

India's strategic restraint demonstrates itself in other manners as well. Today, India's military expenditure makes up a little over 2% of its GDP. While it is growing in real terms, it is still small given the enormity and the range of security threats facing the country. Additionally, India's most significant military operations outside its own borders in recent years have been humanitarian in nature.

Overcoming the Nuclear Hurdle

The U.S.-India nuclear agreement, which benefits India considerably, has barely progressed since the negotiation of the bilateral 123 Agreement last July. Eleven months later, the nuclear deal is being held hostage in New Delhi by the four Left parties upon whom the ruling UPA coalition is dependent for support. There remains a slim chance of the restraints being lifted this year, if elections are set or, even less likely, if the government chooses to pursue the deal against the wishes of the Communist parties. A more likely scenario is that the deal will return in 2009 or 2010 after India's general elections, which must take place before May of next year. In that case, it will be up to the next president and the 111th Congress to see the deal through to its completion by ensuring its approval by the Nuclear Suppliers Group and ratifying the 123 Agreement.

The non-proliferation implications of the deal have been explored in detail by many others. Disputes over India's nuclear program have unfortunately overshadowed other aspects of the bilateral relationship for much of the past 35 years. Actualizing the nuclear deal will enable the two countries to address a host of other urgent matters that are far more deserving of attention. A half-way house for India seems natural, given India's non-proliferation record and the chance for it to be incorporated into the global non-proliferation regime with the international community's acquiescence. I believe the Bush administration was bold and imaginative in developing the deal, but should have specified a number of criteria for such an agreement, thus potentially bringing other countries into such arrangements, and strengthening the overall arms control agenda.

Disputes over India's nuclear program have unfortunately overshadowed other aspects of the bilateral relationship for much of the past 35 years. Completing the nuclear deal will facilitate addressing other matters that are potentially more deserving of attention, although actually implementing the agreement will itself be a difficult process.

Key Areas for Greater Cooperation

There are three areas that in my opinion are ripe for action. All affect India's long term security and prosperity, and thus, indirectly, the United States' long-term prosperity and security. None of these have been priorities for the Indian or American governments in the past few decades, but all are vital to India's sustained growth as a major power. They are: (1) education, particularly higher education; (2) agriculture and (3) the looming environmental crisis in South Asia.

Today India sends more students to American universities than any other country; Indian students account for about a sixth of all foreign university students in the United States.

While this has proven mutually beneficial for both countries, it is in part indicative of the poor state of India's primarily state-run university system. (Interestingly, the ratio of Indian students in America to American students in India is about 80-1).

India lags in primary and secondary education too. Literacy is still untenably low, especially among women. But its problems will be mitigated partially by a growth in private schooling catering to almost every income level. The Indian government can certainly do more to ameliorate the situation, but there are few avenues for the United States to assist India in this regard. By contrast, American universities are eager to establish schools in India, which will benefit both countries considerably by enabling academic exchange and providing many more Indian students with better university educations. Unfortunately, bureaucratic and ideological barriers remain to the expansion of the private educational system, especially at higher levels, and continue to hamper the much needed reform and upgrading of the public college and university system.

A second area which badly needs addressing is Indian agriculture. Due in part to land reforms following independence, which succeeded in breaking old feudal structures, India finds itself suffering from an inability to develop large-scale commercial farming. Over two-thirds of the population is dependent on agriculture, but most have only small farms, often less than half an acre. Continued small-scale farming has limited the potential for agri-businesses, distribution systems and market access for produce. Some estimates indicate that up to half of India's agricultural produce is wasted due to unsatisfactory storage and lack of adequate transport. The United States assisted India in its first agricultural revolution, which enabled it to become self-sustaining. It can now do more to assist India's second agricultural revolution, especially in better managing the delivery chain from farmer to consumer. As in the case of education, this is largely an opportunity for the private sector: there need be no heavy government hand. But enabling legislation, primarily at the state level in India, will be necessary.

The final overlooked area, and one with enormous political and strategic implications, is the potential for cooperation on mitigating environmental degradation. Certainly climate change has been a high-profile issue and is likely to be at the top of the next administration's agenda. But other effects of environmental damage, at a regional or local level, do not receive the attention they deserve. These include problems related to water. Overcrowding and industrialization in India have led to problems concerning India's river systems, including potable water shortages and contamination. This issue affects a colossal number of people. For example, the Ganges-Brahmaputra river basin, which covers most of Bangladesh and Nepal in addition to much of northern India, is home to over 600 million people. If you add Pakistan (160 million people), which is dependent upon water flowing from India into the Indus river system, and if you keep in mind that many of India's rivers (and therefore those of Bangladesh and Pakistan) originate in China, which may have its own plans for rerouting them towards Central Asia, then you have the making of a protracted crisis in years to come even if only the most cautious predictions of climate change come true. In my view, an imaginative American administration will work with India, and other regional states, to attempt a comprehensive treatment of the problem now, and not wait until the cycle of flood and drought drives millions of people off their land, exacerbates disputes between Indian, Nepal, China, Bangladesh, and Pakistan, and—as we have seen already—intensifies disputes within Pakistan and India over access to water. The Kashmir dispute, while important in its own terms, is increasingly an environmental problem, and may paradoxically be easier to deal with in those terms rather than a zero-sum contest between Pakistan and India.

Areas of Disagreement

As with any bilateral relationship, there are areas that will continue to be points of disagreement between the United States and India. These will likely include global issues such as trade and climate change, but also conflicting strategic objectives vis-à-vis states such as Pakistan, Burma and Iran.

Pakistan and India have passed through the period where their conflict was the "most dangerous in the world," as they have adjusted to the existence of nuclear weapons on both sides. It is evident that the four major crises since 1987 constituted a learning experience, just as the U.S. and the Soviet Union learned something from the Cuban Missile Crisis. However, while nuclear weapons make large-scale war unlikely, they do not ensure peace, and there remains a real possibility that another crisis may erupt. In such an event, the United States should be prepared to once again serve as a moderating factor, as we did in 1990, 1999 and 2001-02 (but not in 1987). Our relations with India and Pakistan stem from somewhat different interests, but we cannot ignore the fact that they are each a strategic threat to the other, and we must, at all costs, avoid giving the appearance that we would favor a military solution to their disputes.

Burma has long since ceased to be a coherent state. It is presided over by a military junta that cannot protect its people from known and predictable threats such as the recent cyclone. India has turned to supporting the Burmese generals, in an attempt to reduce Chinese influence there, but both countries are playing by 19th century rules. Yet our policy of isolation and name-calling does not show much promise. It would be wise to consult closely with India, and China, and ASEAN, to see if some middle ground can be worked out that promotes peaceful regime change in Burma.

Among the most high-profile causes of disagreement are India's ties with *Iran.* Much has been made of India's apparent strategic, energy and "civilizational" relationship with Iran Many Indians—particularly those of an anti-American bent—emphasize this connection, while many Americans have serious misgivings about India- Iran ties. India does have some low-level military ties to Iran, Iran remains a major supplier of oil and gas to India, and India is believed to be home to the largest number of Shia outside of Iran. However, other elements of the relationship are frequently overlooked or overstated: India's military relationship with Iran involves little other than some naval training and the renovation of some tanks. In terms of energy, Iran is only the fourth largest oil supplier to India, accounting for only 10% of its imports. Moreover, there are two other reasons why Iran should not be a stumbling block to closer U.S.-India ties.

The first is the India-Israel relationship. Israel is now the second-largest exporter of defense equipment to India in dollar terms, and may surpass Russia as the largest Indians may be liberal in labeling their ties with countries as strategic partnerships, but in the case of Israel, this happens to be apt. In fact, in January this year, India launched an Israeli spy satellite to reconnoiter Iran. The Israel-India commercial relationship is deepening, and Israeli tourists are flocking to India in greater numbers. But despite the threats it faces from Iran's burgeoning nuclear program, Israel does not publicly object to New Delhi's continued dealings with Tehran.

The second reason is the commercial ties with Iran enjoyed by other states, including many of the United States' allies. Japan, Turkey, Italy, Germany and South Korea are among Iran's largest trade partners in 2007. France, Germany, Hungary, Italy, Japan, and Turkey—again U.S. allies—were among the largest investors in Iran in 2006. India lags considerably behind all of these countries in terms of its economic relationship with Iran.

Policy Recommendations

The United States should recognize that two-way trade and economic ties constitute the ballast of the new U.S.-India relationship. This has provided a new floor, so we need not worry overmuch about a return to the dark days of the 1970s, when India saw the U.S. as a hostile, encircling power, and Washington simply forgot about India. Yet, government policy can facilitate or hamper these new economic ties. In this case, the reforms have to be largely on the Indian side, but American business should be sensitive to Indian concerns and Indian practices, and should endeavor to strengthen Indian capacities, especially in areas such as education. American operations in India should not be seen as exploitive, just as Indian operations in the U.S. will be judged as to whether they take away American jobs.

On strategic ties, the motto should be "look before you hop." It would be wrong to expect a close strategic relationship between the two countries on the basis of a hypothetical threat from China. Our relationship should be seen and presented as reinsurance against a malevolent China, a future that may never happen. In the meantime, both sides will be wary of being drawn into the other's conflicts with third parties: India with American concerns about Iran, the U.S. with India's continuing conflict with Pakistan In both cases the root cause is political instability (in Iran and Pakistan), which makes their policies unpredictable, and potentially harmful. We should not demand Indian support for all of our Iranian polices any more than we should allow India to dictate our policy towards Pakistan.

There will be many opportunities for second-tier cooperation, notably in disaster relief, anti-piracy efforts, and in helping stabilize countries that are unable to maintain their own integrity. Naval cooperation is likely to be the most fruitful area, as the Indian navy performs at a very high level of professionalism, and now has a doctrine that encourages such cooperation. India should be invited to join the Task Force 150 in the Gulf, and India's navy and its capacity for power projection should be strengthened

See through the U.S.-India nuclear agreement. The Bush administration and Congress have exerted considerable time and effort in bringing the controversial nuclear deal to fruition. When the political situation in India finally proves favorable to the deal's consummation—be it this year, next year or the year after that—the next U.S. president and Congress should expedite consummation. The bulk of work to enable the deal has already been accomplished, although implementation will be difficult. While it will be imprudent to renegotiate the entire agreement, I do see the possibility of concessions on both sides that make the agreement more attractive. On our part, we can reduce some of the limits on India's use of reactor products (I do not believe that they intend to build a vast arsenal) and accept India formally as a nuclear weapons state. On India's part, the commitment to no more testing could be formalized (preferably by signing the CTBT), they could stabilize their arsenal designs (so no new testing is necessary), and renew earlier commitments to arms control, starting with the revival of the Rajiv Gandhi Action plan, signing on to the Proliferation Security Initiative, and joining a other arms control regimes. The criteria should be: does the agreement not only provide India with enhanced energy resources, but does it, on balance, enhance global arms control and restraints on the development and deployment of nuclear weapons? The U.S. should also translate the India agreement into a criteria-based format, potentially allowing Pakistan and even Israel to enter into a similar arrangement.

Give much greater priority to bilateral cooperation on education, agriculture, and regional water and environmental issues. These are all areas where there has been little cooperation between the United States and India thus far, but which are all vital for India's future. We need to recognize now that these will be the big issues of the next decade, and work towards collaborative mechanisms that include India in their resolution, or amelioration.

For a long time India was seen as an irritant, it did not count economically or strategically. Now that it does, we need to better understand such changes as the caste and class revolutions, the shift of power from the center to the states (India has entered an era of coalition government, which can directly affect foreign policy calculations). Dealing with democracies always requires an extra effort, we must invest in the long-neglected research and scholarly base, a necessary but not sufficient foundation-stone of sound policy.

Mr. Ackerman. Thank you very much.

Ambassador Schaffer?

STATEMENT OF THE HONORABLE TERESITA C. SCHAFFER, DIRECTOR, SOUTH ASIA PROGRAM, CENTER FOR STRATEGIC AND INTERNATIONAL STUDIES

Ms. SCHAFFER. Thank you, Mr. Chairman. And thank you for inviting me to testify.

Before I begin my formal testimony, I would like to say that it is a special honor to appear before the man who was my late mother-in-law's Congressman for many years. Minnie Schaffer passed away about 4 years ago at the age of 101. She was an active participant in Kew Gardens politics until the day she died, and she appreciated your contribution.

There is broad support for a strong relationship with India. Rather than recite our many joint activities, I would like to focus on why India matters to the United States and the potential limitations of the partnership that is emerging.

I want to leave you with two thoughts. First, our partnership and our bond as democracies will prosper only if we focus on our common geopolitical interests. Second, we need to develop a new model for international partnership, different from the Cold War-era alliances. I very much hope the nuclear agreement will be part of this model.

Three factors transformed our relations after 1990: The end of the Cold War, India's booming economy, and the Indian-American community. Both major parties in both countries built today's vibrant relationship.

I see three key building blocks for our new partnership: Asian and Indian Ocean security, economics, and democracy.

We start with the growing convergence of Indian and American interests from the Persian Gulf to the western Pacific. This policy agreement underpins our military cooperation, which both Dr. Cohen and you have made reference to. China and India are both rising powers and will shape Asia's future. India and the United States are engaging peacefully with China, but both are wary of China's growing military strength. Neither one wants Asia to be dominated by a single country. India, the United States, China and the other large Asian countries all play a part in creating a peaceful Asian future. We don't seem to like the term "balance of power" nowadays, but that is what the United States and India want and expect.

Both of us depend on the international energy market. India is the world's second fastest growing energy buyer. Oil represented one-third of its import bill even before the recent hike in prices.

Persian Gulf and Indian Ocean security is critical for both countries. We share concerns about terrorism and radical extremism. India has nearly 5 million workers in the Gulf; they send home one-fourth of India's remittance earnings. The Gulf countries provide two-thirds of India's imported oil and all its imported liquid natural gas.

You mentioned our disagreements over Iran, Mr. Chairman, but even here India and the United States do agree on the big strategic goal, namely not having a militarily nuclear Iran. We disagree about what to do about it.

The IPI pipeline, which you mentioned, faces major commercial obstacles. As I read things, India's policy is not so much pursuing the pipeline as it is refusing to kill off the idea.

The second building block for India and the United States is economics. India has had 3 years of over 9 percent growth. Trade represents 34 percent of India's economy today, compared to only 15 percent in 1990. You have already noted the high profile of United States-India trade and investment. For India, economy is strategy, and the United States is a critical part of India's game plan. And for us, of course, India has become an exciting destination for exports and investment.

Democracy is the third building block for our partnership, but it is also a complication. Take the nuclear deal. I think many Indians were shocked when the Hyde Act turned out to be such a cliffhanger in the United States Congress. And we were stunned when India's coalition politics stalled the next stage of the deal.

Democracy doesn't create partners automatically. The partners need to understand each other's processes and policies. Democratic values have little impact on policy unless they are linked to common interests. That is what is beginning to happen now, and it should give us a kind of foreign policy sweet spot.

So what kind of partnership can we develop? We are not looking at another alliance Our alliances in Europe and Japan arose out of the Cold War, with a single, forceful enemy. Today's world is more diffuse, and the strategic rivalry many predict with China isn't likely to divide the world into two clearly defined camps.

An even more important reason for not trying to create a new alliance is India's strong attachment to strategic autonomy in its foreign policy. Indian governments are not willing to adopt a kind of default position that their foreign policy will align itself with any outside country, even a friend with which India has strong relations. Indian governments that work closely with the United States need to demonstrate to their own people that they can still make decisions that don't match Washington's. Look at the political beating India's Government took after the IAEA votes that you referred to.

In short, I believe that the United States and India will be close partners on some issues but will go their own way on others. This can work well, provided the two governments take the time and energy to understand each other's priorities and figure out which issues lend themselves to common policies and which don't. The experience of the last 10 years suggests that the partnership list will expand.

Our common interests will push us together regardless of the fate of the nuclear agreement. But this breakthrough initiative is the most powerful tool the United States and India have had for putting our partnership on a strong footing India has hesitated since the agreement posed a risk of bringing down the government ahead of schedule. If India now feels able to move ahead, we will have an unparalleled opportunity to recalibrate the way our giant democracies work together and to focus together on the energy and proliferation concerns that we both face.

I should say that I disagree with my distinguished colleague about the feasibility of amending the agreement. If we get into that kind of situation, in all likelihood, the Indian and U.S. Governments will be looking for diametrically opposed kinds of amendments. I spent a lot of my Foreign Service career doing wordsmithing; I think this is a very tough road. And I think the agreement that is before us is the best that both countries are likely to get.

Summing up, India was the missing piece in a United States-Asia strategy for the 21st century. That piece is now being put in place. The next administration will inherit a lot of useful activities: Dialogues on economics, business and energy; military exercises; potential military sales; scientific cooperation; educational exchanges that bring 80,000 Indian students to the United States each year; space cooperation; and hopefully an agreement on civilian nuclear cooperation.

What the new administration needs to do more than anything is to strengthen the strategic context for all this activity by focusing both governments on our common strategic interests and defining the areas where we can act in common.

Thank you, Mr. Chairman.

[The prepared statement of Ms. Schaffer follows:]

Prepared Statement of The Honorable Teresita C. Schaffer, Director, South Asia Program, Center for Strategic and International Studies

Thank you for inviting me to testify, Mr. Chairman Before I begin my formal testimony, I'd like to say that it's a special honor to appear before the man who was my late mother-in-law's Congressman for many years. Minnie Schaffer passed away about four years ago at the age of 101, but she was an active participant in Kew Gardens politics until the day she died, and she appreciated your contribution.

There is broad support for a strong relationship with India. Rather than recite our many joint activities, I will focus on why India matters to the United States, and the potential and limitations of the partnership that is emerging.

I want to leave you with two thoughts. First, our partnership and our bond as democracies will prosper only if we focus on our common geopolitical interests. Second, we need to develop a new model for international partnership, different from the Cold War era alliances. I hope the nuclear agreement will be part of this model.

Three factors transformed our relations after 1990: the end of the Cold War, India's booming economy, and the Indian-American community. Both major parties in both countries built today's vibrant relationship. I see three key building blocks for our new partnership: Asian and Indian Ocean security; economics; and democracy.

We start with the growing convergence of Indian and American interests from the Persian Gulf to the Western Pacific. China and India are both rising, and will shape Asia's future. India and the United States are engaging peacefully with China, but both are wary of its growing military strength. Neither wants Asia to be dominated by a single country. India, the United States, China, and the other large Asian countries all play a part in creating a peaceful Asian future. We don't like the term "balance of power" nowadays, but that's what the U.S. and India want and expect.

Both of us depend on the international energy market. India is the world's second fastest growing energy buyer. Oil represented one-third of its import bill even before the recent hike in prices. Persian Gulf and Indian Ocean security is critical for both countries. We share concerns about terrorism and radical extremism India has almost 5 million workers in the Gulf, sending home one-fourth of India's remittance earnings. The Gulf countries provide two-thirds of India's imported oil and all its imported LNG.

India and the United States have some disagreements on the Middle East and Asia, including some aspects of how we deal with Iran. But we agree on the big strategic goals. This has made possible the expanding U.S.-India military cooperation that you've heard so much about, and it has led India to look on the U.S. presence in the Indian Ocean as a benign one.

The second building block is economics. India has had three years of over 9 percent growth. Trade represents 34 percent of India's economy today, compared to only 15 percent in 1990. Trade with the United States is up to $30 billion a year, plus another $20 billion in services trade. The United States is India's top export destination and buys two-thirds of its Information Technology exports. For India, economy is strategy. This makes the United States a critical part of India's game plan For us, India has become an exciting destination for exports and investment.

Democracy is a building block for our partnership, but also a complication. Take the nuclear deal Indians were shocked when the Hyde Act turned out to be such a cliffhanger in the U.S. Congress. And we were stunned when India's coalition politics stalled the next stage of the deal Democracy doesn't create partners automatically. The partners need to understand each other's processes and policies. Democratic values have little impact on policy unless they are linked to common interests. That's beginning to happen now, and should give us a kind of "foreign policy sweet spot."

So what kind of partnership can we develop? We're not looking at another alliance. Our alliances in Europe and Japan arose out of the Cold War, with a single, forceful enemy. Today's world is more diffuse, and the strategic rivalry many predict with China doesn't divide the world into two clearly defined camps.

An even more important reason for not trying to create a new alliance is India's strong attachment to "strategic autonomy" in its foreign policy. Indian governments are not willing to adopt a "default position" that their foreign policy will align itself with any outside country, even a friend with which India has very close relations. Indian governments that work closely with the United States need to demonstrate that that they can still make decisions that don't match Washington's. Look at the political beating India's government took after it voted twice with the United States and against Iran in the International Atomic Energy Agency (IAEA).

In short, the U.S. and India will be close partners on some issues, but will go their own way on others. This can work well provided the two governments take the time and energy to understand each other's priorities and figure out which issues lend themselves to common policies and which don't. The experience of the last ten years would suggest that the "partnership list" will grow with time.

Our common interests will push us together regardless of the fate of the nuclear agreement, but this breakthrough initiative is the most powerful tool the U.S. and India have for putting our partnership on a strong footing. India has hesitated, since the agreement posed a risk of bringing down the government ahead of schedule. If India now feels able to move ahead, we will have an unparalleled opportunity to recalibrate the way our giant democracies work together, and to focus together on the energy and proliferation concerns that we both face.

Summing up, India was the missing piece in a U.S. Asia strategy for the 21st Century. That piece is now being put in place. The next administration will inherit a lot of useful activities—dialogues on economics, business and energy; military exercises; potential military sales; scientific cooperation on such subjects as HIV research; educational exchanges that bring 80,000 Indian students to the U.S. each year; space cooperation; and perhaps an agreement on civilian nuclear cooperation. What the new administration needs to do is to strengthen the strategic context for all this activity, by focusing both governments on our common strategic interests and defining the areas where the United States and India can act in common.

Mr. Ackerman. Thank you. Dr. Andersen?

Statement of Walter Andersen, Ph.D., Associate Director of the South Asia Studies Program Professorial Lecturer, School of Advanced International Studies, John Hopkins University

Mr. Andersen. Thank you, Chairman Ackerman and members of the committee.

Like Ambassador Schaffer, I have a certain linkage to your consistency as well, having spent the first 4 years of my life there and the remainder of my youth in Bay Ridge, which actually had a different political party representation than yours.

Congressman Scott, you had mentioned the meeting today that the Prime Minister, Manmohan Singh, had with his left colleagues. That meeting has happened, and unfortunately he failed to get his communist allies, which his government needs to sustain the coalition, to back a civil nuclear deal. And it was announced that they would have a subsequent meeting.

Now, the communists and others argue that the deal would undermine the independence of Indian foreign policy. But the very fact that an issue which involves a strategic relationship with the United States has aroused such a debate in India underscores how far the Indo-U.S. relationship has come in the last several years. It also underscores that the difficulty India has in saying "yes" is a sign that Indian moves on the international stage are, by nature, incremental and subject to a number of possible delays in the domestic political system of India, which I will get to in a few minutes.

In fact, the Indo-U.S. relationship has undergone a dramatic transformation over the past 10 years. For the first time since India's independence in 1947, India and the United States can realistically expect to build a partnership that advances their respective foreign policy interests.

And this, in my view, is based on the convergence of interests in several key areas. The first is curbing religiously inspired political radicalism. The second is defeating the forces of the Taliban and al Qaeda in Afghanistan. The third is managing the rise of China. And the fourth is safeguarding the strategically important sea lanes that cross the Indian Ocean and that are used to transport much of the world's oil and gas.

This transformation has occurred so rapidly that we sometimes are tempted to overstate what the relationship can achieve. Phrases like "natural partners," "strategic allies," and "a relationship with no limits" have been used by senior political leaders in both countries. By using these terms, however, I think we risk losing sight of what we can realistically expect. And we also risk a sense of letdown if the results fall short of our expectations.

On security issues, I think we need to start with the assumption that the United States relationship with India will not result in a military alliance or Indian participation in an alliance of democracies. The inequality of power between our two countries, the absence of a habit of cooperation, and the residual bureaucratic and political resistance to deeper engagement will all limit the pace and scope of strategic cooperation.

Still, I think that there is no denying the fact that India will have more in common with the United States than it will with any of the other great powers. And this will produce cooperation when there is a clear alignment of interest and India is treated as an equal partner.

Such cooperation has already started. And because India's rise to major world power is in the long-term interest of the United States, I think we benefit from patience as India works out the precise terms of its relationship with us.

And I completely agree with Ambassador Schaffer that, on the nuclear deal, I think we have to stick with what the deal presently has, because to reopen the negotiations, I think, could create major problems for cooperation in the future between our two countries on this issue and other issues, as well.

There will, however, be significant areas where we continue to differ, most prominently, as you mentioned, Mr. Chairman, on Iran, but also on Myanmar. India maintains good relations with both countries because they are sources of energy and have a strategic value, relating to China from Myanmar and to Pakistan and Afghanistan for Iran.

A note of caution also applies to the economic dimension of the relationship. India is emerging from decades of soft socialism and policies that favored economic self-sufficiency. There remains in India a residual skepticism about whether the market reforms adopted about 15 years ago will result in greater social equity. This skepticism is even stronger regarding the opening of the economy to international competition and to foreign direct investment. Nonetheless, the trend is in the direction of greater openness because it has worked. The question is not whether there will be a greater openness, but the pace of the opening.

What, then, can the U.S. realistically expect of the relationship? I believe the major factor in our relationship is economic, and there are significant opportunities for increased sale of American services and merchandise trade to India.

India's merchandise trade has over tripled since 2000, and the United States has been its largest trading partner every year. While the two-way merchandise trade gap has been in India's favor every year since 2000, the gap is narrowing, as an increasingly prosperous India imports more American machinery and technology. The United States trade deficit with India was cut almost in half, from $11 billion in 2006 to about $6 billion in 2007.

Trade in information technology and services are growing at an even faster pace than merchandise trade. With an estimated $15 billion going in each direction last year, industries in our two countries are developing a close symbiotic linkage in ways that benefits the economies of our two countries. And this trade, in my view, should bc cncouraged.

One of the major opportunities for the U.S. is increased American sale of military equipment. India has embarked on a com- prehensive military modernization program and is spending about $8 billion a year on imported equipment. Some analysts predict it will spend about $60 billion on military imports over the next 5 years. The U.S., for the first time, is a serious competitor because of the appreciation of the high quality of American military equipment.

There is, however, a lack of an Indian Communication Interoperability and Security Memorandum of Agreement. And I hate to use these acronyms, but it is one that has the title of CISMOA, and it is required for U.S. technology sales. And India reportedly has offered a counter draft proposal to enable it to access American arms.

My guess is that the negotiating process on this will require high-level bureaucratic attention, similar to the involvement of Nicholas Burns on the issue of civilian nuclear cooperation where there were similar bureaucratic hurdles to overcome.

A second area where there is a good chance of cooperation with India is Indian engagement with the United States on safeguarding shipping over the critical Indian Ocean sea lanes used to transport a growing percentage of the oil and gas to meet the growing demand from energy-deficient countries like India, China, Japan and Korea. This might be in the form of a memorandum of understanding, preferably multilateral and involving the major users to address a mutual interest in countering terrorism and piracy, providing for search and rescue, and humanitarian assistance.

Unfortunately, sea lane protection in the Indian Ocean is presently covered by a number of ad hoc arrangements. Something more institutional is required. And India, with vital economic and security interest in these sea lanes, would be a good candidate to be a major participant in a multilateral agreement. It possesses the only indigenous blue-water navy in the Indian Ocean, has troops trained in counterterrorism, and, moreover, the Indian navy already has a record of collaboration with the United States on counterterrorism, by providing escorts to American shipping in 2002 at the Malacca Straits and, in 2005, working with the United States, Japan and Australia on tsunami humanitarian relief activities.

The navies of the United States and India, in addition, have a record of joint exercising, starting several years ago, that are geared to anti-piracy and counterterrorism. Such cooperation has the advantage of developing a certain comfort level in India for a security cooperation with the United States, and provides a model that could be used for security collaboration on a larger scale to face crises affecting the interests of both the United States and India.

Finally, India's strategy of using its good relationship with the United States to provide it leverage to reduce the chances of threats from China also gives the United States an opening to push the pace on issues of strategic importance to the United States and which would serve Indian security interests.

Indians, for example, have affirmed their intention of maintaining a security relationship with the United States through the support for Operation Enduring Freedom, a defense framework in 2005 that envisages increased joint military exercises and Indian purchases of United States military equipment. Indian votes twice against Iran at the International Atomic Energy Agency was, in part, prompted by an Indian effort to build a security relationship with the United States.

The lesson of the civilian nuclear deal and other areas where India has delayed action is not that the momentum with the United States has stalled, but that the relationship needs to move incrementally and at a pace that is politically acceptable in India. As mentioned at the beginning, the Indian market is becoming more open because India has benefited from it. And India is building a security relationship with the United States because it is clearly in India's interest to do so.

Thank you.

[The prepared statement of Mr. Andersen follows:]

India and the United States: A Different Kind of Relationship

Distinguished members of the Subcommittee, thank you for asking me to testify today on the US-India relationship. I will focus my remarks mostly on the underlying momentum in this relationship and the challenges we face in sustaining the forward movement.

Indo-US relations have undergone a dramatic transformation over the past decade. The next administration will benefit from the strong underlying momentum behind recently improved bilateral relations.[2] The US and India, for the first time since India's independence in 1947, can realistically expect to build a partnership that advances their respective foreign policy goals. This is based on the strong fundamentals of a convergence of interests on key issues, such as curbing religiously-inspired radicalism, managing the rise of China, defeating the Taliban in Afghanistan, and working towards stability in South Asia and beyond.

The end of the Cold War created conditions that enabled India and the United States to move beyond the suspicions that had soured their bilateral relationship for over four decades. India now views the US as an asset in its quest for great power status. This more positive view of the US shows up in recently released multi-nation public opinion polling data, which show that 66 percent of the Indian public has a favorable opinion of the US (up 7 percent from last year), and 63 percent say that US foreign policy pays attention to Indian interests. Among the 24 countries compared, India is near the top of the chart on both issues, and reflects a major change in Indian opinion of the US.[3] The US, for its part, recognizes India both as a rising power, for it has the world's second largest population and the second fastest growing economy, as well as a stable democracy in an often turbulent Asia.

This transformation occurred so rapidly that leaders on both sides are prone to overstate what the relationship can actually achieve. Leaders have referred to the two countries as "natural partners" (President Bush in 2006), "strategic allies" (Prime Minister Vajpayee in 2004), and in 2005 Prime Minster Manmohan Singh declared that it is a relationship with "no limits'. We risk losing sight of the positive trend in the bilateral relationship if we overstate the possibilities. While there is an element of security in the bilateral relationship, India and the US are not allies in the conventional sense — and are not likely to be so any time soon. The military element in the relationship lacks mutual assistance agreements and basing rights — and none are likely to come about any time soon. India remains committed to the doctrine of strategic autonomy, and it will not become an ally in the mold of the UK or Japan, nor will it be a France, seeking tactical independence within the framework of a formal alliance. It will cooperate only when treated as an equal and only where its own interests are directly involved.[4] On substantive issues, both countries agree that no single power (i.e., China) should dominate Asia, but India will not support an anti-Chinese alliance and rather will seek ways to integrate China more closely into a larger Asian context. While Indians — like Americans — are deeply committed to the democratic process, few Indians see democratic advocacy as a basis for cooperative action. Because of regional security considerations and the need for energy imports, India will conduct a relationship with Iran and Myanmar that is sometimes at odds with the U.S.

The challenge in creating a durable strategic relationship will be for the US to treat India as an equal partner and for India to make itself sufficiently useful to Washington, to justify the political costs needed to implement policies that strengthen Indian power (such as the exception to US non-proliferation policy) In the Indian case, the issue is complicated further by a residue of substantial anti-America opinion in the bureaucracy, in academia and in the press, which while on the decline, often forces the Indian government to be cautious on something new like a security relationship with the United States, a caution that can delay or even stymie initiatives. This caution has delayed Indian agreement regarding to US proposals for a Logistics Support Agreement (LSA), a Communication Interoperability and Security Memorandum of Agreement (CISMOA), and End-User Verification Agreements (EUVA) on military sales because of the physical inspections built into them.

Nevertheless, there is a momentum already established in key areas of the IndoUS relationship that can be used by a new administration to advance US interests. (1) An increasingly open Indian economy with the US playing a significant role in it: (2) increased Indian commitment to the security of the vital sea lanes of the Indian Ocean and its choke points; (3) an Indian security policy of hedging which requires a US element to be effective and thus gives the US some leverage power with India.

I.) The first and perhaps most important element in the bilateral relationship is linked to **India's recent economic prosperity and America's significant involvement in it.** While India's rapid economic expansion is prompted mainly by private activity, a more economically robust India is an important factor accounting for increased US interest in India, and also creates jobs for American workers. The Indian Government in the early 1990s under then Finance Minister—and now Prime Minister — Manmohan Singh removed many of the stifling government controls over the economy and thus unleashed the entrepreneurial potential of the Indian people. The market reforms have produced positive results: the Indian economy grew on an average of 5-6 percent per year during the 1990s (about double the average from independence to 1990) and 7 — 8 percent per year since 2000. Merchandise trade expanded from about 42 billion dollars in 1990-91 to about 311 billion dollars in 2006-2007; foreign currency holdings have gone from only a few hundred million dollars in the 1990s to some 310 billion dollars in mid-2008, an expansion of over a hundred billion in just the past year; and foreign direct investment rose from almost nothing in 1990 to some 20 billion in 2007.

Market reforms were prompted by a balance of payments crisis in the early 1990s, but have survived because, as in China, they are responses to important domestic demands for a better life — in India to substantially enhance the annual economic growth rates in order to address the rising demands for a better life by the vast numbers belonging to the country's historically disadvantaged groups. The challenge, of course, is to avoid quick-fix populist measures that undermine long term growth and the political leadership in New Delhi has a mixed record. The country is still a long way from satisfying the needs of the poor, and democratic politics compel India's leadership to focus on economic development at home.[5] To achieve the desired economic growth rates, the country requires a massive increase in trade and investment in high technology. This objective has been an important factor in the foreign policy of every Indian government since the early 1990s. It translates into pushing for closer ties with countries that can help it economically, such as the US and China. it also translates into a policy of peace with neighbors, most prominently Pakistan and China, so that the country can focus on improving its economy at home. Moreover, it has prompted India to negotiate several free (or preferential) trade agreements, some with individual countries and some multilateral, with countries around the Indian Ocean.

Since the adoption of market reforms, the US has remained India's largest trading partner. Two way merchandise trade with the US has almost tripled just in the past seven years, expanding from 14 billion dollars (out of total trade of 124 billion) in 2000 to 41.6 billion in 2007 (out of total of 311 billion).[6]

The two way merchandise trade has been in India's advantage every year since 2000, though the gap may now be narrowing as an increasingly prosperous India imports more American machinery and technology. The merchandise trade gap of some 11 billion dollars in 2006 in India's favor was almost halved in 2007, as can be seen in Chart 1. This gap is likely to further diminish as India becomes for the first time a significant customer of US military equipment. The Indian military establishment's desire to buy US equipment through the foreign military sales (FMS) route and the US willingness to sell state-of-the-art equipment to India are a convenient convergence of interests, though there is a residue of suspicion in India regarding US reliability as a supplier and in the US about the Indian ability to safeguard its technology. India is now engaged in a comprehensive military modernization program and has been spending about 8 billion dollars a year recently on military imports. Some analysts estimate that India will spend about 60 billion dollars over the next five years on military modernization. Early this year, India signed its biggest defense deal so far with the US with the purchase of six Lockheed Martin C-130 Super Hercules medium transport planes for somewhat more than one billion dollars. Last month, the Indian Air Force opened responses to a global tender of 126 medium multi-role combat aircraft (MRCA) in a deal valued at 10 billion dollars and US firms are among the competitors.[7]

Chart 1. India's Trade Balance with U.S 1998-2007

Year	Exports (Millions U.S. $)	Imports (Millions U.S.$)	Balance (Millions U.S.$)
1998	3,564.5	8,237.2	-4,672.7
1999	3,687.8	9,070.8	-5,383.0
2000	3,667.3	10,686.6	-7,019.3
2001	3,757.0	9,737.3	-5,980.3
2002	4,101.0	11,818.4	-7,717.4
2003	4,979.7	13,055.3	-8,075.6
2004	6,109.4	15,572.0	-9,462.7
2005	7,898.4	18,804.2	-10,814.8
2006	10,056.2	21,830.8	**-11,774.6**
2007	17,588.5	24,073.3	**-6,484.7**

Source: U.S. Census Bureau, Foreign Trade Division, Data Dissemination Branch, Washington, D.C. 20233

Still another promising area for sales is the Indian Navy. India is now embarked on one of the most ambitious naval building and procurement plans in the world, with 35 ships in the works (see Appendix 1). Among the projects is the seven ship Project 17A Shivalik-class frigate, for which three American companies (Lockheed Martin, Northrop Grumman, and General Dynamics) have been sent the initial requests for information. The Indian Navy is looking at ways to augment indigenous information technology with American assistance, a process that would make inter-operability easier between the navies of the two countries. The US (and others, such as Japan and Korea), are more competitive as the Indians have become increasingly skeptical about the reliability of traditional Russian naval suppliers, and it is looking for alternatives.

So far, however, India has not signed the Communication Interoperability and Security Memorandum of Agreement (CISMOA) — permitting the interoperability with US equipment — that is required for it to receive high-tech equipment. Indian interest in American multirole combat aircraft and the P-8i Poseidon long range maritime reconnaissance aircraft appears to be forcing the country to consider a CISMOA, which would in turn enhance the possibilities of even greater Indian purchase of US military equipment. The Indian press reports that the Indian Government has prepared a CISMOA counter draft to submit to the US this month (June 2008) reportedly so that it can buy these big ticket US items. For the Indian counterproposal to be accepted, the US will probably need focused high level bureaucratic attention similar to the involvement of Nicholas Burns, Undersecretary of State for Political Affairs, on the Civil Nuclear Agreement, where there was similar bureaucratic resistance.

The trade volume is in fact larger than the figures noted above because they only include merchandise trade and do not include India's rapidly expanding exports of software and Information Technology services. Much of India's 31 billion dollars of exports in 2007 (and growing recently at about 30 percent a year) have gone to the United States. Indian sources note that the US accounted for over half of India's export markets for information technology and services support.[8] In addition, the US has exported a similar dollar amount of services to India. IT and such support services have created a strong symbiotic linkage between American and Indian companies — and both gain economically from this ever tighter embrace. It also sets up people-to-people networking clusters that each side can use to expand business opportunities in both countries.

II.) The most promising area for India-US military cooperation is **protection of Indian Ocean sea lanes and the vital choke points** leading from that body of water (especially Hormuz and Malacca), which is of strategic importance not only to India and the US, but to the countries of Southeast and East Asia.

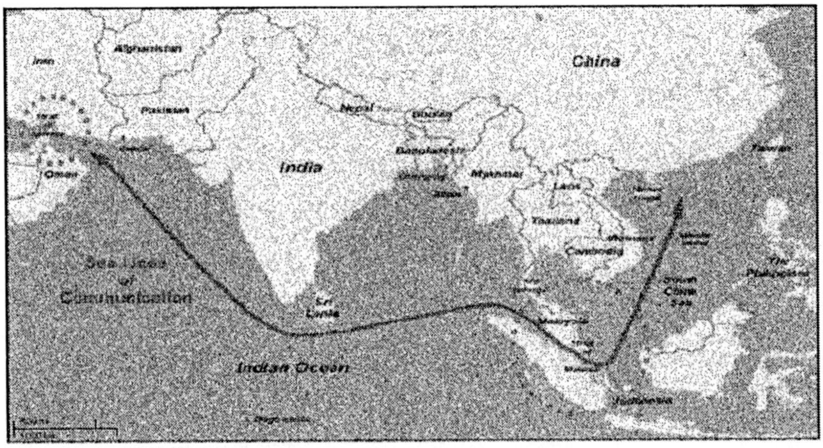

Map. Indian Ocean shipping routes connecting the Persian Gulf to East Asia through the Strait of Malacca (potential choke points highlighted in red dots).

The advantages of maritime cooperation are that it is out of public view and managed by professionals, thus making it less susceptible to politically motivated nitpicking. Maritime cooperation enables India to play a more responsible role in world affairs without directly challenging its doctrine of strategic autonomy. Such cooperation also provides the practical lessons that will make it easier to manage future security cooperation between the US and India (and others) on a larger scale when mutual interests are at stake. Perhaps the US could build on this naval cooperation to work with India in creating multilateral organizations tasked with safeguarding the sea lanes and its increasingly vulnerable choke points. There is presently a hodgepodge of generally ineffective bilateral and multilateral forums to do so, stymied so far by concerns of littoral states with national sovereignty over adjourning waters and perhaps most importantly, by lack of strong leadership to take the initiative.

There is already a growing record of naval cooperation between the US and India, rooted in a 1995 framework agreement on defense and an expanded version of this in 2005 to reflect the objective on both sides for an increased level of military cooperation. In line with a new willingness to cooperate with the US, India took an unprecedented step in April 2002 by lending support to Operation Enduring Freedom in Afghanistan by using Indian Navy ships to protect US supply ships from threats of terrorism and piracy as they moved through the Straits of Malacca. This was followed by several joint IndoUS search and rescue naval missions as well as the "Malabar" naval exercises off India's west coast. The largest in this series took place in early September 2007 in the Bay of Bengal, off India's eastern coast, and involved ships from Japan, the US, Australia, India and Singapore. These exercises, whose goal was to develop joint strategies to combat terrorism and piracy, included two US aircraft carriers and India's sole aircraft carrier. The US and India have also held periodic air and ground exercises both in the US and in India, one of which involved India's largest strategic deployment of its combat aircraft outside the country during the summer of 2004 in Alaska.[9]

The sea lanes are critically important to India, because about 70 percent of its oil is imported from the Persian Gulf- and this dependence is likely to grow as the Indian economy continues to expand and its own domestic energy resources continue to decline. In addition, almost 95 percent of its expanding trade moves by sea across the Indian Ocean. The other rapidly growing economies of Asia (Japan, Korea and China) are also energy deficient and increasingly dependent on energy imports from the Persian Gulf region. This dependence on the Persian Gulf — and the sea lanes leading from it — are likely to grow because this area contains about two-thirds of the world's know oil reserves and a third of the known natural gas reserves. Therefore it is in India's interest to work with the US which, possessing naval and air facilities in the region, has assumed primary responsibility in protecting the sea lanes and the critical Hormuz and Malacca choke points. India has important assets to bring to bear in this effort, besides a growing blue water naval capacity.[10] It has close-at-hand naval and air facilities on the Andaman Islands situated at the mouth of the western approaches to the Straits, and a National Security Guard force created in the mid-1980s for counter-terrorism purposes. India and Indonesia have a bilateral agreement calling for joint patrolling of the western approaches to the Malacca Straits. The Indian Navy conducts regular joint naval exercises with Singapore, Indonesia and Thailand as well as multilateral exercises with several Southeast Asian states.

From the US perspective, India (possessing the only indigenous blue water capacity in the Indian Ocean and strategically located — a huge peninsular that juts down 1500 miles into the middle of that body of water) is a logical candidate to play a role in protecting the Indian Ocean sea lanes. Around the broad swath of Indian Ocean littoral states from east Africa to Indonesia on the east, it is the most politically stable country in a very unstable and strategically important area. Such cooperation would be aimed at the most imminent threats: piracy and terrorism. Most vulnerable would be the choke points. Malacca, for example, handles some 70,000 merchant vessels transporting over 20 percent of the world's seaborne trade and over one third of the world's crude oil shipments. The area around the 500 mile long Malacca Staits is subject to escalating piracy and harbors several terrorist organizations. The ultimate terrorist act, taking a leaf from the 9/11 attack on the US, would be the sinking of hijacked ships in busy channels or at the entrances of major ports. Such an interruption and a prolonged standstill in the Malacca Straits would force shipping to be re-routed through the distant Sunda and Lambok Straits, adding 1.5 sailing days, slowing movement and adding to already high insurance rates for ships in these waters.

III.) India's security strategy of "leveraging", which depends on a good relationship with US, gives the US a "leveraging" power on India. The end of the Cold War gave India an opportunity to break out of the narrow "nonaligned" straitjacket that hampered its ability to protect Indian interests even in South Asia. It almost immediately began to pursue a much broader set of relations with the US, China, Japan, Korea, the European states, and a broad range of other states. Good relations with the great powers, especially the US- the remaining superpower and the strongest power in Asia- offered India the potential to achieve its two major strategic objectives: enhance its international influence and gain leverage with the great powers.[11] Perhaps the most important strategic advantage for India is that it now has the potential to move incrementally closer to the US, should the Chinese take steps that are viewed as threatening- and thus reduce the chances of China taking threatening moves. The importance of the US to Indian strategy also gives the US some leverage with India, and there are several areas where the US could make use of this to push its interests in Asia. Examples of this might be nudging India to support multilateral initiatives aimed at discouraging Iran from developing nuclear weapons, demonstrating greater sensitivity to Pakistani concerns regarding its fears of an Afghan-Indian alliance directed against it, taking a more proactive role in moves to create multilateral bodies that could safeguard shipping to Indian Ocean sea lanes and through its choke points.

While Indian relations with China presently are generally good as it is India's second largest trading partner (with trade presently at a 25 billion dollar level and growing at 40 percent a year), there is a lively debate in India regarding the consequences of a rising China acknowledged to be stronger militarily and economically. [12] Fueling this Indian concern are several issues, most prominently the glacial pace of negotiations on 40 year old border disputes, Chinese efforts to limit Indian participation in Asian multilateral organizations, and what Indians view as deliberate border incursions along the sensitive northeastern areas of dispute- the most recent of which took place a few days ago. Moreover, the two compete for oil and gas as well as for trade along the Indian Ocean littoral. Indians are particularly concerned that China may begin to use the "string of pearls" (a set of naval facilities along the Bay of Bengal and the Arabian Sea with possible military use, and constructed with Chinese assistance) for military purposes. This concern is prompted by the possibility that the Chinese, to safeguard energy sources in the Persian Gulf region, might turn these facilities into forward bases that could threaten the Indian homeland and might use them to nudge local states into supporting Chinese policies that undercut Indian policy.[13] Perhaps the best response to this possible development, within US interests, is to involve the Chinese in multilateral efforts to safeguard the Indian Ocean sea lanes and its choke points.

There is, however, an important caveat to India's policy of leverage: it works only as long as the Indo-US relationship is not perceived in China as a military alliance directed against it. It also works only if relations between the US and China remain cordial. The Indians recognize that China possesses leverage possibilities against India in South Asia. China could try to draw India's South Asian neighbors (who have a record of trying to play China against India), closer to itself. If the US-China relationship turns sour, India almost certainly would try to stay neutral and work to bring about a reconciliation.

US-India efforts to move closer on security issues was set in motion, ironically, by the May 1998 Indian nuclear tests. These tests prompted the US to begin a series of talks between US Deputy Secretary of State Strobe Talbott and Jaswant Singh, Indian External Affairs Minister and confidant to Prime Minister Atal Bihari Vajpayee, that moved beyond nuclear issues and set the groundwork for a significant improvement in the bilateral relations.[14] The greater cordiality and trust was to lead first (in the late 1990s) to American willingness to deal with India as a nuclear weapons power, and then (2007) to an American proposal (backed by strong bipartisan congressional support) that would make India an exception to US nuclear nonproliferation law that had denied India access to nuclear fuel and nuclear technology because it was not a signatory to the 1970 Nuclear Nonproliferation Treaty. This denial regime complicated US efforts to draw India closer to itself strategically, and had stood in the way of Indian involvement in international nonproliferation regimes. The US simultaneously moved incrementally away from a policy of equating India and Pakistan, a stance that had been a major stumbling block in the relationship with India. This approach had long outlived any usefulness it might have had, as it totally overlooked the disparity in national capabilities, the greater contributions India could make to US objectives in Asia, and the potential threat of China to India.

The nuclear deal, offered to India and not Pakistan, underscores the US policy of separating its policy toward the two South Asian Powers. There is, however, a caveat: US policy toward India does affect Pakistan's perception of its security. The US, as noted elsewhere, needs to use its newfound standing with India to encourage it to take a conciliatory policy towards its western neighbor, which would make Pakistan more likely to shift more of its security forces to the turbulent western borderlands that harbor the Taliban and al-Qaeda.

India, recognizing the importance of the US to its security, has taken concrete steps to build a security relationship with the US: naval support for US transport ships supplying Operation Enduring Freedom in 2002, periodic joint military excercises outside the UN framework, Indian participation with the US Navy (and those of Australia and Japan) in the 2004 tsunami relief efforts, a defense framework agreement in 2005 that envisaged substantial Indian purchases of US military equipment and joint military exercises, and Indian votes with the US (twice) against Iran in the International Atomic Energy Agency.

While the government of Prime Minister Manmohan Singh bargained hard for the nuclear deal, it may be a casualty of domestic 'Indian politics. The Communist Party Marxist, whose support is needed to help keep his coalition government in power, have threatened to force new elections if the government signs an India-specific agreement with the International Atomic Energy Agency (IAEA), one of the several steps required before the negotiated agreement with India comes back to the US Congress for action. The nuclear deal would be useful for the overall relationship, but not critical. The relationship with India has advanced to the point that a collapse of the deal would not jeopardize the relationship and not stall moves to advance it in other areas. India is too large, too prosperous, and too strategically located for this to happen. Nonetheless, the lack of Indian action would likely make a future American administration cautious about expending political capital for something comparably innovative and far reaching as the proposed nuclear deal.

Recommendations

(1) Recognize that a security relationship with India — which New Delhi wants — will be different in that India will not permit itself to be militarily dependent on the US and will cooperate on security issues with the US only when there is a significant threat to Indian security interests. This Indian caution is reflected in its reluctance so far to sign a logistics support agreement (LSA), allowing the refueling of aircraft and ships in each other's ports, because of concerns in India that this would undermine Indian policy of not allowing foreign troops on its soil.

(2) Push for a memorandum of understanding on cooperative naval operations to safeguard the sea lanes of the Indian Ocean and critical choke points like the Straits of Malacca and the Hormuz Straits (either bilateral or on a broader multilateral level) to address mutual interest in anti-piracy, counter-terrorism, search and rescue, and humanitarian assistance. This would respond to a virtual absence of such comprehensive institutional mechanisms that would benefit India, the US and other

users of these critical sea lanes. It might also prompt India to sign a Proliferation Security Initiative (PSI) which calls for boarding and searching merchant vessels with suspicious cargo in international waters or to be affiliated with Task Force 150, a multinational task force which pursues vessels as part of the US-led war on terror. India's reluctance to join so far has been because the initiatives are not UN-authorized.

(3) Enhance the scope and depth of military-to-military interaction by increasing the budget for Indian officers to participate in international military education and training (IMET), to increase the level and complexity of joint army exercises to the brigade level (from the present company level) for greater interoperability that would be useful for joint activities in a crisis, and to encourage co-development projects that allow the US and Indian defense industry to collaborate in the development stages of specific Indian weapons programs (i.e., missile defense and over-the-horizon radar) that would also enhance interoperability and possibly sales of US equipment .

(4) Support India as a permanent member of the UN Security Council. This proposal, which has virtually universal support across the Indian political spectrum, would generate enormous good will for the US and go a long way to reduce the suspicion that is a residue from the Cold War period. This step recognizes the present imbalance on the Council for Asia, acknowledges India's growing importance as an economic and military power on the world stage, and would encourage India to assume more global responsibilities befitting the size of its population and economy.

(5) Encourage Tndia to remove restrictions on investment from the US. A prime example is the restriction on investment in the multi-brand retail trade (where American firms are competitive) to bolster infrastructure development of supply and distribution chains. This would help reduce inefficiencies within India's own distribution system, which is a significant drag on the country's economy. There are also similar restrictions on insurance and financial services that stand in the way of investment from the US. Indian regulations make it similarly difficult for collaborative relationships between US and Indian educational institutions.

APPENDIX 1: INDIAN NAVY SURFACE FLEET (DECEMBER, 2007)

TYPE OF VESSEL	CLASS OF VESSEL	FLEET STRENGTH
Aircraft Carriers	Indigenous Aircraft Carrier	1 being built + 1 more projected
	Kiev Class	1 [in refit]
	Centaur Class	1 in service
Guided-Missile Destroyers	Project 15A {Kolkata} Class	1 launched + 3 more planned
	Type 15 Delhi Class	3 in service
	Rajput Class	5 in service
Guided-Missile Frigates	Project 17A Class	7 projected
	P17 {Shivalik} Class	3 launched
	Modified Krivak III Class	2 being built + 1 on orde[r]
	Talwar {Krivak III} Class	3 in service
	Type 16A Brahmaputra Class	3 in service
	Type 16 Godavari Class	3 in service
Guided-Missile Corvettes	Project 28 Class	1 being built + 3 more ordered + 8 more planned
	Type 25A Kora Class	4 in service
	Type 25 Khukri Class	4 in service
	Veer {Tarantul I} Class	12 in service
Frigates	Nilgiri {Leander} Class	4 in service
Corvettes	Abhay {Pauk II} Class	4 in service
Large Patrol Craft	Naval Offshore Patrol Vessel	2 being built + 1 on orde[r]
	Sukanya Class	6 in service + 1 sold to Sri Lanka
	Seaward Defence Boats	6 in service

Fast Patrol Vessels	Car Nicobar Class	2 being built + 8 on order
	Super Dvora Mk.II Class	5 in service + 2 being built
	Bangaram Class	4 in service
	Trinkat Class	2 in service
Amphibious Warfare Vessels	Austin Class	1 in service
	Shardul Class	1 in service + 2 launched
	Mk.3 Landing Craft	8 in service
	Polnochny C/D Class	5 in service
	Magar Class	2 in service
Replenishment Tankers	Jyoti Class	1 in service
	Aditya Class	1 in service
	Deepak Class	1 in service
Mine Countermeasures Vessels	Class Unknown	8 ordered
Minesweepers - Ocean	Pondicherry {Natya 1} Class	12 in service
Survey Vessels	Makar Class	2 in service
	Sandhayak Class	8 in service
Transport Ship	Nicobar Class	2 in service
Research Vessels	Sagardhwani Class	1 in service
Diving Support Vessel	Nireekshak Class	1 in service
Training Vessels	Tir Class	1 in service
	Leander Class	1 in service
Sail Training Vessels	Varuna Class	2 in service
Oilers	Ambika - Diesel Oiler	1 in service
Ocean Tug	Gaj - Ocean Tug	1 in service
	Matanga Class	1 in service
Harbour Tug	Bhim Class	5 in service
	Class Unknown	13 in service
Support Tankers	Poshak Class	6 in service
Water Carrier	Class Unknown	2 in service
Hospital Ship	Class Unknown	1 in service
Torpedo Recovery Vessel	Class Unknown	2 in service
Diving Tender	Class Unknown	3 in service

Source: Bharat Rashak, http://www.bharat-rakshak.corn/NAVY/Surface.htuil. Last accessed June 21, 2008.

Mr. Ackerman. I thank each of you.

First, I think we note that it is two-to-one as to whether or not the 123 Agreement might not be better off compromised or amended by each side in order to get it through.

Dr. Cohen, you are shaking your head?

Mr. Cohen. My view is that, certainly, if the agreement can go through, it should go through. But I suspect—

Mr. Ackerman. All right. Let me ask two questions. One, if it is unchanged, can it pass through the India process?

Ms. Schaffer. I think amendment is irrelevant to getting it through the India process today.

Mr. Ackerman. But can it get through the India process the way it is?

Ms. Schaffer. That I am not at all sure about, because that really depends on what kind of high-stakes poker the leftists are going to play, if they are willing to bring down the government.

What bothers them is the strong relationship with the United States. They are the only significant political element in India that opposes a strong relationship with the United States. And the details don't matter.

Mr. Ackerman. What you are saying—I am trying to understand what you are saying. Is what you are saying that the left, led by the communists, which is the largest bloc, CPM, are they going to vote against it, no matter what, because they are against the relationship with the United States?

Because the 123 Agreement is with the United States. That is not going to be changed It is not going to be with someone else.

Ms. Schaffer. That is what they are threatening to do.

Mr. Ackerman. So it has nothing to do with amending it?

Ms. Schaffer. I don't think so.

Mr. Andersen. No. They are against it because of the developing relationship with the U.S. They see this trend that we have all been talking about, and they see it as dangerous. And the civilian nuclear deal, for them—

Mr. Ackerman. Okay, so there is a bigger question then. Mr. ANDERSEN. Yes.

Mr. Ackerman. Does the left in India have the power to bring down the government if India pursues its positive relationship with the United States?

Ms. Schaffer. It has the power to bring down this government because of the parliamentary arithmetic. Whether it has that power for a future government—

Mr. Ackerman. I know the arithmetic, but does it happen?

Ms. Schaffer. It can happen. If they decide to hang tough, it will happen.

Mr. Cohen. Indians are debating whether an agreement could be concluded by a government that has fallen. And there may be some legal precedent for that. But the larger issue is that Indian governments in New Delhi are going to be coalition governments indefinitely, which means less of a consensus on foreign policy and a degree of unpredictability on the Indian side that we haven't seen in the past. We are unpredictable also, but I think that is a new factor on the Indian side. They may not make an agreement with a foreign country that will stick and the next government may abandon it. It is a new concern that we have with India.

Mr. Ackerman. Do you agree, Ambassador Schaffer?

Ms. Schaffer. I think that, if they make an agreement, the next government will honor it. As Dr. Cohen said, the debate they are having internally is, first of all, whether the government is prepared to take the risk of being brought down by pursuing the nuclear agreement and, secondly, if it does so and if the left follows through on its threat to bring down the government, whether the government can go ahead and sign and implement an agreement under those circumstances.

My best understanding is that, legally, technically, it can. The question is whether, in the Indian political context, this would be considered an act of political chutzpah.

Mr. Andersen. There is a date coming up which is important—

Mr. Ackerman. Now you sound like Minnie Schaffer.

Ms. Schaffer. She was my beloved mother-in-law.

Mr. Andersen. There is a date coming up that is important. The G-8 is meeting next month. The Indian press has said that the Prime Minister would like to speak to President Bush, to say he was able to do something positive about that. If that, in fact, is the case, he may decide to call the bluff of the communists; I am not sure. But if that statement is true, if that attribution to him is true, he will have to do something in the next few weeks.

Mr. Ackerman. Understanding the math is the math, currently. Is there something that, if applied to the 123 process, amending it any way, could that possibly wean off enough votes from the left to change the math? So if the answer is no, that means amending the process is futile to begin with, because it gets you nothing?

Mr. Andersen. Well, the normal or usual suggestions about amendment, at least on our side, is to have something more specific on fissile fuel and no testing I think if you got too explicit about that in the agreement, which is why it was avoided before, I think that almost guarantees that the views of the left would have more support rather than less.

Mr. Ackerman. I have run the clock on myself. And to set an example using me, we will go to Mr. Pence. And that guarantees at least one additional round.

Mr. Pence. Thank you, Mr. Chairman Thank you for calling this important hearing.

And I want to thank this distinguished panel of witnesses for your written testimony as well as your presentations today.

A couple of quick questions, if I may. And I would welcome any member of the panel to take them.

I think some of you reflected this in your statements today. India's economic reform agenda seemed to only have slowed under the Congress Party-led government. My question would be, How important are such issues as fiscal liberalization and trade barrier removal to the further development of a greater United States- India trade and economic relations?

We debate these issues a great deal here on Capitol Hill, but I would like to get a sense from this panel about the importance of those reforms, both internal and external.

Ambassador?

Ms. Schaffer. As far as further reductions of trade barriers are concerned, there has been a tremendous reduction in India's trade barriers already. India is still a more protected economy than a lot of the others in Asia. Certainly, from the point of view of U.S. exporters, this would be a very desirable development.

But the fundamental driver in United States-India economic relations is the private sector. It is private companies that are trading and investing. And we have also always found it easier to work private-sector-to-private-sector, a little bit harder bilaterally, government-to-government, and hardest at the multilateral level, on the economic side.

So anything that happens in that area is a force multiplier. But what has happened already has created a tremendous momentum.

Mr. Pence. Ambassador, if I could step off on something, and then I will go to Dr. Andersen.

How substantive do you consider the complaints that the United States is insufficiently sensitive to India's national constraints, the vulnerability of its farmers to international market penetration? What is your sense about that?

Ms. Schaffer. Congressman, I worked as a trade official for 4 years of my life. I find that trade policy is wonderfully unsentimental about other countries' concerns. We are worried about our farmers; they are worried about their farmers. The officials that are concluding deals need to keep both of those in view. But I think it is inevitable that they will find us less concerned about their farmers than they are.

Mr. Pence. Okay.

Dr. Andersen, whatever part of that you want to speak to.

Mr. Andersen. I was going add to the point that Ambassador Schaffer made about the advances India has made in opening up its trade.

One has to do with the foreign direct investment caps. It used to be virtually impossible to invest in India. And, in fact, you can see that in statistics. In 1990, there was almost no FTI in India. Last year, there was $20 billion. And, in fact, the bulk of that increase has come within the last 3 years, of which a substantial part of that is American.

There are areas, such as retail trade, where there are caps on that. And there is domestic opposition to it, but there is also significant support for it. This is an issue which is now being debated. My guess is that, over time, these caps will be lifted, because it is in India's interest to do so and there are important interests which benefit from it within India. And the U.S. will respond as we have been responding, with foreign direct investment over the last few years.

I mean, this is really a remarkable growth in what has happened in foreign direct investment over the last few years.

Mr. Pence. Great.

Dr. Cohen.

Mr. Cohen. I would agree with that, but I would add a couple of points. As India sees the benefits of trade, as it prospers and it grows, there will be more political support within India to reduce these tariffs.

But there is another factor that Indian politicians are especially sensitive to. The greatest threat to Indian security now does not come from China. It does not come from Pakistan. It comes from within.

There is an enormous, complex insurgency going on in India, raging from South India all the way to the north and up to the northeast. It has nothing to do with outsiders. It has a lot to do with instability and inequities within India itself. And the concern is that uneven growth, malformed growth, will dispossess more people, which will lead them to turn to violence.

The euphemism is the not-so-like revolution. But it is a series of disconnected revolutions which have a common source in social dislocation, and that makes the Indians think many times before opening up and creating greater stresses within Indian society, the stress between the rich and the poor.

So I think that is a factor that the Indian politicians and bureaucrats are very concerned about. They don't have a strategy to deal with this. My own view is that good growth and equitable growth will deal with it, but it is a long-term process; and, in the meantime, a huge amount of violence goes on in India.

Mr. Pence. But that is over time.

But, Dr. Cohen, just to understand your point, that some of the internal resistance to liberalization of trade laws and barriers is because of the concern about increased disparity between the haves and the have-nots within India itself.

Mr. Cohen. Yes. Also, some Indian companies especially in the public sector are highly protectionist. They don't want competition. Mr. PENCE. Thank you.

Mr. Chairman, I am over, so thank you.

Mr. Ackerman. Mr. Scott.

Mr. Scott. Thank you, Mr. Chairman.

First, Dr. Andersen, going back to the recent decision earlier today, the left failing to support this, what does this mean in terms of the next steps? What in your opinion would you expect Mr. Singh to move ahead and try to press on in view of their opposition for the deal?

Mr. Andersen. I am sure right now that whole issue is being debated intensely in India and by the Prime Minister and his closest advisors.

The next step that was announced by the External Affairs Minister was that there would be another meeting, which in effect kicks the issue down, and it was also talked about as if this would be the final meeting, but there have been a number of final meetings over the past several months.

The reality is that if the Communists vote against the government on an issue, if they follow through with their promise to do so, if India signs the India-specific agreement at the IAEA, which is the immediate issue at stake, the government would probably fall. Because the leading opposition party, for its own political reasons, the Bharatiya Janata Party, has said that it doesn't support the agreement as presently written and would like and believes that it can be rewritten somewhat in India's favor, specifically on the issue of testing, nuclear testing.

What will the Prime Minister do? I suspect at the present time he is not quite sure what he is going to do. But he is under enormous pressure because, in a sense, his prestige is at stake. This was something he pushed very hard. He has talked about that. His standing in the international community and his legacy is at stake in this issue.

Mr. Scott. It seems to me that the testing under this agreement will still be allowed. Nuclear testing would still be allowed, is that not true?

Mr. Andersen. No. The agreement doesn't mention testing, and that was a decision not to do so. But it doesn't mean that U.S. law doesn't apply, which is, if there is testing, as I understand U.S. law, then we are required to abrogate the agreement.

Mr. Scott. So, in effect—

Ms. Schaffer. May I add something to that, please?

Mr. Scott. Yes.

Ms. Schaffer. Congressman, there is a very long and detailed passage in the agreement that deals with the termination procedures. And if you read the Hyde Act and the agreement together, it would appear that if India were to decide to test, the United States would be required to start down the road toward the termination procedure. This is driven by a consultative process. It was obviously drafted with great care and with a great deal left between the lines.

The whole plan, the assumption on the Indian side would be that during this consultative process they would be able to persuade the United States that there were some kind of mitigating circumstances that made it okay. The United States clearly did not and could not address those assumptions. But, as a result, the whole question of where testing fits into the 123 agreement is left to a large extent in the spaces between the lines and in the portions of the Hyde Act which obviously are binding on the United States.

Mr. Scott. Okay. I understand that. That is clear.

Now, would you think that another reason for the left being concerned about this agreement would be the strategic position that it would place the United States influence in India vis-à-vis China and their other neighbor, Pakistan?

Ms. Schaffer. Yes. Short answer, that is absolutely what they are concerned about. But there is a large degree of inertia in this This is a party—or the largest parts of the leftist group are parties which for decades were in line with either Moscow or Beijing and which looked on the United States as a hostile power. And while India's foreign policy has turned around, these parties, particularly their representatives in the central Parliament, have not.

Mr. Scott. Now, finally—my time is slipping away, but I would like to find out, would this action—if it is not consummated and the agreement with the United States does not go forward, would this open up a window of opportunity for Iran and Russia, particularly in relationship to both this and additional sources of energy in view of the fact that Russia and China control about half of the natural gas in that region? Would this open up an opportunity for Iran to be able to get in there, particularly in view of the perspective pipeline that is designated to go there?

Ms. Schaffer. Presumably they would try to make that happen. I don't see the Russian energy angle as being particularly relevant in the short run. Russia has lots and lots of gas, but at the moment they have no way of getting it to India, except by very complicated international swap deals.

In the case of Iran though, India already gets 10 percent of its oil imports from Iran. It has, at least in principle, a natural gas import deal, although this has never been implemented. So the energy supply relationship is already well-established with Iran.

Mr. Ackerman. We are going to have to come back on another round.

Mr. Wilson.

Mr. Wilson. Thank you, Mr. Chairman; and thank you all for being here today.

To me, this is just extraordinary to hear your testimony in such a positive manner. The relationship of the United States and India, because those of us who remember the Cold War era, what you are saying here today is truly revolutionary. And particularly I appreciate the chairman pointing out, the last 3 years, the development of our relationship has just been spectacular, and I am really looking forward to the future.

But I do share the concern of the chairman relative to Iran, and I believe that the Iranian efforts to develop a nuclear weapon are an extraordinary threat to India. It would appear to me that, with a land bridge to India, that the threat of nuclear weapons being developed could more easily be delivered to New Delhi than to Washington. And so I would hope that we would be working together more on this issue which is truly a threat to the people of India with the divisions that Dr. Cohen has pointed out across the country. There are plenty of terrorists who would love to, if there was any way of access, to create disruption in the dynamic Republic of India.

Looking at that, I would like to know the position of each of you, each of you relative to the Iran-Pakistan natural gas pipeline. Do you believe this will come to fruition? Is this good for the region? Or is it good, again, for world peace?

Mr. Andersen. Could I start?

Theoretically, it would be good for India, because it desperately needs energy. In fact, I don't think it is going to happen any time soon; and I think the reason is because the prices that the Iranians want are not prices that the Indians are willing to pay. So this is something—my guess—that is quite a way down the pike before it becomes a reality. It is often not stated publicly, but I think this is a major reason for the Indians

Also, the Indians are concerned with the impact it will have on the United States. The very fact that they voted with us twice in the International Atomic Energy Agency is a sign of their concern about the impact on the U.S. But what is really controlling it, I think, is the fact that the pricing is wrong.

Ms. Schaffer. I agree with my colleague's pessimistic assessment of the likelihood of this pipeline.

I think the other reason that it might be good for the region is that it would give India and Pakistan a common stake in some infrastructure that they would want to keep going in somewhat the same manner that the Indus Waters Treaty did. But I don't think this is going to happen. I think the commercial obstacles are likely to sink it.

Mr. Cohen. Let me add that, because it might create a common infrastructure between India and Pakistan, many Indians are opposed to it. They do not want to be dependent on Pakistan. They need the energy. It is a marginal increase if they get it through liquefied form, rather than piped over land.

But I would add a couple of other points that are important. Indians don't see nuclear weapons as threatening. They see them as having stabilized the region. They see them as the equalizer with China.

We may see nuclear weapons, nuclear theft as a scary thing But from the Indian experience, they have gone through four crises, three of which were nuclear crises. They have come out better off than they were before. So their relations with Pakistan are better now. Their relations with China are good. They don't see nuclear weapons as quite the kind of threat or danger that we do.

I think there is a nuclear risk, but I think we may have exaggerated it. But I do think that Indians have underestimated the dangers of accident and theft.

And there is a third factor; and that is, what have the Israelis said about the Indian-Iranian relationship publicly? Not much. Not anything, as far as I can tell.

So I think from an Israeli point of view, and I am not quite sure what their policy is, if they are talking to the Indians it is very private. And what they are saying privately I do not know, but publicly they are quiet. It is a big issue here, but it is not a public issue in Israel.

Mr. Wilson. And I indeed see the difference between a nation having nuclear weapons but terrorists having access to nuclear weapons. And a country that has been attacked for 60 years, with attacks recently as last month, I just can't imagine that people wouldn't realize that, if they had access, how extraordinarily dangerous that would be.

But a final question before the chairman is so brutal in calling my time; and that is, the Nation of Pakistan—I am glad you mentioned it. What is the latest in regard to the peace process between India and Pakistan, particularly with the new government?

Ms. Schaffer. Both countries want to have a peace process. Neither government is strong enough to do very much with it.

Mr. Wilson. Thank you very much.

Mr. Ackerman. That was pretty good. Exactly on time.

I want to go back to the question that Mr. Scott raised or the answer that he received, which had something to do with the question that I asked. Was there something that would change the agreement, that would change the math? And I thought we had a consensus after I asked the question, but after Mr. Scott asked the question, the discussion came around to testing and whether India's right to test changes something. Did I miss something or does—if the United States announced that we have no objection to India testing and nobody was concerned about that, does that change the dynamic?

Ms. Schaffer. Not with the leftists, Mr. Chairman.

There are three sources of opposition to the nuclear deal in India. The opposition BJP it would have an influence on. The nuclear scientists, who have largely been brought on board by the 123 agreement, would be delighted. I don't think it would make a difference to the leftists, who are the only opponents whose position really makes a difference now.

Mr. Andersen. There is the larger issue that was mentioned before, and that is the left is opposed to any move that gets closer to the U.S. so it doesn't really make any difference. They see this deal in the context of the larger move of India toward the United States that has been taking place in the last 10 years. They want to stop it.

Mr. Ackerman. Accepting that there are three points of opposition and possibly others or nuances of each, as an old math teacher I am just interested in the math. If the Communists walk out, their only objection is us. The deal is with us. If they walk out, the math is the government can fall or the government will fall. And they are going to walk out, no matter what, as long as we are the other half of the agreement, which it seems to me we are the other half of the agreement. So everything else is just rhetoric. They are walking out on this deal.

Mr. Andersen. But there is an additional problem. The major opposition party, the Bharatiya Janata Party, has increasingly, for its own political reasons, come out against the deal. So if this were a vote that was placed in Parliament, which in fact the deal is the issue, the BJP would probably vote against the government as well. So that is the bigger issue. The Communists alone, in terms of the math that you referred to, wouldn't be enough to bring down the government. You would have to have the major part of the opposition also vote against the government.

Mr. Ackerman. So I am getting a different answer than I got before. If the BJP steps in, the Communists don't bring down the government mathematically.

Ms. Schaffer. Mr. Chairman, if the BJP steps in and decides to support the deal, then the government doesn't fall, even if the Communists vote against it.

Mr. Ackerman. Well, that is a different answer than I got the first time.

Ms. Schaffer. But then the BJP has other equities involved. They think an early election will favor them.

Mr. Ackerman. So the answer to the question—I am not telling you what the answer is, but it seems to me you are telling me the answer is now that there are things that can be done to change the math, despite the fact that the Communists are going to walk out no matter what, and that is if the deal is amended or clarified or changed in any way, that brings the BJP aboard—and I don't know exactly how you do that—that the Communists don't have enough votes to bring the government down.

Mr. Andersen. But I think what the BJP wants is something that would be very difficult for us to do. I think that they would want language which was more specific on allowing India to have the option of testing

Mr. Ackerman. Yes. That goes under the category is there anything that can be amended to change it to keep them in.

Yes?

Ms. Schaffer. Mr. Chairman, they have another issue as well. That doesn't necessarily bring them on board, because everything depends on whether they think that they basically want to bring the government down because they think they are going to win the election.

Mr. Cohen. There are also some in the BJP who feel that they tested once in 1998. There is a nuclear deal that they don't like. But if they test again and refine their designs they might get a better nuclear deal. I don't like that logic, but there are some who argue that in the BJP.

Mr. Ackerman. I am going to relinquish the other half-minute that I have, because this wasn't even the question that I wanted to ask. And I am going to go to Mr. Pence, and we are going to break after that.

The pipeline, I want to come back to the pipeline. We can both ask.

This deal with the pipeline is sticky, and I think it is more controversial on our side as a deal breaker than it is on their side. But certainly it is problematic on both sides. And it also seems to me that the Indians go first.

The discussion that we are hearing—and one of the quotes was it is not going to happen any time soon—is not soothing to the American politicians' political palate. If we are going to enter into a marriage with the Indians over this and in taking the vows when you get to the part whether or not you are going to be faithful and the answer is I am not going to be unfaithful any time soon, I think that indicates a problem.

Mr. Pence. Will the chairman yield?

Mr. Ackerman. I would be happy to yield at that point.

Mr. Pence. It is—on these issues, it is not surprising when the chairman and I are in strong agreement; and the panel no doubt knows Chairman Ackerman and I have authored legislation encouraging strong action for further economic sanctions against Iran. It has been widely misinterpreted in some quarters, but it is very much in harmony with action taken by the European Union recently.

I want to acknowledge that India's vote against Iran in the IAEA, despite what appeared to be its own public's opposition to that vote. But I want to associate myself strongly with the chairman's comments and phrase it as a question, about what—it is, I think, the almost unanimous opinion of this subcommittee and the overwhelming opinion of this Congress that we have to be further isolating Iran economically, and India's engagement or potential engagement with regard to this pipeline sends precisely the opposite message than what the world community should be sending.

So I will yield back to the chairman, and he can yield to you to respond to the question appropriately. But that would be—it is very disconcerting.

Mr. Ackerman. If somebody would like to react to that.

Mr. Cohen. I think there are two points.

One is, what is the total value of—presumed value to Iran of some kind of pipeline agreement, compared with what Iran gets vis-à-vis its trade with Europeans and other Asian countries now.

I suspect it is fairly small. It doesn't figure high up in the Iranian bankbook.

Ms. Schaffer. Perhaps I could add what I have been thinking India does not want a nuclear Iran. We disagree on what to do about it. India recognizes that we are strongly opposed to the pipeline but then observes that we are giving them a hard time and we are not giving the Pakistanis a hard time, and so we are sending mixed messages to them.

From India's point of view, Iran is, unfortunately for us, one of the cases where they feel it necessary to demonstrate their independent foreign policy. The fact that Iran supplies 10 percent of their imported energy is very important in that. There are other things they get from Iran. They look to Europe and see that the Europeans are able to trade in energy with Iran and say, why not us?

So we really don't see eye to eye on the question of further isolation of Iran. I think their willingness to work with us is going to have to be much more narrowly focused on the question of Iran's nuclear program.

I am not sure the marriage analogy is one that the government in Delhi would be altogether comfortable with. It gets back to what we were saying about the difference between an alliance and a more selective partnership.

Mr. Cohen. My second point was that we are providing Pakistan—

Mr. Ackerman. I don't know that we are ready to enter into an open marriage situation with them, either.

Mr. Cohen. My second point was that we are providing Pakistan with about $1 billion a year in aid, much of it military aid. The Indians have been very quiet about that. In years past, this was a key issue which strained our relationship. They have been silent so far. In a sense, I think that shapes our Iran policy, also.

Mr. Ackerman. Mr. Scott has a question.

Mr. Scott. Real quickly, if I could get your quick opinions on, India is pursuing a permanent seat on the U.N. Security Council, which I think very important. What is the likelihood of that, in each of your opinions, in the next 5 years?

Ms. Schaffer. Low. I think their strongest backer among the current permanent five is probably Russia. They have formal support from Britain and France but not much enthusiasm. The present administration I think basically doesn't want to enlarge the Council, and I am not sure that a future administration is going to want to put much work into the enterprise.

Mr. Cohen. I would add to that that, from an Indian point of view, they may not want to be on the Security Council they are going to be asked to take positions on a whole range of issues that they have sidestepped so far. So there are Indians who argue that would be good for prestige and status, they would like it. But they would have to commit themselves as a Security Council member in a way they have not had to do in the past.

Mr. Andersen. I don't agree with that. I think this would get support across the political spectrum of India. It is something that they very much want. It would be a sign of respect for them and their arrival as a great power on the world stage, and I think we should push it ourselves. I know there are structural reasons, but that doesn't mean we can't push it. On the civil nuclear deal there were structural reasons, too, and we continued because it was good for us, and it was good for India, and I think we should do so.

Mr. Scott. Thank you.

Mr. Ackerman. If anybody has any reason to object to why these two countries should not be joined, do not speak now.

We are going to recess for two votes.

[Recess.]

Mr. Ackerman. The subcommittee will come back to order. Thanks for your patience.

I just wanted to follow up a little bit on the pipeline. The Indians officially respond to those of us who press them on the issue that it is really not going anywhere and that the Iranians have reneged on the original pricing of it. And, as a matter of fact, it was stated here, the pricing is wrong for the deal to happen. That is also not something that gives us any great comfort level, that it is not going to go through because the pricing is bad. Because prices can always change. It is the intent that a lot of us are concerned about.

And Mr. Pence referenced some legislation that he and I are sponsoring. I think those who want to avoid a major conflict with Iran should be onboard.

The only strategy that I could think of, because we are not getting their attention in any other way, to economically get their attention and to put an economic stranglehold on them, if necessary, which does not talk to the issue of blockading the ports or anything like that but does talk about already agreed to inspections of things going from places headed for Iran. Use the tool of economic diplomacy, if you will, leverage, if you would, to try to affect behavior in Iran.

The Indians move counter to that in continuing to talk about a pipeline. It is troublesome, because it runs counter to the notion of what a lot of us are trying to do, and that is to dissuade others from investing in Iran, whether it be the energy sector or anywhere else, and to isolate them economically so that they feel the full pressure of the international community.

I am not sure how much of that India really gets and just reads that as personal against them, but certainly the pipeline would cause a lot of concern as to whether or not we would then pass the 123 agreement on our side, assuming that the Indians did and came to their agreements with those with whom they had to conclude agreements.

Reaction?

Ms. Schaffer. Mr Chairman, I guess it makes a difference who you think the primary beneficiary would be were the pipeline to go through. As I said, I don't expect it to go through.

I think that if—I am not trying to be an advocate for the Indian Government's position but trying to interpret it as best I can. I think they feel that if the conditions are right for such a deal to go—for such an agreement on the pipeline to go through, they, rather than Iran, would be the main beneficiaries; and so with-holding it is something they would be doing to themselves rather than to the Iranians.

Now one can look at that in both directions; and presumably any major economic agreement has to, in some sense, benefit both sides. But I also think that India, philosophically, is out of step with us on this question in the sense that they see their own energy requirements as a very important driver of policy, not that they are rushing in to do something with Iran but that they are unwilling to kill off the possibility that both the commercial conditions and the political conditions might be suitable at some point down the road.

Mr. Ackerman. Dr. Andersen.

Mr. Andersen. There is another issue here with India and Iran that we can actually do something about. Is Pakistan now denies India the right to transship to Afghanistan or, via that, to Iran. India now is required, because of that, to—or to Central Asia—to ship its stuff via Iranian ports and then use the Iranian rail system to get its products, imports and exports to Iran and the Central Asian republics and Afghanistan as well.

So we could do something about that. We could press Pakistan to lift its restrictions on India.

And I am surprised that—I know in theory we say it is a good thing, but we really—I think we have something to gain, and on this we have something important to gain.

Mr. Ackerman. And what do we give Pakistan?

Mr. Anderson. Is to get Pakistan to lift the restriction.

Mr. Ackerman. No. What do we give them in order to get that from them?

Mr. Andersen. We are already giving them a lot. I think they owe us something, given the extent of the support that we give them and, you know, are continuing to give in terms of military assistance and economic assistance.

Mr. Ackerman. Dr. Cohen.

Mr. Cohen. I think that the way I would put it, "Does an agreement help India more than it hurts Iran?" What is in that balance of hurt and help? My own judgment is it probably helps India more than the continuing sanctions hurt Iran.

In the case of Pakistan, I don't think the Pakistanis are ready for that kind of agreement with India, and I don't think the Indians are ready for that kind of agreement with Pakistan. They still deeply distrust each other.

In Pakistan, the root of that problem is the military In India, the politicians and the strategists have yet to decide whether they want to see Pakistan shrivel up and go away or they would like to finish it off militarily once and for all or whether they will try to ignore Pakistan. So we are caught in their primary disputes. There is no clear way out for us.

But in the case of India and Iran I think there is a balance of benefit and harm which probably comes out on the side of the pipeline. But I don't think the pipeline will be built, in any case.

Mr. Ackerman. Are you suggesting there is not a hiatus in at least rhetoric between India and Pakistan?

Ms. Schaffer. I actually disagree somewhat with my colleague here on this. Yes, there certainly has been a hiatus in a lot of the rhetoric on Pakistan, and I think it goes deeper than that. I think the Indian Government has consciously avoided commenting on Pakistan's domestic troubles for the past 6 months because they didn't want to make themselves the issue at a time when Pakistan's politics were in turmoil. They are quite troubled by what is going on in Pakistan.

I don't doubt that there are a few politicians in India, who would, as Dr. Cohen put it, like to see Pakistan shrivel up and die, but I think mainstream opinion is actually not there at all. I think mainstream opinion in India and government policy is that they would like to see Pakistan stabilized. I think they would dearly love to get Pakistan to agree to land transit through to Afghanistan. I think that would be a tough sell for the U.S. to persuade them, although in the grand scheme of things it would be a good thing.

Mr. Cohen. The Indians want Pakistan strong enough to hold together but not so strong that it threatens India. And they are trying to calibrate their policies. To have a weak government in Pakistan is acceptable but not a government which allows the country to fall apart and then disperse people and nuclear weapons through the subcontinent. They are very concerned about that.

Mr. Ackerman. Dr. Andersen, you note Indian suspicion when it comes to arms sales from the United States. What steps can the U.S. take to overcome that suspicion or do we have to build up a track record of such sales before the suspicions disappear?

Mr. Andersen. Well, we are starting to do that now. But, of course, we have certain restrictions on arms sales that depend on India signing end user agreements; and I think the Indians, because they think that our arms are good, are prepared to negotiate on that. I think this could create, as I mentioned in my formal comments, some bureaucratic problems; and I think it will take high- level intervention on our part to get these negotiations moving.

If the Indian press is right, the Indians have already sent a counterproposal to us; and this requires negotiations. That has been an impediment. I think it is one that we need to remove.

Mr. Ackerman. Let me say this panel has been excellent; and the members have commented to me on the way to vote that they found it very, very helpful. On behalf of all of us, let us thank you.

Your written statements are in the record. They will be carefully scrutinized by experts, scholars and even Members of Congress.

And the committee now stands adjourned.

[Whereupon, at 4:33 p.m., the subcommittee was adjourned.]

Appendix
Material Submitted For The Hearing Record

Prepared Statement of the Honorable Mike Pence, A Representative in Congress from the State Of Indiana

Mr. Chairman, thank you for calling this important hearing, and I welcome our distinguished witnesses. As always, this subcommittee is ahead of the curve.

The emerging power that is India, the world's second largest country with fully one sixth of the earth's population, will command international attention for the next century. I view India as a stable and benign rising power. India has a booming economy and vibrant democracy, itself no small feat. In fact, as our witness Dr. Cohen points out, "Every time India goes to the polls, it is the world's largest organized human activity."

Mr. Chairman, the decisions taken by this democracy are not always to my liking. Leftist minority parties within India have blocked the 123 civil nuclear Agreement with the U.S. Given Secretary Rice's assurances to this committee that this agreement is in keeping with the Hyde Act, I view this as a disappointment and a missed opportunity. This agreement had the potential to show the way to peaceful nuclear cooperation and development among the US and its allies.

In this vein, India's prospective natural gas pipeline deal with Iran concerns me. Given the EU's recent actions sanctioning Iran, the world should be moving toward isolating Iran. India should join this international effort. I must give credit where it is due, however, in appreciating India's vote against Iran at the IAEA despite its own public's opposition.

Mr. Chairman, US foreign assistance toward India for many decades has been heavily centered on food aid programs. And, yet, in a case of the left hand not knowing what the right hand is doing in our foreign policy, tariffs on US agriculture products remain prohibitively (and unwisely) high. Just this month, our Commerce Department raised concerns about India's commitment to WTO requirements. And, given their status as the world's fourth largest emitter of greenhouse gases, I could do without their criticism of our environmental policies.

There is still much good news. The US is India's largest trading and investment partner, and our military-to-military cooperation is the greatest India has ever had with any country. Although India may not view itself primarily in these terms, it can potentially serve as a strategic counterweight to China, especially given recent reports of Chinese escalation in a space arms race. Dr. Andersen correctly says, India "is the most politically stable country in a very unstable and strategically important area."

India is in a pivotal region, along the path where much of the world's energy resources and commerce flow. As Ambassador Schaffer says, "Democracy doesn't create partners automatically." I am pleased this subcommittee is doing its part in forging a useful partnership with India.

Mr. Chairman, thank you for calling this hearing; I look forward to hearing from our witnesses.

END NOTES

[1] A 24-Nation Pew Global Attitudes Survey released earlier this month showed that Indians have a 66% favorability rating of the United States, behind only South Korea and Poland. Indians are also the most positive about U.S. economic influence (41%), the personal benefits of trade (87%) and foreigners buying domestic companies (59%), underscoring the importance of the economic relationship.

[2] For a comprehensive discussion of the momentum in the Indo-US relationship, sec Pratap Bhanu Mehta, "Going in Two Directions in South Asia" *Current History,* May 2008.

[3] Data released by the Pew Global Attitudes Project on June 12, 2008, available at: http://pewglobal.org/reports/display.php?Report1D=260. Last accessed June 22, 2008.

[4] For a discussion of India's developing security policy. sec S. Raja Mohan, "India and the Balance of Power" *Foreign Affairs,* Jul/Aug 2006, vol85, issue 4, pp. 17 -32.

[5] Leahy, Joc. "India's Report Card Fails to make the Grade," Financial Times June 19, 2008. Also sec Jim O'Neill and Poddar Thushar's "Ten Things for India to Achieve its 2050 Potential," Global Economics Paper no. 169, June 16, 2008.

[6] The percentage increase in lndo-U S trade is significantly less than the 40 percent growth of two way trade with China recently. China, with some 25 billion in trade in 2007, could surpass the US as India's leading trading partner if current rates of increase hold.

[7] Sec report of India's growing arms imports in "China. India largest imporlcrs of military hardware," *The Economic Times,* June 10, 2008.

[8] NASSCOM. Kcy Highlights of the IT-BPO sector pctionnance in FY 2007-08, available at http://www.nasscom.in/upload Review Feb2008.pdf. Last accessed June 21, 2008.

[9] For a description of these military exercises, sec Robert a Blake. "US-India Relations: The Making of a Comprehensive Relationship", an August 23, 2004 speech released by the US Embassy in India. (Ambassador Blake) was at that time the US Charge in New Delhi.)

[10] See Appendix 1 for a chart of the Indian fleet disaggrated by ship types.

[11] Mohan, 2006.

[12] For a much more comprehensive view of the India-China relationship, see my "Rise of India and China and its Impact on Asia", a paper given at the May 24th - 280' Shanghai Forum, and published in the proceedings of the Forum.

[13] For a good study of Indian concerns, see Ashley Tellis, "China and India in Asia in Francine R. Frankel and Harry Harding (cds.) *The India-China Relationship: the United States Needs to Know,* (Washington D.C: The Woodrow Wilson Center Press, 2004).

[14] Strobe Talbott has provided an excellent analysis of these talks in *Engaging India: Diplomacy Democracy, and the Bomb,* (Washington D.C., Brookings Institution Press, 2004), a book he wrote several years later. A key result of those talks was India's acknowledgement that the US was not seeking to prevent India from playing a more important role on the international stage.

CHAPTER SOURCES

The following chapters have been previously published:

Chapter 1 – This is an edited, reformatted and augmented version of a report from the Economic Research Service, United States Department of Agriculture, Economic Information Bulletin Number 37, dated July 2008.

Chapter 2 – This is an edited, reformatted and augmented version of an Electronic report from the Economic Research Service, United States Department of Agriculture, Economic Research Report Number 17, dated April 2006.

Chapter 3 - This is an edited, reformatted and augmented version of a Congressional Research Service publication, Report Order Code RL33016, updated November 3, 2008.

Chapter 4 - This is an edited, reformatted and augmented version of a Congressional Research Service publication, Report Order Code RL33529, updated August 12, 2008.

Chapter 5 - This is an edited, reformatted and augmented version of a Congressional Research Service publication, Report Order Code RL34312, dated January 7, 2008.

Chapter 6 – This is an edited, reformatted and augmented version of remarks delivered during a Hearing before the Subcommittee on The Middle East and South Asia of the Committee on Foreign Affairs, House of Representatives, One Hundred Tenth Congress, second session, on June 25, 2008, Serial No. 110-188.

INDEX

A

academic, 244
access, 2, 24, 26, 35, 44, 60, 72, 82, 111, 114, 115, 118, 128, 142, 176, 177, 189, 196, 199, 202, 216, 219, 233, 235, 236, 245, 253, 260, 270, 271
accidental, 159
accommodation, 241
accountability, 129
accounting, 9, 10, 11, 17, 20, 22, 31, 34, 44, 45, 53, 134, 139, 178, 190, 193, 245, 255
achievement, 121, 126, 127, 128, 210
acid, 98
ACM, 38
ad hoc, 118, 253
adjustment, 52, 75, 150
administration, x, 105, 109, 122, 130, 151, 231, 236, 237, 241, 244, 249, 251, 254, 255, 261, 273
administrative, 99
adulthood, 11
adults, 201
advocacy, 255
AEA, viii, 101, 102, 103, 105, 116, 120, 125, 127, 129, 131, 132, 133, 135, 143
aerospace, 178, 181, 210
Afghanistan, 153, 155, 166, 206, 208, 220, 252, 254, 258, 275, 276
Africa, 202, 207, 259
afternoon, 237
age, 11, 185, 211, 247, 249
agents, 24, 198
aggression, ix, 216, 224
aggressive behavior, 228
aging, 179
agricultural, vii, 1, 2, 3, 4, 5, 6, 7, 8, 9, 11, 13, 15, 16, 17, 18, 19, 20, 22, 24, 25, 26, 27, 28, 29, 30, 31, 32, 33, 34, 35, 36, 41, 44, 45, 77, 185, 187, 188, 189, 190, 202, 244
agricultural commodities, 2, 30, 35, 36
agricultural exports, 34, 41
agricultural market, 2, 18, 19, 22, 34, 36
agricultural sector, 3, 5, 9, 15, 185, 187
agriculture, vii, 1, 2, 3, 4, 5, 6, 7, 8, 9, 11, 13, 15, 16, 20, 21, 24, 25, 27, 29, 31, 32, 36, 41, 187, 191, 240, 244, 247, 277
aid, ix, 116, 119, 146, 166, 167, 183, 201, 211, 273
AIDS, 201, 204
air, 34, 178, 179, 180, 207, 211, 220, 225, 226, 242, 259
air pollution, 211
aircraft, 167, 168, 179, 181, 183, 186, 207, 226, 242, 256, 257, 259, 261
airplanes, 227
airports, 187
Al Qaeda, 183, 252
Alaska, 259
allies, ix, 104, 109, 141, 149, 166, 169, 177, 209, 215, 216, 222, 225, 229, 237, 246, 252, 255, 277
alternative, 45, 61, 80, 120, 121, 166, 171, 191, 216
alternative energy, 166
alternatives, 105, 129, 257
alters, 98
ambiguity, 142
amelioration, 240, 247
amendments, 18, 38, 109, 142, 151, 174, 249
amino, 98
amino acid, 98
amino acids, 98
analysts, vii, viii, ix, 18, 116, 145, 146, 147, 151, 152, 157, 159, 161, 162, 163, 166, 169, 171, 174, 175, 180, 181, 182, 183, 184, 185, 193, 194, 196, 198, 206, 207, 215, 216, 217, 225, 226, 228, 253, 256
analytical framework, 69, 80
anger, 154
animal husbandry, 27
annual rate, 49

anomalous, 126
anti-American, 149, 241, 245
anti-Americanism, 149, 241
anti-terrorism, 159, 160, 204
apartheid, 148, 172
APEC, 225
APP, 191
apparel, 186
appendix, 61, 65, 80, 81, 82, 87, 88
application, 112, 173
appraisals, 184
appropriations, 189
aquaculture, 48
Areva, 174
Argentina, 19, 53, 74, 79
argument, 115, 174
Ariel, 208
arithmetic, 266
Armed Forces, 199
arms control, 156, 239, 243, 247
arms transfer agreements, 179
Army, 207, 212, 220
ASEAN, 216, 218, 229, 245
ash, 190
Asia, ii, v, viii, ix, 44, 46, 140, 145, 157, 168, 174, 180, 183, 184, 190, 191, 210, 215, 216, 217, 218, 219, 220, 221, 222, 224, 225, 228, 229, 230, 237, 238, 248, 250, 251, 255, 259, 261, 262, 267, 278
Asia Pacific Economic Cooperation, 225
Asian, i, ii, iii, ix, 45, 142, 143, 149, 154, 157, 158, 185, 209, 213, 215, 216, 217, 218, 219, 223, 224, 226, 228, 229, 230, 248, 250, 255, 260, 273, 275
Asian countries, 248, 250, 273
Assam, 19, 20, 155, 195, 196, 206
assassination, 167, 170
assessment, 78, 82, 127, 156, 188, 210, 217, 219, 270
assets, 17, 259
assimilation, 166
Association of Southeast Asian Nations, 216
assumptions, 61, 64, 65, 69, 72, 74, 98, 269
atmosphere, 228, 237
Atomic Energy Act, viii, 101, 102, 125, 128, 137, 139, 173, 174, 204
Atomic Energy Act (AEA), viii, 101, 102
Atomic Energy Commission, 119
attachment, 249, 251
attacks, 153, 158, 160, 194, 197, 198, 199, 200, 212, 271
attention, ix, 155, 158, 171, 184, 191, 192, 198, 215, 216, 218, 243, 244, 253, 254, 257, 274, 277
attribution, 266
Australia, v, ix, 19, 33, 168, 180, 191, 215, 216, 218, 219, 220, 222, 223, 224, 225, 226, 227, 228, 229, 230, 253, 258, 261
Austria, 142
authority, 15, 16, 17, 18, 26, 59, 102, 126, 128, 129, 137, 170, 175, 211
autonomous, 193
autonomy, 106, 138, 148, 193, 195, 249, 251, 255, 258
availability, 5, 7, 15, 16, 17, 20, 21, 22, 28, 29, 35, 60, 69, 98
average costs, 59, 74, 80, 99
average variable cost, 83
averaging, 6, 9, 46, 65
aviation, 182
avoidance, 18
awareness, 201, 224

B

background information, 229
balance of payments, 46, 66, 256
ballast, 222, 239, 246
ballistic missile, viii, 145, 160, 161, 177, 179, 183, 221, 225
ballistic missiles, viii, 145, 179, 183, 225
Bangladesh, 157, 167, 195, 206, 240, 243, 244
banking, 24, 153, 186, 188, 233, 235
banks, 20, 139, 187
barrier, 267
barriers, vii, 1, 16, 44, 45, 69, 71, 77, 82, 99, 184, 187, 217, 244, 267, 268
barter, 7
base year, 87, 88
battery, 181
beating, 249, 251
behavior, 61, 274
Beijing, ix, 161, 162, 163, 165, 207, 216, 218, 219, 220, 223, 224, 225, 228, 229, 269
benchmark, 152, 184, 185
benchmarks, 183
benefits, vii, 26, 43, 45, 58, 59, 64, 65, 67, 69, 72, 74, 75, 76, 77, 78, 82, 84, 91, 92, 93, 94, 95, 96, 97, 98, 104, 109, 112, 147, 157, 173, 174, 182, 185, 187, 223, 225, 243, 253, 268
benign, 250, 277
Bhutan, 157, 195
bilateral relations, 156, 159, 161, 165, 173, 177, 179, 219, 221, 222, 223, 224, 228, 233, 235, 241, 243, 245, 254, 255, 260
bilateral trade, 186, 187, 222, 223, 237
binding, 132, 176, 177, 191, 269
biological, 107

biological weapons, 107
biometrics, 182
biotechnology, 32
bioterrorism, 182
bipartisan, 174, 221, 231, 234, 260
birth, 197, 201
black, 16, 111
black market, 16, 111
blame, 158
board members, 118
Board of Governors, 102, 106, 107, 118, 124, 142, 148, 150
Boeing, 181, 210
bomb, 118, 153, 154, 155, 192
bonus, 26
border crossing, 162
borrowing, 24
Boston, 229
boys, 200
Brazil, 5, 6, 19, 53, 74, 79, 108, 189, 223
Brazilian, 6, 78
breakdown, 193
breeder, 118
bribery, 152, 188
Bribery, 205
Britain, 179, 273
British, 160, 200, 211, 224, 241
brokerage, 98
Buddhist, 163, 167
building blocks, 248, 250
Bureau of Economic Analysis, 10
Bureau of Industry and Security, 178, 210
bureaucracy, 186, 255
Burma, 161, 163, 164, 180, 195, 202, 207, 217, 222, 229, 243, 245
Burma Freedom and Democracy Act, 207
buses, 192, 195, 197, 198, 199, 208
Bush administration, 130, 242, 243, 246
Bush Administration, ix, 104, 105, 111, 146, 150, 151, 156, 163, 165, 166, 172, 173, 174, 175, 181, 184, 202, 210, 211, 215, 218, 219, 221, 222, 225, 228
business, iv, viii, ix, 22, 26, 38, 74, 78, 145, 146, 148, 150, 153, 157, 166, 173, 184, 185, 187, 188, 190, 212, 217, 236, 239, 246, 249, 251, 258
business costs, 22
buyer, 248, 250

C

calculus, 228
California, 238
caloric intake, 11
Cambodia, 229
campaigns, 201
Canada, 19, 123
canals, 31
Canberra, ix, 215, 220, 222, 223, 224, 225, 228, 229
candidates, 123, 146, 169
capacity, 28, 29, 30, 32, 34, 44, 45, 46, 56, 57, 58, 59, 60, 64, 65, 67, 69, 70, 72, 73, 74, 77, 78, 80, 81, 82, 83, 84, 86, 89, 98, 99, 105, 115, 137, 148, 157, 179, 182, 190, 202, 229, 239, 242, 246, 259
Capacity, 34, 40, 57, 63, 66, 68, 71, 73, 76, 83, 85, 86, 89
capacity building, 32, 229
capital, 4, 5, 6, 8, 9, 10, 17, 34, 46, 57, 60, 78, 154, 169, 180, 184, 188, 190, 221, 261
capital markets, 188
Capitol Hill, 267
carbon, 173, 174, 191
cargo, 34, 262
carrier, 167, 179, 259
cast, 171, 225
Catholic, 170
caucuses, 157
cease-fire, 153, 161, 167, 196
cement, 159, 175
Census Bureau, 12, 257
Central Asia, 244, 275
central bank, 185
ceramic, 137
cereals, 12, 13, 16, 17, 30
certification, 134, 135
certifications, 103, 134
channels, 2, 24, 36, 121, 259
charm, 216, 218
chemical, 107, 108, 140, 164, 186
Chicago, 206, 210, 212, 237, 238
child labor, 198
Child Survival and Health, 204
children, 11, 154, 198, 199, 201, 211, 241
Chinese, 6, 161, 162, 163, 180, 184, 188, 189, 207, 216, 219, 222, 224, 228, 230, 245, 255, 260, 277
chloride, 107, 140
Christians, 199
chronic, 28, 46, 198
CIA, 108, 147, 183, 211
citizens, vii, viii, 145, 146, 163, 185, 198, 233, 235, 236
civil liberties, 168
civil society, 198
civil war, 243
Civil War, 213
civilian, vii, viii, 104, 112, 114, 115, 116, 117, 118, 119, 130, 132, 134, 136, 137, 140, 145, 146, 147,

148, 153, 156, 160, 172, 173, 175, 177, 186, 221, 222, 224, 228, 237, 249, 251, 253, 254, 265
classification, 26
classified, viii, 9, 101, 102, 126, 224
clean energy, 191, 202
clean technology, 191
cleaning, 24
climate change, 138, 155, 191, 217, 244, 245
Clinton administration, 231
Clinton Administration, 183, 209, 234
closure, 60, 98, 99
clusters, 258
coal, 105, 190
coastal areas, 164
cohesion, 109
Cold War, ii, 155, 161, 185, 221, 242, 248, 250, 254, 259, 262, 270
collaboration, 3, 36, 104, 156, 176, 180, 232, 234, 253, 254
colonial, 174, 195
combat, 138, 179, 180, 181, 182, 199, 201, 203, 225, 226, 227, 256, 257, 259
commerce, 104, 110, 114, 156, 162, 170, 175, 177, 178, 180, 277
Commerce Department, 178, 187, 189, 277
commercial, 16, 17, 20, 24, 29, 49, 53, 60, 123, 143, 152, 159, 172, 177, 186, 187, 190, 199, 202, 207, 216, 232, 234, 244, 246, 248, 270, 275
commercial bank, 20, 60
commercialization, 20
Committee on Intelligence, 211
commodities, 2, 16, 17, 30, 35, 36, 59
commodity, 8, 16, 17, 35, 41, 44, 67, 80, 87
commodity markets, 35
communalism, 152
communication, 193, 216
Communist Party, 118, 142, 171, 196, 209, 261
communities, 198
community, viii, 138, 145, 146, 148, 157, 233, 235, 236, 243, 248, 250, 269, 273, 274
community support, 148
comparative advantage, 45
compatibility, 225
compensation, 26, 65, 188
competition, 24, 45, 56, 78, 161, 217, 221, 227, 253, 268
competitive advantage, 72
competitiveness, 22, 53, 191
competitor, 253
complement, 87
complementary, 7
complexity, 69, 262
compliance, 22, 104, 116, 210
components, 44, 45, 130, 131, 178
composite, 45, 61, 74, 161
composition, 12, 44, 46, 53, 98
comprehension, 189
Comprehensive Test Ban Treaty, 110
computer, 155
computer technology, 155
computerization, 20
computing, 41
concentrates, 32
concentration, 141
concrete, 112, 261
confidence, 3, 36, 87, 117, 119, 152, 155, 156, 160, 166, 221, 236, 237
confidentiality, 11, 210
conflict, viii, 77, 145, 157, 158, 161, 166, 180, 183, 193, 197, 199, 217, 218, 220, 239, 241, 245, 246, 274
conflict of interest, 161
conflict resolution, 166, 180
confrontation, 217
congress, 208
Congressional Research Service, 279
congruence, 174, 180
connectivity, 117
consensus, 2, 16, 102, 109, 118, 122, 173, 193, 266, 271
consent, 121, 126, 128, 135
conservation, 191
consolidation, 45, 60, 74, 78, 91, 92, 93, 94, 95, 96, 97, 98, 158, 166
constant rate, 74
Constitution, 15, 125, 129, 175, 193
constitutional, ix, 119, 129, 216, 227
constraints, 11, 13, 17, 115, 148, 155, 172, 190, 267
construction, 5, 34, 60, 117, 122, 123, 130, 136, 161, 165, 166, 167, 179
consulting, 104
consumer expenditure, 13
consumer goods, 17
consumer markets, 15
consumers, vii, 12, 16, 26, 34, 43, 44, 45, 47, 50, 53, 57, 59, 61, 65, 69, 72, 74, 75, 77, 78, 80, 82, 173
consumption, 12, 26, 32, 35, 47, 48, 52, 61, 64, 65, 67, 69, 72, 74, 75, 80, 190
contamination, 244
continuing, 44, 112, 149, 159, 160, 175, 179, 184, 186, 198, 202, 221, 226, 239, 246, 274, 275
contracts, 18, 35, 60, 165, 174
control, 16, 18, 40, 59, 102, 105, 110, 111, 113, 116, 120, 124, 129, 138, 139, 161, 170, 172, 178, 181, 201, 202, 204, 239, 247, 269
controlled, 27, 155, 160, 192

convergence, 189, 209, 221, 248, 250, 252, 254, 256
conversion, 139, 199
coordination, 20, 32, 34, 183, 220
copyright, 188
corn, 25, 49, 87, 265
corporations, 242
corruption, 182, 188, 198, 199, 205
cost curve, 59, 80, 81, 82, 84
cost of power, 29
cost saving, 60
cost-effective, 30
costs, vii, 4, 7, 13, 26, 28, 29, 31, 43, 44, 56, 58, 59, 60, 61, 64, 65, 66, 67, 69, 70, 71, 72, 74, 75, 77, 78, 80, 82, 83, 84, 86, 90, 98, 99, 149, 152, 204, 245, 255
cotton, 32, 186
Council on Environmental Quality, 212
counterbalance, 152, 163, 180
counterfeiting, 188
countermeasures, ix, 216
counternarcotics, 202
counter-terror, 234, 259, 261
counterterrorism, 146, 156, 167, 179, 181, 182, 202, 207, 222, 224, 232, 253
country of origin, 11
courts, 199
coverage, 41, 80
CPI, 79
credentials, 170, 192
credibility, 123, 151
credit, 2, 7, 11, 15, 16, 20, 21, 36, 46, 55, 60, 152, 187, 277
credit rating, 152
critical infrastructure, 182
criticism, 149, 152, 170, 176, 183, 210, 224, 277
crops, 19, 32, 46, 54, 56, 67
cross-border, viii, 145, 159, 166, 167, 192
CRS, 139, 140, 141, 142, 143, 144, 146, 194, 203, 204, 206, 208, 209, 210, 211, 212, 229, 230
crude oil, 259
cruise missiles, 179
CSH, 203, 204
Cuba, 158, 171
cultivation, 27, 56
cultural, 158, 198, 241
culture, 170, 198, 236
currency, 256
current account, 46
current account deficit, 46
cyclone, 164, 245

D

dairy, 34, 48
dairy products, 34
dairy sector, 48
danger, 152, 217, 270
data collection, 1, 35
database, 13, 31, 47, 48, 52, 53, 79, 213
dating, 27
death, 26
deaths, 167, 182, 193, 195, 196, 212, 242
debt, 187
decision making, 153
decisions, 35, 107, 121, 124, 188, 224, 242, 249, 251, 277
defense, viii, ix, 101, 102, 112, 126, 127, 128, 145, 146, 156, 157, 160, 162, 164, 167, 172, 175, 178, 179, 180, 181, 182, 207, 215, 216, 219, 220, 222, 223, 224, 225, 227, 228, 232, 234, 236, 241, 242, 245, 254, 256, 258, 261, 262
deficit, 28, 44, 77, 187
definition, 5, 6, 136
degree, ix, 149, 199, 216, 221, 228, 237, 242, 266, 269
delays, 30, 58, 167, 252
delivery, 18, 116, 181, 183, 184, 211, 244
demand, vii, 1, 3, 11, 12, 13, 22, 31, 32, 36, 44, 45, 46, 47, 48, 49, 53, 56, 57, 61, 62, 64, 65, 77, 78, 80, 84, 85, 86, 87, 89, 99, 149, 177, 190, 193, 210, 239, 246, 253
democracy, vii, viii, 145, 146, 157, 163, 164, 168, 182, 196, 207, 221, 236, 248, 250, 255, 277
Democratic Party, 154, 195
democratization, 158
demographic, 154
demographics, 3, 11, 12
denial, 260
Department of Agriculture, 19, 32, 34, 39, 279
Department of Commerce, 10, 147, 210
Department of Defense, 211
Department of Energy, 212
Department of State, viii, 101, 102, 143, 209, 210, 212, 213
depreciation, 62
depressed, 81
deregulation, 185
derived demand, 47
desire, 105, 168, 174, 179, 207, 224, 228, 237, 256
desires, 194
destroyers, 225, 226
destruction, 138
deterministic, 84
deterrence, 179, 183, 218

developing countries, 19, 44, 45, 189, 191
development assistance, 202
Development Assistance, 204
diesel, 31
diet, 11, 47, 53
dietary, 11
diets, 11
diffusion, 200
direct investment, 10, 186
direct taxes, 22, 24
Director of National Intelligence, 156
disappointment, 277
disaster, 167, 202, 216, 221, 222, 226, 239, 243, 246
disaster assistance, 216
disaster relief, 167, 221, 239, 246
discipline, vii, 43, 67
discomfort, 161, 182
discounts, 35
discrimination, ix, 146, 198, 200, 201
discriminatory, 103, 106, 107, 112, 138, 184
disequilibrium, 80, 81, 82
dislocation, 268
displacement, 198
disposition, 240
disputes, 24, 26, 158, 159, 163, 167, 170, 187, 222, 245, 260, 275
distribution, 7, 16, 27, 29, 143, 244, 262
diversification, 11, 12, 13, 32, 36, 167, 190
diversity, 195
dividends, 27
division, 37
doctors, 200
Doha, 189, 190, 212
domestic demand, 11, 26, 49, 57, 185, 256
domestic investment, 10
domestic policy, 1, 2, 77
dominance, 169, 216, 223
donations, 204
donor, 189, 201
draft, 32, 112, 118, 120, 121, 124, 141, 142, 150, 151, 184, 189, 253, 257
drought, 64, 245
dual-use items, 130, 139
duration, 125, 150
duties, 82, 129

E

early warning, 179, 181
earnings, 9, 66, 248, 250
earth, 191, 277
East Asia, 10, 216, 223, 228, 229, 230, 258
economic assistance, 275
economic boom, 187
economic cooperation, 223
economic development, 157, 187, 191, 196, 256
economic growth, vii, 1, 2, 22, 156, 187, 190, 236, 256
economic growth rate, 256
economic integration, 162, 163, 168
economic policy, 155, 241
economic problem, 153
economic reform, 153, 171, 184, 185, 186, 187, 267
economic reforms, 185, 187
Economic Research Service, 40, 41, 43, 79, 279
economic security, 190, 193, 203
Economic Support Fund, 204
economics, 69, 248, 249, 250, 251
economies, 2, 5, 11, 44, 45, 46, 78, 161, 185, 189, 224, 241, 253, 259
economy, 2, 3, 4, 5, 9, 15, 17, 24, 28, 44, 46, 49, 72, 152, 153, 157, 184, 185, 188, 189, 202, 228, 236, 239, 241, 248, 250, 253, 255, 256, 259, 262, 267, 277
ecosystem, 191
ecosystems, 191
education, 157, 186, 201, 202, 239, 240, 244, 246, 247, 262
Education, 39, 105
educational institutions, 262
efficacy, 159
egg, 48, 49, 53, 64
eggs, 12, 26, 46, 48
elasticity, 87, 88
election, 153, 169, 200, 229, 272
electoral process, 160
electrical, 9, 28, 105, 190
electrical power, 28
electricity, 7, 80, 115, 117, 118, 123, 137, 152, 173, 190
electronic, 181
electronic warfare, 181
elephant, 40
embryonic, 219
emitters, 192
employees, 26
employers, 26
employment, 3, 15, 17, 26, 44, 74, 188, 191
employment growth, 15
encouragement, 223
endurance, 194
energy efficiency, 190, 191
Energy Information Administration, 212
energy markets, 173, 174, 190
energy supply, 269

engagement, ix, 156, 159, 160, 163, 165, 167, 168, 186, 192, 215, 219, 227, 243, 252, 253, 273
English, 147, 224
Enhancement, 103, 133
enlargement, 98
enterprise, 273
entertainment, 188
enthusiasm, 226, 227, 273
entrepreneurial, 157, 236, 255
environment, vii, 1, 2, 8, 11, 15, 16, 22, 27, 29, 32, 36, 131, 156, 157, 173, 177, 202, 220, 224, 229
environmental, 186, 240, 244, 247, 277
environmental crisis, 244
environmental degradation, 186, 244
environmental issues, 240, 247
epidemic, 201
equality, 162
equating, 261
equipment, 5, 9, 17, 59, 108, 120, 121, 122, 126, 127, 128, 130, 131, 132, 134, 135, 138, 139, 141, 164, 167, 176, 177, 181, 182, 186, 196, 207, 227, 242, 245, 253, 254, 256, 257, 261, 262
equities, 272
equity, 187, 252
ERS, 45, 59, 62, 63, 64, 66, 68, 71, 73, 76, 80, 83, 87, 92, 94, 96, 97, 98
ESF, 204
ethnic groups, 168, 195
Europe, 248, 250, 273
European, 10, 46, 181, 259, 272, 273
European Union, 10, 46, 272
Europeans, 273
evidence, 3, 7, 17, 36, 112, 115, 148, 152, 153, 158, 159, 172, 180, 197, 199
evolution, 34, 242
excess demand, 67
exchange rate, 3, 11, 45, 61, 88
exchange rates, 45, 61
excise tax, 22, 23
execution, 213
exercise, 102, 117, 121, 129, 131, 137, 138, 225, 226, 227
exogenous, 45, 61, 69, 83
expanded trade, 189, 222
expenditures, 13, 14, 15, 33
expertise, 238, 240
experts, 115, 130, 149, 174, 175, 190, 276
exploitation, 16, 18, 196, 199
explosions, 142, 154
explosive, 103, 113, 121, 126, 127, 129, 130, 131, 133, 136, 139
explosives, 128
export competitiveness, 46
export controls, 104, 109, 112, 138, 184
export subsidies, 189
exporter, 46, 53, 245
exports, vii, 17, 24, 41, 45, 46, 49, 53, 64, 65, 66, 67, 72, 74, 80, 85, 86, 89, 99, 101, 103, 108, 110, 111, 115, 117, 120, 121, 122, 125, 127, 128, 129, 130, 132, 137, 139, 143, 144, 147, 179, 186, 192, 202, 228, 248, 250, 257, 275
exposure, 11
extraction, 31, 53, 56, 57, 58, 59, 60, 69, 83, 84, 86, 88, 89, 90, 98, 107
extremism, 180, 182, 232, 235, 237, 248, 250
eye, 273

F

F-16, 180, 181
fabrication, 116, 137, 139
failure, 126, 127, 150, 151, 156, 166, 170, 190, 198, 199, 241
faith, 111
family, 201
family planning, 201
FAO, 41
Far East, 230
farm, vii, 1, 2, 3, 4, 5, 8, 16, 17, 21, 28, 29, 30, 32, 35, 36, 37, 59, 65, 69, 76, 80, 81, 82, 83, 87, 189, 190
farmers, vii, 1, 2, 3, 4, 7, 8, 11, 15, 16, 18, 20, 21, 24, 29, 32, 34, 36, 50, 55, 60, 61, 65, 67, 80, 82, 188, 189, 190, 196, 200, 211, 212, 267
farming, 18, 19, 34, 244
farmland, 2, 19, 20
farms, 19, 244
Fast Breeder Reactors, 117
faults, 241
FBI, 183, 211
FDI, 9, 10, 11, 27, 36, 223
fear, 134, 168, 207, 218, 219, 224
fears, 166, 218, 222, 260
February, 35, 40, 107, 108, 115, 118, 122, 132, 139, 141, 142, 144, 150, 153, 159, 160, 164, 169, 178, 180, 192, 193, 201, 203, 204, 205, 206, 207, 209, 210, 211, 213
federal government, 154, 189, 197
Federal Register, 141
fee, 18, 24, 30, 34
females, 200
fertilizer, 7, 49, 55
fertilizers, 9, 186
fetuses, 201
fiber, 98
fighters, 179, 180, 181, 196, 232, 234

finance, 156, 169, 185, 188
financial crisis, 185
financial distress, 60
financial institution, 187
financial institutions, 187
financial markets, 202
financial sector, 188
financing, 30, 182, 187
fire, 151, 167, 179, 188, 197
fires, 159
firm size, 2
firms, 2, 3, 11, 15, 17, 18, 20, 22, 24, 26, 27, 28, 29, 34, 35, 47, 59, 60, 74, 103, 123, 164, 165, 167, 186, 188, 232, 234, 256, 262
fish, 23, 48
fish production, 48
fisheries, 27
fissile material, 102, 110, 112, 113, 116, 118, 151, 175, 183, 184
fission, 183
fixed costs, 58
flexibility, 26, 46, 52, 195
flight, 179
flood, 189, 196, 245
flow, 9, 180, 216, 237, 240, 277
fluctuations, 29, 41
focusing, 32, 249, 251
food, vii, 1, 2, 3, 7, 8, 9, 11, 12, 13, 15, 16, 17, 18, 20, 22, 23, 24, 27, 32, 34, 36, 37, 41, 46, 47, 67, 80, 83, 152, 154, 164, 201, 202, 241, 277
food aid, 201, 204, 277
food commodities, 24
food industry, 27
food intake, 11
food processing industry, 18, 24, 27
food products, 11, 16, 23, 34
foodstuffs, 152
forced labor, 199
foreign affairs, 129, 164
foreign assistance, 124, 201, 223, 277
foreign direct investment, 3, 4, 9, 36, 186, 187, 223, 232, 234, 253, 256, 267
Foreign Direct Investment, 9, 10, 27, 39
foreign exchange, 9, 66, 69, 186
foreign firms, 27
foreign investment, ix, 3, 4, 11, 27, 36, 146, 153, 167, 174, 184, 185, 186, 187, 188
Foreign Military Financing, 202
foreign policy, vii, viii, 106, 127, 145, 146, 151, 167, 174, 175, 176, 208, 217, 220, 233, 235, 237, 241, 247, 248, 249, 250, 251, 252, 254, 256, 266, 269, 273, 277
foreigners, 278
fragmentation, 59
France, 104, 113, 114, 122, 132, 136, 140, 141, 143, 174, 179, 180, 181, 205, 207, 208, 210, 211, 212, 246, 255, 273
free trade, 190, 202, 216, 222
freedom, 20, 149, 153, 157, 159, 182, 188, 192, 197, 199, 200
freedom fighter, 192
Freedom Support Act, 165
freedoms, vii, ix, 146
freight, 30, 86, 87, 90, 204
freshwater, 48
friction, 161
friendship, 160, 236
fruits, 24
frustration, 153, 188
FTA, 222, 223
fuel, 102, 103, 104, 106, 107, 108, 109, 110, 113, 114, 115, 116, 117, 119, 120, 121, 123, 126, 128, 129, 130, 132, 133, 134, 136, 137, 139, 141, 144, 148, 149, 150, 152, 154, 173, 176, 177, 181, 260, 266
fuel cycle, 102, 103, 106, 107, 108, 109, 113, 128, 129
full capacity, 82
funding, 34, 166, 191, 201
funds, 10, 15, 191
fusion, 104
futures, 34, 35, 60

G

G8, 109, 150, 155
GAO, 143
gas, 106, 107, 165, 166, 167, 190, 245, 252, 253, 260, 269
gasoline, 152
GDP, 4, 5, 6, 11, 12, 41, 46, 86, 88, 89, 147, 184, 185, 187, 243
GDP deflator, 88
gender, ix, 146, 200, 201
General Accounting Office, 143
general election, 243
generation, 28, 29, 173, 185, 190, 221, 241
Generation IV, 104
Geneva, 112, 184
Germany, 37, 108, 120, 141, 185, 223, 246
gestures, 158, 171
GHG, 191
girls, 200, 201, 213
global economy, 188, 191, 236
Global Insight, 147, 211
global markets, 2, 26

global trade, 45, 98, 172
globalization, 185, 241
Globalization, 40
goals, vii, ix, 15, 43, 61, 74, 78, 104, 117, 153, 156, 160, 175, 183, 191, 194, 211, 215, 216, 217, 225, 250, 254
goods and services, 18, 189
governance, 170, 193
government budget, 67, 184
government intervention, 16
government policy, 35, 239, 246, 276
government revenues, 22
government-to-government, 267
governors, 118
grades, 34, 35
grading, 2, 18, 28, 35, 36
grains, 35, 36, 67
grants, 135, 201, 204
grapes, 25
grassroots, 197
greenhouse, ix, 146, 173, 191, 192, 277
greenhouse gas, ix, 146, 173, 191, 192, 277
greenhouse gases, ix, 146, 173, 191, 277
grids, 187
gross domestic product, 4, 11, 46
Gross Domestic Product (GDP), 5, 87, 147
groundnut oil, 17
groundwater, 29, 31
grouping, ix, 215, 225, 226, 227
groups, 12, 41, 158, 164, 170, 171, 193, 195, 196, 197, 198, 199, 213, 216, 241, 242, 256
growth, vii, 1, 2, 3, 4, 5, 7, 9, 11, 12, 13, 16, 20, 26, 27, 30, 32, 34, 36, 41, 44, 45, 46, 47, 49, 52, 53, 54, 61, 62, 64, 77, 78, 98, 105, 147, 152, 184, 185, 186, 187, 188, 190, 202, 244, 248, 250, 256, 267, 268, 278
growth rate, 41, 105, 147, 185, 186, 187, 256
Guam, 218, 229
guidance, 165
guidelines, 102, 103, 105, 109, 111, 112, 121, 124, 129, 130, 138, 147, 148, 150, 173
Gujarat, 19, 20, 34, 37, 108, 154, 170, 190, 195, 197, 198, 200, 213
guns, 207

H

habitat, 191
Hainan Island, 163
handling, 30, 67, 69, 70, 72, 87, 90, 98, 99
hands, 149
harm, 199, 228, 272, 275
harmful, 150, 173, 210, 239, 246
harmonization, 105, 138
harmony, 199, 272
harvest, 56, 58
hate, 253
head, 141, 181, 199, 265
health, 155, 202, 213
healthcare, 211
hearing, 105, 106, 109, 113, 115, 121, 123, 133, 139, 140, 141, 142, 150, 232, 234, 235, 236, 266, 272, 277
Heart, 213
heavy water, 103, 107, 117, 120, 128, 130, 137, 139, 142, 151
Hebrew, 238
hedging, 35, 228, 255
hegemony, 161, 241
helicopters, 181, 227
hexane, 58, 83, 98
hibernation, 151
high tech, 178, 234, 256
higher education, 244
high-level, 153, 154, 156, 160, 161, 176, 193, 208, 226, 253
high-tech, 148, 172, 178, 181, 184, 232, 257
highways, 164, 187
hip, 165, 195, 219, 221, 222, 223, 224, 228, 241, 243, 254, 255, 256
hips, 155, 219
hiring, 26
HIV, ix, 146, 156, 198, 201, 202, 203, 213, 251
HIV/AIDS, ix, 146, 156, 198, 201, 202, 203
homes, 193
horizon, 262
Horticulture, 25, 34
host, 243
hostage, 243
House, v, viii, x, 79, 102, 103, 104, 105, 106, 109, 111, 113, 115, 116, 120, 128, 130, 133, 134, 135, 139, 140, 141, 142, 144, 150, 168, 169, 173, 174, 175, 192, 200, 201, 202, 203, 204, 205, 207, 208, 209, 210, 221, 231, 279
household, 28, 29, 31, 32, 87
household income, 32
households, 11, 29
hub, ix, 117, 215, 216, 218, 223
human, vii, ix, 146, 155, 163, 164, 185, 192, 193, 195, 197, 198, 199, 200, 207, 213, 241, 277
human activity, 241, 277
human development, 185
human development index, 185
human rights, vii, ix, 146, 155, 163, 164, 192, 195, 197, 198, 199, 200, 207, 208, 213
humanitarian, ix, 183, 216, 226, 243, 253, 261

Hungary, 246
hybrid, 32

I

IAEA, 102, 104, 106, 107, 108, 109, 110, 111, 112, 113, 114, 116, 117, 118, 119, 120, 121, 122, 123, 124, 127, 128, 129, 131, 132, 134, 135, 136, 137, 139, 140, 141, 142, 148, 149, 150, 164, 176, 205, 209, 233, 235, 249, 268, 273, 277
IBM, 186
ice, 129, 173, 176, 208
id, 39, 41, 99, 116, 139, 140, 143, 209, 211, 213
identification, 119
identity, 80, 85, 228
ideology, 200
Illinois, 181, 237
images, 38
imaging, 210
imaging systems, 210
IMET, 204, 262
immigrants, 157
immigration, 236
imperialism, 149, 152
implementation, 9, 16, 21, 27, 77, 109, 117, 121, 124, 178, 188, 221, 239, 246
import prices, 52, 84
import substitution, 15
importer, 3, 24, 46
imports, vii, 3, 9, 37, 41, 43, 44, 45, 46, 47, 49, 51, 52, 53, 54, 56, 57, 60, 63, 64, 65, 66, 67, 68, 69, 71, 72, 73, 74, 75, 76, 77, 78, 80, 81, 82, 83, 84, 85, 86, 89, 90, 99, 147, 179, 186, 189, 207, 245, 253, 255, 256, 259, 269, 275, 278
IMS, 89
incentives, 8, 11, 13, 24, 44, 57, 59, 60, 77
incidence, 188, 200, 201, 211
INCLE, 204
inclusion, 128
income, 2, 3, 11, 12, 22, 24, 36, 44, 45, 47, 61, 77, 80, 185, 211, 244
income tax, 24
incomes, 1, 2, 3, 11, 12, 36, 44, 46, 47
increased access, 237
independence, 17, 106, 151, 154, 167, 176, 192, 193, 195, 207, 208, 212, 244, 252, 254, 255, 256
Indian Ocean, 157, 161, 167, 168, 207, 221, 222, 224, 226, 238, 248, 250, 252, 253, 255, 256, 258, 259, 260, 261
Indiana, 277
Indians, 3, 27, 111, 153, 154, 161, 171, 185, 193, 199, 201, 211, 238, 240, 241, 245, 248, 250, 254, 255, 257, 260, 266, 268, 270, 271, 272, 273, 274, 275, 276, 278
indication, 210
indicators, 194
indigenous, 113, 115, 116, 117, 137, 141, 142, 179, 189, 193, 196, 210, 253, 257, 259
Indonesia, 218, 220, 229, 259
induction, 182
industrial, 3, 8, 11, 17, 28, 29, 31, 143, 171, 186, 187, 190, 191, 223
industrial sectors, 186
industrialization, 244
industry, vii, 11, 17, 18, 27, 31, 34, 37, 43, 45, 46, 49, 57, 58, 59, 60, 64, 74, 78, 114, 140, 148, 163, 185, 194, 201, 262
inefficiency, 4, 58
inelastic, 98
inequality, 252
inertia, 269
infection, 201
infectious diseases, 202
Infiltration, 212
inflation, 22, 152, 169, 178, 185
information asymmetry, 35
information sharing, 182
information technology, 27, 184, 253, 257
Information Technology, 250, 257
infrastructure, vii, 1, 2, 3, 5, 6, 11, 13, 18, 24, 28, 36, 46, 158, 163, 184, 186, 188, 191, 211, 262, 270
inheritance, 19
inhibitor, 98
injury, 26
innovation, 27, 191
Innovation, 32
INS, 125, 179, 181
insecurity, 161
inspection, 2, 28, 30, 35, 36, 128, 141, 142
inspections, 111, 112, 139, 148, 182, 255, 274
inspectors, 128
instability, 167, 195, 207, 217, 220, 268
institutions, ix, 28, 158, 187, 215, 216, 219, 233, 235
instruments, 178
insurance, 86, 90, 153, 259, 262
integrated unit, 59
integration, 20, 45, 196, 202
integrity, 239, 246
intellectual property, 32, 187, 188
intellectual property rights, 187, 188
intelligence, 153, 158, 182, 183, 206, 211, 219, 225
intelligence gathering, 182
intensity, 30, 57, 191, 218
intentions, 115, 161, 175
interaction, 177, 220, 262

interactions, 164, 233, 235
interest groups, 188
interest rates, 22
interference, 106, 153, 158, 176
internal processes, 234
International Atomic Energy Agency, vii, 101, 126, 136, 148, 172, 177, 251, 254, 261, 270
International Atomic Energy Agency (IAEA), 126, 136, 148, 251, 261
international law, 172, 222
international markets, 3, 32
International Military Education and Training, 204
International Monetary Fund, 211
International Narcotics Control and Law Enforcement, 204
international relations, 155
international standards, 29, 58, 59, 138
international trade, 44
International Trade, 219
interoperability, 180, 217, 220, 221, 226, 257, 262
interpretation, 130, 225, 227
interstate, 4, 15, 60, 158, 160, 179, 192
interval, 131
intervention, 36, 46, 167, 276
interviews, 3, 45, 142, 143, 212
investigative, 159
investment, vii, 1, 2, 3, 4, 5, 6, 7, 11, 13, 15, 16, 17, 18, 19, 20, 22, 24, 26, 27, 28, 31, 32, 34, 36, 59, 60, 78, 81, 99, 152, 153, 155, 165, 171, 184, 185, 186, 187, 188, 191, 217, 232, 234, 236, 248, 250, 256, 262, 277
investment bank, 185
investment rate, 153
investors, 3, 4, 13, 16, 17, 18, 22, 25, 27, 28, 35, 36, 164, 171, 185, 196, 246
Iran, 106, 107, 108, 109, 128, 140, 141, 149, 164, 165, 166, 175, 176, 180, 208, 209, 210, 233, 235, 239, 245, 246, 248, 250, 251, 252, 254, 255, 260, 261, 269, 270, 272, 273, 274, 275, 277
Iran Sanctions Act, 208
Iraq, 180, 218, 220, 221, 222, 228, 242
Ireland, 121, 142
irrigation, 5, 7, 29, 31, 187, 190
Islam, 221
Islamic, ix, 160, 167, 192, 215, 216
Islamist terrorism, 209, 224
island, 10, 167, 225
isolation, 176, 245, 273
Israel, 179, 181, 206, 240, 242, 245, 247, 271
ISS, 212
Italy, 246

J

Japan, v, ix, 108, 141, 150, 151, 155, 162, 168, 180, 191, 205, 215, 216, 217, 218, 219, 220, 221, 222, 223, 224, 225, 226, 227, 228, 229, 230, 237, 246, 248, 250, 253, 255, 257, 258, 259, 261
Japanese, 168, 220, 221, 222, 223, 225, 226, 227, 230
jewelry, 186
jihad, 206
jobs, 17, 174, 239, 246, 255
John McCain, 146, 204
joint ventures, 27, 181
judgment, 127, 241, 275
jurisdiction, x, 120, 136, 231, 233
justice, 197, 198, 200
justification, 67, 164

K

Kashmir, viii, 19, 20, 145, 153, 154, 155, 158, 159, 160, 161, 181, 192, 193, 194, 195, 196, 198, 199, 206, 212, 238, 245
Kazakhstan, 123, 226, 229
King, 181
Korea, ii, 225, 229, 253, 257, 259
Korean, 217, 229
Kuwait, 221
Kyoto protocol, 191
Kyrgyzstan, 226, 229

L

labeling, 35, 245
labor, 15, 16, 26, 74, 80, 83, 98, 186, 188, 199
labor-intensive, 15, 74
land, 5, 15, 16, 19, 20, 24, 30, 37, 46, 56, 154, 188, 220, 225, 241, 244, 245, 270, 276
language, 119, 121, 143, 151, 153, 176, 224, 272
Laos, 185, 229
large-scale, 17, 36, 44, 56, 99, 241, 244, 245
Latin America, 45, 202
law, viii, 17, 26, 101, 102, 103, 110, 114, 125, 129, 130, 132, 133, 134, 136, 137, 147, 150, 166, 167, 173, 175, 182, 197, 198, 208, 209, 210, 242, 247, 249, 260, 266, 269
law enforcement, 182
laws, vii, 2, 16, 17, 19, 20, 24, 26, 27, 29, 36, 101, 104, 108, 124, 130, 133, 172, 173, 182, 188, 199, 268

lead, ix, 18, 24, 44, 54, 60, 61, 77, 81, 99, 109, 131, 148, 158, 169, 170, 176, 177, 185, 193, 215, 217, 260, 268
leadership, 149, 166, 169, 170, 221, 223, 256, 258
learning, 245
Lee Kuan Yew, 237
legal systems, 16, 182
legislation, viii, 16, 26, 27, 102, 103, 105, 125, 128, 133, 138, 147, 157, 164, 169, 173, 174, 175, 176, 200, 221, 244, 272, 274
legislative, 16, 27, 114, 125, 129, 143, 149, 177, 183
lending, 21, 152, 258
lens, 221
liberal, 44, 46, 205, 245
liberalization, 45, 46, 54, 56, 61, 69, 70, 72, 75, 76, 77, 91, 92, 93, 94, 95, 96, 97, 98, 187, 189, 267, 268
Libya, 165, 208
licenses, 17, 127, 134
licensing, 125, 127, 143, 178
life-threatening, 198
lifetime, 113, 120, 132, 133, 144
likelihood, 157, 249, 270, 273
limitations, 36, 88, 115, 175, 247, 250
linear, 80
linear function, 80
linkage, 251, 253, 257
links, ix, 60, 162, 167, 182, 183, 215, 216
liquefied natural gas, 190
liquidity, 35
literacy, 202
literature, 3, 87
liver, 98
livestock, 98
LNG, 250
loans, 201, 223
lobby, 150, 190
lobbying, 157
local government, 18, 27, 60
location, 60, 72, 224, 225, 226, 228
Lockheed Martin, 181, 210, 256, 257
locus, 169
logging, 31
logistics, 220, 221, 261
London, 60, 198, 205, 206, 210, 211
longevity, 160
long-term, 98, 155, 157, 161, 165, 168, 184, 194, 196, 243, 252, 268
long-term impact, 98
losses, 69, 74, 77, 188, 190
love, 224, 270, 276
Low cost, 28
low tech, 58, 59
lower prices, 53, 67
low-income, 57
low-level, 245
low-tech, 57

M

machinery, 9, 17, 253, 256
mainstream, 106, 173, 276
maintenance, 24, 28, 99
Malaysia, 205, 229
management, 34
management practices, 34
manners, 243
mantle, 189
manufacturer, 181
manufacturing, 2, 8, 15, 103, 110, 185, 196, 210
marginal costs, 58
marginal revenue, 71
marginalization, 193, 194
maritime, 180, 181, 207, 220, 223, 224, 226, 257, 258
market access, 162, 187, 189, 244
market opening, ix, 146
market penetration, 267
market prices, 2, 52, 55, 56, 67, 98
market structure, 18
market value, 58
marketing, vii, 1, 2, 3, 4, 15, 16, 17, 18, 20, 22, 24, 32, 34, 35, 36, 61, 78, 86, 90
markets, 2, 4, 5, 15, 16, 18, 19, 20, 24, 34, 35, 36, 37, 38, 53, 60, 98, 185, 189, 196, 232, 234, 242, 257
marriage, 272, 273
Marxist, 118, 142, 171, 209, 261
Maryland, 181
Mauritius, 10
meals, 44, 46, 49, 53, 56, 61, 62, 64, 67, 72, 77, 80, 86, 87, 88, 99
meanings, 133, 143
measures, 15, 46, 49, 112, 113, 114, 119, 120, 132, 141, 155, 183, 185, 187, 256
meat, 13, 23, 26, 46, 48, 53
mechanical, 57
media, 40, 211, 212, 213
mediators, 192
megawatt, 107, 167
membership, 136, 139, 168, 193, 223, 224
memorandum of understanding, 253, 261
men, 159, 199
merchandise, 253, 256, 257
messages, 273
Microsoft, 186

middle class, 149, 185
Middle East, v, x, 190, 231, 233, 235, 250, 279
migrants, 167
militant, 167, 181, 192, 193, 195, 196
Militant, 213
military aid, 273
military junta, 245
militias, 166
milk, 12, 14, 23, 46
millet, 56
million barrels per day, 190
minimum wage, 26
minorities, 164, 198, 199, 200, 242
minority, 154, 167, 170, 197, 199, 277
missile defense, 172, 180, 181, 220, 225, 232, 234, 262
missiles, 183, 225, 227
missions, 191, 258
modalities, 159
models, 241
moderates, 193
modernization, 34, 220, 222, 253, 256
mold, 255
momentum, 159, 161, 169, 222, 223, 227, 254, 255, 267, 278
money, 163
monks, 163
monsoon, 55, 240
moratorium, 104, 110, 111, 112, 121, 122, 138, 176, 183
Morocco, 185
mosaic, 168, 195
Moscow, 122, 167, 238, 269
motion, 152, 188, 260
motives, 180
mountains, 192
mouth, 259
movement, ix, 4, 15, 16, 17, 36, 59, 60, 146, 158, 159, 160, 161, 163, 194, 196, 197, 207, 236, 241, 242, 254, 259
MRCA, 210, 256
MSP, 56, 67, 69, 74, 77
multilateral, ix, 67, 102, 111, 112, 128, 138, 168, 173, 180, 186, 189, 216, 227, 228, 229, 232, 233, 234, 235, 253, 256, 258, 259, 260, 261, 267
multinational companies, 60
multinational firms, 74
multiplication, 83
multiplier, 267
muscle, 169, 218, 243
Muslim, 147, 152, 154, 170, 171, 192, 193, 195, 197, 199, 212, 213, 217, 233, 235
Myanmar, 207, 208, 252, 255

N

NADR, 204
NAM, 106, 107
narcotics, 157, 158
nation, 10, 107, 121, 126, 127, 135, 139, 157, 165, 167, 168, 170, 199, 225, 226, 254, 271
national, 20, 29, 32, 38, 121, 122, 129, 131, 135, 138, 149, 150, 152, 153, 155, 157, 158, 163, 164, 165, 169, 170, 171, 176, 177, 180, 184, 190, 191, 192, 197, 199, 200, 206, 211, 217, 218, 233, 235, 236, 242, 258, 261, 267
national action, 155, 191
national interests, 150, 180, 217
national security, 129, 131, 149, 153, 177, 180, 197, 206, 218, 233, 235, 236, 242
National Security Council, 141
National Security Strategy, 156
National Strategy, 118, 142
nationalism, 169, 170, 238
nation-building, 170
NATO, 226
natural, vii, viii, ix, 70, 115, 145, 146, 163, 165, 166, 168, 190, 191, 216, 221, 226, 243, 248, 252, 255, 259, 269, 270, 277
natural disasters, ix, 216
natural gas, 163, 165, 166, 190, 248, 259, 269, 270, 277
natural resources, 191
Navy, 167, 208, 225, 230, 257, 258, 259, 261, 263
Near East, 238
necrosis, 98
negative consequences, 177
negotiating, 119, 253
negotiation, 138, 151, 174, 193, 196, 243
Nepal, 157, 166, 190, 195, 206, 208, 240, 242, 243, 244
Netherlands, 142
network, 20, 34
networking, 258
Nevada, 180
New South Wales, 230
New York, 197, 198, 205, 206, 207, 208, 210, 211, 212, 213, 233
New York Times, 205, 206, 208, 210, 211, 212, 213
New Zealand, 122, 142, 219, 229
NGO, 201
NGOs, 34, 201
Niger, 123
Non-Aligned Movement (NAM), 106, 221, 228
non-binding, 124, 164, 176
nongovernmental, 34, 149, 200
nongovernmental organization, 34, 149

non-human, 183
nonlinear, 84
non-nuclear, 103, 104, 109, 110, 111, 113, 114, 125, 126, 127, 128, 131, 135, 136, 137, 139, 151, 212
nonproliferation, viii, 103, 106, 107, 108, 109, 111, 112, 116, 117, 121, 122, 127, 128, 133, 138, 139, 145, 146, 147, 149, 151, 156, 173, 174, 175, 176, 183, 184, 210, 260
nontariff barriers, 44, 54, 56, 60, 78, 81, 99
non-tariff barriers, 187
normal, 88, 266
normalization, 194
norms, 149
North Korea, ii, 108, 109, 110, 183, 217, 221, 225
Northeast, 195, 213
Norway, 142
NPT, vii, 101, 103, 104, 107, 109, 110, 111, 112, 113, 114, 122, 125, 129, 134, 136, 137, 139, 140, 141, 143, 151, 172, 224
NRC, 103, 126, 127, 134
NSG, 102, 103, 104, 105, 108, 109, 110, 111, 112, 115, 120, 121, 122, 124, 129, 130, 132, 133, 134, 139, 142, 148, 149, 150, 151, 172, 173, 205
nuclear arms race, 138, 149, 154, 174
nuclear energy, vii, viii, 101, 103, 104, 105, 107, 108, 111, 123, 132, 145, 146, 147, 162, 173, 191, 224
nuclear material, vii, 101, 105, 110, 111, 113, 117, 120, 125, 126, 127, 131, 135, 136, 137, 138, 139, 141, 143, 150, 154
Nuclear Nonproliferation Treaty, vii, 101, 103, 106, 136, 140, 172, 184, 260
nuclear power, 103, 105, 115, 122, 123, 132, 134, 141, 148, 173, 190, 224, 237
nuclear power plant, 122, 141
nuclear program, 106, 107, 115, 124, 128, 140, 164, 184, 210, 217, 243, 246, 273
nuclear reactor, 104, 115, 117, 119, 139, 167, 173
Nuclear Regulatory Commission, 103, 126, 127
Nuclear Suppliers Group, vii, 101, 121, 138, 148, 172, 205, 224, 243
Nuclear Suppliers Group (NSG), vii, 101, 148, 172
nuclear technology, 103, 104, 107, 108, 114, 117, 127, 130, 147, 173, 231, 234, 237, 260
nutrition, 211

O

obligation, 109, 126, 176
obligations, 116, 129, 134, 156, 191
observations, 87
occupational, 200
OCT, 140
OECD, 186
offenders, 200
oil, 17, 25, 35, 44, 45, 46, 47, 49, 50, 51, 52, 53, 54, 56, 57, 58, 59, 61, 62, 64, 65, 66, 67, 69, 70, 72, 73, 74, 75, 77, 78, 80, 83, 84, 85, 86, 87, 88, 89, 90, 91, 92, 93, 94, 95, 96, 97, 98, 162, 165, 167, 190, 245, 248, 250, 252, 253, 259, 260, 269
oil refining, 57
oils, 3, 13, 14, 16, 23, 44, 45, 46, 47, 49, 52, 53, 54, 56, 57, 58, 59, 60, 61, 64, 67, 72, 75, 77, 80, 84, 86, 87, 88
oilseed, vii, 26, 43, 44, 45, 46, 49, 50, 52, 54, 55, 56, 57, 58, 59, 60, 61, 62, 63, 64, 65, 66, 67, 68, 69, 70, 71, 72, 73, 74, 75, 76, 77, 78, 80, 81, 82, 83, 84, 87, 89, 92, 94, 96, 97, 98, 99
online, 3, 140
openness, 154, 166, 253
Operation Enduring Freedom, 254, 258, 261
operator, 83
opium, 196
opposition, 106, 107, 118, 119, 149, 150, 152, 154, 164, 165, 166, 169, 171, 175, 188, 205, 233, 235, 267, 268, 271, 273, 277
oppression, 196
optimism, 150, 153, 174, 189
optimists, 185
optimization, 84
organization, 129, 141, 170, 171, 193, 228, 229
Organization for Economic Cooperation and Development, 186
organizations, 217, 258, 260
orientation, 161, 172, 182
outrage, 152, 165, 209
oversight, 16, 105, 173, 174, 218
ownership, 9, 15, 19, 20, 27, 45, 60, 74
oxide, 137

P

Pacific, ix, 180, 191, 215, 218, 219, 220, 222, 223, 225, 226, 229, 230, 248, 250
Pacific Region, 229
packaging, 35
Pakistani, 110, 111, 153, 154, 155, 158, 159, 160, 161, 166, 183, 192, 193, 194, 206, 211, 260
Palestine, 180
palm oil, 25, 45, 52, 80, 87
paper, 241, 278
Paper, 38, 40, 78, 79, 138, 278
Paris, 186, 192
Parliament, 112, 114, 137, 141, 148, 149, 151, 160, 166, 176, 177, 188, 205, 210, 269, 271
partition, 160

partnership, vii, viii, 101, 104, 105, 106, 112, 123, 145, 146, 148, 156, 157, 162, 164, 167, 168, 172, 173, 174, 176, 182, 191, 198, 208, 221, 222, 223, 224, 232, 234, 235, 236, 247, 248, 249, 250, 251, 252, 254, 273, 277
partnerships, 3, 32, 36, 216, 220, 226, 228, 229, 245
passive, 207
Patent and Trademark Office, 188
peace process, 153, 159, 160, 271
peacekeeping, 224
peanuts, 46, 61, 62, 65, 69, 71, 72, 75, 76, 80
pearls, 186, 260
penalties, 200
Pentagon, 180, 181, 202, 210, 218
PEPFAR, 201, 204
per capita, 11, 47, 86, 147, 184
per capita income, 11
percentile, 13, 14, 15
perception, 158, 192, 217, 221, 261
perceptions, 161, 170, 180, 188, 217
performance, viii, 3, 18, 41, 61, 77, 101, 102, 129
periodic, 167, 199, 259, 261
permit, 3, 27, 36, 54, 109, 148, 178, 261
Persian Gulf, 248, 250, 258, 259, 260
personal, 22, 121, 142, 170, 236, 274, 278
personal benefit, 278
personal communication, 142
persuasion, 192
Pervez Musharraf, 153
pesticides, 55
pests, 54
petroleum, 9
Phalcon, 181
Philippines, ix, 216, 229
philosophy, 170, 221
pilots, 180
piracy, 180, 188, 239, 246, 253, 258, 259, 261
pitch, 181
planning, 29, 237
plants, 28, 57, 58, 59, 60, 71, 72, 74, 77, 78, 81, 99, 116, 117, 118, 121, 122, 137
platforms, 179
play, 15, 46, 50, 156, 174, 223, 224, 248, 250, 258, 259, 260, 265
pluralism, vii, viii, 145, 146
plutonium, 115, 117, 120, 126, 148, 183
pneumonia, 201
point of origin, 54
Poland, 278
police, 154, 155, 158, 182, 183, 188, 196, 197, 198, 199, 213
policy choice, 174
policy initiative, 169
policy instruments, 57
policy making, 157, 170
policy reform, 61
policymakers, 3, 18, 52, 61, 69, 168, 221, 228, 242
political crisis, 159
political instability, 166, 239, 246
political leaders, 195, 252, 256
political legitimacy, 160
political parties, 193
political power, 228
political uncertainty, 221
politicians, 151, 169, 268, 272, 275, 276
politics, 152, 170, 171, 228, 247, 248, 249, 250, 256, 261, 276
polling, 254
pollution, 186, 191
poor, 2, 3, 18, 28, 30, 49, 58, 60, 87, 98, 170, 186, 190, 217, 244, 256, 268
poor performance, 3
population, 3, 11, 123, 152, 157, 161, 185, 191, 199, 201, 211, 244, 255, 262, 277
portfolio, 186
portfolio investment, 186
ports, 71, 72, 99, 187, 259, 261, 274, 275
positive relationship, 7, 266
post-Cold War, 167, 221
posture, 115, 207, 218, 220, 222, 228
potatoes, 34
poultry, 19, 23, 26, 46, 48, 49, 53, 64
poverty, 2, 3, 11, 12, 160, 161, 169, 184, 191, 202, 211
poverty line, 3, 211
poverty rate, 211
poverty reduction, 2, 12, 191
powder, 25
power generation, 28, 29, 190
power relations, 223
powers, 161, 164, 169, 192, 216, 217, 223, 225, 227, 228, 248, 252, 259
PPP, 147
pragmatic, 114, 163
preference, 57, 64, 243
premiums, 35
preparation, 47
preparedness, 160
presidency, 129, 169
president, 108, 162, 165, 168, 170, 195, 229, 233, 243, 246
President Bush, vii, viii, x, 101, 102, 103, 104, 108, 116, 122, 129, 132, 133, 134, 137, 145, 146, 147, 149, 150, 151, 155, 156, 172, 173, 174, 175, 178, 182, 183, 184, 191, 208, 212, 218, 221, 225, 227, 231, 233, 234, 255, 266

President Clinton, 156, 183, 211, 231, 234
President Vladimir Putin, 167
pressure, viii, 7, 19, 26, 36, 107, 108, 112, 145, 176, 268, 274
prestige, 184, 268, 274
pretrial, 198
prevention, 158, 201, 202
preventive, 182
price elasticity, 99
price instability, 7
price movements, 62
prices, vii, 2, 3, 4, 7, 8, 15, 16, 22, 24, 35, 37, 43, 44, 45, 47, 49, 52, 53, 54, 55, 56, 58, 59, 61, 62, 64, 65, 67, 69, 70, 71, 72, 74, 75, 76, 77, 78, 80, 81, 82, 83, 84, 86, 87, 88, 98, 99, 152, 248, 250, 270, 274
priorities, 32, 77, 108, 217, 243, 249, 251
private, vii, 1, 2, 4, 5, 6, 7, 8, 11, 15, 16, 17, 18, 19, 20, 24, 28, 29, 30, 31, 32, 34, 35, 36, 47, 49, 69, 186, 187, 191, 217, 223, 242, 244, 255, 267, 271
private education, 244
private investment, vii, 1, 2, 3, 4, 7, 8, 11, 15, 16, 18, 19, 28, 29, 30, 32, 34, 36, 223
private sector, 18, 31, 32, 35, 244, 267
private-sector, 19, 267
privatization, 185
proactive, 40, 260
procedures, 113, 127, 133, 135, 269
producers, vii, 4, 8, 21, 26, 28, 43, 44, 45, 49, 50, 52, 53, 54, 55, 57, 58, 59, 61, 64, 65, 67, 69, 70, 72, 74, 75, 76, 77, 78, 80
product market, 57
production costs, 26
production technology, 130
productivity, 2, 3, 7, 31, 36, 44, 46, 54, 77, 185
productivity growth, 7, 31, 54
professionalism, 239, 246
profit, 63, 66, 68, 71, 73, 76, 84, 92, 93, 95, 97
profitability, 8, 28, 49, 60
profits, 24, 27, 64, 65, 69, 72, 74, 75, 76, 77, 81, 82, 84, 98, 99
program, 67, 106, 107, 108, 110, 112, 113, 114, 115, 116, 117, 125, 128, 129, 137, 141, 142, 148, 149, 163, 171, 177, 178, 183, 201, 253, 256
proliferation, viii, 104, 105, 106, 108, 109, 110, 126, 128, 129, 138, 139, 141, 142, 145, 155, 157, 178, 180, 221, 222, 224, 232, 234, 243, 249, 251, 255
promote, viii, 17, 32, 60, 101, 102, 162, 183, 192, 203, 212, 216
property, 185, 188
property rights, 188
prosperity, 168, 186, 219, 243, 255
prostitution, 198
protection, vii, 25, 43, 49, 50, 52, 58, 69, 70, 77, 78, 139, 166, 174, 181, 188, 198, 222, 253, 258
protectionism, 186
protein, 44, 46, 57, 61, 77, 88
proteins, 45
protocol, 109, 124
protocols, 142
prototype, 117
PSI, 109, 262
psychological, 173, 174
public, 2, 4, 5, 6, 7, 11, 20, 28, 29, 31, 32, 34, 35, 36, 108, 128, 129, 147, 148, 152, 154, 158, 159, 161, 187, 191, 195, 209, 210, 211, 217, 227, 244, 254, 258, 268, 271, 273, 277
public debt, 187
public expenditures, 7
public finance, 152, 187
public funds, 36
public investment, 7, 11, 31, 32, 36
public opinion, 154, 254
public sector, 5, 20, 31, 268
public service, 211
public support, 195
public view, 258
pulse, 17
pulses, 3, 12, 16, 24, 56
pumps, 29, 31
Putin, 167

Q

question mark, 241
questioning, 129, 226
quotas, 52

R

R&D, 242
race, 138, 163, 183, 277
radar, 181, 217, 262
radical, 153, 221, 248, 250
rail, 30, 72, 99, 275
rainfall, 50, 55
range, 11, 15, 18, 35, 54, 99, 154, 156, 177, 178, 179, 183, 191, 193, 207, 219, 222, 229, 231, 232, 234, 243, 257, 259, 274
rape, 198
ratings, 227
raw materials, 26, 45, 46, 50, 58, 60, 67, 72, 73, 78, 80, 82, 98, 196
reaffirmation, 138
real estate, 27
real terms, 3, 9, 20, 22, 32, 64, 83, 243

realist, 161
reality, 200, 268, 270
reasoning, 106, 134
reciprocity, 181
recognition, 112, 114, 202, 231, 234
reconcile, 229
reconciliation, 151, 164, 260
reconstruction, 166, 222
recovery, 28, 202, 232, 235
recruiting, 196
reduction, 22, 24, 73, 75, 82, 187, 194, 195, 201, 267
reelection, 170
refining, 9, 57
reforms, vii, 1, 2, 3, 8, 9, 11, 16, 18, 19, 29, 46, 153, 155, 164, 185, 186, 239, 244, 246, 252, 256, 267
refuge, 207
refugees, 167, 193
regular, 110, 121, 156, 223, 242, 259
regulation, 15, 27, 31, 40
regulations, vii, 1, 15, 18, 19, 27, 49, 59, 60, 124, 130, 184, 187, 262
regulatory framework, 27
reinsurance, 239, 242, 246
rejection, 169, 184
relationship, 7, 105, 106, 107, 111, 129, 138, 148, 149, 155, 156, 160, 161, 162, 172, 175, 176, 180, 208, 218, 219, 220, 221, 222, 223, 224, 225, 228, 231, 232, 233, 234, 235, 236, 237, 238, 239, 240, 241, 242, 245, 246, 247, 248, 250, 252, 253, 254, 255, 259, 260, 261, 265, 269, 270, 271, 273, 278
relative prices, 47
relatives, 241
relevance, 164, 194
reliability, 152, 256, 257
religion, 199
religions, 195
religious, vii, ix, 146, 153, 168, 182, 192, 193, 197, 198, 199, 200, 232, 235, 237
religious groups, 193
renewable energy, 105, 191, 192
repatriation, 9, 27
reporters, 114
repression, 163
reprocessing, 102, 105, 108, 111, 112, 116, 117, 118, 120, 121, 122, 126, 128, 129, 130, 134, 135, 136, 138, 139, 148, 150, 175, 176, 177, 209
research, 20, 28, 31, 32, 33, 103, 104, 107, 117, 137, 140, 211, 212, 236, 240, 247, 251
Research and Development, 107, 178
research funding, 33
resentment, 169
reservation, 59
reserves, 113, 115, 133, 186, 259
reservoirs, 31
residuals, 80
resistance, 3, 147, 154, 176, 177, 184, 227, 252, 257, 268
resolution, 102, 104, 106, 107, 126, 127, 131, 135, 143, 153, 161, 163, 193, 194, 195, 196, 204, 221, 233, 235, 240, 247
resources, 29, 115, 116, 123, 141, 155, 161, 162, 165, 187, 190, 196, 201, 217, 221, 222, 239, 247, 259, 277
respiratory, 211
respiratory disorders, 211
responsibilities, 104, 112, 157, 236, 262
responsiveness, 98
restaurants, 47
restructuring, 217
retail, 3, 22, 36, 186, 262, 267
retirement, 26, 170
returns, 2, 4, 32, 44, 49, 65, 67, 69
revenue, 22, 52
revolutionary, 241, 242
rhetoric, 167, 271, 275
rice, 2, 7, 8, 17, 31, 35, 54
risk, viii, ix, 2, 16, 17, 18, 20, 35, 36, 55, 59, 60, 101, 102, 118, 139, 152, 159, 166, 198, 201, 216, 223, 249, 251, 252, 255, 266, 271
risk factors, 36
risk management, 2, 35, 36, 60
risks, ix, 28, 36, 60, 99, 186, 216, 223, 228, 237
river systems, 244
rivers, 207, 244
robustness, 221
rocky, 237
rolling, 175
rule of law, vii, viii, 145, 146, 157, 168
rural, 2, 5, 6, 19, 169, 171, 187
rural development, 187
rural population, 19
Russia, 104, 110, 113, 114, 122, 132, 136, 139, 141, 163, 167, 174, 179, 181, 185, 191, 208, 210, 226, 229, 230, 241, 245, 269, 273
Russian, 136, 140, 167, 179, 180, 217, 257, 269

S

safeguard, 136, 182, 189, 256, 260, 261
safeguards, vii, 101, 102, 103, 104, 106, 107, 108, 109, 110, 111, 112, 113, 114, 115, 116, 117, 118, 119, 120, 121, 122, 124, 125, 126, 127, 128, 131, 134, 135, 136, 137, 139, 141, 142, 148, 149, 150, 172, 173, 175, 177
safety, 110, 112, 113, 118, 120, 139, 156, 157, 227

sales, viii, 20, 22, 24, 51, 53, 60, 69, 80, 84, 108, 111, 120, 145, 146, 156, 157, 163, 164, 165, 173, 181, 182, 202, 224, 232, 234, 242, 249, 251, 253, 255, 256, 257, 262, 276
salinity, 31
sanctions, ix, 107, 108, 112, 125, 140, 141, 146, 163, 164, 165, 180, 183, 185, 207, 211, 224, 233, 235, 272, 275
satellite, 172, 177, 210, 220, 225, 246
satisfaction, 161, 164, 165, 171, 178
savings, 69
scale economies, 72
school, 244
schooling, 244
science, 27, 167, 177, 237
scientific, 20, 27, 32, 156, 175, 176, 178, 249, 251
scientific community, 175, 176
scientists, 103, 107, 141, 148, 151, 164, 174, 176, 210, 271
scores, 153
search, 193, 225, 253, 258, 261
searching, 262
seasonal factors, 56
secondary data, 3
secondary education, 244
secretariat, 118
Secretary of Commerce, 188
Secretary of Defense, 180, 209
Secretary of State, viii, 102, 103, 106, 114, 117, 121, 123, 129, 140, 141, 148, 150, 151, 156, 157, 163, 165, 173, 176, 177, 186, 187, 208, 209, 238, 260
Secretary of the Treasury, 187
Secretary-General, 150
secular, 199, 205
secularism, 171
securities, 185
Security Council, 105, 106, 107, 223, 235, 262, 274
seed, 20, 49, 54, 80, 83, 86, 87, 89, 96
seeds, 27, 32, 54, 55, 90
segregation, 198
Self, 79, 220, 222
senate, 140, 206, 211
Senate, viii, 102, 103, 104, 106, 116, 117, 121, 128, 129, 133, 134, 135, 139, 140, 141, 143, 144, 153, 163, 173, 174, 175, 180, 183, 184, 192, 202, 203, 204, 209, 210, 211, 212, 218
Senate Foreign Relations Committee, 102, 103, 106, 117, 121, 128, 134, 135, 139, 140, 141, 143, 144, 192, 204, 209, 212
sensitivity, 16, 53, 181, 260
sensors, 181
separation, 26, 102, 113, 116, 117, 119, 124, 134, 135, 136, 140, 141, 173, 175
September 11, 122, 142
series, 87, 156, 167, 172, 180, 183, 201, 211, 223, 232, 234, 258, 260, 268
services, 1, 2, 3, 5, 9, 18, 24, 27, 28, 34, 35, 36, 158, 180, 181, 185, 186, 187, 189, 198, 202, 206, 232, 233, 234, 235, 250, 253, 257, 262
sesame, 17, 59
sex, 200, 201
sexuality, 201
SEZ, 24, 27, 188, 212
shame, 200
Shanghai, 216, 226, 228, 229, 278
Shanghai Cooperation Organization, 216, 226, 228, 229
shape, ix, 11, 82, 159, 215, 224, 225, 226, 248, 250
shaping, 15, 57
shares, 9, 45, 49, 233, 235, 236
sharing, 67, 179, 222, 224
shipping, 253, 258, 259, 260
shocks, 110, 153
shoot, 225
short run, 59, 99, 174, 269
short supply, 67
shortage, 28, 35, 197
short-range, 179
short-term, 60, 67, 185
shoulder, 156
sign, viii, 103, 104, 123, 136, 139, 145, 159, 210, 239, 252, 261, 262, 266, 270, 274
signaling, 165
signals, 15, 237
signs, 4, 116, 150, 155, 169, 171, 176, 183, 185, 206, 217, 242, 261, 268
Silicon Valley, 208
simulation, 88
simulations, vii, 43
Singapore, 168, 180, 206, 213, 218, 226, 228, 229, 230, 237, 258, 259
singular, 176
sites, 123, 163
skeptics, 148
smuggling, 196
social, 155, 158, 160, 168, 189, 198, 200, 252, 268
social development, 156, 158, 160
social structure, 198
socialism, 252
socialist, ix, 146, 185
socialist economy, ix, 146, 185
socially, 200, 227
society, 37, 196, 201, 241, 268
software, 188, 257
soil, 207, 261
solar, 191

solar energy, 191
solutions, 69, 84, 107
solvent, 17, 53, 56, 57, 58, 59, 60, 98
South Africa, 37, 201
South America, 78
South Asia, v, vii, viii, x, 30, 40, 41, 79, 141, 145, 146, 156, 157, 158, 160, 161, 166, 174, 181, 182, 183, 184, 206, 207, 208, 209, 210, 211, 224, 230, 231, 233, 237, 238, 240, 242, 244, 247, 249, 251, 254, 259, 260, 261, 278, 279
South Asian Association for Regional Cooperation, 161
South Korea, ix, 180, 191, 216, 218, 229, 246, 278
Southeast Asia, 45, 161, 238, 259
sovereignty, viii, 111, 142, 145, 162, 192, 195, 207, 258
Soviet Union, 143, 155, 221, 241, 242, 245
soy, 78, 84, 88
soybean, 25, 35, 45, 46, 47, 49, 50, 52, 53, 54, 56, 62, 64, 65, 72, 74, 75, 78, 83, 84, 87, 88, 99
soybeans, 43, 44, 45, 46, 49, 50, 53, 57, 58, 59, 62, 71, 72, 75, 77, 78, 80, 82, 84
space exploration, 177
Speaker of the House, 207
spectrum, 155, 262, 274
speech, 108, 123, 186, 209, 278
speed, 241
spent nuclear fuel, 134
spheres, 241
spices, 17
spiritual, 207
Sri Lanka, 153, 167, 207, 238, 243
SSI, 17, 18, 59
stability, viii, ix, 35, 145, 157, 165, 180, 182, 195, 216, 222, 226, 233, 235, 254
stabilize, 25, 239, 246, 247
stages, 34, 179, 262
stakeholder, 228
stakeholders, 195
standards, 16, 27, 34, 35, 49, 64
state borders, 60
State Department, 108, 116, 119, 120, 123, 124, 130, 132, 133, 141, 142, 143, 165, 166, 172, 181, 182, 196, 197, 198, 199, 200, 201, 210, 213, 237, 238
state-owned, 210
statistics, 39, 211, 267
statutory, 119
stock, 16, 35, 83, 185, 186
stockpile, 120, 160, 183
stockpiling, 138
storage, 2, 4, 5, 7, 16, 17, 18, 34, 36, 59, 60, 67, 99, 126, 137, 244
strategies, 191, 237, 259
strength, ix, 168, 170, 215, 217, 223, 228, 248, 250
stress, 153, 223, 268
strikes, 152
strong force, 197
students, 244, 249, 251
submarines, 168, 179
subsidies, 2, 4, 7, 8, 28, 29, 31, 36, 152, 189, 190
subsidy, 7, 11, 34
substitutes, 80
substitution, 87
Sudan, 180
suffering, 244
sugar, 16, 17
suicide, 153, 155, 166, 209
summer, 151, 190, 259
Sun, 88, 230
sunflower, 45, 53, 57, 64, 65, 72, 75, 80, 83, 87
superpower, 241, 259
suppliers, 18, 45, 52, 53, 109, 121, 122, 133, 167, 174, 179, 257
supply, 3, 16, 22, 28, 29, 32, 34, 36, 44, 45, 47, 49, 61, 65, 69, 80, 87, 88, 98, 109, 114, 115, 119, 120, 132, 133, 134, 139, 141, 150, 151, 164, 177, 186, 190, 191, 258, 262
supply chain, 3, 16, 22, 28, 32, 36
supply disruption, 69, 133
support services, 173, 201, 257
Supreme Court, 125, 143, 197
surging, 185
surplus, 31, 44, 60, 71, 77, 78, 84, 91, 93, 95, 97, 162, 181, 204
surprise, 156, 166, 169, 189
surveillance, 207
suspects, 199
sustainability, 3, 123
sustainable development, 191
sustainable growth, 186
Sweden, 181
Switzerland, 142
symbiotic, 253, 257
symbolic, 111, 148, 160, 163, 174, 176
symbols, 184
synthetic, 87
systems, 2, 17, 30, 31, 36, 116, 155, 181, 182, 183, 190, 222, 244

T

tactics, 197
Taiwan, 217, 220, 230
Taiwan Strait, 217
Tajikistan, 226, 229
Taliban, 166, 252, 254, 261

tangible, 156, 172
tanks, 179, 207, 245
targets, 21, 115, 227
tariff, vii, 16, 25, 28, 29, 43, 44, 46, 50, 51, 52, 54, 56, 57, 65, 67, 69, 71, 72, 74, 75, 77, 78, 81, 82, 84, 86, 88, 89, 99, 123, 185, 187, 189
task force, 262
tax exemptions, 60
tax incentive, 24, 60
tax incentives, 24, 60
tax rates, 22, 23
tax receipt, 22
tax system, 22
taxation, 4, 10, 15, 36, 196
taxes, 2, 16, 18, 22, 24, 36, 60, 98
tea, 27, 159
Tea, 23
technical efficiency, 58
technological, 80
technology, 2, 17, 18, 26, 34, 55, 59, 105, 107, 108, 111, 113, 116, 121, 122, 128, 130, 132, 134, 138, 139, 141, 164, 177, 178, 179, 180, 184, 200, 222, 232, 234, 253, 256
technology transfer, 116, 179, 180, 232, 234
Tehran, 106, 107, 155, 164, 165, 208, 210, 246
Tel Aviv, 238
telecommunications, 9, 186
television, 115
tenants, 20
tension, 132, 217, 223
tenure, 174, 175
terminals, 34
territorial, 153, 158, 159, 162, 163, 192
territory, 159, 161, 163, 192, 225
terrorism, viii, ix, 139, 145, 155, 156, 157, 158, 159, 160, 180, 182, 192, 206, 213, 215, 216, 218, 232, 234, 242, 248, 250, 253, 258, 259
terrorist, 118, 153, 156, 158, 159, 160, 167, 182, 183, 196, 197, 206, 227, 237, 259
terrorist acts, 153, 159
terrorist attack, 153, 156, 159, 160, 167, 183, 206, 237
terrorist groups, 158, 167, 183, 196
terrorist organization, 259
terrorists, 196, 236, 270, 271
testimony, 113, 236, 240, 247, 249, 266, 270
textiles, 186, 189
Thailand, ix, 216, 217, 229, 259
theft, 28, 190, 270, 271
theoretical, 87, 116
theory, 161, 275
thermal, 28, 143
thinking, 157, 193, 229, 238, 240, 273
threat, ix, 106, 107, 119, 138, 166, 167, 193, 195, 196, 215, 216, 218, 221, 225, 233, 235, 239, 242, 245, 246, 261, 266, 268, 270
threatened, 31, 118, 150, 166, 167, 194, 196, 197, 229, 261
threatening, ix, 147, 149, 151, 152, 216, 260, 265, 270
threats, 156, 180, 186, 217, 243, 245, 246, 254, 258, 259
thyroid, 98
Tibet, 162, 207
timber, 9
time periods, 87
time series, 87
time-frame, 108
timing, 135
title, 232, 234, 241, 253
Tokyo, ix, 168, 215, 221, 222, 223, 224, 225, 226, 229, 230
tolerance, 199
torture, 198
total employment, 74
total energy, 190
total factor productivity, 32
total revenue, 22, 187
tourism, 159
tourist, 194
tracking, 225
trade agreement, 217, 256
trade deficit, 253
trade liberalization, 43, 45, 78, 82
trade policies, 59, 74, 83, 188
trade policy, 1, 3, 46, 49, 54, 56, 267
Trade Representative, 187, 189
trading, 3, 9, 17, 18, 27, 34, 35, 36, 47, 60, 65, 155, 162, 207, 232, 234, 236, 253, 256, 260, 267, 277, 278
trading partners, 65
tradition, 106, 199
traffic, 30
trafficking in persons, 199
training, 179, 180, 181, 182, 183, 192, 199, 202, 221, 224, 242, 245, 262
traits, 224
trans, 70, 78, 256
transaction costs, 35
transactions, 18, 22
transfer, 75, 76, 82, 107, 108, 111, 113, 121, 122, 125, 126, 129, 130, 132, 134, 151
transformation, 188, 221, 236, 252, 254, 255
transition, 195
transmission, 28, 29, 190
transparency, 18, 118, 211

transparent, 27, 117, 184, 185
transport, 2, 9, 28, 30, 34, 36, 60, 61, 67, 69, 70, 72, 84, 90, 99, 165, 181, 242, 244, 252, 253, 256, 261
transport costs, 84, 99
transportation, 72, 86, 87
travel, 166
Treasury, 211
treaties, viii, 146, 191
trend, 8, 60, 74, 80, 206, 253, 255, 265
tribal, 195, 197, 198
tribal rights, 195
tritium, 107
trucks, 30
trust, 154, 162, 260
tsunami, 167, 202, 221, 226, 242, 253, 261
turbulent, 255, 261
Turkey, 246
turnover, 60
two-way, 110, 180, 207, 232, 234, 239, 246, 253

U

U.N. Security Council, 106, 107, 162, 165, 168, 184, 203, 233, 237, 273
U.S. Agency for International Development, 202, 204
U.S. Department of Agriculture, 35, 38, 40, 41, 79
U.S. Department of the Treasury, 183
U.S. dollar, 62
U.S. military, 180, 218, 220
U.S. Treasury, 187
ubiquitous, 198
UK, 37, 255
UN, 138, 140, 211, 213, 235, 261, 262
UN General Assembly, 138
uncertainty, 36, 220
unclassified, viii, 101, 102, 108
undergraduate, 237
uniform, 179
uniformity, 241
unilateral, 104, 110, 111, 121, 122, 138, 176
unit cost, 65, 80, 81, 82
United Kingdom, 114, 123, 132, 136, 219
United Nations, 105, 163, 201, 223
universities, 32, 244
university education, 244
university students, 244
upload, 278
upward mobility, 157
uranium, 103, 107, 111, 113, 114, 115, 118, 121, 126, 128, 130, 134, 137, 141, 148, 165, 183, 224
uranium enrichment, 107, 111, 128, 130, 165
uranium oxide, 137
urban, 11, 30, 149, 169, 170, 186
urban areas, 11
urbanization, 3, 11, 12, 46
USAID, 201, 202
USDA, 1, 3, 38, 41, 43, 47, 48, 51, 52, 53, 61, 79, 80, 88, 98
users, 28, 29, 31, 178, 253, 262
Uzbekistan, 123, 226, 229

V

vacuum, 228
value added tax, 23
value-added tax (VAT), 22
values, vii, viii, ix, 52, 87, 145, 146, 168, 180, 215, 216, 217, 218, 220, 222, 228, 248, 250
variable, 60, 80, 83, 87, 171
variables, 35, 45, 61, 69, 80, 189
VAT, 22, 23
vector, 88
vegetable oil, 12, 24, 43, 44, 46, 51, 56, 58, 64, 77
vegetables, 12, 15, 24, 25, 27, 46
vehicles, 178, 184, 227
vein, 277
venue, 186, 217, 219
vertical integration, 26, 78
vessels, 168, 223, 226, 259, 262
Vice President, 176, 218
victims, 198, 200, 234
Vietnam, 229
vigilante, 197
village, 35, 196, 242
violence, 160, 170, 193, 194, 195, 196, 198, 199, 206, 207, 212, 268
violent, 154, 163, 182, 189, 196, 197, 198, 207, 232, 235
visa, 197
vision, ix, 105, 138, 215, 216
voters, 169
voting, 152
vulnerability, 267

W

wages, 26
walking, 271
Wall Street Journal, 116, 140, 141, 205, 209, 210, 212
war, 158, 159, 160, 161, 162, 167, 179, 192, 196, 220, 221, 236, 237, 240, 242, 243, 245, 262
war on terror, 236, 237, 262
warfare, 226

Washington Post, 140, 141, 142, 204, 206, 207, 208, 209, 210
waste, 80, 83, 123
waste management, 123
wastes, 98
water, 7, 28, 29, 31, 37, 130, 158, 164, 186, 191, 202, 222, 240, 244, 247, 253, 258, 259
water resources, 31, 37, 191
water supplies, 29, 31
waterways, 164
weakness, 46
weapons, 103, 105, 108, 110, 112, 113, 114, 115, 116, 117, 138, 141, 148, 151, 155, 160, 161, 163, 164, 176, 178, 180, 181, 182, 183, 184, 196, 197, 207, 222, 232, 234, 235, 239, 245, 247, 262, 270, 271
weapons of mass destruction, 105, 164, 176, 180, 222, 232, 234
Weapons of Mass Destruction, 107, 118, 138, 142
web, 212, 213
welfare, 49, 69, 82
wells, 31
wheat, 2, 3, 7, 8, 17, 25, 31, 35, 54, 56
White House, 139, 141, 229
wholesale, 3, 27, 35, 36, 56, 65, 83, 84, 87, 88, 90
wind, 28
winning, 148
winter, 56
Wisconsin, 237
withdrawal, 154, 175
witness, 106, 277
witnesses, 139, 237, 266, 277
WMD, 107, 109, 140, 164, 180, 182, 184
women, 26, 170, 198, 199, 201, 221, 244
workers, 26, 166, 201, 248, 250, 255
World Bank, 11, 17, 18, 23, 24, 30, 32, 34, 40, 41, 60, 79, 83, 211
World Trade Organization, 24, 67, 189, 212
World War, 216, 220, 236
worry, 153, 164, 239, 246
WTO, vii, 43, 49, 52, 65, 67, 69, 74, 77, 156, 189, 212, 277

X

X-axis, 80

Y

Y-axis, 80
yield, 4, 56, 62, 65, 80, 86, 89, 237, 272, 273
young adults, 11